Jeanne Wolff Bernstein

The Lure of the Gaze and the Past

A Psychoanalytic Exploration of Édouard Manet's Works

Jeanne Wolff Bernstein, Ph.D., lives and works as a psychoanalyst in Vienna. She is Vice President of the Vienna Psychoanalytic Association, former President of the Psychoanalytic Institute of Northern California (PINC) and Chair of the Scientific Advisory Board of the Sigmund Freud Museum in Vienna. She teaches at the Vienna Psychoanalytic Association, the New York University Postdoctoral Program for Psychoanalysis and Psychotherapy and she is on the faculty at PINC.

Jeanne Wolff Bernstein

THE LURE OF THE GAZE AND THE PAST

A Psychoanalytic Exploration of Édouard Manet's Works

Alexander Verlag Berlin

Alexander Wewerka, Fredericiastrasse 8, 14050 Berlin, Germany
www.alexander-verlag.com · info@alexander-verlag.com

Copyediting: Andrew Ellis, Reuben Loewy
Proofreading: Katja Karau
Index made by: Elaine Taylor
Design, Layout, Typesetting: Antje Wewerka
Cover image: Édouard Manet, *Olympia* (1863)

ISBN 978-3-89581-623-9
Printing and Binding: FINIDR s.r.o., Český Těšín
Printed in the Czech Republic (February) 2025

Contents

Acknowledgement

A book does not write itself on its own. One needs the company and generous advice of others to complete the process of writing it. I will not say that it takes a village, but it takes a good circle of friends and numerous discussions with smart minds to shape and reshape one's work. Many years were spent thinking about different psychoanalytic perspectives and languages from within one could speak about Édouard Manet's oeuvre, and the conversations with others, inside and outside the psychoanalytic field, became a central source of inspiration for me. Without the tremendous support and encouragement of so many colleagues and friends, this book would never have seen the light of day. Let me thank the three people who were there at the very beginning of this endeavor. My late husband, Michael André Bernstein was the first to stir me into the direction of Manet, evoking my interest and evolving passion for the artist's oeuvre. Subsequently, Eli Zaretsky and Alan Swope were most attentive and supportive readers for my treatise on Manet, as were my dear friends in Berkeley, Martine Aniel, Elin Sowle, Barbara Baer, Jane Burka, Maureen Murphy, Victor Bonfilio, Rachael Peltz and Joyce Lindenbaum. A very special thank you goes to Ruth Fallenbaum and Zeese Papanikolas who were there from the beginning, giving me their undivided support in so many special ways. A heart-felt thank you also goes to Thomas H. Ogden, a trusted friend and teacher from whom I have learned a great deal over so many years and who was one to support me in my writing on art from early on.

As Manet crossed the ocean with me from Berkeley, California to Vienna, Austria, new friends came along and agreed to read first drafts of my manuscript, such as Johannes and Elisabeth Schlebrügge and Marcel Drach. Their insightful comments were most helpful to me as the manuscript progressively took on the shape of a book. Wolfgang Martin Roth also deserves a big thank you for repeatedly reminding me to remain focused on Manet, to recognize the importance of my work, and not to be diverted by other professional obligations. I also want to thank Cecilia Taiana, Angela Sowa and Pina Attinucci, our little "Vienna Group," for their wonderful suggestions and exacting criticism. I benefitted a great deal from their comments and the close scrutiny with which they read my text. I want to thank Françoise Davoine, my wonderful friend from Paris, who was one of the first to read through the entire manuscript and her honest and spontaneous enthusiasm helped me bring this book to fruition. I also want to express a deep gratitude to Vera Ligeti for her appreciative comments as well as Beate Hofstadler for patiently and repeatedly assisting me with the insertion of Manet's paintings into a text, August Ruhs for giving me a chance to hold several talks about Manet in German, Gabriele Braunsberg for giving me sound advice whenever I needed it and Marlene Roth-Greussing for being a good friend throughout this final process, and the late Elly Mayer for encouraging me all along to continue writing on "my Manet". Last, not least I want to thank my cousin Eva Hehemann for her encouragement in this whole endeavor.

My greatest gratitude goes to Andrew Ellis, my editor in Milan, who worked through several drafts of my book and helped me transform it into good English. Being sometimes hopelessly lost and stuck between two languages, I turned to Andrew, who knew how to "kick this text into shape." He was tirelessly committed to my endeavor, patient and funny at the same time, sending me encouragements and the occasional cartoon, along with anecdotes of his life alongside the young migrants he shares his home with as they integrate into Italian society. Thank you Irad Malkin for recommending Andrew to me, your referral provided me with a very special link.

Subsequently, it was one of my oldest friends, Geoffrey Layton, who directed me to Alexander Verlag Berlin, a very wonderful publisher with whom it has been a joy to work. Antje Wewerka's sensitive aesthetic mind and tireless efforts have contributed in essential ways to the final shape and design of the book, and I am most grateful for her suggestions and guidance. Alexander Wewerka is to be much thanked for agreeing to take on my Manet project in the first place, and to see it through in such an generous and respectful way. In addition, I would like to express my sincere gratitude to Katja Karau for lending her exquisite skills to editing my book one more time and I also would like to thank Xenia Andrä and Christin Heinrichs-Lauer of the Alexander Verlag Berlin for providing further patient and professional assistance to completing my book. A thank you also goes to Paulina Buhda for finding some missing references in a truly detective style. Much gratitude also goes to Elaine Taylor for crafting a most comprehensive index for my book. I would also like to express my gratitude to Judy Fox for allowing me the right to publish her picture of *Olympia*.

I want to thank Bernard Toboul in no small measure for the continuous support he has lent me throughout the years, for the many incisive discussions we had about Manet, Lacan, Bourdieu, Mallarmé and others, too numerous to mention here. His astute mind has helped me understand the depth of psychoanalytic thinking at a more judicious level. Last but not least I want to thank my daughter Anna-Nora for her help with this book, for the many visits upon which she accompanied me to view Manet's paintings at the Musée d'Orsay in Paris and the Metropolitan Museum in New York, and for simply being there from the very beginning.

Jeanne Wolff Bernstein
Vienna, January 2025

Abstract

This book examines the works of the French painter Édouard Manet from a psychoanalytic perspective. Unlike standard psychobiographic approaches that tend to neglect the artworks themselves and instead use them merely as clues to delve into the artist's unconscious, this treatise develops a psychoanalytic pictorial analysis through an exploration of Manet's oeuvre from three distinct viewpoints: personal, historical, and identificatory.

Rather than speculate about the artist's childhood experiences, this treatise matches the available biographical data against the paintings in which Manet frequently posed relatives and friends as models, and adopts the psychoanalytic technique of a dream or joke analysis to study the relationship between the painterly depictions and the biographic descriptions of the figures portrayed.

Manet's references to Old Masters are interpreted as memories from his painterly heritage. Comparing the techniques used in painting with those of the joke-work compresses a multiplicity of such references into a single work achieved through condensation, displacement, and indirect representation. In this way, Manet's recontextualizations of traditional sources are discussed in terms of the artist's personal interpretation of his era's painterly genealogy. This technique reveals how Manet's expression of the contradictions inherent to his epoch subtly veiled his criticism of the world around him.

For the analysis of the artist-painting-spectator relationship, the primary model is Freud's essay "Jokes and Their Relation to the Unconscious" (1905), whereby the joker calls upon his audience to complete a joke regarding a third figure: here the artist implicates the viewer's unconscious processes to complete the scene portrayed in the canvas. Much like the way an infant identifies with the mirrored representation of their own or their mother's body, the viewers seek aspects of themselves and their desires in the painting before them. This book will show how, unlike traditional painters, who tend to invite or exclude the spectator from the painted spectacle, Manet unsettles his viewer's identificatory desires by drawing them in and out of the scene depicted, thereby making them aware of the process in which they are engaged. Together, the three perspectives open a new domain for psychoanalytic studies in art, suggesting a methodology that can expand the interpretive techniques of both psychoanalytic and art-historical discussions of painting.

Introduction

Art historians and psychoanalysts alike have lamented and criticized the paucity of psychoanalytical contribution to the field of aesthetics. Following in Freud's footsteps, many psychoanalysts have relied upon highly speculative psycho-biographies to interpret a given painter's artwork. This line of approach not only raises the question of whether such a transposition can be affected with sufficient methodological rigor, but also whether it delivers any significant insights into the artwork itself.

Such standard psychoanalytic biographies have been used largely as a pretext for clinical studies of particular personalities and have shed scarcely any significant light upon the artworks themselves.

Does this mean that psychoanalytic criticism cannot make a significant contribution to the realm of aesthetics? The answer is clearly "no," as this treatise on Édouard Manet will show.

Using Freud's "Leonardo da Vinci and a Memory of his Childhood" (1910) as the primary model for aesthetic psychoanalytic investigations, post-Freudians have more or less shunned other crucial texts by Freud, despite the fact that these could have offered an alternative approach to painting than the psycho-biographic model. Consequently, as an object the artwork has been indicated merely as a clue for the psychological portrait of a painter.

A strictly pictorial analysis can only be undertaken if one sheds the constraints of a psycho-biographic approach, and instead consults texts like Sigmund Freud's "The Interpretation of Dreams" (1900); "Jokes and Their Relation to the Unconscious" (1905); "Delusions and Dreams in Jensen's Gradiva" (1907); and "Creative Writers and Day-Dreaming" (1908). In conjunction with writings by Jacques Lacan and D.W. Winnicott, in addition to different sources drawn from the world of art history, sociology, and semiotics, these texts form the wider body of writings which have enabled me to undertake a largely pictorial analysis of Édouard Manet's work.

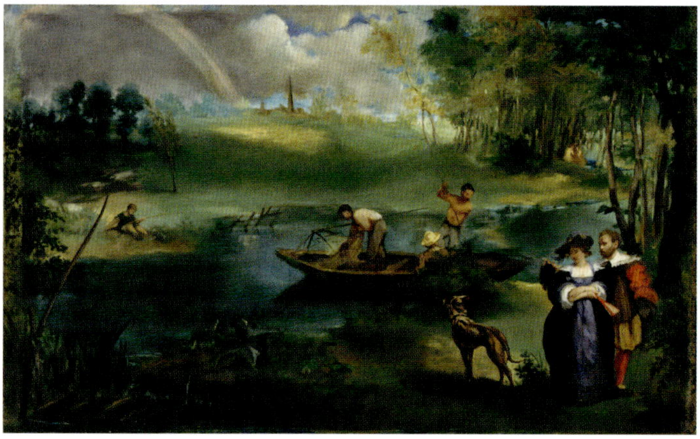

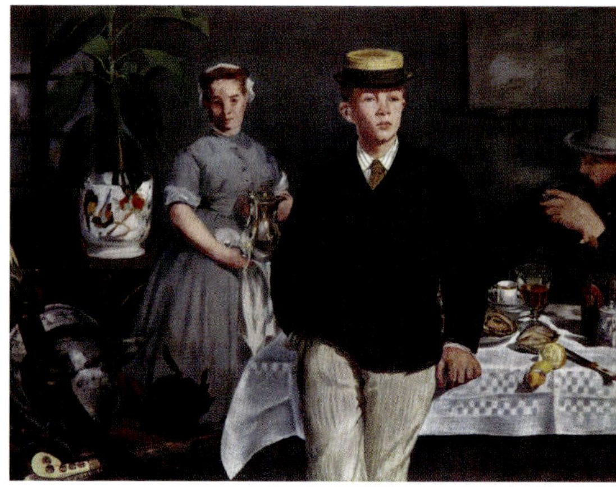

Plate 1: Édouard Manet, *La Pêche* (1861–1863)
Plate 2: Édouard Manet, *Le Déjeuner dans l'atelier* (1868)

It is no coincidence that I have selected Manet's oeuvre: his paintings irresistibly invite a psychoanalytic study precisely because they raise fundamental issues relevant to the analytical field of study such as the process of identification, the constitution of the subject through the Other, the status of the subject/interpreter in relation to the Other, the production of meaning, and the search into the past for an understanding of the present. In contrast to traditional aesthetic psychoanalytic examinations, which attempt to unlock a painting's unique hidden meanings, this book proposes that layers of meaning are continually created and re-created through a dialectical relationship between the painter, the painted object, and the spectator. In this relationship, a painting shares key characteristics with the structure of the spoken joke. For a joke to achieve its desired outcome, there also has to be a joker, along with the object of the joke, and not least a listener. While the common elements linking a painting with a joke will be discussed at greater length in Chapter I, it is important to note from the outset that I will use the same methods to explain Manet's paintings that Freud established in his research into humor in "Jokes and Their Relation to the Unconscious" (1905) and in "The Interpretation of Dreams" (1900).

In Chapter II, I will examine the principal details of Édouard Manet's life and artistic career. As I embarked on my research into the life of Manet, a few biographical oddities emerged. Recent research has revealed an indecipherable relationship between Manet and his alleged godson, Léon Édouard Koëlla Leenhoff. Was he Édouard Manet's son born out of wedlock, or was he instead his half-brother, the product of an alleged affair between his father and the then unmarried piano-teacher Suzanne Leenhoff, who would later become Édouard's wife? Léon's paternity has never been definitively resolved, and even his maternity was left cryptic since his mother Suzanne Leenhoff declared him to be "her younger brother" and only acknowledged him as her son in 1906, shortly before her own death. Notably, Léon Leenhoff appears as Manet's model in no less than seventeen of the painter's 420 works, but two of these in particular, *La Pêche* (1861–1863) [Plate 1] and *Le Déjeuner dans l'atelier* (1868) [Plate 2], might shed some light on Léon's elusive parenthood.

Meanwhile, Manet's paintings themselves constitute a major source for our psychological portrait of the artist, along with the many anecdotes narrated by his friends and contemporaries, letters written by him, and reviews of his works. Since Manet was in the habit of getting family members and friends to model for his paintings, the artworks themselves offer insights into Manet's private and social life. However, in order to situate Manet squarely in his epoch, we also need to look at the social environment in which he grew up and worked as an artist. By contextualizing our investigation we can reflect not only upon socio-historical events, but also probe the debates, conflicts, and issues dominating artistic circles during the man's life.

Chapter III examines the themes of Manet's paintings with a special focus on the artist's shrewd use of references taken from past painterly tradition: unlike earlier or contemporary painters, Manet strategically borrowed specific themes, figures, motives and compositions from the Old Masters, such as Velázquez, Goya, Rubens, Titian, Giorgione, and remodeled their themes and depictions for his own time.

A great many modern art-historians have researched Manet's references in considerable detail and have demonstrated convincingly which early paintings served as resources for his works. Hence, today one can no longer look at Manet's *Le Déjeuner sur l'herbe* (1863) [Plate 3] without comparing it to Giorgione's/Titian's *Le Concert*

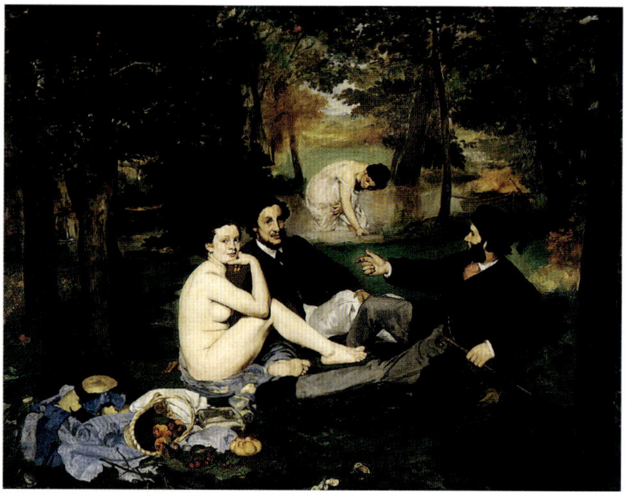

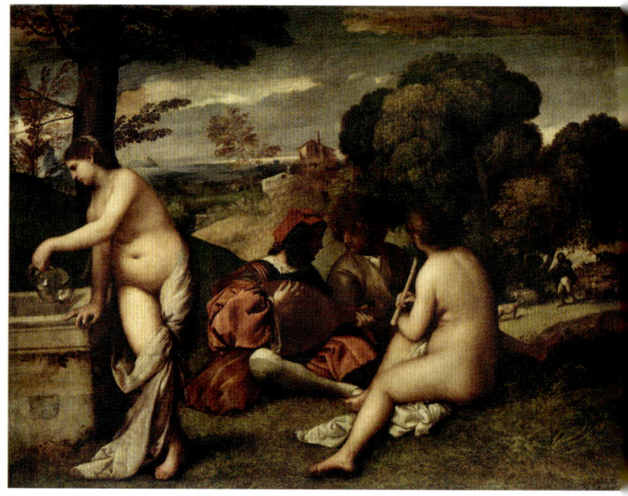

Plate 3: Édouard Manet, *Le Dejeuner sur l'herbe* (1863)
Plate 4: Giorgione/Titian, *Le Concert Champêtre* (1509)

Champêtre (1509) **[Plate 4]**, or Manet's *Olympia* (1863) **[Plate 5]** without referencing Titian's *Venus of Urbino* (1538) **[Plate 6]**.

Conventional art-historical research questions whether these past reference points were the true inspiration for Manet's works, or whether still others might be included, and if Manet effectively drew upon Velázquez or Goya, given that his first visit to Spain was not undertaken until 1865.[1]

I believe the correct question to address is why Manet so explicitly borrowed themes from earlier painters. While his contemporary critics either failed to recognize his use of traditional references or believed that Manet lacked imagination and therefore had to "copy" the Old Masters, more recent scholars have generally agreed that his use of existing compositions was itself a deliberate stratagem rather than a remedial device. While they also agree that Manet remained so modern because he was able to insert daily contemporary life in the place of historical subjects, few critics have discussed the specific methods by which he transformed traditional themes into scenes of modern life. With the exceptions of George Mauner's study *Manet, Peintre-Philosophe, A Study of the Painter's Themes* (1975) and Michael Fried's article "Manet's Sources, Aspects of his Art,

1 Notably, at the time, reproductions of any kind were virtually inexistent.

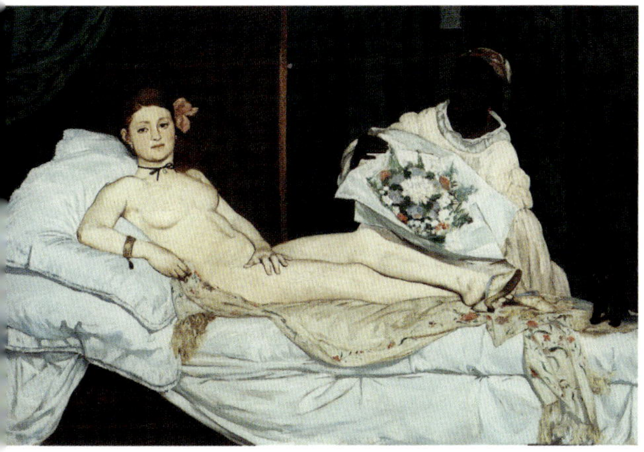

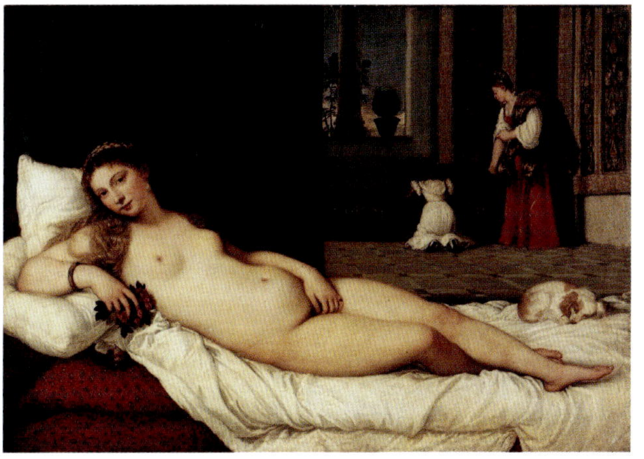

Plate 5:
Édouard Manet,
Olympia (1863)
Plate 6:
Titian,
Venus of Urbino (1538)

1859–1865" (1969), few critics have explored the particular meanings embodied in Manet's transformations.

What I intend to demonstrate here is that psychoanalysis proves to be a particularly incisive method to decipher Manet's transformations of old into new. Manet's creative translations of classical prototypes into contemporary modern scenes parallel the mechanisms at play in the unconscious activity of dreams. As the dream-work uses the process of condensation "to combine all the sources which have acted as stimuli for the dream into a single unity in the dream itself,"[2] so the painter has to fuse various references and current impressions and transfer them to a one-dimensional picture plane. Since the painter/dreamer also injects key latent meanings into details that seem insignificant, the same goes for the process of displacement. "[T]he psychical intensity," noted Freud, "passes over from the thoughts and ideas to which it properly belongs on to others which in our judgment have no claim to any such emphasis."[3] Moreover, like a dream, a painting cannot express causal relationships, logical connections or "either/or" options. Instead, "they [the dreams] reproduce *logical connections* by *approximation in time and*

2 Freud 1900: 179.
3 Freud 1900: 654.

space, just as a painter will represent all the poets in a single group in a picture of Parnassus."[4]

These metaphoric and metonymic relationships will be analyzed in detail below, and—as Freud suggested when he described his method of interpreting dreams—not en masse.[5] Manet's paintings lend themselves to such a pictorial analysis precisely because he regularly provides his viewer with explicit references to the original and canonical pictorial scenes. An analysis of *Olympia* (1863) therefore invites a comparison with Titian's *Venus of Urbino* (1538), which in turn allows us to unravel the deliberate distortions and transformations that Manet bestowed upon the finished works.

The fact that the same analytic method developed by Freud for the interpretation of dreams is used here for Manet's oeuvre does not imply that a painting functions like a dream. Nor does it suggest that the *Venus of Urbino* should be regarded as the latent content vs. the manifest content of Manet's *Olympia*.

Instead, "The dream thoughts and the dream content are presented to us like two versions of the same subject-matter in two different *languages*."[6] In this sense, the meaning of *Olympia* does not reside in the notion that she represents a nineteenth-century version of Titian's *Venus of Urbino*. Actually, the links arising from the comparison of these two paintings reveal a multiplicity of meanings embedded in the new work. Analogous to Bakhtin's conception of a text "as a mosaic of quotations [...] and as the absorption and transformation of other texts,"[7] Manet's paintings are replete with quotations of the past that represent reinterpretations of the Old Masters as well as oft-hidden, satirical, and sometimes political commentaries on the artist's contemporary world. Adopting Lacan's concept of language as a sliding chain of signifiers to the realm of painting, I argue that Manet's subject matter constitutes a link in the ever-shifting interconnection of pictorial representations across

---

4 Freud 1900: 661 (emphasis in the original).

5 See Freud 1900: 104.

6 Freud 1900: 277 (author's emphasis).

7 Kristeva 1986: 37.

generations. As a result, his paintings cannot be interpreted as mere representations of his own particular personal and social environment, but—as the painter himself well understood—as elements in the sliding circuit of pictorial productions. Meaning is generated therefore not only by sifting through past resources, but also in the relationships that the artist's paintings evoke and arouse in the spectator, then and now.

The way in which his figures gaze out of the canvas has puzzled art critics and often disconcerted his admirers—from the first viewers of his day to his critics of more recent date. The apparent immediacy of the figures is belied by the aloofness of their gaze, a factor that prompts our awareness that not only are they involved in the process of returning our gaze, but that our "voyeurism" is predicted by the figures themselves.

This process of observing/being observed is explored further in Chapter IV and reveals how Manet strategically positioned his spectators in his compositions. While previous painters tended to maintain a certain distance from their future viewers—never overtly challenging the relationship between the artwork and the beholder—Manet makes this crucial bond part of the work itself, endowing it with an innovative emotional thrust. While the viewer is at first drawn into some private relationship with the figures in the painting, they soon become aware that they are privy to a form of public exposure that also involves their own.

I maintain that the reason why Manet's paintings elicit such a complex and enigmatic relationship with their viewer is that they thematize the process of identification, which Lacan defines as the process through which the subject is constituted by the Other.

One of the texts behind Lacan's mirror stage may have been Freud's analysis of Michelangelo's statue of Moses in Rome. Freud did not intend his text to focus on identification (unlike his "Group Psychology and the Analysis of the Ego" of 1921), but rather as a covertly autobiographical essay in which he reveals his distrust toward his followers after the rift with C.G. Jung in 1913. Yet, as he stands there in the Vincoli church in Rome, Freud unwittingly identifies with the sculpture discussed in his essay "The Moses of Michelangelo" of

1914. Freud relates a scenario based upon his painstakingly detailed evaluation of the statue's specifics, in which

> Suddenly the clamour strikes his ear; he turns his head and eyes in the direction from which the disturbance comes, sees the scene and takes it in. [...] His rage, distant as yet from its object, is meanwhile directed in a gesture against his own body.[8]

While traditionally the "Moses of Michelangelo" text has been viewed as one of Freud's most telling autobiographical revelations, few theoreticians have considered examining the identificatory process as a necessary and unconscious process by which the viewer interiorizes a work of art and at times *"completes"* it, filling in the blanks, as it were.

The objective here is to show how Manet's paintings require a closer study of the viewers' identification with the figures portrayed, and how the artist implicates and enframes the spectators' participation, particularly in his most enigmatic works. While he invites his viewer to cross the threshold and don the guise of one of the figures portrayed, at the same time he makes it clear that the scenario he or she enters is the viewer's own invention. While previous painters arrested their viewers in an imaginary position, Manet upends this approach and makes us aware of the complex and intricate dynamic he applied in order to induce his audience to engage with the work before them.

It is my hope that this book will contribute to the enduring legacy of Édouard Manet's work, which remains unrivaled in its enigmatic use of classic works of the past while prompting a complex and baffling challenge regarding how the viewer engages with any artwork, both past and present.

---

8 Freud 1914b: 225.

Chapter I

PSYCHOANALYTIC APPROACHES TO ART

If in making these statements I have provoked the criticism, even from friends of psycho-analysis and from those who expert in it, that I may have merely written a psycho-analytic novel, I shall reply that I am far from over-estimating the certainty of these results. Like others I have succumbed to the attraction of this great and mysterious man [...].

Sigmund Freud, "Leonardo da Vinci and a Memory of his Childhood" (1910)

[...] Freud's essay on Leonardo [...] is primarily a study in psychoanalytic biography: and the connection with art is *almost* exhausted by the fact that the subject of the biography happens to be one of the greatest, as well as one of the strangest artists in history.

Richard Wollheim, *On Art and the Mind* (1974)

Sigmund Freud's essay on Leonardo continues to offer the cornerstone of psychoanalytic art criticism, despite Freud's own misgivings about "the certainty of these results."[1] The question that logically arises for any contemporary investigation is to what extent the techniques developed by Freud in the Leonardo paper offer an explanatory force, such that post-Freudians saw no reason to question their methods when analyzing a work of art. It may be that some

1 Freud 1910a: 134.

post-Freudians recognized the flaws in Freud's essay on Leonardo, but decided that the psychoanalytic theory itself was inherently limited to offering a series of more or less subtle psycho-biographic accounts of the genesis of works of art. The issue, then, for those writers who seek to challenge the privileged status of the artistic psycho-biography is primarily methodological in nature, that is, in addition to those elaborated by Freud, what other methods can be introduced to widen the horizon of psychoanalytic art theory.

To answer this question, one has to revisit Freud's text on Leonardo da Vinci and evaluate the strengths and weaknesses of his procedure. Freud's primary goal was to solve the riddles that had already perplexed Leonardo's contemporaries. Like them, he was intrigued by Leonardo's complete withdrawal from painting after a successful artistic career, and by his seeming indifference to the fate of his artworks once he had begun to devote himself to scientific research. Puzzled by the contrast between Leonardo's striking lack of concern towards his paintings and drawings, and his fierce pursuit of scientific research, Freud believed that his psychoanalytic method might explain these inconsistencies and gaps in Leonardo's life and oeuvre.

Such a decision was, of course, a natural extension of Freud's prior work, since the analysis of inconsistencies, contradictions, and lacunas in human behavior had led Freud to revolutionary discoveries in his works on dreams, jokes, and the myriad pathological phenomena of everyday life. Following the same strategies as the ones pursued in these studies, he suggested: "If a biographical study is really intended to arrive at an understanding of its hero's mental life it must not—as happens in the majority of biographies as a result of discretion or prudishness—silently pass over its subject's sexual activity or sexual individuality."[2]

Freud subsequently concluded that Leonardo's artistic inhibition was paralleled by a sexual inhibition, even though Leonardo is rumored to have actively practiced his homosexuality. Freud deduced that Leonardo's sexual energy was now being primarily channeled into his scientific research. Having established these two important

2 Freud 1910a: 69.

elements in Leonardo's life—the artistic and sexual inhibition on one hand, and the alleged homosexual proclivity and thirst for scientific knowledge on the other—Freud drew upon his research of childhood sexuality to establish a structure for his own investigation. Yet, before he began the reconstruction of Leonardo's childhood in terms of fixation points and successive regressions, he searched for material from the artist's early years that could provide him with the necessary insights into his fantasy life. He found such a source in the man's only documented childhood memory: "I recall as one of my very earliest memories that while I was in my cradle a vulture came down to me, and opened my mouth with its tail, and struck me many times with its tail against my lips."[3]

In the same manner that the analyst's work involves the dream-text narrated by a patient, Freud dissected this statement into its component elements, and drawing upon his research in mythology, anthropology, and archaeology, he arrived at the following analysis: the vulture is a replacement for the mother, and the insertion of the vulture's tail is a fantasy that conceals "a reminiscence of sucking—or being suckled—at his mother's breast". The symbol of the striking tail, corresponding to the act of fellatio, is an act that Freud most characteristically associated with homosexuality. This explanation led Freud to assess that Leonardo, as an illegitimate son, initially experienced the undivided love of his mother, who seduced him into sexual precocity; in the absence of a father, the mother became the only object of Leonardo's desire. The move to the household of his noble father and stepmother, however, led to the repression of Leonardo's erotic feelings toward his mother. Leonardo preserved these feelings for his mother by identifying himself with her and by seeking sexual relationships with other boys. This way, he could hold onto his mother and only love boys, in the same way as he was loved by his mother. It is with this childhood reconstruction in hand that Freud reviewed the successive stages of Leonardo's adult life. Freud linked the initial phase of the man's artistic career to the first years of unbounded love for his mother. But gradually, parallel to the loss

---

3 Freud 1910a: 82.

of his love object and entrance into his father's house, Leonardo withdrew from painting and devoted himself to the rigid pursuit of scientific research. Freud found that "the effect which Leonardo's identification with his father had on his paintings was a fateful one. He created them and then cared no more about them, just as his father had not cared for him."[4]

In a sense, Leonardo's thirst for knowledge not only emanated from his early sexual curiosity, but it also served as a defense mechanism against his erotic desires toward his mother. Even a seeming violation of this schema—Leonardo's brief return to painting toward the latter part of his life—is incorporated by Freud without any noticeable strain on the general argument. He suggests moreover that the model for the *Mona Lisa* portrait—the Florentine lady Lisa Gherardini del Giocondo—elicited memories of his mother's love in a way that unleashed new creative forces in him. Yet, before I address Freud's analysis of the *Mona Lisa* and the *Madonna and Child with St. Anne* paintings per se, some comments are required about the general reliability of Freud's interpretive methods in the essay.

It has been widely documented that Freud committed two major factual mistakes in his interpretation of Leonardo's childhood memory. The first error is his mistranslation of the Italian word "nibbio"[5] as vulture rather than as kite. This initial mistake led him to the erroneous assumption that the Egyptian hieroglyph for the word mother ("mut"), which correctly represents a vulture, would further confirm his findings. The fact that the very core of Freud's analysis of Leonardo da Vinci—the interpretation of the artist's childhood dream—is itself governed by a mistranslation into German of the dream text's crucial symbol, has by now become a commonplace in discussions of the Leonardo essay. But the full implications of this error have received surprisingly little rigorous scrutiny. Indeed, once one becomes aware of the factual mistake, the truly curious

---

4 Freud 1910a: 121.

5 For a detailed discussion of Freud's mistranslation of the Italian word "nibbio" as "vulture" rather than as "kite", see Schapiro 1956; Spector 1974; Fuller 1980; and-Strachey 1978.

thing is how Freud actually pays very little attention to the symbolic significance of the vulture image. He selects an ancient legend, by which female vultures are said to be inseminated by the wind, in order to underscore the significance he attributed to the illegitimacy of Leonardo's birth and the absence of the father during the artist's infancy. At the same time, however, Freud does not refer to the vulture as a bird of prey or, figuratively speaking, as "something which preys upon a person, the mind, etc.; a consuming or torturing passion; a person of a vile and rapacious disposition" (*Oxford English Dictionary*). Since vultures are more commonly associated with predatory beasts rather than with their particular method of becoming impregnated, Freud's decision to treat only the most arcane of the bird's characteristic associations is itself a leap that requires some explanation. Meyer Schapiro is one of the few art historians who evaluates the implications that a correct translation would have had on the interpretation of Leonardo's childhood fantasy. He states:

> "Of the kite we read that when it sees that its children are too fat, it pecks their sides out of envy and keeps them without food." The kite here is not the model of the good mother who wishes to have her child her own forever; she is the opposite of the vulture which, according to tradition (ignored by Leonardo) is the best of all mothers, protecting her young for a hundred and twenty days and scratching herself to give her blood to her young—an emblem of compassion like the pelican which symbolizes Christ's sacrifice. [...] A psychologist could infer [...] that Leonardo did not forgive Caterina his illegitimacy and her willingness to abandon him to a step-mother.[6]

While the correct translation of "kite" might have led Freud to a different interpretation of Leonardo's childhood, what this error demonstrates most strikingly is the deliberate manner in which Freud assembled his material relating to the discussion of Leonardo. Without pursuing the issue of the multiple interpretations of the vulture image, one may justifiably be surprised by Freud's decision

6 Schapiro 1956: 156–157.

to choose the sole interpretation which would support his basic argument for Leonardo's homosexuality. In response to the factual mistakes Freud made in his essay and troubled by the insufficient biographical information available to him, post-Freudians have tried to refine their methodology so that the same criticism could not be leveled against them.[7] As a result, painters like Van Gogh, Picasso, and Michelangelo are preferable as subjects of study, because they left behind a wider range of biographical data. While recognizing Freud's somewhat halting research, few psychoanalysts have questioned the psycho-biographic method per se as a privileged approach to art criticism. On the contrary, they have extended Freud's claim even further by arguing that psycho-biographic techniques might be applied to analyze not only the artist, but also the art object.

Since Freud never presumed to write a psychoanalytic study of Leonardo's works but only of his character, one is struck by the post-Freudians' insistence on using the Leonardo paper as their model for aesthetic studies. Freud himself emphasizes throughout the Leonardo text that "[t]he aim of our work has been to explain the inhibitions in Leonardo's sexual life and in his artistic activity."[8] In other words, the Leonardo monograph is not primarily a study about art. Instead, the artist's life history serves as an excuse for Freud's real purpose of showing how adult capacities are dependent upon early infantile experiences.

The study of Leonardo emerged from Freud's desire to exhibit another case history that could demonstrate the universal importance of early infantile sexuality as postulated in "Three Essays on the Theory of Sexuality" (1905), and to show clearly that psychiatric research was not limited to the study of "frailer men," but could equally examine

---

7 The minutes of the Vienna Psychoanalytic Society which document Freud's first presentation of the Leonardo material to his psychoanalytic circle also indicate that neither Freud nor his colleagues were primarily interested in the artistic aspects of Leonardo da Vinci. Instead, their discussion focused on the diagnostic aspects of Leonardo's personality. See *Minutes of the Vienna Psychoanalytic Society*, eds. Herman Nunberg and Ernst Federn, vol. II, 338–352 (New York: International Universities Press, 1976).

8 Freud 1910a: 131.

"one who is among the greatest of the human race […]."[9] Furthermore, the particular case history of Leonardo furthermore gave Freud the opportunity to set the stage for two theories he would develop later in more detail: the theory of homosexuality and that of narcissism. In a sense, therefore, the Leonardo text served several purposes, and paradoxically it is the least significant of these for which it has subsequently become best known, namely, for the study of art.

Despite the fact that Freud never intended the Leonardo text to serve as a template for psychoanalytic studies of art, this is precisely what it has become. As a result, post-Freudians have continued to argue that a work of art cannot be adequately understood without an in-depth knowledge of the artist's life history. And more importantly, they have persisted in treating the artwork per se as an object whose hidden meanings are to be unlocked by establishing the secret autobiographical key to its structure. By this reckoning, an artwork cannot signify formal terms on its own, but must be examined for clues about the artist's inner life. This conviction not only vitiates the analysis of an artwork on its own formal terms, but it also severely hampers the potential to analyze the oeuvre of artists who have not left behind significant biographical material to work from. In the absence of exploring verbal statements as they might with a patient's free associations, psychoanalysts have tended to remain silent when discussing artworks on their own. Instead of seeking a suitable methodology vis-à-vis a painted object, psychoanalysts have been inclined to limit their attention to those artists who left behind an abundance of biographical material—such as letters, diaries, and autobiographical documents—and then used these particulars to analyze a particular artifact. And yet, numerous texts by Freud lend themselves for the interpretation of objects of art, irrespective of whether they are publicly acknowledged as inquiries into aesthetics.

---

9 Freud 1910a: 63.

The Moses of Michelangelo

At first glance, Freud's "The Moses of Michelangelo" (1914) appears to focus solely on aesthetics. Unlike the Leonardo paper, in which Freud probes the artist behind the work, and the canvases themselves are marginal to his analysis, in the Michelangelo piece Freud focuses on the statue's expressive character as well as on the spectator's personal reaction to the monument. Interestingly enough, Freud confines his observations to the statue itself and strangely omits any considerations on Michelangelo's personal life, although a far greater amount of biographic material is available on Buonarroti than on his contemporary Leonardo da Vinci. To my mind, Freud so keenly identified with the figure of Moses that he failed to reflect upon the person who had created this magnificent sculpture. In a way, Freud neglected his own inclination to craft a psycho-biographic tale and instead remained fixated on the sculpted figure itself.[10]

Since the Moses study represents an alternative to the psycho-biographic method, the question arises why this text is so rarely treated as a study in aesthetics, whereas the Leonardo paper—which was written largely as a psycho-biographical case study—is still considered the standard psychoanalytic text for any discussion on art. The conventional neglect of "The Moses of Michelangelo" paper is largely due to the text being identified as an autobiographic statement by and about Freud himself. It is a well-known fact that the Moses study was writ-

10 Freud published the Moses study anonymously in 1914 in *Imago*. It was only in 1924 that he agreed to publish it under his own name. According to Ernest Jones, Freud gave three reasons for his decision to write the essay without signing it. "The reasons he [Freud] gave for his decision seem rather thin. 'Why disgrace Moses by putting my name to it? It is a joke, but perhaps not a bad one.' To Abraham he gave three reasons: (1) 'it is only a joke,' (2) 'Shame at the evident amateurishness of the essay,' (3) 'Lastly because my doubt about my conclusion is stronger than usual; it is only because of editorial pressure (Rank and Sachs) that I have consented to publish it at all'." (Jones 1953, II: 366). It is interesting to note that *Fragment of an Analysis of a Case of Hysteria* (1905) was also published with a delay. Freud wrote down the Dora case in 1901, but waited four years before publishing it. The curious coincidence might be explained by the fact that Freud in both papers inadvertently exhibits his transference relationship to Dora, his patient, and to Moses, the human figure externalized in the Michelangelo statue.

ten at the height of the controversy and eventual break-up with C.G. Jung. Like the Moses he describes, in 1914, Freud was ready to throw down the Tablets of the Law (i.e., his psychoanalytic works) and take vengeance upon his faithless followers. As Ernest Jones aptly puts it:

> Was Moses on descending from Sinai unable to control his anger, as the Bible related, or could he attain the heights of self-control which Freud maintained Michelangelo depicted? We know that this preoccupation coincided with the time when he was suppressing his own indignation at the way his Swiss followers had suddenly repudiated his work, and that merely confirms what his intense preoccupation alone would have taught us: namely, that he had emotional reasons for identifying himself with his mighty predecessor.[11]

Peter Fuller adds another interesting note to the historical circumstances surrounding Freud's conception of the Moses study. Since the Moses text was written at about the same time as Freud's essay "On Narcissism: An Introduction" (1914), Fuller argues that the Moses study represented Freud's counter-piece to the more "revolutionary" study "On Narcissism," and that in it, Freud pledged his allegiance to scientific methods and the truth. While "On Narcissism" was a purely speculative, meta-psychological endeavor, the Moses essay was devised to be a "strictly scientific enterprise." All these viewpoints suggest that in the course of this exegesis, the Moses of Michelangelo was subsumed into the Moses of Freud.

While personal interests and attractions seem to have influenced both of Freud's studies in aesthetics, the Michelangelo paper remains the one most typically linked to his personal concerns. Classifying the Moses paper as an autobiographical document has resulted in a widespread disregard for the important aesthetic issues Freud raises in the essay. In a sense, the traditional perspective on this study is fairly justified, since Freud himself clearly intended the text to be a thinly disguised warning to his errant followers and allowed his tendency for polemic to derail the development of a more strictly pictorial psychoanalysis. However, potential traces of that reluctant

---

11 Jones 1953, III: 368.

analysis can be found amidst the more transient concerns of the essay, and it is those traces that a closer reading of "The Moses of Michelangelo" can help bring to the surface.

Freud is guided by a complex mesh of motives in his study of Michelangelo's statue, which contained multiple strands that are absent from his earlier texts on art. Whilst he emphasized his personal fascination with the figure of Leonardo da Vinci and studied the painter/scientist from the perspective of "the conscious communion of one great man with another,"[12] in the Michelangelo text Freud admits that "no piece of statuary has ever made a stronger impression on me than this."[13] From the beginning, Freud establishes a relationship not so much between himself and the hidden artist, as between himself and the visible sculpture. Unlike the distant clinical stance Freud assumes when he analyzes Leonardo's paintings, he commences the Michelangelo piece with a powerful emotional confession:

> Nevertheless, works of art do exercise a powerful effect on me, especially those of literature and sculpture, less often of painting. This has occasioned me, when I have been contemplating such things, to spend a long time before them trying to apprehend them in my own way, i.e. to explain to myself what their effect is due to. Wherever I cannot do this, as for instance with music, I am almost incapable of obtaining any pleasure. Some rationalistic, or perhaps analytic, turn of mind in me rebels against being moved by a thing without knowing why I am thus affected and what it is that affects me.[14]

By seemingly taking the reader into his confidence, Freud establishes two important principles which hitherto had never figured in his speculations on art: first, the study of works of art as self-sufficient entities; and second, the effect of the artwork upon the observer.

Let me now turn to the first principle and examine the methods by which Freud approaches the artwork in questioning the statue of Moses in the church of San Pietro in Vincoli, Rome. In a letter

---

12 Wollheim 1974: 205.

13 Freud 1914b: 213.

14 Freud 1914b: 211.

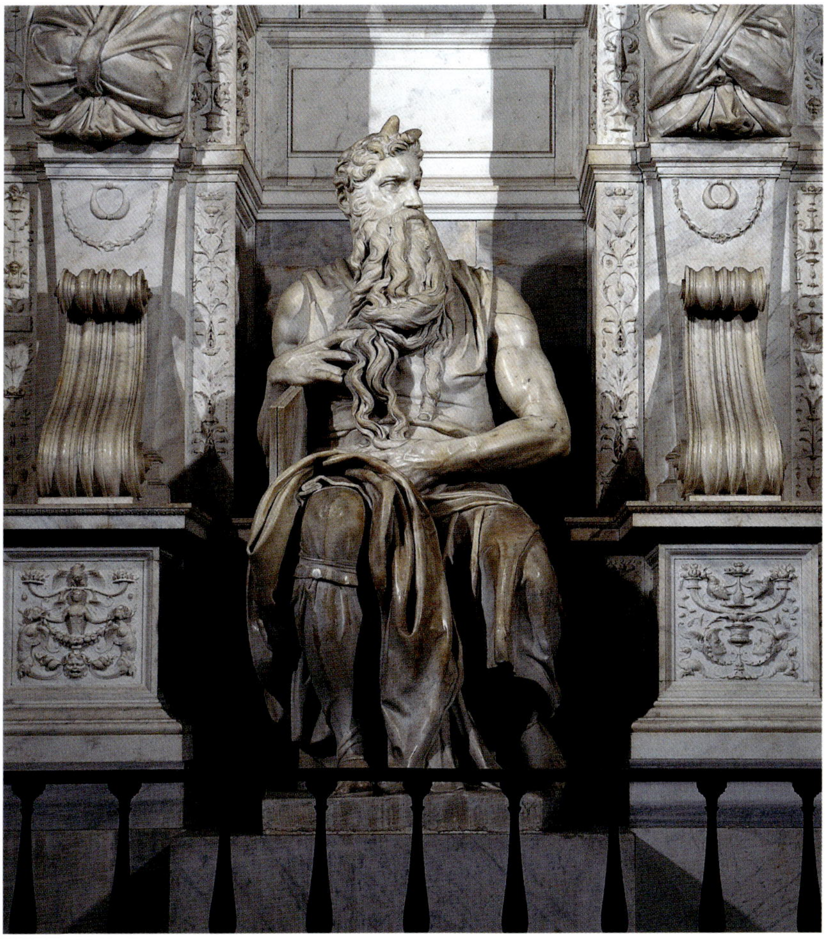

Plate 7: Michelangelo, *Moses* (1513–1515)

to Eduardo Weiss, Freud emphasizes the empirical undertone of the Moses paper: "For three lonely September weeks in 1913 I stood every day in the church in front of the statue, studied it, measured it, sketched it until I captured the understanding for it which I ventured to express in the essay only anonymously."[15]

In his attempt to unravel "the meaning and content" of what is "represented"[16] in Michelangelo's *Moses* (1513–1515) **[Plate 7]** from a scientific psychoanalytic viewpoint, Freud finds support for his project

15 Jones 1953, II: 367.
16 Freud 1914b: 212.

in the research of Giovanni Morelli, an Italian art connoisseur, who had invented a new method for distinguishing original works of art from copies.[17] Freud succinctly describes Morelli's method, which consisted of:

> [...] insisting that attention should be diverted from the general impression and main features of a picture, and by laying stress on the significance of minor details, of things like the drawing of the fingernails, of the lobe of an ear, of halos and such unconsidered trifles which the copyist neglects to imitate and yet which every artist executes in his own characteristic way.[18]

Freud uncovered certain similarities between Morelli's and his own psychoanalytic technique, in their common refusal to be swayed by the general impression of a painting/dream, and insistence upon the examination of details as opposed to facile global themes. Based on this, Freud concludes that the Morelli method of inquiry "is closely related to the technique of psycho-analysis. It, too, is accustomed to divine secret and concealed things from despised or unnoticed features, from the rubbish-heap, as it were, of our observations."[19] The impression that these two methods share common features is seemingly further sustained if one compares the Morelli technique with Freud's description of the interpretation of dreams:

> Our first step in the employment of this procedure teaches us that what we must take as the object of our attention is not the dream as a whole but the separate portions of its content. If I say to a patient who is still a novice: 'What occurs to you in connection with this dream?', as a rule his mental horizon becomes a blank. If, however, I put the dream before him cut up into pieces, he will give me a series of associations to each piece, which might be described as the 'background thoughts' of that particular part of the dream.[20]

---

17 For a detailed study of the Morelli method, see Richard Wollheim's essay, "Giovanni Morelli and the origins of scientific connoisseurship," (Wollheim 1974: 177–201).

18 Freud 1914b: 222.

19 Freud 1914b: 222.

20 Freud 1900: 103–104.

I believe, however, that these apparent similarities obscure the fundamental differences between the Morellian and Freudian techniques. Whereas Morelli was keen to distinguish copies from originals and to establish the authenticity of authorship, Freud was not concerned with questions of attribution. Rather, he wanted to analyze rationally why this particular statue exerted such a powerful effect upon him. In fact, Freud not only used the Morelli method for a different purpose than its creator intended, but applied it to unravel the *meaning* rather than the *provenance* of the Moses statue, and failed to take into account the theoretical contradictions between the hermeneutic essence of psychoanalysis and the natural-scientific orientation of Morelli's method. Jack Spector argues:

> [...] Freud's comparison of his method with Morelli's is not wholly accurate. Whereas the analyst, assuming that beneath the formal surface lie the depths of emotion, looked *through* the detail, and used it as a peephole onto secrets of the mind, the connoisseur, assuming that in art the formal surface is the main thing, looked *at* the detail, and grouped it with other details to establish the artist's stylistic identity.[21]

What were the principal features of the Morelli method? According to the Italian scholar, the task of a connoisseur consists of the study of individual works, what they represent, and to whom they should be attributed. He criticized art historians for their lack of scientific research and believed that

> [...] all art-historians, from Vasari down to our own day, have only made use of two tests to aid them in deciding the authorship of a work of art—intuition, or the so-called general impression, and documentary evidence; with what result you have seen for yourself.[22]

Showing ill-concealed contempt for his fellow art historians, Morelli developed complex schemata of so-called *Grundformen*, those signa-

21 Spector 1969: 68 (emphasis in the original).
22 Morelli 1892, I: 21.

ture forms and shapes characteristic to each artist. He drew up a series of schedules, each based on independently authenticated works of art which illustrated how a particular detail of the body—an ear, a hand, a foot or thumbnail—were painted by individual artists. Based upon this catalogue of hallmarks, Morelli could, for example, distinguish a Bellini from a Botticelli depiction. Morelli's method was based on the belief that each artist possessed signature traits, and that these traits were consistently repeated throughout the artist's entire oeuvre. This quest for distinguishing hallmarks is reminiscent of the very popular nineteenth-century discipline of graphology, and, as Spector argues, also of the science of physiognomy.

> Like Morelli, physiognomists such as the famous Lavater were especially interested in the permanent qualities of personality, rather than in pathography or the momentary moods and passions [...].
> One might also compare Morelli's methods of detecting forgeries obviously to the work of criminologists, but also to the increasingly popular genre of detective stories. One thinks especially of Poe, whose methods of detection included criptography along with graphology, and who made small overlooked details into the major clues.[23]

When Morelli studied a painting, he essayed to detect the artist's stylistic identity—in other words, his signature—by examining isolated details within the canvas. Had Morelli been commissioned to examine the Moses statue for authenticity, he would have been satisfied to certify that it was an autograph work of Michelangelo, and unlike Freud this would have been the purpose of his examination.

Driven by his life-long need to appear scientific, especially after the rather speculative and emotive text "On Narcissism" (1914), in his own scrutiny of the monument Freud was prompted to choose a technique that closely resembled his own detailed observational style, and he settled upon Morelli's procedure and approached the statue of Moses in the role of a scientific observer. Like a physician, Freud "treats" the Moses as a specimen figure that undergoes a close

23 Spector 1969: 71–72.

physical examination, not unlike the bodily inspections that the title character had to endure under the doctor in Georg Büchner's famous play, *Woyzeck*.[24]

Where Morelli would cross-reference specific patterns shared between different paintings, Freud instead establishes and analyzes the connections between the particular elements within the single statue. Freud's method of linking specific configurations within the Moses statue and creating an imaginary scenery for Moses's prior movements before he was captured in the pose in which Michelangelo portrays him has been compared to a cinematographic technique.

"Others have prised Freud's methods even further away from the early 19th century spiritual modes of analysing a work of art," notes Peter Fuller, "and claimed, I think convincingly, that Freud's interpretation is '*cinematographic*': i.e. the very way in which he looks at the Moses and perceives it as forming part of a 'readable' continuum of events suggests that his perception has been conditioned by the photograph."[25]

Indeed, Morelli's failure to analyze the juxtapositions of the bodily details represents one of the major flaws in his theory. As Wollheim observes: "[T]he same configuration can in different circumstances, that is to say in different contexts or in different wholes, look very different."[26] It is precisely this "adjustment" of the Morellian method that leads Freud to an entirely different analysis of the artwork, one that Morelli would likely never have endorsed. Moreover, since it was not Freud's goal to confirm the authorship of the Moses statue, but rather to explain the discrepancy between the statue's "outward" calm and "inward" emotions,[27] Freud interpreted Michelangelo's characteristic traits not as signatures validating authenticity, but as

---

24 Doctor: "Woyzeck, you have the finest *aberratio mentalis partialis* of the second category, quite pronounced. Woyzeck, I'm going to give you a raise. Second category: fixed idea but otherwise rational. Apart from that, going on as usual? (...) Eating your peas? (...) Carrying out your duties? (...) You're an interesting case, Woyzeck. You'll get a raise. Just keep it up. Let me feel your pulse. Yes." (Büchner 1996: 22–23).

25 Fuller 1980: 46 (author's emphasis).

26 Wollheim 1974: 188.

27 Freud 1914b: 221.

signs of a specific artistic intention. In other words, each detail encumbered meaning, and it is only through a rigorous examination of these details that the statue's intentions and effect upon the spectator can be unveiled.

From the outset, Freud agreed with those art historians who argued that Michelangelo had portrayed a particular moment in Moses's life rather than "a timeless study of character and mood."[28] Had Michelangelo captured the instant before Moses springs to his feet and takes action? Or had he portrayed Moses in the moment before he hurls the Tablets of the Law to the ground upon seeing his people dancing around the Golden Calf? This psychological inscape trapped in the figure was what intrigued Freud.

While Freud ostensibly adopted the Morellian method to uncover the true meaning—or, as I prefer, the underlying *plot* of the Moses statue—, he in fact used this scientific discipline to screen his identification with the mythical story of Moses's deeds and character.[29] This ostensible scientific method served a deeper function, however. In Freud's clinical recommendations, crafted around the same time as "On Narcissism" of 1914 and "The Moses of Michelangelo," he strongly warned against the influence of the analyst's countertransference in the analytical process. Countertransference, the analyst's personal, emotive responses to a given patient, were in his thinking something to be overcome, an interference with the analyst's dispassionate, "neutral" and objective view of the patient. Succumbing to a highly emotional reaction in front of the Moses sculpture had to be counterbalanced and disguised behind the kind of dispassionate tone employed by Morelli.

What makes Freud's text on the Moses statue so crucial, is that it provides us with a formidable document in which Freud unintentionally illustrates the conflict between a purely pictorial and a

28 Freud 1914b: 215.

29 As Ernest Jones observes: "There is every reason to suppose that the grand figure of Moses himself, from Freud's early Biblical studies to the last book he ever wrote, was one of tremendous significance to him. Did he represent the formidable Father-Image, or did Freud identify himself with him? Apparently both, at different periods." (Jones 1955, II: 364–365).

highly subjective analysis of a work, foreshadowing the later much more extensive discussion about the relevance of countertransference in the comprehension of the patient's unconscious dynamics. Was the analyst the sleuth or the co-author of the patient's/art object's construction?

A close reading of Freud's procedure reveals how intimately the two seemingly antithetical types of evaluations are often related. In the first part of his investigation, Freud still adheres strictly to the dictum of the Morellian and psychoanalytic principle of paying close attention to the minutiae of an artwork. He observes, for instance, that, "the thumb of the hand is concealed and the index finger alone is in effective contact with the beard," or that the "other three fingers are propped upon the wall of his chest and are bent at the upper joints [...]."[30]

This itemization of the sculpture uncovers certain seemingly insignificant inconsistencies, such as the precarious position of the tablets held against the body and the anatomically implausible droop of Moses's beard. In addition, Freud is perplexed by the position of the man's right hand, his fingers threading through a clump of beard that trails down from the left side of his jaw. He remarks "how strangely unsuitable as a means does the pressure of a single finger appear to be!" Assuring the reader that "[t]here is a solution which will remove our difficulties", Freud infers that "there had been a retreating motion of the right hand. This one assumption necessarily brings others with it. In imagination we complete the scene of which this movement, established by the evidence of the beard, is a part [...]."[31]

The change in Freud's language from a pedestrian physical description to the informal style of inviting the reader on stage "to complete the scene" is paralleled by the different stance Freud himself assumes vis-à-vis the sculpture.[32] Drawing up sketches of the imagined previ-

---

30 Freud 1914b: 223.

31 Freud 1914b: 224.

32 Freud used a similar terminology in his studies on hysteria. Describing the hysteric's remembrance of repressed incompatible ideas, he frequently described this process as the patient's reproduction of past scenes. The theatricality of his language might have been partially influenced by the rhetoric of Anna O. (Josef

ous movements of the Moses sculpture, Freud suddenly imbues the statue with life and creates a stormy, even melodramatic scenario:

> [...] Moses desired to act, to spring up and take vengeance and forget the Tables; but he has overcome the temptation, and he will now remain seated and still, in his frozen wrath and in his pain mingled with contempt. Nor will he throw away the Tables so that they will break on the stones, for it is on their especial account that he has controlled his anger; it was to preserve them that he kept his passion in check. In giving way to his rage and indignation, he had to neglect the Tables, and the hand which upheld them was withdrawn. [...] He remembered his mission and for its sake renounced an indulgence of his feelings.[33]

Freud becomes so entangled in this fictional account that at one point he expects to see the statue rise, "dash the Tables of the Law to the ground and let fly its wrath." Almost doleful, Freud affirms that "[n]othing of the kind happened," and "that something was represented here that could stay without change."[34] At the point at which he feels compelled to hazard a solution and decipher the content and meaning of the sculpture before him, he conjures up a dramatic backstory and mistakes his subjective experience for an objective account of the work. In other words, he confuses the two principles he set out to study, the meaning and content of the work and the emotional effect the Moses statue exerted upon him. While he began to unravel the former, he enacted the latter and used this emotional enactment in place of an analytical interpretation. Freud's interpretive technique of intermixing his subjective experience with the objective representation of an artwork and using the former as analytical evidence for the latter, is a strategy that he also employs in "The Interpretation of Dreams" (1900). In his paper "Freud and the Inter-Penetration of Dreams" (1979), David Willbern exposes how Freud frequently in-

---

Breuer's famous hysterical patient), who described her systematic day-dreaming as her "private theatre" (See Freud 1895: 21–47).

33 Freud 1914b: 229–230.

34 Freud 1914b: 220–221.

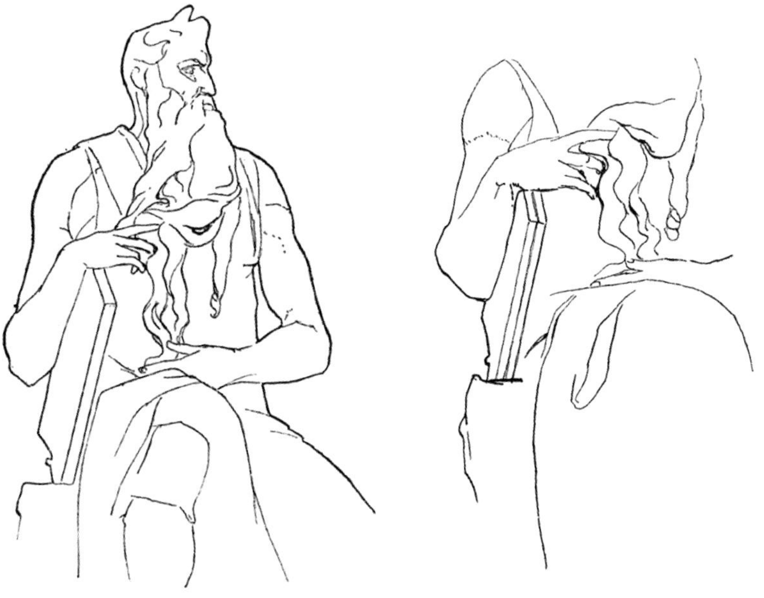

Plate 8: Sketches of Michelangelo's *Moses* (1513–1515) in Freud's *The Moses of Michelangelo* (1914)

troduces his own associations into the reported dream text, translates that text into his own terms, and reconstructs the dreamer's dream by way of his own interpretive inclinations. Willbern remarks that Freud tends to interpolate his own idiomatic phrases whenever he observes a gap in the patient's account—which he then reverses and interprets. In the final analysis, Freud "re-presents the dream to its dreamer [...] in such a way that the dreamer accepts the representation as her own creation."[35] It is important to recognize that Freud not only interjects his own associations, but his relationship to the patient as well. In this way "the dream under investigation, the text which is subjected to interpretation, becomes in practical reality a co-creation of the dreamer and the interpreter."[36]

Whilst Willbern considers Freud's interpretive style as "a technique of interpolation and interpenetration," Freud defined his interpretive process as the constructive task of the analyst: "His task is to make out what has been forgotten from the traces which it has left behind

35 Willbern 1979: 105.
36 Willbern 1979: 105.

or, more correctly, to *construct* it." These constructions "constitute the link between the two portions of the work of analysis, between his own part and that of the patient."[37]

In this text, "Constructions in Analysis" (1937), Freud recognizes that much less attention has been directed towards the position of the analyst than to the behavior of the patient. Although he realizes that the work of analysis involves "two separate localities" with two distinct tasks, he does not pursue the ramifications of this complex relationship in any detail. Freud's remark that "the task performed by the analyst, has been pushed into the background,"[38] eventually led to the crucial, ongoing, and central debate that emerged after Freud's death regarding the importance of the transference-countertransference relationship between the analyst and the patient, as noted earlier. For fear of losing an objective and hence "neutral" stance, Freud had always urged psychoanalysts to analyze away any subjective and personal feelings. For him, such responses invariably clouded the full picture of the patient's psyche. However, thanks to post-Kleinian evolutions and writings by the Relational school, this offspring of the psychoanalytic process eventually begat the royal road toward a fuller understanding of these unconscious parts of the patient.[39]

But back to Freud's reaction to the marble sculpture of Moses. We can detect that he had unwittingly engaged in a compromising counter-transferential process by identifying with the Moses figure. And while at the time he dramatically enacted his identification in the original analysis of the Moses statue, later he explicitly thematizes the process in two papers: "Group Psychology and the Analysis of the Ego" (1921), and "A Child is Being Beaten" (1919). In the first text, Freud describes different types of identification, and it is the "identification via a symptom" and the "identification through the introjection of the lost object" that most closely parallel his identificatory process with the statue.

37 Freud 1937: 258–259 (emphasis in the original).

38 Freud 1937: 258.

39 For a more in-depth discussion of the unfolding history of the use of countertransference in psychoanalytic practice, see Wolff Bernstein 1999: 275–300.

In the identification via a symptom formation, Freud states that this type of identification "leaves entirely out of account any object-relation to the person who is being copied."[40] He cites the example of a young girl who reacts hysterically to "a letter from someone with whom she is secretly in love which arouses her jealousy [...]."[41] Her girlfriends react with the same fit of hysteria, not because they are sympathetic towards their friend, but because they desire to put themselves in the same situation. Experiencing a sense of guilt over their rival feelings, they accept the suffering involved and identify themselves with the symptom.

By the same token, one may argue that Freud does not really identify with the physical mass of the Moses sculpture since it is, after all, just a piece of statuary and not the living prophet. Yet, he undeniably identifies with the emotions elicited by the sculpture. As Freud explains: "One ego has perceived a significant analogy with another upon one point [...], an identification is thereupon constructed on this point, and, under the influence of the pathogenic situation, is displaced on to the symptom which the one ego has produced."[42]

The analogy that Freud perceived in the figure of Moses was the shared frustration with their faithless followers. Yet, it is important to keep in mind that Freud did not identify himself with the biblical Moses, who "actually fell into a fit of rage and broke the Tablets," but rather with the sculptured representation of the prophet. Based upon his reconstruction of Moses's movements, Freud creates an idealized version of the prophet, but attributes—in other words, re-introjects—his own idealized image of Moses onto the statue's creator. " [...] Michelangelo has placed a different Moses on the tomb of the Pope, one superior to the historical or traditional Moses."[43]

Previously, I have argued that Michelangelo's Moses became Freud's Moses. Let me expand this statement now by saying that Freud identified with the sculpture by projecting his own idealized self-image

---

40 Freud 1921: 107.
41 Freud 1921: 107.
42 Freud 1921: 107.
43 Freud 1914b: 233.

of a man who was "struggling successfully against an inward passion for the sake of a cause to which he has devoted himself."[44]

The process of identification that we witness in Freud's analysis of the Moses sculpture is crucial for an analysis of a similar process, unfettered by the figures in Manet's paintings. Freud's essay "A Child is Being Beaten" (1919) goes even deeper into the analysis of identification, as it focuses upon the triadic process of a fantasy formation. In this text, Freud attempts to explain why so many of his patients reported a fantasy about "a child is being beaten." In order to make sense of this fantasy, he subdivides the process into three stages:

(1) My father is beating the child;
(2) I am beaten by my father;
(3) A child is being beaten.

Upon further analysis, Freud extends the first phase to:

My father is beating the child whom I hate.[45]

Between the first and second phases, Freud remarks that a profound transformation has taken place, "The person beating the child remains the same (that is, the father); but the child who is beaten has been changed into another one, and is not invariably the child producing the fantasy [...] Now, therefore, the wording runs: 'I am beaten by my father'."[46]

In other words, the witness of the fantasy has become the author of the fantasy. The third fantasy resembles the first, with the exception that it is no longer the father who is beating the child, but some *representative* of the father—such as a schoolteacher—a shift that can be translated into the phrase "a child is being beaten." In this last phase, "the child who is producing the beating" fantasy no longer itself features in it, but steps back into the role of a spectator,

44 Freud 1914b: 233.
45 Freud 1919a: 185.
46 Freud 1919a: 185.

distancing him/herself. In short, the position of the child changes with each stage: from (1) the author of the fantasy, to (2) the object of the fantasy, to (3) the spectator of the fantasy.

While the first and third phases represent fantasies reported by his patients, the second phase, which Freud calls the most important, is a theoretical construct that Freud introduces to make the fantasy of "a child is being beaten" intelligible. Freud leaves it somewhat unclear whether the second phase existed but "never succeeded in becoming conscious," or, as he says, "is a *construction* of analysis, but [...] no less a necessity on that account."[47] In "The Moses of Michelangelo," Freud follows a strikingly similar path to the one mapped out in "A Child is Being Beaten." In the first part of the essay, Freud assumes the fictional role of an art critic: he introduces the sculpture to the reader and presents a detailed art-historical account of the Moses statue. He is the one who examines the statue on the reader's behalf. Yet, when he begins to decipher the intention and movement concealed within the marble figure, he seems almost to change places with Moses, and is no longer the one looking at the work, but the one looked at by Moses: "Sometimes I have crept cautiously out of the half-gloom of the interior as though I myself belonged to the mob upon whom his eye is turned [...]"[48]

Two events have occurred here: (1) Freud has taken the place of Moses (by identifying with him) in order to scrutinize what lies behind the affective power of the statue. As mentioned earlier, the shift from Stage I to Stage II—that is, from author to object of the fantasy—was also reflected in the change in Freud's own writing style, which turned from a strictly scientific discourse into a speculative and affect-laden narrative. (2) By identifying with or "putting oneself in the same situation"[49] as Moses, Freud temporarily turned himself into a sculpture, an object that can be contemplated by the readers of the Moses study. It is only at the end of the Moses essay that Freud re-adopts the position of the spectator/interpreter. He illustrates this

47 Freud 1919a: 185 (author's emphasis).
48 Freud 1914b: 213.
49 Freud 1921: 107.

return to the third state (the spectator of the fantasy) by citing an art-historical essay that largely confirms his own interpretation of the statue. Thus, by rejoining the ranks of art historians, Freud once more becomes the spectator of the sculpture. By now it seems as though I have used the process of identification as additional evidence to confirm the standard opinion that Freud's "The Moses of Michelangelo" is essentially no more than a thinly disguised autobiographical statement. While this opinion undoubtedly contains a strong measure of truth, my own reasons for focusing on the process of identification are of quite a different nature. While the Moses text has been rather exclusively seen as a biographical document and ignored as an important essay about the identificatory process between a spectator and a painted figure, I want to argue that this subtle process of identification is crucial to an understanding of the relationship Manet constructs between his painted figures and his imagined spectators.

Freud seemed to recognize that an artwork could not be understood if one merely studied its thematic and descriptive content, but that its true meaning could only be unlocked if one included the effect the painting or sculpture exercised upon its beholder.

Jokes and their relations to aesthetics

Stéphane Mallarmé, a close and faithful friend of Manet's, had already claimed for his own field that the aim of poetry was "peindre non la chose, mais l'effet qu'elle produit" (do not paint the thing, but the effect it produces). In other words, the content cannot be separated from the reaction it elicits. Mallarmé, whom Manet later depicted in *Portrait de Stéphane Mallarmé* (1876) **[Plate 9]**, also advocated that the medium through which the effect was produced "was to be so thoroughly enmeshed in the fabric of the work that the reader would be unaware of the mechanics by which the poem was created."[50]

This same principle has governed the realm of painting for centuries. Spectators were always to be aroused and emotionally moved by the

---

50 In Harris 1964: 559.

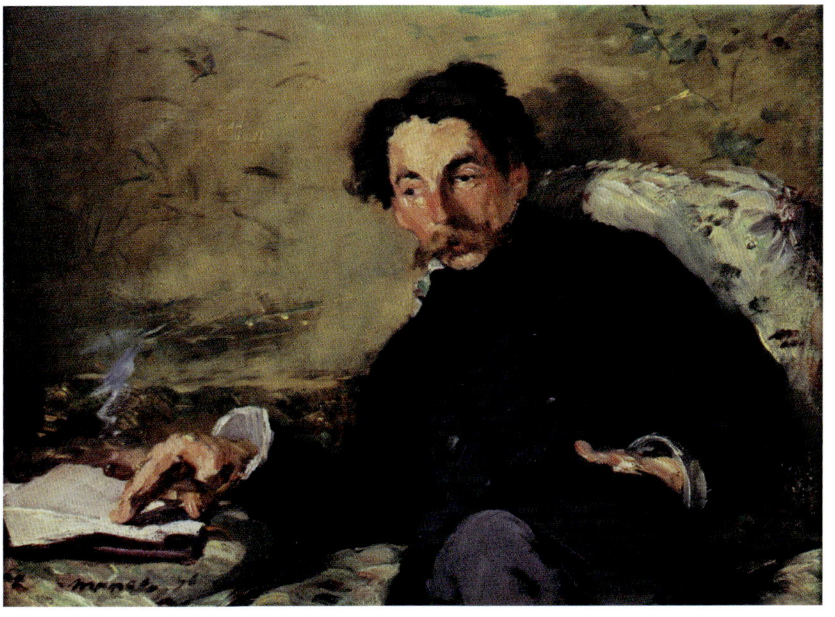

Plate 9:
Édouard Manet,
Portrait de Stéphane Mallarmé (1876)

subject matter represented in the artwork. But the techniques through which the painter achieved these emotional effects were disguised, because it was believed that the conspicuous presence of the artist's personal imprint upon the painting would destroy the very effect the painting was designed to elicit. If the painter focused too blatantly on the means by which he manipulated the viewer's emotional response, he was considered an unaccomplished and technically clumsy artist.

Manet broke with this long-existing convention. Unlike his predecessors, he openly revealed the methods by which he enmeshed the observer in the painted spectacle. He deliberately drew attention, both to his position as the painter having intended the effect, and to the spectator as the recipient and object of his intention. Michael Fried argues that Manet heightened the spectator's self-awareness *qua* spectator by making his own self-awareness "an essential part of the content of his work."[51] By narrowing the distance that is usually maintained between a painting and its beholder—a distance that allows the viewers to unleash their own fantasies—Manet restrained

51 Fried 1969: 49.

them from engaging in their fantasy world. He methodically drew attention to the fact that the viewer was not looking at a real figure, but at a painted representation of a figure. Paradoxically enough, by collapsing the distance between the painting and the spectator, Manet heightened the inner tensions and anxieties within the viewer, which in turn leads to the general impression that his figures possess an estranging and enigmatic quality. By shortening the distance between the painted canvas and the spectator, he contracted the symbolic realm within which his viewers could retreat into their separate fantasy worlds and muse about their desires. Manet was too confrontational, however, too engaging with the outer world to allow room for that separate internal space. It is my contention that with this ploy Manet was unknowingly addressing the identificatory process which develops once a spectator is confronted with a painted figure.

His unconscious use of this complex identificatory process between spectator and painted figure can be analyzed particularly well from a psychoanalytic perspective. Accordingly, the identification Freud was enacting when looking at Michelangelo's *Moses* can offer a potentially fruitful portal into the complex problematics of a psychoanalytic study of Édouard Manet's oeuvre. Freud's texts "On Narcissism" (1914), "A Child is Being Beaten" (1919), and "Group Psychology and the Analysis of the Ego" (1921) will serve as further material for analyzing the process of identification, even though none of them were planned for this purpose. The same is true for Freud's early paper "Jokes and Their Relations to the Unconscious" (1905), which was devised to analyze the unconscious structure of jokes and provide a companion to "The Interpretation of Dreams" (1900), his grammar of the unconscious. In 1914, Freud himself recognized, however, that the structure of the joke could also offer a richly powerful key to the structure of an artwork. "The first example of an appliciation of the analytic mode of thought to the problems of aesthetics," he wrote, "was contained in my book on jokes."[52]

The tendentious joke, in particular, lends itself to comparisons with an artwork, especially in so far as it highlights the relationship

52 Freud 1914d: 37.

between the spectator and the art object. In contrast to the jest, the puzzle, the pun, or the un-tendentious joke, the tendentious joke requires the same three positions or objects as those Freud adopts when he scrutinizes the Moses statue.

"Generally speaking," he writes, "a tendentious joke calls for three people: in addition to the one who makes the joke, there must be a second who is taken as the object of the hostile or sexual aggressiveness, and a third in whom the joke's aim of producing pleasure is fulfilled. [...] it is not the person who makes the joke who laughs at it and who therefore enjoys its pleasurable effect, but the inactive listener."[53]

Even though the painter is rarely if ever present when his artworks are exhibited, he nonetheless abides by a similar three-figure dynamic. The obscene joke—or, as Freud calls it, "*Zote*" (smutty insinuation)—illustrates this structure particularly well. In a smutty story, a particular person—usually a woman whose attention the relator wants to gain—is shoved under the spotlight and teased. The woman is anything but impressed by such antics, whereas the men (in the exclusive company of other men) enjoy swapping smutty tales as a means of staving off the act of seduction. "A person who laughs at smut [...] is laughing as though he were the *spectator* of an act of sexual aggression."[54] The longer the woman rebuffs the man's overtures, the more he turns to obscene banter and derives perverse pleasure from the rebuttal. In this scenario, it is the third person who acquires particular importance in the successful telling of an obscene joke. While at first merely an outsider intruding on the man's erotic pursuits, he later becomes the narrator's most significant ally.

Freud summarizes this process as follows:

> In the case of smut, the three people are in the same relation. The course of events may be thus described. When the first person finds his libidinal impulse inhibited by the woman, he develops a hostile trend against that second person and calls on the originally interfering third person as his ally. Through the first person's smutty speech

53 Freud 1905b: 100.

54 Freud 1905b: 97 (author's emphasis).

> the woman is exposed before *the third*, who, as listener, has now been bribed by the effortless satisfaction of his own libido.[55]

When smutty insinuations become a joke proper, all the technical rules of humor need to be obeyed. In other words, the more refined the joke, the subtler the allusions to the original obscenity. Moreover, the object of the original sexual inferences retreats even further into the background of the tale. Meanwhile, the woman necessary to the original seduction scene in the joke is actually felt in and through her *absence*—by the effects she continues to generate upon the joke-teller and the listener. Thus, what is now only *implied* gives substance to the joke.

Freud's detailed description of the mechanisms of humor allows us to look not only at the spectator's role, but also at the relationship between the artist, his object, and the spectator. Freud's theory about the joke and its relation to the unconscious introduces another angle from which one can analyze the matrix a painter like Manet constructs to enlist the attention and engagement of the spectator in a shared play at the expense of the depicted object. Taking Manet's work *Olympia* **[Plate 5]** as an example, we may argue that Manet takes possession of his model Victorine Meurent as she lounges back on the couch, embodying the role of the mythical Olympia. Manet somewhat bluntly makes us realize that we as the viewers will never be in a position to possess this prized object the way he did. In this way, the artist whets our appetite while vicariously satisfying his own erotic impulses, indirectly luring his spectators to share the awkward pleasure of gazing at an exposed yet unattainable naked female object. Although I have chosen *Olympia* to illustrate the parallels in the dynamics between artist-object-spectator and joker-object-listener, this does not imply that such a triadic relationship exists only in paintings whose contents are considered lewd or provocative. On the contrary, I intend to show that the joker-object-listener dynamics that Freud analyzes as being necessary for the successful outcome of a tendentious suggestive joke is equally valid for other paintings. Simply put,

---

55 Freud 1905b: 100 (author's emphasis).

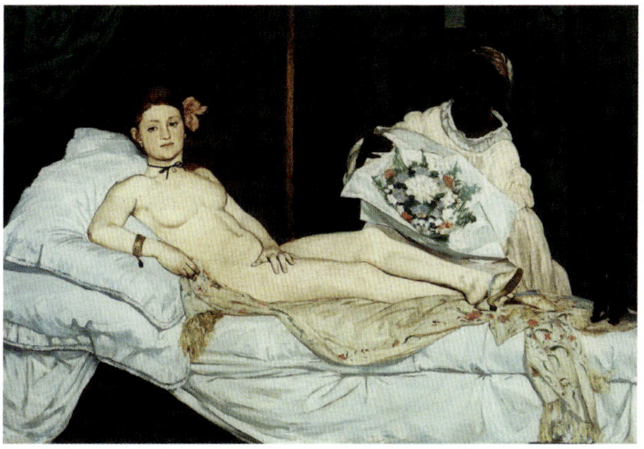

Plate 5:
Édouard Manet,
Olympia (1863)

this underlying triadic structure holds true not only for paintings with sexual or confrontational subtexts, but also for paintings that contain no overt sexual or audacious contents, such as Manet's *Le Balcon* (1868–1869) **[Plate 10]**, *Le Buveur d'absinthe* (1859) **[Plate 11]**, or *Le Déjeuner dans l'atelier* **[Plate 2]**. For each of these paintings, an analysis of the spectator's position vis-à-vis the depicted scene is crucial in order to comprehend fully the emotional as well as the structural force of each canvas. As Lacan notes:

> "[…] in the picture, something of the gaze is always manifested. The painter knows this very well—his morality, his search, his quest, his practice is that he should sustain and vary the selection of a certain kind of gaze. Looking at pictures, even those most lacking in what is usually called the gaze, and which is constituted by a pair of eyes, pictures in which any representation of the human figure is absent, like a landscape by a Dutch or a Flemish painter, you will see in the end, as in filigree, something so specific to each of the painters that you will feel the presence of the gaze.[56]

When Freud compares the joke with a dream, he emphasizes that "as a result of the part played by the third person, jokes are bound by a certain condition which does not apply to dreams."[57] Unlike the joke, the dream is

> […] a completely asocial mental product; it has nothing to communicate to anyone else; it arises within the subject as a compromise between the mental forces struggling in him, it remains unintelligible to the subject himself and is for that reason totally uninteresting to other people. […] A joke, on the other hand, is the the most social of all mental functions that aim at a yield of pleasure. It often calls for

56 Lacan 1978: 101.
57 Freud 1905b: 173.

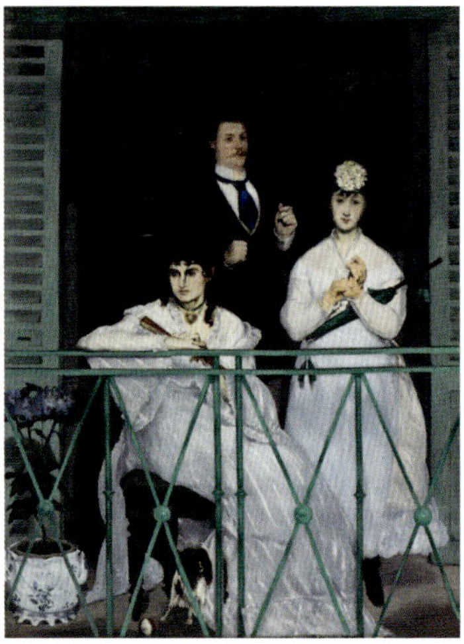

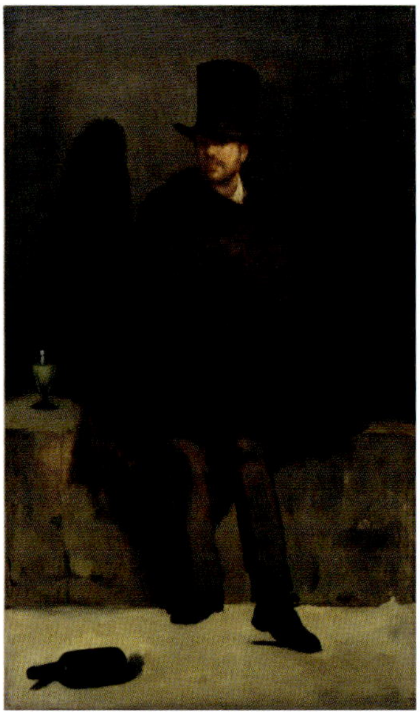

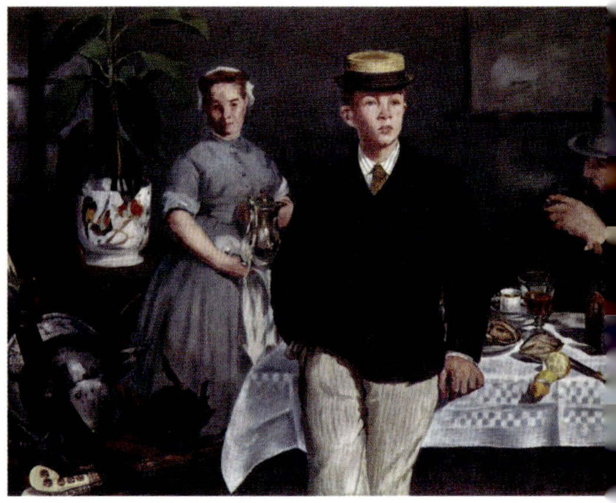

Plate 10: Édouard Manet, *Le Balcon* (1868–1869)
Plate 11: Édouard Manet, *Le Buveur d'absinthe* (1859)
Plate 2: Édouard Manet, *Le Déjeuner dans l'atelier* (1868)

> three persons and its *completion* requires the participation of someone else in the mental process it starts. The condition of intelligibility is, therefore, binding on it; it may only make use of possible distortion in the unconscious through condensation and displacement up to the point at which it can be set straight by the third person's understanding.[58]

The position of the third person which Freud claims to be critical for the *completion* of a joke has also become a central issue for the literary theoreticians of the Reader-Response School. They argue, for the field of literature, that a text cannot be fully analyzed without a knowledge of its effects upon its readers. Janet Wolff observes:

> The reader, viewer, or audience is actively involved in the construction of the work of art, and without the act of reception/consumption, the cultural product is incomplete. This is not to say that consumption is simultaneous with production, but that it complements and completes it.[59]

---

58 Freud 1905b: 179 (author's emphasis).
59 Wolff 1981: 95.

Manet's paintings greatly complicate this need to make sense of interactivity with the object, unlike the interaction with the *Moses* statue, whose representational inconsistencies invited Freud to fill in the gaps and establish the missing connections by creating a miniature drama fueled in large measure by Freud's own projections, whether conscious or inadvertent. Manet's canvases are constructed like a modern text, in which, as Wolfgang Iser describes, "one detail appears to contradict another, and so simultaneously stimulates and frustrates our desire to 'picture', thus continually causing our imposed '*gestalt*' of the text to disintegrate."[60]

It is interesting to note that the Reader-Response theoreticians not only focus on the actions in responding to a text, but, like Freud, they also stress the importance of the reproductive and recreative aspects of the reader's interpretive response. Defining a text as a dynamic entity, they argue that a work of art can only be constructed by the mediation of past and present and of author and reader, and that creation is inherently a recreation of previous entities. The scene which Freud asks his readers to imagine when he proposes a solution to the contradictory configurations in his Moses essay is equivalent to the scenario that the joke-teller invites his listeners to construct. It is in this in-between realm—or what D.W. Winnicott calls the "transitional space"—that the self-object boundary between the artist and the spectator becomes blurred. While the passage through the transitional space is usually an unconscious process in the spectator–object relationship, Manet consciously thematizes this process and captures viewers in this "precarious play" which wavers precariously between subjectivity and objectivity. As a consequence, viewers are simultaneously engaged and caught in the transitional realm when contemplating Manet's paintings. They are both spectators of and actors in the mise-en-scène that Manet establishes in his covert and largely unconsciously assumed role as the director. We know that Manet made use of friends and family members in his scenes from urban life (see Maryanne Stevens, 2013), but we also know, as noted by Michael Lüthy, that "the scene of the picture is much less [...]

60 Iser 1980: 59.

the internal stage upon which the spectator looks. Rather, the space in-between the painting and the spectator becomes the actual stage."[61]

The psychoanalyst D.W. Winnicott devoted much of his writings to this intermediate space, an element that becomes critically important for our understanding of Manet's canvases. With his concept of the transitional object and the transitional space, Winnicott injects a new vocabulary to conceptualize the fluid interchange between subject and object, in other words between the artist, his object (the painting), and its beholder. Winnicott defines the transitional object as an

> "intermediate area of *experiencing*, to which inner reality and external life both contribute. It is an area that is not challenged, because no claim is made on its behalf except that it shall exist as a resting-place for the individual engaged in the perpetual human task of keeping inner and outer reality separate yet interrelated."[62]

This transitional object, according to Winnicott, serves as an important stepping-stone in the gradual differentiation of inner and outer world, of me and non-me, of illusion and reality testing. Weaning the child from its omnipotent illusion that the mother's breast is an extension of itself, the child uses the transitional object to "master" the separation from the mother's breast, and to experiment with the "me" and "non-me" parts of itself. Later on, the infant's acquisition of verbal language fulfills a function similar to that of the transitional object. In this way, the transitional object becomes the mother's magical symbolic representative lending assurance to the child in the absence of the mother. The transitional object is the child's first non-me possession, an object that simultaneously symbolizes the child's desire for union with and the drive for separation from the mother. Through the use of the transitional object, the child begins to be able to form images and to think symbolically.

While I would not describe a painting as a transitional object per se, I would argue that a painting shares certain characteristics

---

61 Lüthy 2016: 14 (author's translation).

62 Winnicott 1980: 3 (emphasis in the original).

with a transitional object. Unlike early transitional objects, such as a blanket or a teddy bear, a painting is not a found object but an object deliberately presented by the artist to his audience. As Winnicott emphasizes:

> Of the transitional object it can be said that it is a matter of agreement between us and the baby that we will never ask the question: "Did you conceive of this or was it presented to you from without?" The important point is that no decision on this point is expected. The question is not to be formulated.[63]

Similar to the transitional object, the painting exists in the intermediate area where it belongs neither to the artist's inner world nor to the externally shared world of the spectator and the artist. Yet, while it does not belong to either, it nonetheless encompasses attributes of both. Moreover, the viewers project their fantasies onto the painted canvas and bring the figures alive, just as little children project their fantasies into a transitional object. In this way, we might venture to state that the scenario which Freud constructed when contemplating the Moses statue, compares to the child's creation of a transitional object. Both phenomena arise from the need to bridge the gap between the external object and oneself, that is the need to make the unfamiliar familiar. Winnicott recognized that transitional phenomena exist throughout life and are not limited to the child's early development. "This intermediate area of experience, unchallenged in respect of its belonging to inner or external (shared) reality," he notes, "constitutes the greater part of the infant's experience, and throughout life is retained in the intense experiencing that belongs to the arts and to religion and to imaginative living, and to creative scientific work."[64]

It is my contention that it is this intermediate transitional area that is repeatedly addressed, questioned, and challenged in Manet's paintings. The beholder of his works is regularly diverted in and out of this intermediate space, and suspended between subjectivity and

63 Winnicott 1980: 14.
64 Winnicott 1980: 16.

objectivity, the world of the me and the not-me, the realm of illusion and reality. Winnicott defined psychotherapy as "the overlap of two areas of playing, that of the patient and that of the therapist. Psychotherapy has to do with two people playing together."[65] This idea of a common field of play is reminiscent of Freud's famous notion of transference as a playground ("Tummelplatz," 1914: 154), the space of rough-and-tumble in which one "is allowed to expand in almost complete freedom"[66] and permitted to unfold one's fantasies and desires, as he himself did while contemplating the Moses statue. This freedom of play, of actor and director, of subject and object, of projection and introjection in Manet's works will be examined later, with a particular emphasis upon the artist's intricate way of engaging the viewer in an uncanny play of provocation and estrangement, unleashing all the familiar rules by which the spectator-artist relationship had existed thus far.

---

65 Winnicott 1980: 44.
66 Freud 1914a: 154.

Chapter II

ÉDOUARD MANET: A PSYCHOANALYTIC PICTORIAL ANALYSIS

> Analyzing an artist's personality piece by piece is a delicate business. Such an undertaking is always difficult and can only be properly accomplished for artists whose work is completed, and who has already achieved what was expected of them. Their entire career can be studied and all aspects of their genius can then be examined and an accurate and definite likeness can be portrayed without fear of overlooking any details. And for the critic there is the absorbing pleasure in pretending that he can afterwards reconstruct the living man complete with limbs and nerves and heart, with body and soul intact.
>
> Émile Zola, *Mes Haines*, 1866[1]

> But the subject should not be entirely abandoned. It should be reconsidered, not to restore the theme of an originating subject, but to seize its functions, its intervention in discourse, and its system of dependencies. [...] In short, the subject (and its substitutes) must be stripped of its creative role and be analysed as a complex and variable function of discourse.
>
> Michel Foucault, *Language, Counter-Memory*, Practice 1977

Even now, some 130 years after the completion of Manet's oeuvre, the job of analyzing the artist's personality is no easy task. Besides a small number of letters, Manet left few significant documents

1 Zola 1879.

from which we might derive insights into his personality or attitudes. Hence, Manet the person is known to us largely through the eyes of others. Antonin Proust, his long-time friend, is the central chronicler of Manet anecdotes, but as Anne Coffin Hanson points out, these memories of Manet, published in 1913, might not be entirely objective, colored as they are by "Manet's eventual achievement, and also by the eventual justification of [his] faith in the artist."[2]

A scrupulous biographer who eschews indulging in the pretense of being able to reconstruct "the living man," must first acknowledge that any account of Manet's life remains a fragmentary undertaking, a puzzle in which many pieces are permanently missing. George Heard Hamilton is correct when he writes that "[i]ndeed, in quite a literal sense we can know this man only by studying his work [...]."[3] One potentially fruitful way to begin to piece together the elements of this puzzle is to study those paintings in which Manet depicts his family and intimate friends, in light of the anecdotes handed down by this circle of acquaintances.

Since Manet never expounded any particular theory of art—despite his friends' urgings that he become the leader of their Batignolles school—,he appears to have deliberately evaded the role of the "master," preferring instead to be seen as part of a broader system of dependencies. The standard portrait that emerges of Manet is perhaps neatly summarized by Hanson's description of a man who was

> [...] not himself well-read, a friend of the important literary figures of his day; politically naive in a period of political turmoil; hard-working but playful; painfully sensitive but self-assured—, a man of duality, of paradox, attempting to reconcile his love of tradition with his compulsion to create the new.[4]

Other critics, like John Richardson or George Mauner, have also emphasized the Janus-like aspect of Manet's character. Richardson describes him as the "forward-looking rebel" and the "backward-

---

2 Hanson 1977: 44.

3 Hamilton 1969: 4.

4 Hanson 1977: vii.

looking bourgeois;"[5] whereas Mauner characterizes him as a "homo duplex,"[6] and Émile Zola considered him a "rebellious painter who worshipped society."[7] The polarizing tensions of Manet's personality are reflected not only in his life-long struggle to have his paintings accepted by the Salon (his work was wholly or partially rejected six out of twenty-one times) and even those accepted frequently met with vitriolic outbursts of outrage and denigration. His complex nature is also mirrored in his fraught relationships with his family, friends, and critics. These numerous accounts of Manet's paradoxical personality raise at least three important questions:

(1) How accurate is this collective depiction of Manet?
(2) Are the contradictions that emerge a characteristic of the painter, or may they also be considered as a particular sign of his era?
(3) Do Manet's paintings hold the clues to an understanding of the dynamics governing his contradictory nature?

To find some answers to these three preliminary questions, we need to begin with an examination of the man's life history.

Édouard Manet was born in Paris on January 23, 1832 to Auguste Manet and Eugénie-Désirée Fournier as the eldest of three children. His father was the chief of personnel at the Ministry of Justice, and his mother the daughter of a French diplomat who had assisted Marshall Bernadotte to assume the Swedish throne. As a result, the king of Sweden acted as Eugénie's godfather. The curious union of Manet's parents—the stern conservator of French law marrying a woman linked to a rebel who had deserted Napoleon in order to keep his Swedish crown—is a remarkable historical coincidence emblematic of the recurring divided loyalties that followed Édouard Manet throughout his career.

Manet engaged his two younger brothers, Eugène (born 1833) and Gustave (born 1835), many times as models for his paintings;

5 Richardson 1958: 6.
6 Mauner 1975: 17.
7 Zola, quoted in Courthion 1960: 59.

Le Déjeuner sur l'herbe constituted the most famous of his "double portraits," since Manet used both brothers interchangeably as models for the one dressed gentleman seated opposite the undressed woman.

No material is available about Manet's childhood, not even written reminiscences which might enlighten us about his early years. We know only that Manet entered the school of Canon Pouilop at the age of seven, and that he subsequently enrolled at the Collège Rollin aged ten. Although his father had envisioned a legal career for him, it was Manet's maternal uncle Edmond Fournier who interfered with these paternal plans and took charge of the artist's early education.

Troubled by Édouard's early scholastic failures, his uncle assumed responsibility for the boy's unpromising enrollment in the prestigious Collège Rollin. These efforts were not immediately rewarded, since the boy showed no particular enthusiasm for any of his classes and performed poorly in all subjects—except gymnastics and history. According to George Heard Hamilton, Manet was described in his school reports as a "caractère difficile."[8] However, Fournier, a connoisseur of art, did not give up on Édouard and encouraged him to enroll in drawing classes and to visit the museums of Paris. It was in one of these early drawing classes that Manet met Antonin Proust, who remained his lifelong friend and who (thanks to his position as the Minister of Arts under Gambetta's brief government) was instrumental in Manet being awarded the Légion d'honneur medal later in 1881.

According to Pierre Daix's account of Manet's early life, his father never forgave Fournier for having encouraged his son to become a painter.[9] When Manet graduated from the Collège Rollin at the age of sixteen in 1848, Manet *père* again insisted that his eldest son study law, and again the boy rejected his father's career choice. Heated discussions erupted between father and son, and a compromise was

---

8 Hamilton 1969: 20.

9 See Pierre Daix 1983: 28; Pierre Schneider also argues that the tensions between Auguste Manet and Edmond Fournier dated back to earlier political disagreements. Fournier was a monarchist who had resigned from the army in 1848 out of loyalty to the dethroned king Louis-Philippe, whereas Auguste Manet was a staunch Republican supporting the downfall of Louis-Philippe (see also: Schneider 1968: 13–14).

eventually reached when the father allowed Édouard to enter the Naval Training School. However, the youth failed his entrance exam for the Academy and enlisted instead in the Merchant Marines, which promised a naval career after six months of service.

In December 1848, two days before the fall of Louis-Philippe's government, Édouard went to sea as a cadet on the training ship *Havre et Guadeloupe*, bound for Rio de Janeiro. In a letter to his mother, whose role in the father-son dispute remains undocumented, Édouard expressed both sorrow and pride over his impending departure:

> I would have liked you to come with me as far as Le Havre if I hadn't so dreaded the thought of another parting and the "good-byes"—always so hard to bear. You could have seen our splendid ship. We couldn't be better off; we've got everything—not only all we need but even a certain amount of luxury as well—and all this comfort consoles and reassures the poor mamas who come to say "good-bye" to their children.[10]

The jaunty and somewhat sardonic tone Manet adopts towards his mother seems to be deliberate, even self-consciously mature for a sixteen-year-old separating from his parents for the first time, to embark upon what is even now considered a very long journey. While admitting his pain over their separation, Édouard seems eager to humor his mother and at the same time to reassure her of his good spirits. One gains the impression that he is more concerned about his mother's well-being than about his own anxieties about sailing for distant shores. Émile Zola describes Manet's embarkment for Brazil as follows:

> At the age of seventeen, on leaving college, he fell in love with painting. What a terrible love that is—parents tolerate a mistress, even two; they will close their eyes if necessary to a straying heart and senses. But the Arts! Painting for them is the Scarlet Woman [*la grande impure*], the Courtesan, always hungry for flesh, who must drink the blood of their children, who clutches them, panting, to her insatiable lips. [...] So, of course, at the age of seventeen, Édouard Manet was embarked as a cadet on a ship bound for Rio de Janeiro. Undoubtedly,

---

10 Courthion 1960: 13.

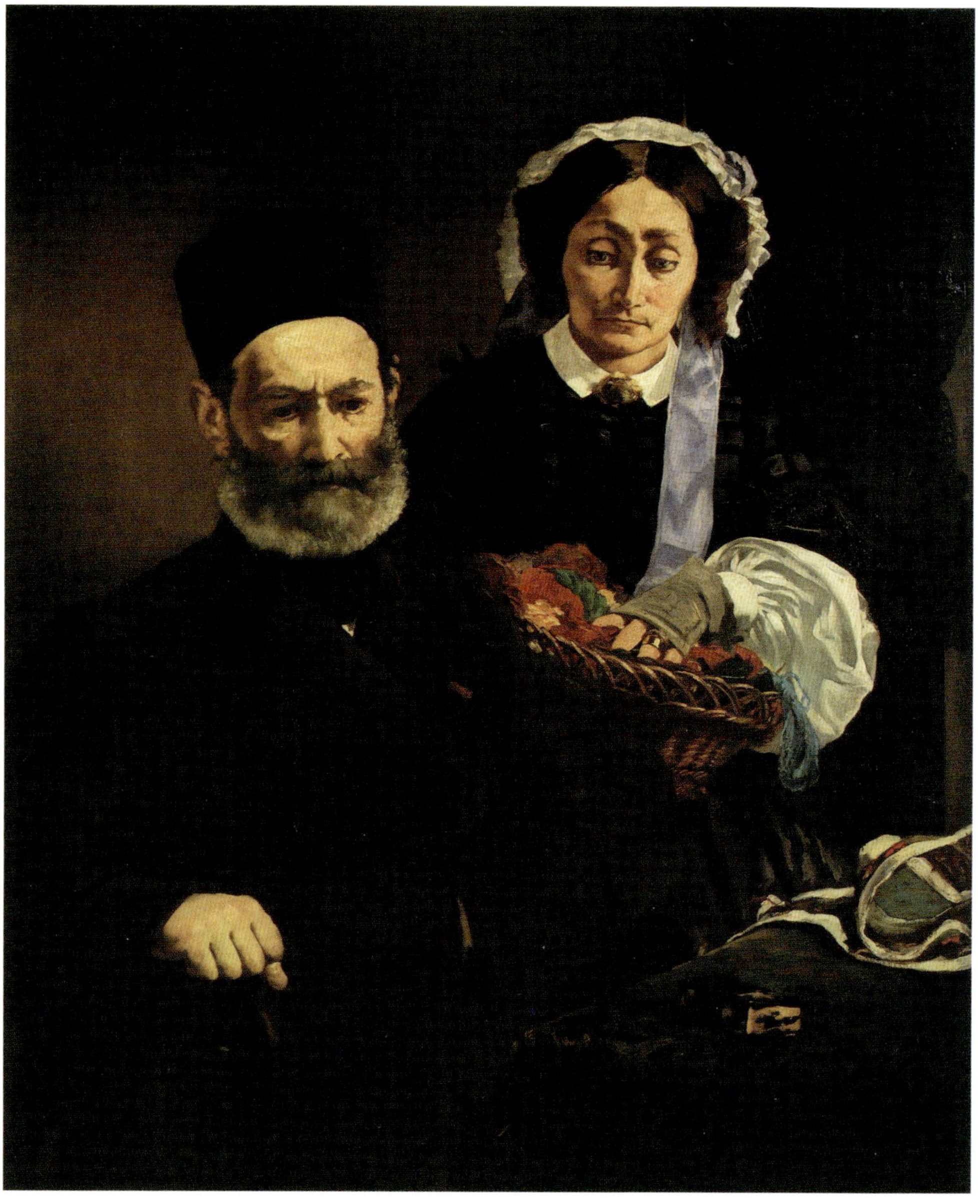

Plate 12: Édouard Manet,
Portrait de Monsieur et Madame Auguste Manet (1860)

> the Scarlet Woman, that Courtesan, always hungry for fresh blood, embarked with him, and surrounded by the clear, empty vastness of sky and ocean, succeeded in seducing him. [...] On his return, Manet was given up entirely to Infamy.[11]

Upon his return from Brazil, Manet was once more rejected as a candidate for the Naval Academy, and his father finally consented to the youth's wishes to pursue a career in painting. Two years before his father's death, Manet painted his mother and father in the *Portrait de Monsieur et Madame Auguste Manet* **[Plate 12]** in 1860.

At first sight, Manet's depiction of his mother and father suggests a conventional bourgeois couple, the patriarch presiding sternly in the foreground, while the mother stands respectfully behind her husband. Manet's father is prominently identified by his professional class affiliation, sporting the bright red Légion d'honneur medal pinned to his black waistcoat. Théodore Zeldin remarks upon the bourgeois attire:

> He [the bourgeois] had to show taste, which meant knowing what was *correct*, and inclining therefore to conservatism and understatement. That is why for so long the bourgeois wore a black uniform, pointing out his precise rank only with details of cut and cloth.[12]

In contrast, Eugénie holds a basket of colored balls of wool—a common symbol of quiet domesticity. Yet, this painting of a respected bourgeois couple was greeted by contemporary critics with howls of derision. Léon Lagrange decried its appearance at the Salon of 1861 in the following terms:

> But what a scourge to society is a realist painter! To him nothing is sacred! Manet tramples under foot even the most sacred ties. The *Artist's Parents* must more than once have cursed the day when a brush was put in the hands of this merciless portraitist.[13]

11 Zola, quoted in Courthion 1960: 116.
12 Zeldin 1973: 15 (emphasis in the original).
13 Lagrange, quoted in Hamilton 1969: 26 (emphasis in the original).

While the painter's technique drew flak for its "photographic bluntness and the harsh extremes of lighting,"[14] the major grounds of objection were found in the sentiment (or lack thereof) the canvas conveyed. In its unpitying record of the imperfections of form and character it is a cold work, and indiscreet in its declaration of the couple's uneasy modus vivendi. Writers were quick to assail what they perceived to be Manet's lack of filial reverence. But this criticism already admits a great deal—that conditions prevailed in the family that a dutiful son would not typically have exposed to public view. "The sacred ties" are undone between these two figures, who are visibly neither coherently related nor strictly separate. The only sign of their union is the oversized wedding band on Eugénie's left hand.[15]

The palpable lack of harmony and affection between Manet's parents is rendered even more pronounced by the difference in the portrayal of the two parental figures. Mme. Manet's aloof demeanor, her eyes distractedly cast downward, seems ill-matched with the prominence accorded to her figure. Combined with the large-scale, frontal presentation, her faraway gaze creates an unnerving effect, a foretaste perhaps of later figures with similar cold or completely disengaged stances that became a hallmark of Manet's work. The mother's rather artificially flattened form prevents the spectator from plunging into a factitious depth behind the picture plane. Her strongly etched features express no particular sentiment, nor does she consciously strike a particular pose for her son, the painter. Her stale, somewhat resigned presence sharply contrasts with the cheery and slightly bemusing tone Manet adopted in his letter to her twelve years earlier when he left for Brazil.

The suppressed air of anxiety which George Heard Hamilton detects in this elderly couple is confirmed, I believe, by the expression Manet has assigned to his father's visage. Unlike his wife, Auguste seems to be acutely self-conscious about being captured for the canvas. Given his vocal objections to his son's choice of profession, the

---

14 Hanson 1977: 76.

15 The French word *alliance* for wedding band possibly captures the uneasy alliance underlying Monsieur and Madame Manet's "union."

act of submitting himself to being portrayed by his son is a public sign hinting at capitulation. In a way, the finished painting of the artist's parents offers a testimony to the son's victory over his father. I think that Manet beautifully captured his father's authoritarian and powerful attitude, while giving full play to the fragile and resigned sentiment of his age. The man's right fist clenched on his cane, the oversized black greatcoat, the left hand thrust inside the fold, the imposing cap and stiff pose, all of theses suggest an air of frustrated power and authority. This forcefulness, however, is subtly counter-balanced by the troubled expression in his downcast eyes. Unlike his mother's lost gaze, the father intentionally stares downward, as if determined to ignore his son's scrutiny—and that of the spectator.

Curiously, in his way the painter has managed to establish a keener connection between the father and the spectator than the one binding the two parents. One can only wonder whether this covert yet more intimate relationship with the viewer is indicative of further unrevealed complications between father and son. Unlike the reverse voyeurism of the portraits in which his figures openly challenge the viewer's stance, here both of his subjects—his parents—decline to engage either with the spectators or with each other, which may be an allusion to Manet's uneasy relationship with his mother and father.

In other words, what is not already captured in the content of the painting is projected into the relationship Manet sets up between the painted figure, in this case his father Auguste, the judge and the imagined viewers. This technique of injecting undeclared emotions into the relationship—feelings not ready yet to be articulated in the painting—becomes another trademark of Manet's ensuing works. We can think of this intersubjective dynamices as an equivalent to the process of projective identification in which concealed or "unacceptable" experiences or fantasies are unconsciously assigned to the other person (in this case the spectator), who in turn experiences them as their own identification with the projections. If we translate this process to Manet's works, we could think that the painter, who was known to be reluctant to inject ideas into his paintings, felt anxiety and anger towards his parents, emotions he could not openly express. Instead, he unconsciously projected these affects onto his spectators,

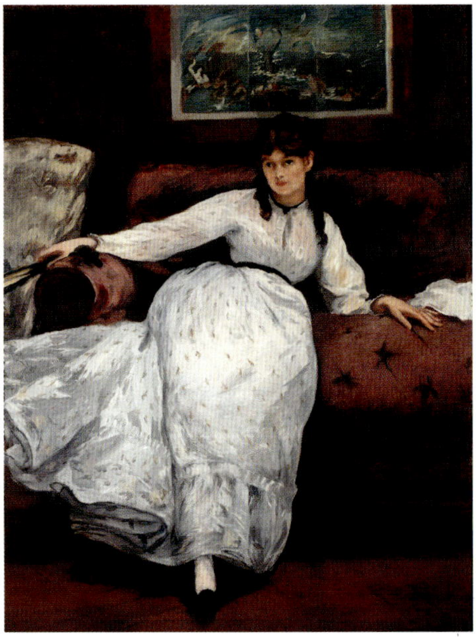

Plate 13: Édouard Manet, *Le Repos* (1870–1871)

generating a nervous apprehension that they experience as their own at the sight of Manet's parents.[16]

By the same token, what inferences can be made from the situation in which Manet placed his mother? Unfortunately, there is no significant information available about Manet's relationship to his mother – other than that she appeared to be supportive and at times actively engaged in furthering his reputation, even after her son's death in 1883. A recent exhibition held in 2021 about his niece Julie—the daughter of Berthe Morisot and Eugène Manet—included a letter from Manet's mother to Jules de Jouy that reveals a more embittered and contentious aspect of her personality.

After Édouard's death on April 30, 1883, Eugénie Manet writes to de Jouy: "I have ruined myself enough for my two sons [Édouard and Eugène] without going to reduce me to nothing." For the world of the Leenhoffs, she has particularly harsh words:

> They are adversaries, to put it mildly. [...] There are things I won't go into again, it's the crime that made her commit the affection she has for this brave boy who is only the victim of his sad birth. She [Suzanne] wants more than she ought to have, it is the punishment of her crime, and she must submit to it.[17]

---

16 Projective identification has evolved as a key concept in the psychoanalytic literature in conjunction with the increased acceptance of countertransference as a welcome and necessary mechanism to absorb and comprehend the disavowed and unconscious affects and fantasies of your counterpart and, in a clinical setting, of your patient. Originally conceived by Melanie Klein as a primitive defense mechanism to ward off unbearable and hostile feelings, it has been transformed by Wilfred Bion into a defense mechanism by which the infant/person can project into the Other unwanted and terrifying feelings with which the other identifies and which s/he mistakes as their own. It is only after some time and much reflection that these affects are realized to come from the other and help to understand the other person's most terrifying feelings. As a consequence, projective identification does not just serve as a defense mechanism but as a means of empathic understanding between two people.

17 1883, quoted in Mathieu/d'Arnoult/Gooden, *Julie Manet – La mémoire impres-*

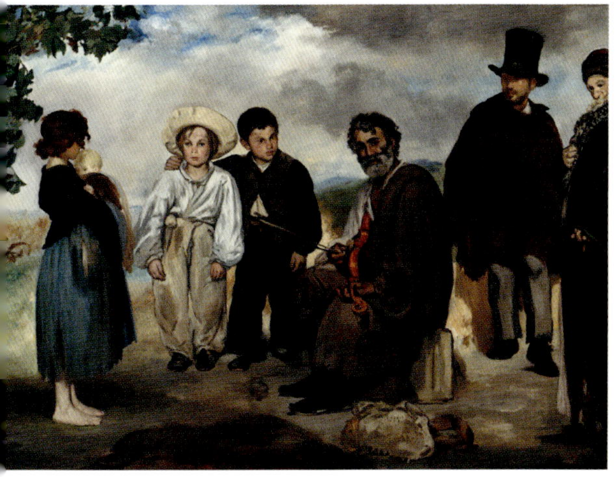

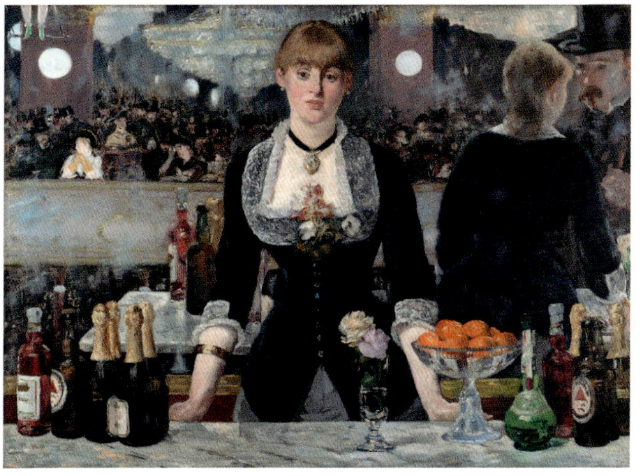

Plate 14:
Édouard Manet,
Le Vieux Musicien (1862)
Plate 15:
Édouard Manet,
Un Bar aux Folies Bergère (1881–1882)

Given this recent information about his mother, it is perhaps clearer why Manet portrayed her so aloof, her attitude offering a degree of self-preservation and a screen for her resentments towards her daughter-in-law—and possibly also towards her husband. By concealing her animosity towards the "Leenhoffs," she probably rendered it difficult for her son Édouard to decipher the cause of her underlying bitterness. It is possible that her demeanor intrigued Édouard, prompting him to paint canvas after canvas in which this residue of detachment was repeatedly echoed. Elsewhere, such works as *Le Balcon* **[Plate 10]**, *Le Repos* (1870–1871) **[Plate 13]**, *Le Vieux Musicien* (1862) **[Plate 14]**, *Le Déjeuner dans l'atelier* **[Plate 2]**, and *Un Bar aux Folies Bergère* (1881–1882) **[Plate 15]** capture this same vacant and distracted look in his mother's eyes. The two people most frequently

---

sioniste (Paris: Hazan, 2021): "Je me suis assez ruinée pour mes 2 fils [Édouard et Eugène] sans aller encore me réduire à rien." (Letter from Eugénie Manet to Jules de Jouy, January 24, 1883 - Musée Marmottan Monet, Paris, inv. DV-1986.2013.591 [23/135], author's translation); "Ce sont des adversaires, pour ne pas dire autre chose. [...] Il y a des choses sur lesquelles je ne reviendrai pas, c'est le crime que lui a fait commettre l'affection qu'elle porte à ce brave garçon qui n'est que la victime de sa triste naissance. Elle [Suzanne] veut plus qu'elle ne devait avoir, c'est la punition de son crime, et il faut qu'elle le subisse." (Comment regarding Eugénie Manet's rapport with her son Gustave in a letter to Jules de Jouy, June 28, 1883 - Musée Marmottan Monet, Paris, inv. DV-1986. 2013. 625 [23/135], author's translation).

depicted in this manner are Berthe Morisot and Léon-Édouard Leenhoff Koëlla, individuals whose relationships to Manet remained veiled in mystery throughout his life.

Berthe Morisot, herself an accomplished Impressionist painter, was one of the women to whom Manet was greatly attracted and who in turn was a fervent admirer of his art. Critics have speculated wildly about the degree of intimacy in their relationship, yet thus far no one has found an adequate explanation for the abrupt termination of their friendship in 1874, sealed by the shift of Manet's attention to Eva Gonzalès, a much less attractive and much less talented painter.

Berthe's later marriage to Manet's younger brother Eugène has widely—and probably correctly—been perceived not so much as the cause but the consequence of the sudden estrangement between Édouard and Berthe.

Manet's relationship with Léon Leenhoff Koëlla, however, raises far more troubling questions than his possible affair with Berthe Morisot. Léon was born in 1852, the same year in which his mother Suzanne Leenhoff joined the Manet household as Édouard's and Eugène's piano teacher. Although Édouard and Suzanne were married in 1863—after what one assumes was a thirteen-year-long affair—Manet never acknowledged his paternity of Léon and instead acted as the boy's godfather at a Protestant christening in Suzanne's Dutch hometown of Zalt-Bomel. Nonetheless, throughout his lifetime, Manet treated Léon like a son and, moreover, made him and Suzanne the sole beneficiaries of his fortune.

However, there may be another important and far more scandalous reason why Manet depicted his father so taut and withdrawn, as if shunning the scrutiny of others. While it had been assumed for some time that Léon was Édouard's illegitimate son, information surfaced in the late 1980s that it was not Édouard who had sired the boy but the patriarch Auguste himself. That made Léon not the illegitimate son of Édouard but his younger half-brother—a far greater scandal than the initial one presumed.

In her book *Manet and the Family Romance* (2001), Nancy Locke delves deeply into this issue and in a footnote details how she obtained this shocking information:

> The late Mina Curtiss published a claim that "a highly distinguished and reliable writer" who had married into the Manet family confided the paternity to a close friend. [...] In light of other events of the previous year, it seems quite plausible that Auguste, like so many men of his society, might have sought a clandestine mistress. [...] it was not unusual for artists in Manet's circle to father illegitimate children and subsequently to legitimize them (as Monet, Renoir, Pissarro and Cézanne did, and as Édouard Manet did not when he married Suzanne Leenhoff). [...] What is without doubt is how scandalous it would have been for a civil judge, who was often called upon to determine the validity of paternity claims, to have fathered an illegitimate child.[18]

According to Locke's research, socially Auguste Manet would have found himself in an extremely indefensible situation, had the truth leaked out.

Although Suzanne was above the age of consent when Léon was conceived, Auguste would have found himself in a precarious position, both legally and socially. In the circumstances, the birth of a child would have put many things at stake: Auguste's reputation, the name of the Manet family in the Paris courts, his Légion d'honneur award, his salary, and not least his retirement pension. The Penal Code prescribed a lifetime sentence of forced labor for persons guilty of rape if they had been in positions of authority, a rule that applied to teachers, ministers, and public functionaries.[19]

Thus, Édouard was the bearer of a monumental secret that needed to be guarded at all times and at all costs, neither casting a shadow upon his father's reputation, nor jeopardizing his own career as an artist. The powerful unconscious and conscious dynamics of family secrets are described by Nicholas C. Avery (1982–1983):

> The issue of what constitutes exploitation of one member's secret has a built-in contradiction. From the vantage of the family's "ego ideal," members do not expose each other's painful feelings to outsiders; they are instead discrete. On the other hand maintaining the secret as just

18 Locke 2001: 188.
19 See Locke 2001: 47.

> described involves perpetuating one's own internal exploitation of the secret and this violates one's own superego and ego ideal standards.[20]

The duality that arises provides the family a stake both in the maintenance of the secret and in its responsible revelation. This inherent contradiction may explain a salient feature of family secrets: although they are tenaciously maintained, given the proper conditions they are surrendered with astounding equanimity. Manet *fils* was certainly tenacious in keeping this potentially explosive family secret and generously provided for the boy's welfare. Meanwhile, his testament may shed some light upon the complicated position in which he found himself: protecting his father's reputation, shielding his mother, and providing for his half-brother, whom he officially identified as his godson throughout his life. His last will and testament eloquently summarizes his thoughts on the matter:

> I hereby appoint Suzanne Leenhoff, my lawful wife, as my general devisee and legatee. She will bequeath, by testament, everything I have left to her to Léon Koëlla, called Leenhoff, who has cared for me most devotedly, and I believe that my brothers will find these dispositions quite natural. A sale of pictures […] From the total proceeds of the sale of my pictures will be deducted a sum of 50,000 francs which will be given to Léon Koëlla, called Leenhoff. The rest will go to Suzanne Leenhoff, my wife. […] If I die before my properties at Gennevilliers are sold, I would like for my wife to continue to live with my mother. […] Drawn up in Paris and completely written in my hand, 30 September 1882. Édouard MANET. It is agreed that Suzanne Leenhoff, my wife, will leave by testament to Léon Koëlla, *called Leenhoff*, the estate I have left to her.[21]

It is of course startling to read to what extent Manet identifies each inheritor not only by name but by familial link as well, mother, wife, brothers. Only the lad Léon lacks any familial epithet, even that of "godson." What does it mean, "Léon Koëlla, called Leenhoff"? "Koëlla" was probably a pure invention and "called Leenhoff" established the

---

20 Avery (1982–1983): 471.

21 Quoted in Locke 2001: 116–117 (author's emphasis).

single true link with his mother Suzanne, who had actually identified him as Édouard's brother when the boy was born in Holland. What does he mean when he says that his two younger brothers will "find these positions *quite natural*"? One answer may be that in exchange for selecting the older son Édouard to be the carrier of this high-level paternal/family secret, Edgar and Gustave agreed not to be the co-inheritors of their brother Édouard's fortune. However, Locke provides another fascinating reason for Manet's refusal to legitimize Léon after his marriage to Suzanne and the death of his father. She explains:

> It is possible […] that Léon was not eligible for legitimization. According to the Napoleonic Code, Article 331, children who were the offspring of adulterous or incestuous unions could *never* be legitimized, even upon the subsequent marriage of the parents. […] Even if Manet *père* had wanted to claim Léon as his son, such an avowal would not only have been a social and professional disaster: it would also have been legally null and void.[22]

But let us return to the *Portrait de Monsieur et Madame Auguste Manet* **[Plate 12]** before we search for further clues about Manet's relationship with Léon and Suzanne Leenhoff in the paintings in which they appear. That eerie and elusive presence of his mother was a forerunner of later prominent canvases, such as *Olympia* (1863) **[Plate 5]**, *La Chanteuse de rue* (1862) **[Plate 16]**, and *Un Bar aux Folies Bergère* (1881–1882) **[Plate 15]**. Manet used his favorite model Victorine Meurent to stage scenes that recaptured the resigned, aloof and forlorn look he assigned to his mother. In all likelihood, his mother was privy to the family secret. She was aware that her husband had sired a son with the young Dutch piano teacher, and yet there was nothing that she could do. Her reaction to the "Leenhoffs", however, suggests that she primarily blamed Suzanne for the "unfortunate birth of Léon,"[23] and considered her culpable for the disgrace and dishonor that would inevitably befall her if she did not continue to

22 Locke 2001: 117.

23 Quoted in Mathieu/d'Arnoult/Gooden 2021: 23.

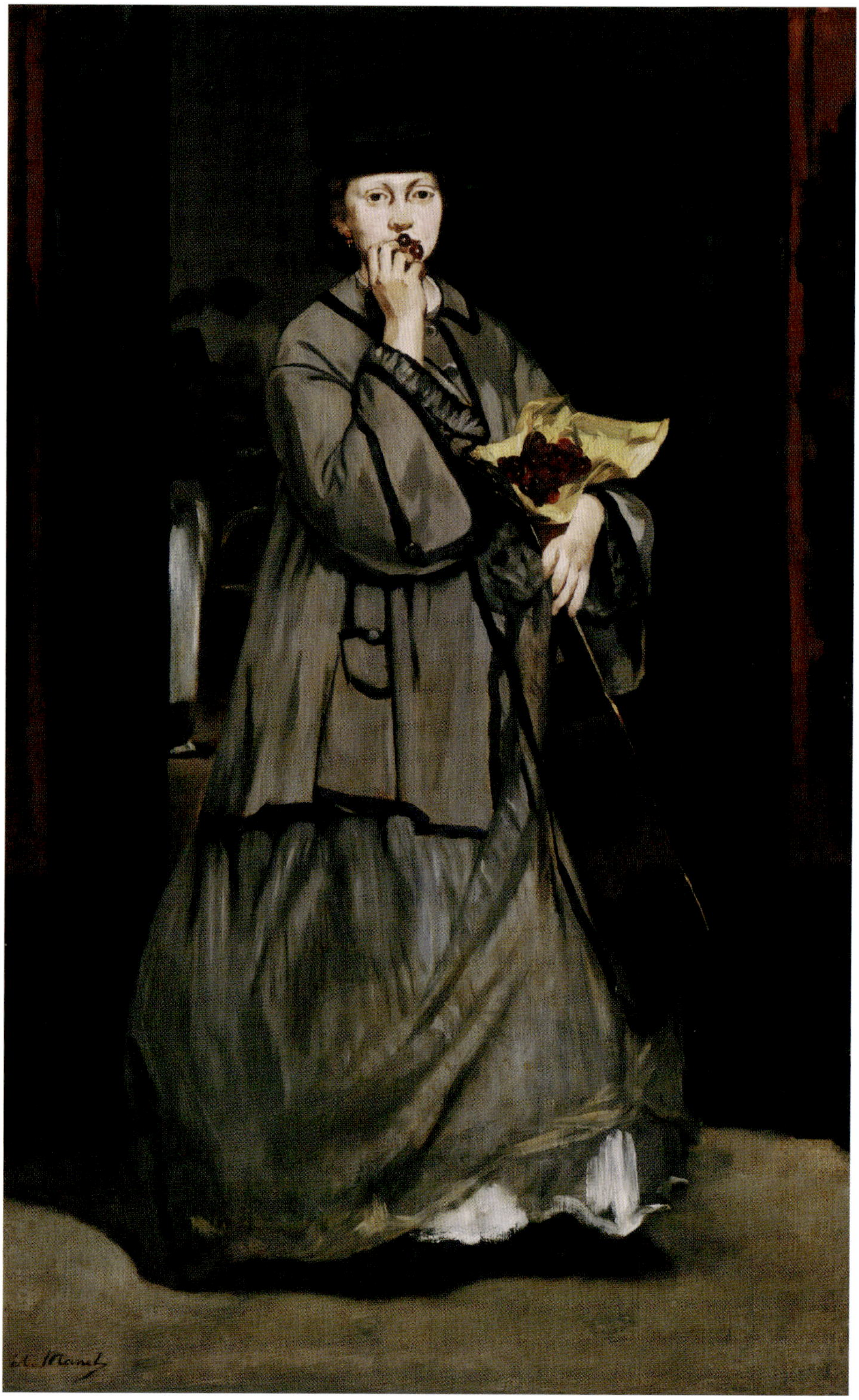

play the dutiful wife to Auguste. At the same time, though, she was powerless to protect her eldest son from carrying the burden of his father's philandering. Therefore it was Édouard who professed to be Léon's godfather, and it was he who married his father's mistress. In other words, Édouard was the only one to legitimize the immoral and illegitimate acts of his father, and he became the only one to eventually assume the role of surrogate father and thereby assume the symbolic position of the Third in this rather incestuous triangle.

In the *Portrait de Monsieur et Madame Auguste Manet*, Manet places his father squarely between himself and his mother. With this arrangement, the father forms a kind of barrier, blocking access to the mother, as if endorsing the symbolic role of the father and of the official representative of the French law. Yet, if our information is correct, and Auguste Manet was indeed the true father of Léon, the man had miserably failed in his paternal duties. On the contrary, he is the father who, instead of upholding the laws on incest, undermines them within his own family, using his eldest son as a cover-up for his own unlawful conduct. Rather than upholding the family honor, Auguste Manet sets himself above the law, instrumentalizing his entire family as a smoke-screen of sorts, in particular Édouard and his wife. A closer examination of Manet's painting *La Pêche* **[Plate 1]**, which I will discuss in a moment, may shed further light upon the painter's relations with Suzanne and Léon and the intricacies of their secretive family affairs.

In 1850, Manet joined the studio of Thomas Couture, a history painter who in 1837 had won the "Prix de Rome" aged twenty-two and had reached the pinnacle of artistic success with the painting *Les Romains de la décadence* (1847) **[Plate 17]**. Couture was hailed as "roi de la peinture" and slated for a brilliant future as France's Titian. Although Couture might have "seemed the painter who could best set young Manet on the path to official honors and financial success,"[24] Manet quickly developed a lasting antipathy towards his teacher. Throughout this six-year apprenticeship, Couture and his famous pupil were consistently at odds because of their artistic disagreements. Antonin Proust, who also enrolled as a student in Couture's studio, remembers

page 74: **Plate 16:**
Édouard Manet,
La Chanteuse de rue (1862)

24 Hamilton 1969: 21.

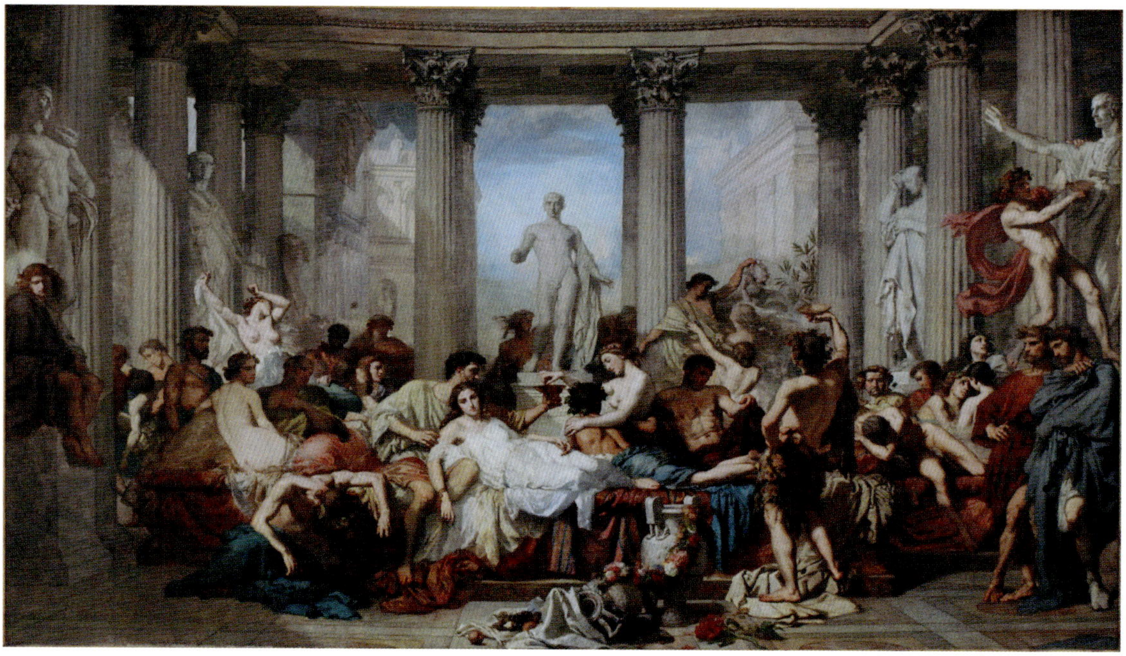

Plate 17: Thomas Couture, *Les Romains de la décadence* (1847)

Manet saying: "I can't think why I am here, […] everything we see here is absurd; the light is false, the shadows are false. When I arrive at the studio, I feel as though I'm entering a tomb."[25]

From an early age, Manet was guided by two essential principles: to paint what he saw around him, and to record it as sincerely and truthfully as possible. Zola described the artist as someone who "just looked at Nature and his whole ideal was to force himself to record it truthfully and forcefully."[26] Courbet's famous aphorism that he would not paint angels because he had never seen any is echoed in Manet's refusal to paint the models in Couture's studio who posed like Roman statues.

He asked them to put their clothes back on and to stand naturally, exclaiming: "What! Can't you be natural? […] Is that the way you would buy a bunch of radishes at the greengrocers?" When the model Mlle Dubosc objected and angrily responded: "Monsieur Manet,

25 Proust, quoted in Courthion 1960: 3.

26 Zola, quoted in Courthion 1960: 163.

thanks to me there is more than one student who has gone to Rome,"[27] Manet replied: "We're not in Rome now and we don't want to go there. We're in Paris—let's stay here." When Couture later entered the studio and discovered that his model was partly clothed because of Manet's suggestion, he exclaimed: "My poor boy, [...] my poor boy, you will never be anything more than the Daumier of your day."[28]

Among his fellow students Manet was famous for his brash and rebellious attitude towards his teacher. A description by Antonin Proust helps us visualize the young Manet during his beginning career as a painter:

> At that time [1850], Édouard Manet was of medium height and physically very strong. [...] he could never succeed in being vulgar. One was always conscious of his breeding.
> His forehead was broad, his nose was drawn in a bold straight line. His mouth, turned up at the corners, was mocking. His glance was keen; his eyes small but very mobile. When he was very young, he wore his hair, which was naturally curly, long and swept back. At eighteen his hair had receded from his forehead, but he had grown a beard which lent a softer look to the lower part of his face. ... Few men have been as attractive as he.[29]

Given the vehemence of their disagreement, the length of Manet's apprenticeship under Couture is something of a puzzle, yet, despite Zola's initial misgivings, Couture's tutoring evidently exerted a crucial effect upon Manet's later works. Like many of Manet's early champions, Émile Zola felt that Manet had wasted his time at Couture's atelier; he also believed that Couture's influence was a hindrance to Manet's career:

> For three years, [...] he remained bruised by the caning he had received. He had the new answer in his mind and it was on the tip of

27 Courthion 1960: 4. The model's comment was an allusion to Thomas Couture, who had won the prestigious "Prix de Rome"award, which included a journey to the Italian capital.

28 Courthion 1960: 4.

29 Courthion 1960: 38–39.

> his tongue, as they say, but he was unable to pronounce it. Then, his vision cleared; he was able to see things distinctly; he no longer had an impediment in his speech and he was able to speak.[30]

However, recent criticism sheds a different light on Couture's influence upon Manet's work. Having carefully researched Couture's teaching methods, Anne Coffin Hanson paints a picture of Manet's teacher that sharply contradicts the standard view of Couture as an artist mired in academic convention. Although he still clothed his models in Greek and Roman costumes, Couture exhorted his students to paint their own period and to look around themselves and draw inspiration from life, rather than from the nostalgia of the past: "Soyez donc Parisiens comme on étoit Athéniens. Ayez confiance dans vos forces, ne vous suicidez pas dans le passé."[31]

Similarly, he reminded his students to recognize the changing modern world and to be aware that art was, as Thoré Burger had already stated, no longer "made for gods and princes"[32], since "the railroads and the great businesses will give important work to the artist, and the State will no longer have to nourish monumental art alone."[33]

Even Manet's famous aphorism "I paint what I see, and what I see is modern life" reveals a definite link to Couture's ideas and didactic principles, since Couture regularly "urged his students to carry a sketch book at all times and to draw men, women and children in natural poses, going about the normal task of their daily life."[34] This advice contradicts Proust's account of Couture's teaching methods: his techniques emerge as both flexible and wide-ranging. He encouraged his students to learn from and copy the Old Masters, yet, at the same time to not lose sight of the modern world and its subject-matter. His painting techniques incorporated a similar mixture of traditional methods of color application and preparatory

---

30 Zola, quoted in Courthion 1960: 118–119.

31 Couture 1897: 266; "Be Parisians as if you were Athenians. Have confidence in your strengths, don't suicide in the past." (author's translation).

32 Burger, quoted in Hanson 1977: 9.

33 Quoted in Hanson 1977: 14.

34 Hanson 1977: 146.

studies with new concepts of palette harmonization and a preference for spontaneity in both drawing and painting. And although as a painter Couture continued to render his subjects in an idealized and sentimental fashion, Rosen and Zerner note that his subject-matter covers both high art and popular culture, leans toward the Academy while acknowledging the avant-garde, looks back into the past and forward into the future, and even references contemporary events.[35]

Couture's celebrated *Les Romains de la décadence*, which currently hangs near Manet's *Olympia* in the Musée d'Orsay in Paris, illustrates his muddled attempts to integrate past themes with modern life. Although the work was intended as a comment on the decadence of contemporary French society, his intention is scarcely discernible in the finished painting. The fascination with pseudo "Roman" props and poses as well as the classic painterly execution vitiate the criticism Couture intended to make: the painting itself serves as an illustration of the very decadence it was meant to rebuke. A comparison of Couture's *Les Romains de la décadence* with Manet's *Olympia* illustrates the reason for their artistic disagreements, which ultimately led to their break-up.

In *Olympia*, Manet depicts his model in a fashion similar to that chosen by Couture for his central figure: an elongated Venus draped on a couch. Yet, while Manet uses a contemporary model, "the sort of girl we meet every day on the pavements, with thin shoulders wrapped in a flimsy faded woolen shawl,"[36] Couture chooses an ideal figure who bears no mark of modern allure. Instead, he adheres to the rules of classicism proclaimed by David, which Werner Hofman summarizes in the following way:

> [...] it is symptomatic of the whole process that David should confess in a note on his 'Rape of the Sabine Women' to having set himself the aim of reproducing the antique way of life with such meticulous care that if Greeks or Romans were to stand before his pictures, they would recognize in them the work of one thoroughly familiar with their usages.[37]

35 See Rosen/Zerner 1982: 51.

36 Zola, quoted in Courthion 1960: 131.

37 Hofman 1961: 63.

What Couture can only express implicitly and vaguely, Manet exhibits explicitly in *Olympia*. Although both artists depict a scene of sexual depravity and decadence in French bourgeois society, Manet paints what he knows to lie behind the respectable façade of married life, a secret life like the one his father had led behind a façade of respectability. The prostitute's role was all the more important since divorce was forbidden by French law until 1886. As Théodore Zeldin reports:

> In the 1850s it was estimated that London had about 24,000 prostitutes but Paris, with almost half the population, was said to have 34,000. [...] Public opinion was less outraged by their trade, than by their trade being carried on publicly and in a manner which constituted a nuisance for those who did not require their services.[38]

Couture's painting did not shatter the thin veneer of bourgeois respectability, but actually teased the bourgeois appetite for sexual indulgence. The fact that his *Les Romains de la décadence* received the Salon's most prestigious award, while *Olympia* was greeted with shock and opprobrium, not only illustrates the hypocrisy and pretension of official morality, but poignantly underscores the rift between Couture and Manet. Although Couture protested against the monopolizing control of the Salon and warned his students not to be intimidated by the past, his public works show no trace of his avant-garde attitude; on the contrary, they reveal a man who was always ready to compromise and who rarely succeeded in transforming his modern ideas into artistic productions.

The official break between Couture and Manet occurred in 1859 when Manet invited his teacher to comment on his first major painting, *Le Buveur d'absinthe*. Couture dismissed the work with the comment: "An absinthe drinker! And they paint abominations like that! My poor friend, you are the absinthe drinker. It is you who has lost your moral faculty!"[39] Couture's objection to the *Buveur* was shared by the Salon, which rejected it in 1859 despite Delacroix's vote of approval. It is generally believed that Couture and the public disap-

---

38 Zeldin 1973: 307.

39 Couture, quoted in Hamilton 1969: 22.

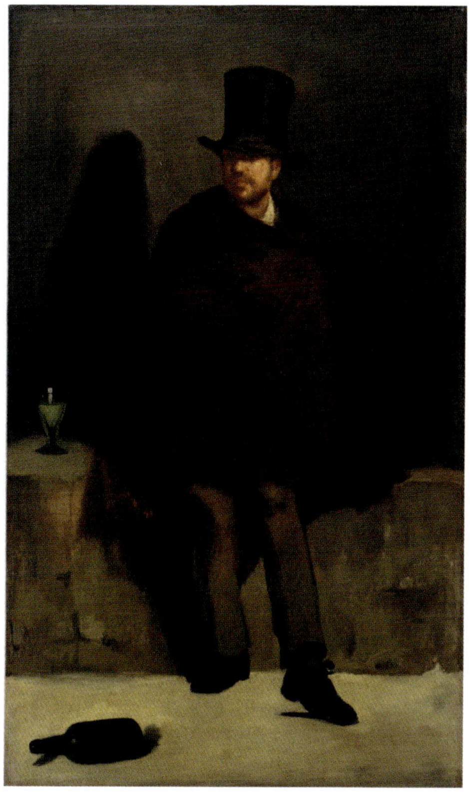

Plate 11:
Édouard Manet,
Le Buveur d'absinthe
(1859)

proved of *Le Buveur d'absinthe* because it depicted a contemporary subject, a rag-picker whom Manet had encountered at the Louvre. Hamilton remarks that "in painting the *Absinthe Drinker* Manet placed himself in opposition not only to the idealizing academic subject but also to the typical Romantic subject with its overtones of imaginative escape from present time and place. Only two years before, Delacroix had noted in his journal (January 13, 1857) that 'modern subjects are difficult to treat in the absence of the nude and the poverty of modern costume'."[40]

Couture's reaction to *Le Buveur d'absinthe* (1859) [Plate 11] also crystallized the hypocrisy of his own didactic principles. Although he had advocated that contemporary subjects be painted in their natural poses, he had also warned his students that "'Men and women of the lower classes draped in old curtains and coverlets' are not natural."[41] It is important to notice that by depicting an ordinary subject, Manet paid an implicit tribute to the School of Realism. The entire canvas serves as an endorsement of Champfleury's view that the "'serious representation of present-day personalities, the derbies, the blackdress-coats, the polished shoes or the peasants' sabots' had a far greater interest than the frivolous knick-knacks of the past."[42] Thus, in one stroke Manet was able to expose the weakness and opportunism of Couture's art, to pay an initial allegiance to the School of Realism, to show his genuine indebtedness to Velázquez (a painter who had been admired but never successfully used by Couture), and to venture a subtle statement about his own position as a beginning painter, isolated and denigrated by his master.

---

40 Hamilton 1969: 23.

41 Couture in Hanson 1977: 146.

42 Champfleury, quoted in Nochlin 1971: 28.

After the Salon's rejection of *Le Buveur d'absinthe*, Manet disclosed his intentions:

> I painted a Parisian character whom I had studied in Paris, and I executed it with the technical simplicity I discovered in Velázquez. No one understands it. If I painted a Spanish type, it would be more comprehensible.[43]

Manet's statement not only reveals his acute perception of the public's refusal to comprehend art outside the firmly established Academic conventions, but it also points towards his own identification (via Velázquez) with the rag-picker as an emblem of the artist-philosopher. By composing *Le Buveur d'absinthe* in a manner strikingly similar to that of Velázquez's paintings of *Aesop* (1640) **[Plate 18]** and *Menippos* (1640) **[Plate 19]**, Manet consciously drew upon the convention prevalent in Spanish art, that philosophers were regularly portrayed as beggars. Although *Le Buveur d'absinthe* has never been identified as a self-portrait, I believe that it is such, and has a distinctly polemical thrust. This identification becomes even more compelling if one considers the iconographic implications of Manet's borrowings from Velázquez: both philosophers represented were slaves whom their masters eventually freed in recognition of their brilliance, and both Aesop and Menippos were pre-eminent writers of satire. Now, if one considers the fact that Manet deliberately followed the studio techniques insisted upon by Couture, while basing his model upon Velázquez's philosophers, the ironic implication becomes clear: it is Couture who has become the object of satire, who has, as it were, made a farce out of his own ideals when he decided to reject Manet's *Le Buveur d'absinthe*.[44]

One could argue that Couture's harsh dismissal of *Le Buveur* confirmed Manet as an independent artist, just as his father's initial

---

43 Manet, quoted in Hamilton 1969: 24.

44 Peter Gay remarks upon the schism between Manet and Couture, saying that "The break between Couture and Manet had more subtle and more poignant causes than fundamental disagreements over art. Manet committed a grave offense: he dared to carry out his teacher's program. The man who performs what others promise cannot expect them to forgive him." (Gay 1976: 78.)

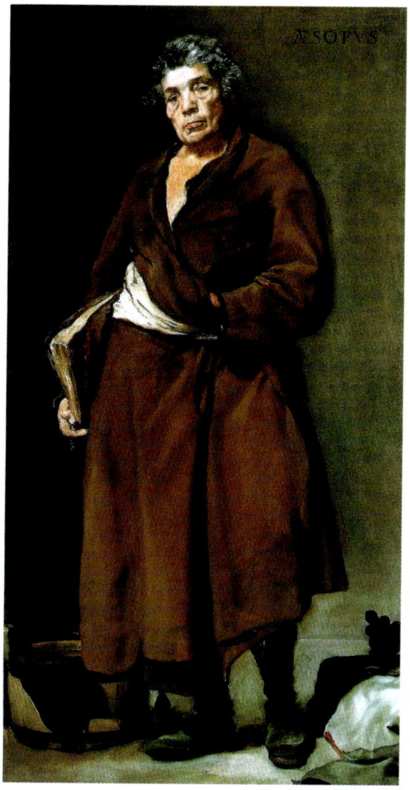

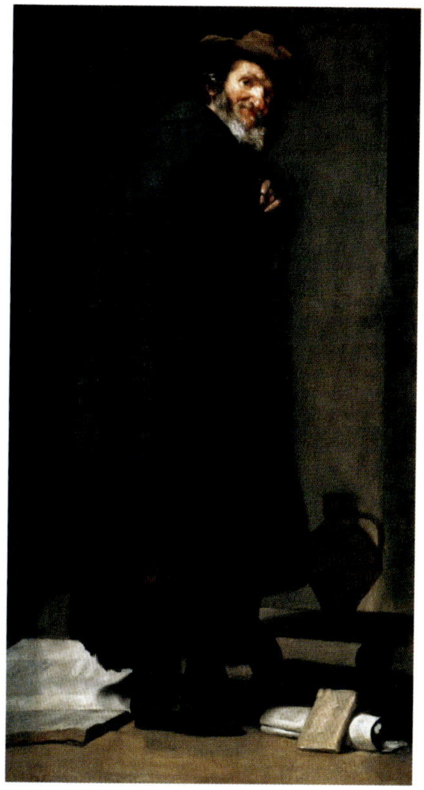

Plate 18:
Diego Velázquez,
Aesop (1640)
Plate 19:
Diego Velázquez,
Menippos (1640)

refusal to allow him to become a painter merely strengthened his determination. It seems therefore that conflict and resistance actually spurred Manet's ambition, to the extent that in the ensuing years, he deliberately sought this conflict by submitting his paintings to the Salon, time and time again. In truth, Manet had ample opportunities to exhibit his works at other gatherings, especially in the 1870s, when the Impressionists had formally founded a group and were showing their works at private galleries. However, Manet declined to exhibit his works with his Impressionist friends, despite their frequent invitations. I believe his insistence on the Salon was dictated by a desire to challenge his adversaries on their own ground, and to force them to recognize the shallow hypocrisy of their own stance. Given our knowledge of his father's deceit, a man who probably made Édouard swear to secrecy about the adulterous relationship with the young Dutch woman who bore his son, Manet exercised his rancor and

explains: "By Article 148 [of the Napoleonic Code] parental consent was essential for men wanting to marry up to 25 and girls up to 21; but even up to the ages of 30 and 25 respectively, consent had to be asked, though it could be ignored after three refusals."[48] Thus, Manet would have been legally obligated to ask for his father's consent to marry until 1862, the year of his father's death. One does not have to speculate wildly in order to understand why Manet decided not to ask for his father's permission, since Auguste Manet might not have agreed to this official union. Behind the upright façade, Manet *père* appears to have been a stern upholder of bourgeois principles, hypocritically adhering to all the conventions that such a household implied.

> […] Auguste, Edouard's father, was not the sort who left anything to improvisation. […] The role [of a judge] suited him ideally: he was a man of duty, sternly honest, unflaggingly virtuous. He was enormously self-righteous: a confirmed republican […]. Auguste's life was a web of inexorable routines. Twice a week he held receptions, not because he was sociable, but because it was expected of a well-salaried civil servant.[49]

By all accounts', Manet's father was a person who would not likely smile upon such a match, and one can safely assume that he would have refused his consent to Édouard's union with Suzanne, which constituted the kind of misalliance the bourgeoisie most feared. Again, according to Zeldin:

> The marriage of their children was a public valuation placed on the parents' position, and it was also a method of improving that position. The great problem was to avoid a *mésalliance*, which was why love was the great enemy, the rebel against parental authority which could bring disaster on all their plans.[50]

Suzanne was two years older than her prospective husband and came from a humble, artistic background, and in assuming her capacity as a

---

48 Zeldin 1973: 361.
49 Schneider 1968: 13.
50 Zeldin 1973: 287.

piano teacher, she belonged for all intents and purposes to the servant class. Given the official bourgeois conventions, she was simply not an eligible choice. Since marriage was largely considered as a business contract and the ideal marriage as a fair bargain between families, Manet's liaison with Suzanne Leenhoff would have thwarted all of Auguste's plans to increase the family's fortunes through his son's bride. However, had Manet disclosed his marriage plans before his father's death, Auguste might well have retaliated by cutting him out of his will. Such a loss would have been catastrophic, not merely to Édouard's material condition, but also to his very career as a painter. It was only because of his inheritance that Manet found himself in a privileged position among his fellow artist friends. "He was able to live without the necessity of selling his pictures [...] and he was able to set aside enough to provide for the necessary expenses for a studio and models."[51]

After his father's death and the obligatory one-year mourning period, Manet could properly marry Suzanne without disclosing to a soul the full circumstances of his thirteen-year liaison with her. He further obscured an already murky and secretive affair by convincing friends like Charles Baudelaire that he was traveling to Holland to fetch a wife. The painter who defined himself as an artist of "sincerity and truth" was anything but sincere and truthful in his own private affairs. Through his father's hypocrisy and deeds he was embedded in a network of lies and secrecies that he could perhaps only exorcise through his paintings, constructing a more honorable line of genealogy—such as the Spanish and Italian Old Masters—than the one he had inherited through his father Auguste.

Manet's duplicity was not an exception from French bourgeois conventions, but rather an example for them. As Richard Sennett explains:

> People lived so that they would avoid detection on the street, sought, as Thackeray so beautifully put it, to "deny to probing eyes knowledge that should come to none indiscriminately in the city." Theirs was a world of shaded lamps, hooded bonnets, rides in closed carriages. [...]

---

51 Courthion 1960: 49.

> the very belief that appearance is an index of character would prompt people to make themselves nondescript in order to be as mysterious, as little vulnerable, as possible.[52]

This concurs with Édouard's elaborate efforts to conceal from the public his long-standing affair with Suzanne Leenhoff, and his intention to present her at the time of their marriage in such a way that would not let slip any compromising information about the complexities of their shared history.

His painting *La Pêche* [**Plate 1**] was the vehicle for Manet's formal introduction of his wife to society, and at the same time constituted his announcement of their marriage. This is the only canvas which depicts Édouard and Suzanne together. Manet completed it in 1863 (the year of his marriage and the year of *Olympia*), and the work resembles a traditional marriage portrait. Since Manet had officially announced to his friends that he was going to be married in Holland and then return to Paris with his bride, it is evident that he was attempting through *La Pêche* to lend verisimilitude to his improbable story, and to paint an attractive picture that would disguise and glaze over the elements that could reveal the real nature of their liaison.

Unlike any other painting by Manet, *La Pêche* recalls the classical Dutch landscape tradition, evoking an atmosphere of calmness and serenity. The Baroque style is further underscored by the seventeenth-century costumes in which the couple poses. The personal elements Manet included here become clearer when one traces the subtle echoes of other works that Manet introduced into this particular canvas. Rubens's etchings *Château de Steen* and his *Landscape with Rainbow* have been identified as the two principal sources for *La Pêche*. Manet and Suzanne stand in the same position as Rubens and his second wife, Hélène Fourment, in *Château de Steen*. The overall composition of the landscape, the rainbow and the dog looking backward at the couple, echoe faithfully Rubens's *Landscape with Rainbow*. In *La Pêche*, the references to Rubens not only signify Manet's tribute to the venerated Old Master, but allude by happy coincidence to the

---

52 Sennett 1977: 169.

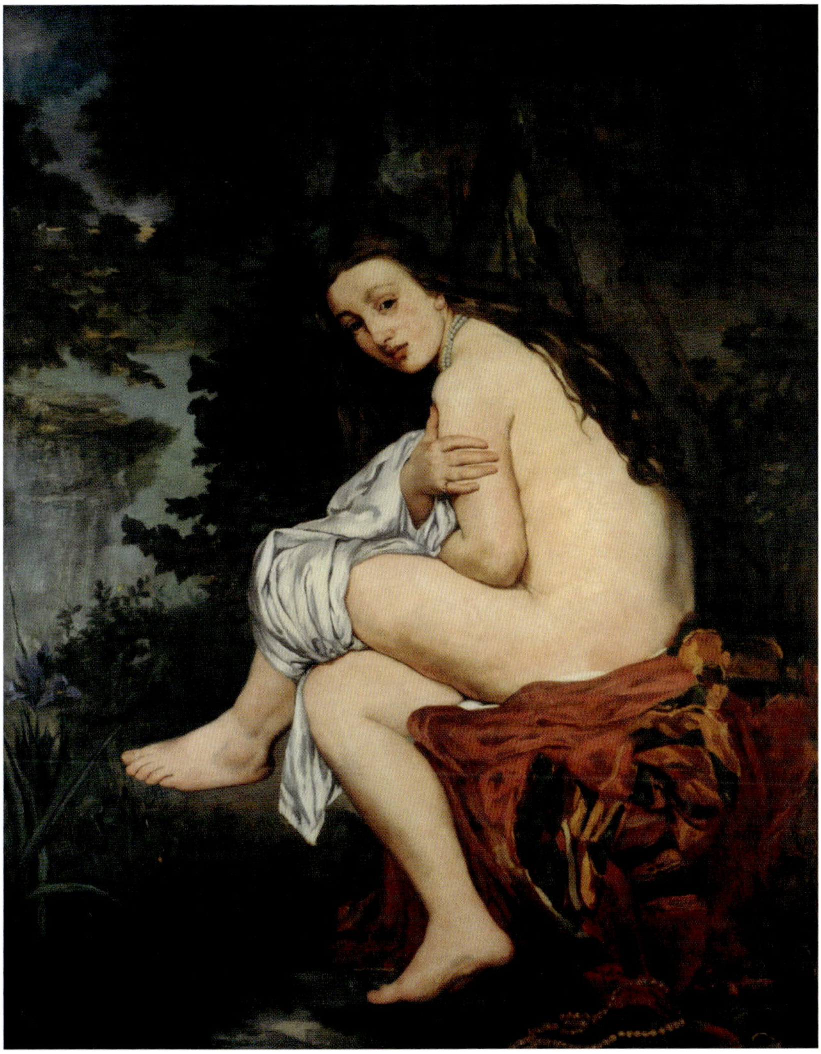

Plate 20:
Édouard Manet,
La Nymphe surprise
(1859–1861)

Dutch origins of Suzanne Leenhoff. By placing himself and his wife in the same position as Rubens and Hélène Fourment in *Château de Steen*, Manet may have been making an optimistic comparison of his recent marriage to that of Rubens, a union that had conspicuously rejuvenated Rubens's artistic career and inspired many of his greatest works. Moreover, Manet may have wanted to allay doubts about Suzanne's origins by creating the impression that Suzanne Leenhoff had come from a family as respectable and well-placed as that of Rubens's wife.

The rainbow (a symbol of union), the dog (a symbol of fidelity), and the church in the background can be interpreted as Manet's attempt to depict these qualities in his loving relationship with Suzanne. These direct and unambiguous references all bolster the official version of Manet's marriage as he himself wished it to be portrayed. George Mauner observes that, besides *La Pêche*, Suzanne had been portrayed in connection with water in two other paintings—*La Nymphe surprise* (1859–1861) **[Plate 20]** and *Le Déjeuner sur l'herbe* **[Plate 3]**, where she is thought to be the model for the figure wading in the background. While the symbolism of water usually suggests immortality, birth and the fountain of youth, the association of purity seems to be the one most consistently linked to Suzanne. She is clearly the model for *La Nymphe surprise*, in which she strikes a pose similar to that of Susanna in Rubens's many versions of *Susanna and the Elder* and Rembrandt's *Susanna in the Bath*. Manet was well aware of the biblical parable of Susanna and the Elders, which tells the story of a chaste and beautiful woman who bravely resists an attempt on her virtue and the false accusations of a pair of corrupt older men, and he includes a lily in *La Nymphe surprise*, the traditional Christian symbol of purity as a visual echo of the parable.

> The crouching figure, striving to cover her nudity, becomes the incarnation of spiritual love in the more complex *Déjeuner sur l'herbe* of two years later. In that work, Manet has provided her with a suitable garment which she holds shut, while the nude who has retained Susanna's outward glance, is essentially derived from another set of figures.[53]

page 91: **Plate 21:** Édouard Manet, *La Lecture* (1865–1873)
Plate 22: Édouard Manet, *Madame Manet au piano* (1867–1868)
Plate 23: Édouard Manet, *Portrait de Madame Édouard Manet sur un canapé bleu* (1874)

Le Déjeuner sur l'herbe was initially called *Le Bain*, and I believe that the change in title bears more significance than is generally assumed. In this painting the spectator's eyes are initially directed towards the nude woman sitting on the grass in the company of two fully clothed men. However, by naming the painting *Le Bain*, Manet confounded this immediate focus upon the nude woman in the foreground and shifted the attention instead to the woman bathing, whose presence is less disquieting than that of the three figures on the grass.

---

53 Mauner 1975: 23.

This potential loss of focus is remedied once Manet renamed the painting *Le Déjeuner sur l'herbe* and thereby validated the spectator's natural impulse to focus on the sexually provocative picnic scene. Is it possible that this displacement from the bather to the nude woman also corresponds to Manet's own drifting attention, away from his wife towards the other woman who served as the model for his painting? Unlike Rubens, who used his young wife as a model for numerous paintings after their marriage, Manet rarely portrayed Suzanne Leenhoff after 1863.

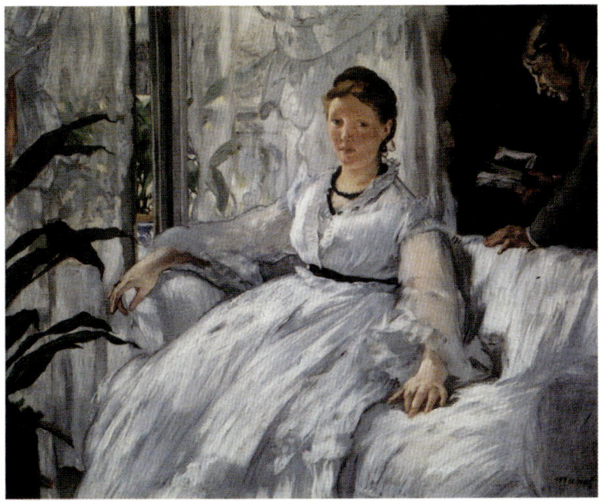

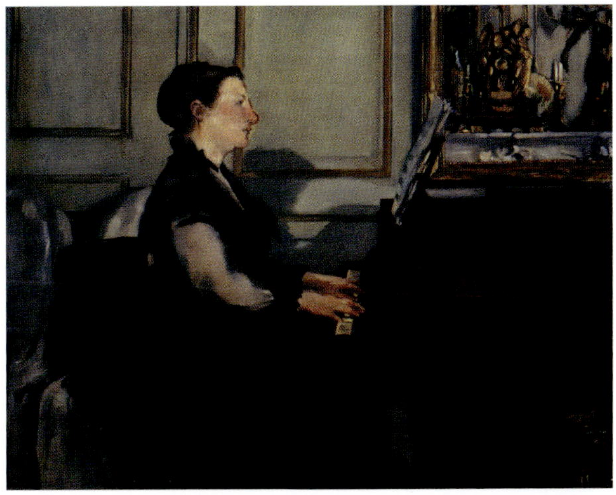

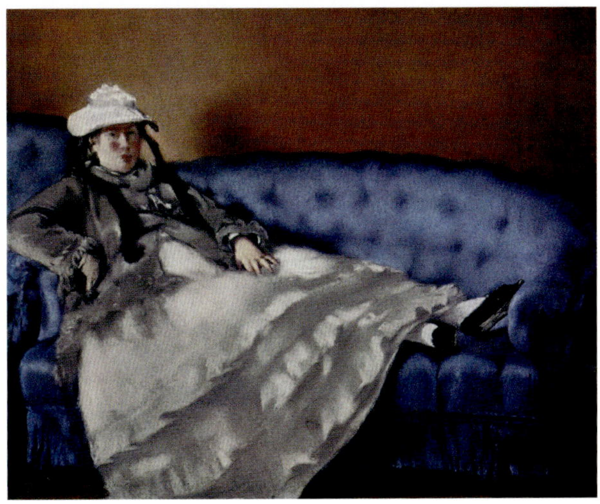

This led Mme. Morisot, the mother of Berthe, to remark in a letter to her younger daughter, Edna: "He [Manet] has reproduced his wife. I think it was high time."[54] However, Manet's decision to portray Suzanne in only a small number of paintings, such as *La Lecture* (1865–1873) **[Plate 21]**, *Madame Manet au Piano* (1867–1868) **[Plate 22]**, *Sur la Plage* (1873), and *Portrait de Madame Édouard Manet sur un canapé bleu* (1874) **[Plate 23]** and *Madame Édouard Manet dans la serre* (1879), does not seem to be a strictly negative comment upon their personal relationship, since their marriage remained a happy one throughout Manet's life. It is possible though, that Manet was no longer interested in using Suzanne as a model for his paintings

54 Rouart 1957: 29.

since her physiognomy changed with increasing age. As Françoise Cachin points out: "Since posing for Reading [...] Mme Manet had put on weight, and her kind, placid features, always somewhat ruddy, had coarsened."[55]

Even Berthe Morisot remarked upon this in a letter to her sister, Edna, in 1873: "I saw our friend Manet yesterday; he left today with his fat Suzanne for Holland and in such a bad humour that I do not know how they will get there."[56]

It is clear that, for whatever reasons, Suzanne Leenhoff's social standing substantially changed once she became Manet's lawful wife. In accordance with bourgeois ideas of decorum, a wife was relegated to the role of an unpaid housekeeper. Her domain was the home, and she was to keep to it. Indeed, Manet's wife took no active part in her husband's professional career and was seldom seen in his atelier. He explicitly illustrates this change in her social position by portraying her exclusively in bourgeois surroundings, confining her to performances at the piano, comfortable settings in the parlor, or leisurely times at the beach.

The setting for *Madame Manet au piano* was aptly described by Théodore Zeldin:

> A bourgeois must spend his money to maintain a certain decorum in his clothes, his accommodation and his food. [...] He had to have a *salon*, furnished with a piano, paintings, candelabras, clocks and bibelots, in which to receive visitors and to show that he possessed a surplus of wealth, dedicated to cultured living, beyond the basic necessities.[57]

Irrespective of the effort involved, Manet did succeed both in obscuring the real circumstances of his premarital affair and in integrating his Dutch wife into bourgeois Parisian life. He continued frequenting his parents' home as before, and like them, he and his wife held weekly salons in their own residence. Often Suzanne would play the

---

55 Cachin 1983: 437.

56 Rouart 1957: 77.

57 Zeldin 1973: 15.

piano, and Manet's mother Eugénie would hold recitals which were frequently attended by such prominent friends as Baudelaire, Degas, Stevens, the Morisots, Zola, etc.[58]

Returning for a moment to *La Pêche* (1861–1863) **[Plate 1]** a description of this painting—at least from a biographical perspective—would not be complete without noticing the little fishing boy at the opposite end of the pond from where Manet and his bride are situated. This figure is commonly believed to represent Léon Leenhoff. It is interesting to note that Manet decided to include rather than simply omit the "product" of his pre-marital relationship, or at least the reminder of an incestuous, illegitimate affair of his father with Suzanne Leenhoff, in his "official" wedding portrait. Although the boy's features are barely recognizable, his isolated position within the painting commands a certain centrality. Moreover, as in the case of *Le Bain*, the title of the painting prepares the viewer to focus on the only person who is actually being portrayed as "fishing," namely the boy Léon. Another indirect reference to Léon's importance in the wedding canvas is contained in the Rubens/Manet figure, who, while casually holding his hat in the hand behind the Hélène/Suzanne figure's shoulder, is actually pointing with the sketchily painted index finger of that hand beyond the fisherman in his boat to the opposite shore, where a seated child is also engaged in fishing. "This child, then, takes on a special meaning, which we can only associate with the idea of innocence and purity."[59]

Another, more circuitous connection can be detected between the child and the Manet couple. Édouard's index finger also points towards the raft on which he has prominently signed his name, and it is from this signed raft that a single reed, rising from the water, leads the

---

58 Not everyone seemed to have enjoyed the evening's entertainment at the house of the Manets as the description of Berthe Morisot's mother illustrates: "I found the Manet salon in just the same state as before, it is nauseating. If people were not interested in hearing individual accounts of public misfortunes, I think little would have been said. The heat was stifling, everbody was cooped up in the one drawing room, the drinks were warm. But Pagans sang, Madame Édouard played, and Monsieur Degas was there." (Rouart 1957: 70).

59 Mauner 1975: 25.

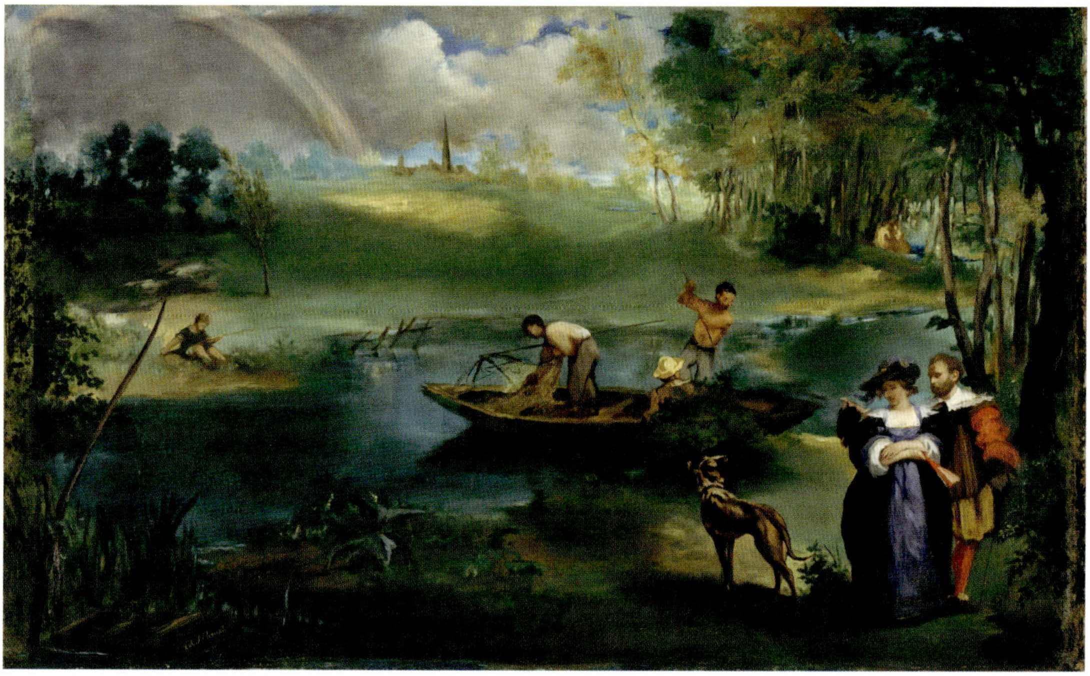

Plate 1:
Édouard Manet, *La Pêche* (1861–1863)

eye towards the child. It is therefore only through the name Manet that Édouard placed upon the wooden board, that a symbolic link of kinship is to be established to the boy. Whether it was Auguste or Édouard himself who had fathered Léon, the boy should have borne the name Manet, but for fear of breaking many taboos and risking scandal, Léon was assigned an invented name, placing him squarely into a perverse matrimonial lineage.

Although Léon is surrounded by icons which I previously identified as symbolic for the theme of domesticity and fidelity, he remains apart, isolated on the other bank of the pond and separated from the couple. He is also set apart from the three fishermen in the bark, who are preoccupied with their fishing. Could those three fishermen possibly stand for the three older Manet siblings whose younger half-brother was left alone, busy with his own fishing expedition? Could the man in the boat wearing a white straw hat, his head turned away, be a metaphor for the father deliberately ignoring Léon and leaving his sons, particularly Édouard, to clear up his messy affair?[60]

An alternative reading of *La Pêche* leads to a similar conclusion. Besides the circuitous link via the signed raft and reed, the fishing-boat constitutes the most direct connection between the Manet couple and the Léonfigure. The boat is not tied to either shore, and it is not clear whether the boatman wielding the bargepole is pushing the vessel in the direction of Léon, or toward the Manet couple. If one thinks of the boat as a sort of ferry linking two opposite banks, its destination seems deliberately ambiguous. I wish to argue that *La Pêche* is of great symbolic import and provides important clues to the Manet family's troubled question of paternity. Jacques Lacan defines the paternal metaphor as the process by which the father, in the position of the symbolic father, helps the child navigate from one bank of the river to the other, from the maternal/imaginary/dualistic bank to the symbolic/paternal/societal bank, where the child is in-

60 The white straw hat foreshadows the hat Maximilian wears in *L'Exécution de Maximilien*, but in an inverserelationship. Rather than pointing towards a sense of innocence, in this case with the figure's face turned around, it may mark the father's faceless culpability towards his three sons.

troduced into language and into kinship relationships. "The father, the Name-of-the-father, sustains the structure of desire within the structure of the law—but the inheritance of the father is that which Kierkegaard designates for us, namely, his sin."[61]

In French, the word *pêche* has a double meaning, it means both "fishing" and, with a slightly different spelling (*péché*) but similar sound, it means "sin." If we put all these "pictorial signifiers" together—Manet's signature on the wooden craft, the single reed, the lone boy fishing, the boat with its crew of three, one turning his back to us, and the Manet couple dressed in Dutch costumes—they all seem to hint at a sinful act of paternity: Léon had to be sacrificed in order to maintain the honor and reputation of Auguste Manet. His true origins were camouflaged with the fictional name of "Koëlla" to cover up the misdeed. There is a chance that the figure of the gentleman in the bright straw hat whose face is concealed is the son's way of portraying the lie, the family shame. If so, this would be Manet's most blatant statement about his father and the troubled origins of Léon's birth.

In subsequent paintings featuring Léon, such as *Le Vieux Musicien* (1862) **[Plate 14]**, *Les Bulles de savon* (1867) **[Plate 24]**, and *Le Déjeuner dans l'atelier* (1868) **[Plate 2]**, Manet accentuated this quality of disconnectedness conveyed in *La Pêche*. In *Le Vieux Musicien*, for instance, Léon is portrayed as a Pierrot, "[a]n actor without passion, without words and almost without a face, he says everything, expresses everything, makes fun of everything."[62] In *Le Fifre* (1866) **[Plate 25]**, a similarly expressive silence and distance are embodied, which led Paul Mantz—a critic of Manet's era known to be particularly harsh—to compare *Le Fifre* with a playing card: "*Le Fifre*, an amusing specimen of primitive illustration, is like a Jack of Diamonds, stuck on a door."[63] Léon, however, strikes a still more uncanny pose in *Le Déjeuner dans l'atelier*, where the immediacy of the foreground figure is belied by his inscrutable pose and a radical lack of affect in his expression, which renders him emotionally aloof from the other two figures portrayed, and also from the spectator.

---

61 Lacan 1978: 34.

62 Janin, quoted in Mauner 1975: 55.

63 Mantz, quoted in Courthion 1970: 173.

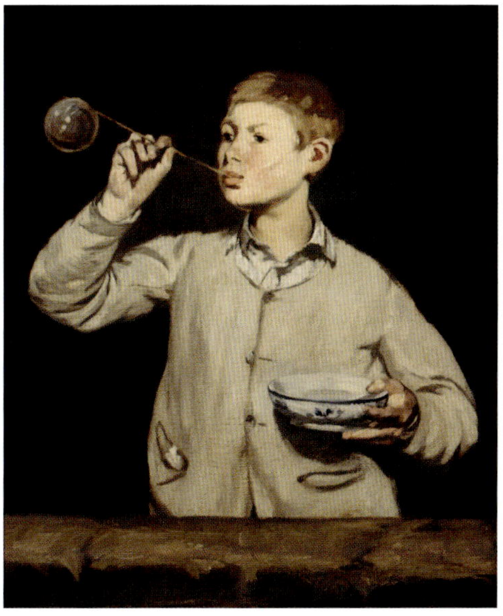
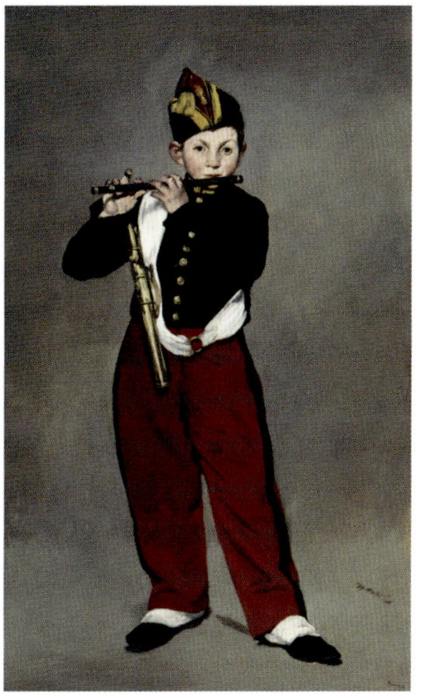

Plate 24:
Édouard Manet,
Les Bulles de savon (1867)
Plate 25:
Édouard Manet,
Le Fifre (1866)

In this painting Manet reiterates the enigma which surrounded Léon in his real life, and the artist thereby continued to "deny to probing eyes a knowledge that could come to none indiscriminately."[64] Through a matrix of detached connections, Manet imbues *Le Déjeuner dans l'atelier* with another set of confusing signifiers which substantiate, I believe, the deceitful paternal lineage of the lad's birth, but I will take another look at this dilemma when I return to this work in Chapter IV where I will discuss further the gazes which avoid one another in this painting.

Manet was a master at constructing a façade analogous to the one instrumental in a joke—or dream work—to shield himself from the critics' probing into his private life. Freud remarked that "thanks to their façade, they [the jokes] are in a position to conceal not only what they have to say but also the fact that they have something—forbidden—to say."[65] In light of the forbidden nature of a thirteen-year affair and the conception of an illegitimate son who may ultimately have been Édouard's younger half-brother, it seems that the artist unconsciously experienced an additional pressure and desire to com-

64 Thackeray, quoted in Sennett 1977: 169.
65 Freud 1905b: 106.

plicate the techniques by which he simultaneously unveiled and concealed his relationship to Léon and his wife Suzanne. As we have seen, in both *Le Déjeuner sur l'herbe* and *La Pêche*, Manet uses the technique of displacement to establish a sophisticated interplay between the pictorial and verbal representations of his young wife and (god-)son/half-brother. He employs the technique of "indirect representation" when he substitutes his own figure and that of his wife for the figures cited from Rubens's *Le Château de Steen*. Moreover, as a sub-species of the indirect representation technique, Manet uses the method of "representation by something small or very small—which performs the task of giving full expression to a whole characteristic by means of a tiny detail"[66] when he points out the signed raft to the son on whom he never wished to bestow his or his father's name. Taking all these techniques together in conjunction with Manet's hesitation over the title for *Le Déjeuner sur l'herbe*, one may deduce that these two familial canvases were of particular emotional significance to him and called forth his most subtle skills.

Léon himself never provided any additional information, even after the death of both parents. He never got married, but became the publisher of the newspaper *L'Impartial*. In addition, he was later involved in a series of unsuccessful business ventures. Recent research unveiled another side of Léon, that of a dubious art dealer who may have been inadvertently involved in selling forgeries in order to increase the market value of Manet's originals. A cousin of Suzanne's by the name of Édouard Vibert—along with Suzanne's brother Rodolphe, himself a painter—apparently made replicas of Manet's works once they had been purchased "allegedly so that she [Suzanne] would not feel the loss as painfully. After Suzanne's death in 1904, however, Léon, as if he were ignorant of Vibert's enterprise, sold a few of the copies as original second versions by Manet himself. When Léon died in 1927 he was involved in a lawsuit over a second version of *La pêche* that he had sold in 1910, after securing written authentication for it from the aging Duret."[67] Given my analysis of *La Pêche*, it may not be an ac-

66 Freud 1905b: 80.

67 Stuckey 1983: 174.

cident that it was this very picture that Léon attempted to counterfeit twice. It seems as if Léon was never really much welcomed by Manet's mother into her household after Édouard Manet's death. She clearly preferred her grandchild, Julie Manet, to whom she bequeathed what was left of her fortune. In a letter to Julie, Eugénie writes that "as for Léon, he is not entitled to more consideration than those reserved for servants! I will give to Léon my vanity-stand and the vases which are underneath it, and thank him again for the tender and devoted care he took the two cruel months of suffering of my poor Édouard."[68]

The years of 1862/1863 marked the beginning of one of Manet's most productive creative periods. Up to the outbreak of the Franco-Prussian war in 1870, during which Manet served as a soldier in the National Guard, Manet produced numerous masterpieces in rapid succession. It was also during this eight-year period that Manet gained the public reputation as an eccentric, a madman, and a sort of subversive bohemian character, "a rogue" and "ridiculous bogey," even. As Hamilton points out, "neither his work nor his appearance was ever regarded as other than shabby, willfully untidy, and arrogantly contemptuous of public opinion."[69] To correct this view of his work and personality, Manet's literary friends published numerous articles defending and explaining the nature and character of his work, and attempting at the same time to polish the public image of his personality. Unlike Zola, who figures as the staunchest and most prominent supporter of Manet's work, Charles Baudelaire rarely defended Manet's art in public. Although he had access to the major journals, having reviewed the Salon exhibitions for nearly twenty years, Baudelaire abstained from including Manet's works in his art reviews or from using him as the representative example of the modern painter in his famous essay *Le peintre moderne*. And yet Manet fulfilled the ideal of what a modern painter should be, according to Baudelaire's ideas, far better than did Constantin Guys, whom Baudelaire chose to champion:

68 "Je donne à Léon mon armoire à glace et les vases à fleurs qui sont dessus et le remercie encore des soins si tendres et dévoués qu'il a donnés pendant les deux cruels mois de souffrance, à mon pauvre Édouard." Mathieu/d'Arnoult/Gooden 2021: 24 (author's translation).

69 Hamilton 1969: 51.

> The painter, the true painter for whom we are looking, will be he who can snatch its epic quality from the life of today and can make us see and understand, with brush or with pencil, how great and poetic we are in our cravats and our patent-leather boots.[70]

Why, the question inevitably arises, did Baudelaire refrain from publicly supporting Manet? Baudelaire's stance vis-à-vis Manet did not parallel his private relationship with the painter. On the contrary, Baudelaire remained one of Manet's most faithful friends, never ceasing to encourage the painter's developing career. However, instead of publicizing his alliance with Manet, Baudelaire worked behind the scenes, asking other critics and gallery owners to review favorably Manet's exhibitions, or to show his paintings in prominent locations. In private, Baudelaire scolded Manet for being too influenced and demoralized by the public's vitriolic rejection of *Olympia*. On May 11, 1865, he writes:

> I see I've got to have another word with you about yourself. I've got to make an effort to impress your own value upon you. Confound it, but you expect a lot! It's really fantastic. They laugh at you, do they? Their pleasantries exasperate you … Do you suppose you're the first man to find himself in this situation? Are you a greater genius than Chateaubriand or Wagner? And do you think they weren't laughed at? Well, it didn't kill them. And so as to keep your pride within limits, let me tell you that these two men, each in his own way, are paragons in a period exceedingly rich. As for yourself, you are only the first in the decline of your art. I hope you won't take offense at the rough handling I'm giving you. I'm your friend, you know that.[71]

Baudelaire's straightforward and well-intended remark helped rally Manet's spirits, acting as a kind of positive counterbalance to Couture's dismissal of *Le Buveur d'absinthe* in 1859. In Baudelaire, Manet not only found a sincere friend but also an extremely important teacher. *Le Buveur d'absinthe*, *La Musique aux Tuileries, La Chanteuse de rue* **[Plate 16]**, *Lola de Valence* and *Olympia* can be seen as

---

70 Baudelaire 1845: 32.

71 Baudelaire, quoted in Bataille 1955: 9.

Manet's testament to the crucial influence the poet had exerted upon him. Yet, it would be too simplistic to view these particular paintings as mere illustrations of Baudelaire's aesthetic ideas and poems, since they go beyond a painterly representation of Baudelaire's poetry.

Manet's paintings seem to engage the Baudelarian verses in an open dialogue, they question the poems, express them, challenge them, and finally embody them in their own particular way. Baudelaire responded to this challenge by re-interpreting Manet's paintings which already embodied his own ideas with new poems. In a sense, their respective ideas are so tightly interwoven that one can no longer trace a primary source of influence.[72] Manet's paintings capture this complex relationship between poetry and the visual arts, as Baudelaire had described it as early as 1846:

> To make a deliberate point of looking for poetry during the conception of a picture is the surest means of not finding it. It must come without the artist's knowledge. It is the result of the art of painting itself; for it lies in the spectator's soul, and it is the mark of genius to awaken it there.[73]

Returning to the question of why Baudelaire rarely publicized his support for Manet, it is interesting to notice that Manet responded in a parallel manner by never using Baudelaire as a central model for a major canvas. In contrast to the large portraits of his literary friends and supporters like Émile Zola, Zacharie Astruc, Stéphane Mallarmé and Antonin Proust, Baudelaire is memorialized in only two small etchings and as one among many figures in the crowd represented in *La Musique aux Tuileries*. While it is possible that Manet was prevented from painting a major portrait of Baudelaire

---

72 Paul Valéry remarks upon the affinity between Manet and Baudelaire: "Manet, with his fondness for the picturesquely exotic, still paying tribute to the toreador, the guitar, and the mantilla, though already half wonover to everyday objects, to models found in the street, must have seemed to Baudelaire like a close reflection of his own problem: the crucial condition, for an artist, of being subject to several opposing temptations and actually capable of expressing himself in a variety of admirable styles." (Valéry 1960: 107).

73 Baudelaire 1981: 98.

by the poet's flight to Brussels in 1864 and his death three years later, one may also view Manet's reluctance as being psychologically determined. Embroiled too deeply with Baudelaire's aesthetic ideas, Manet might not have found the distance necessary to embark upon a portrait of the friend to whom he was both emotionally and intellectually so intimately indebted. In addition, however, the very paintings seemingly conceived along the lines suggested by Baudelairian motifs also served as an occasion for Manet's attempt to challenge some of the poet's most famous theories. As a bourgeois painter, for instance, Manet's whole career disproved Baudelaire's notion that:

> If there is one thing a thousand times more dangerous than the Bourgeois, it is the Bourgeois-artist who was spiritually created to come between the public and the genius; he blocks one from the others.[74]

In addition, Manet undermined the force of Baudelaire's assertion that "like all our arts, [painting] is too inclined to be satisfied with the imitation of the old masters"[75] by transposing exact scenes from the Old Masters without losing the immediacy or modernity which Baudelaire was searching for in the painters of his time. In *Olympia,* Manet synthesized these two apparently contradictory themes. By basing his contemporary nude portrait on Titian's *Venus of Urbino,* Manet proved that the imitation of an Old Master would not necessarily lead to an idealization of the past, as Baudelaire had feared, but that instead it could result in a shockingly direct comment on the present.[76] And yet it was Baudelaire who persuaded Manet to exhibit *Olympia* at the Salon of 1865. Having completed the painting in 1863, Manet had hesitated to submit it because he feared that it would provoke as much notoriety as *Le Déjeuner sur l'herbe* had

---

74 Baudelaire 1981: 39–40.

75 Baudelaire 1981: 81.

76 Curiously enough, Baudelaire's practice of quoting lines from past poems and reworking traditional themes—for instance, in his poem *Le Cygne*—closely parallels Manet's own technique of reworking themes from Old Masters.

caused in 1864 at the Salon des Refusés.[77] Of course, Manet's fear was amply justified. No other painting had unleashed such torrents of abuse as *Olympia*. Paul de Saint-Victor wrote in *La Presse* in 1865:

> The mob, as at the Morgue, crowds around the spicy *Olympia* and the frightful *Ecce Homo* by Manet. Art sunk so low doesn't even deserve reproach. "Do not speak of them; observe them and pass on," Vergil says to Dante while crossing one of the abysses of hell. But Manet's characters belong rather to Scarron's hell than to Dante's.[78]

Ernest Fillonneau of *La Moniteur des arts* reviewed the painting as follows:

> An epidemic of crazy laughter prevails in front of the canvases by Manet … [It is] a subject of general surprise that the jury accepted these works. Olympia is a nude, recumbent woman to whom some sort of Negress offers a bouquet voluminously wrapped in paper. At the foot of the bed crouches a black cat, its hair on end, who probably doesn't like flowers since it cuts such a pathetic figure. Moreover, the heroine herself seems indifferent to the homage of the Negress. Is Olympia waiting for her bath or for the laundress?[79]

While the journalists enjoyed inventing new sorts of insults to describe *Olympia*, and the public laughed, screamed and brandished sticks and umbrellas in front of the painting, Manet's circle of friends reaffirmed their support of him. At the Café du Bade or the Café Guerbois in the 18th arrondissement, a favorite meeting place for artists and writers, Manet had become the center of a little court. Twice a week he would meet with the regulars like Alphonse de Gros, Whistler, Fantin-Latour, Baudelaire, Zola, Duranty, Degas, Zacharie Astruc, as well as Renoir, Monet and Pissarro

---

77 Napoleon III and his wife had also visited the Salon des Refusés and after pausing in front of *Le Déjeuner sur l'herbe*, they apparently turned away with a gesture of dismissal, since they considered the painting an offense against public morality. This imperial rebuke intensified the outrage at Manet's depiction of a nude woman in the midst of two dressed men.

78 Saint-Victor, quoted in Hamilton1969: 71.

79 Fillonneau, quotedin Hamilton 1969: 71–72.

> They discussed the recent exhibitions; they were interested in budding talent, and especially in potential works; in their conversations there was no place for petty jealousies, envy and gossip. They were all artists who upheld the highest tradition of art.[80]

This group soon became known as "The Batignolles School" which Fantin-Latour portrayed in *Hommage à Delacroix* and in *Un atelier aux Batignolles* (1870) **[Plate 26]**. In both canvases Manet is granted the central location, in the former as the successor to Delacroix, and in the latter as the painter in progress of portraying Zacharie Astruc with Monet, Renoir, Zola, Bazille, Maître, and Scholderer forming a circle around him. Although Manet's disciples desired to found a formal school, Manet did not wish to institutionalize these weekly meetings which Monet later recalled as the most exciting discussions in which he had ever participated. "Nothing was more interesting than these discussions, with their perpetual clash of opinions. They kept one's spirit awake, encouraged one to disinterested and sincere research, enabled one to store away reserves of enthusiasm, which nourished one for weeks and weeks."[81]

For Manet, the Batignolles group constituted a gathering place where he could try out and discuss his ideas, and, more importantly, renew his courage to paint what he saw. He writes to Fantin-Latour: "I believe [...] that if we would stick together and, above all, not lose courage, it would be possible to react against this mediocre world, whose only strength lies in its unity."[82]

Paul Valéry points out how these writers and artists of entirely different temperaments, backgrounds and political opinions would sometimes have nothing else in common but their belief in Manet and a passion for painting. Indeed, each painter and writer found something in Olympia which coincided with their own intellectual bias, ranging from the naturalist writer, Émile Zola, to the realist theoretician Champfleury to the symbolist, Baudelaire. Their inter-

80 Courthion 1960: 66.

81 Manet, quoted in Schneider 1968: 87–88.

82 Manet, quoted in Schneider 1968: 88.

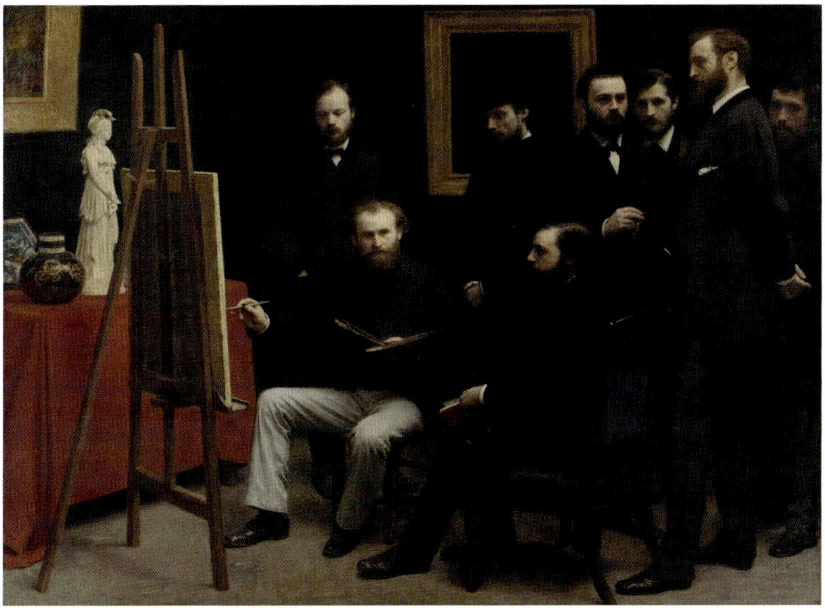

Plate 26:
Henri Fantin-Latour,
Un atelier aux Batignolles
(1870)

pretations of *Olympia* and understanding of Manet's artistic intentions sometimes differed to such a degree that it is hard to imagine that they were discussing the same canvas.

In Zola's defense of Manet, published in 1866 in *L'Événement*, a portrait of the painter emerges which entirely contradicts Manet's affinity with Baudelaire. Zola writes:

> I take this opportunity to denounce the relationship some people have wished to establish between Manet's paintings and Baudelaire's poetry. I know that a warm friendship exists between the poet and the painter, but I believe I can say that the latter has never been guilty of the stupidity committed by many others of wishing to put ideas into his paintings.[83]

Instead, Zola viewed Manet as a painter who was guided by the same scientific methods as the writer himself. Zola categorizes Manet as an analytical painter who does not "share this preoccupation with subject matter which frets the public above everything else," but who

83 Zola, quoted in Hamilton 1969: 94.

is only attempting "to obtain vivid contrasts and free disposition of masses."[84] From this formalist perspective, Zola analyzes *Olympia* as a painting in which Manet had undertaken a purely painterly exercise in the disposition of colors and shapes:

> You needed a nude woman and you chose Olympia, the first-comer. You needed some clear and luminous patches of color, so you added a bouquet of flowers; you found it necessary to have some dark patches so you placed in a corner a Negress and a cat. What does all this amount to—you scarcely know, no more do I. But I know that you have succeeded admirably in doing a painter's job, the job of a great painter; I mean to say you have forcefully reproduced in your own particular idiom the truths of light and shade and the reality of objects and creatures.[85]

The appearance of Zola's article in one of the leading journals was of great importance to Manet, who had grown increasingly desperate over the hostile reception of his works. He immediately responded to Zola's article with a letter:

> You have given me a first-rate New Year's present, and your remarkable article pleases me very much. It comes at an opportune time, for I have been considered unworthy to benefit, as so many others, by the advantage of the invitation list, and as I augur nothing good from my judges I shall take good care not to send them any paintings.[86]

Manet welcomed Zola's review not just because it represented the first major favorable notice of his work, but also because he saw it as an opportunity to gain finally the recognition of a famous critic. Although Baudelaire had rarely reviewed Manet's work, his association with him had been widely known and this did not always cast a favorable light upon Manet. Indeed, the scandals surrounding Manet's reputation were reminiscent of Baudelaire's frequent altercations with the

---

84 Zola, quoted in Hamilton 1969: 97.

85 Zola, quoted in Courthion 1960: 131.

86 Manet, quoted in Hamilton 1969: 104; It is ironic that Émile Zola, a writer who emphasized so strongly the sociological context in his own novels, would praise Manet for his attention to pure form. See also Theodore Reff, "Manet's portrait of Zola", *Burlington Magazine* (January 1975): 41.

authorities. Baudelaire's publication of *Les Fleurs du Mal* in 1857 had brought him to trial and six of his poems were suppressed as indecent. His twenty-year relationship with Jeanne Duval, a Mulatto woman, "a priestess of debauchery," his acknowledged consumption of opium and alcohol, and his dying as an incoherent and paralyzed syphilitic, gave Baudelaire a reputation that Manet did not want to inherit through a kind of guilt by association. Therefore, an association with Zola, a critic of the bourgeois society but a respectable bourgeois himself, better suited Manet's public image. By describing Manet as a painter who did not "put ideas" into his paintings, Zola also authenticated Manet's self-description as an artist who did not interpret but represented reality in his canvases. According to Jacques-Émile Blanche, Manet vehemently protested whenever his friends remarked that his paintings bore little resemblance to nature but revealed his powerful imagination.

In the *Portrait d' Émile Zola* (1868) **[Plate 27]**, Manet memorializes his gratitude to the writer by including specific compositional elements frequently mentioned by Zola. The writer is seated before a desk cluttered with papers and books, among them his celebrated pamphlet on Manet. On the wall to the right is a rack with three prints, a Japanese print which, according to Zola, resembles Manet's works in its "strange elegance and magnificent spots of color"; Goya's etching after Velázquez's *Los Borrachos*, which alludes to Zola's comment that the Spanish masters had given Manet "the Spanish accent with which he spoke for the first time";[87] and a reproduction of *Olympia*, a reference to Zola's staunch defense of the painting. At first glance, these references appear to be simple allusions to Zola's much-appreciated role as Manet's defender; yet, upon closer scrutiny, they are more ambiguous and double-edged. Theodor Reff has correctly noted how the eyes of the reproduced *Olympia* swerve towards the sitter, as though in gratitude for his defense of her reputation.[88]

Linda Nochlin remarks:

---

87 Hamilton 1969: 115.

88 It is ironic that Émile Zola, a writer who emphasized the sociological context in his own novels so strongly would praise Manet for his attention to pure form. See also Reff 1975: 41 (emphasis in the original).

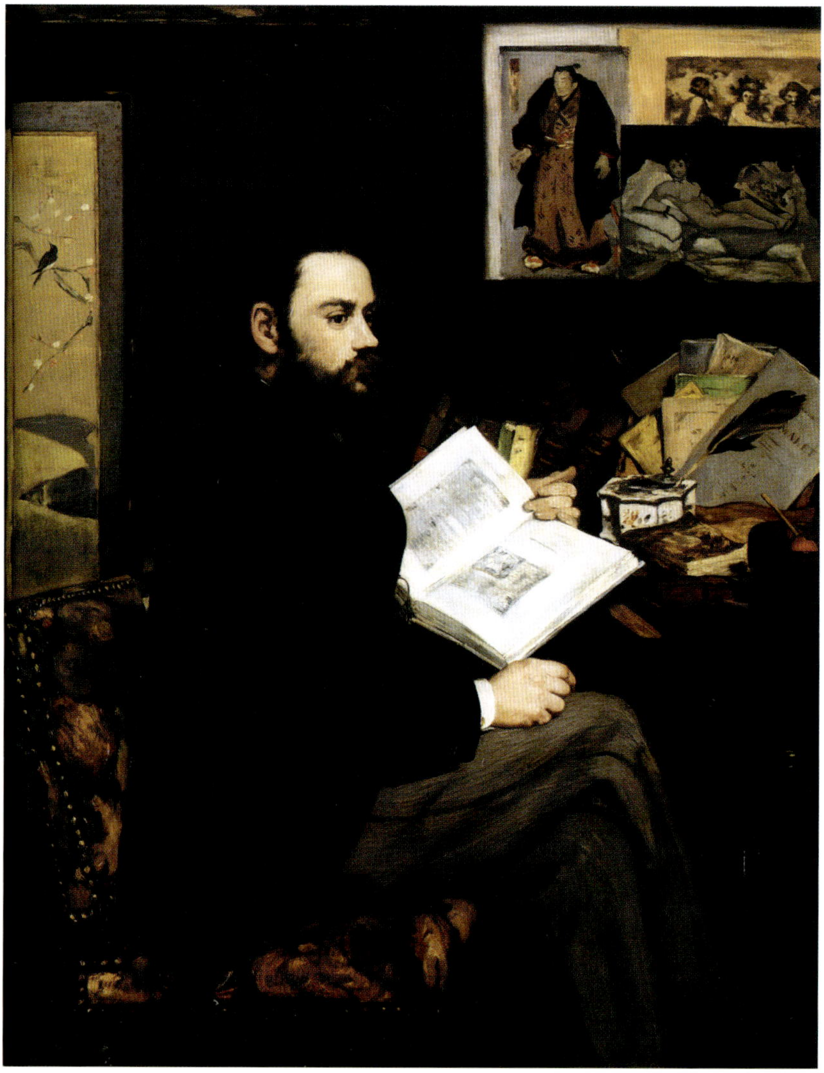

Plate 27:
Édouard Manet,
Portrait d' Émile Zola
(1868)

The cut-off is a way of making the Olympia in the Zola portrait more modest, less sexually charged in the presence of her knight-at-arms. The rather prim Zola had stoutly denied that *Olympia* was in any way obscene or sexually provocative. It is certainly possible that Manet, an inveterate *blagueur,* substituted a chastened as well as grateful Olympia for the original—a private visual joke between himself and his friend.[89]

89 Nochlin 1983: 193.

Manet also included other elements in the portrait which subtly undermine the terms of Zola's defense of the painter. The mere fact that Manet so carefully selected the various references to Zola contradicts the man's theory that Manet was a pure painter who did not interject ideas into his painting. Secondly, the fact that Manet singles out the reproduction of *Olympia* as the only print devoid of any color ridicules Zola's contention that Manet was interested only in the composition of colors when creating the work. Lastly, as Nochlin observes:

> […] the margin of the photograph within the painting has been itself cropped on the right immediately against the body of the black cat, which almost disappears into the background rather than standing out with memorable perversity, as in the original.[90]

Moreover, since the black cat was a symbol equally connected to Baudelaire's *Les Fleurs du Mal* and Manet's painterly oeuvre, its omission not only attenuates the sexual provocativeness of Olympia, but it also points towards Zola's mistaken claim that Manet was not influenced by Baudelaire. As with *La Pêche*, in this canvas Manet again chose to include indirect references that undermine the manifest content of his painting, in this case, his declared gratitude for and agreement with Zola's defense of his works. Unlike in his other paintings, in which Manet leaves it up to the spectator to recognize the traditional sources with which he intends to form a link, in *Portrait d' Émile Zola* he explicitly makes the connection between Zola and the novelist's pamphlet about *Olympia*. Rather than condensing the traditional source with his own interpretation of the quoted work, in *Portrait d' Émile Zola* Manet arranges side by side all the elements—the novelist, the pamphlet, the reproduction of Velázquez's *Los Borrachos* and the Japanese print—among which he intends to construct a logical relationship. Thereby Manet shows how the artwork parallels what Freud described as the dream-work's method of producing a logical connection by simultaneity in time: "Whenever [the dreams] show us two elements close together, this

90 Nochlin 1983: 193.

guarantees that there is some specially intimate connection between what correspond to them among the dream-thoughts."[91]

However, once the connection has been made between the different dream-thoughts or elements in a painting, both the dreamer and the artist can still use a variety of methods to contradict, modify, or subvert the apparently intended connection. As we have seen, Manet undertook only very subtle changes in the *Portrait d'Émile Zola*, using such "dream-or-joke" techniques as "omitting" the colors and leaving out the famous cat in the reproduction of *Olympia*, and "representing the opposite" by replacing the subject's distant gaze with a more intimate and less provocative one. By so effectively manipulating his imagery, Manet exhibited that he could play as skillfully with images as a joker plays with words. Freud identified the re-arrangement of verbal material as one way of playing upon the multiple meanings of words, and remarked that "one can take the same verbal material and merely make some alteration in its *arrangement*. The slighter the alteration—the more one has the impression of something different being said in the same words—the better is the joke technically."[92]

I think that Manet's use of subtle alterations to criticize while seeming to laud Zola confirms the accuracy of Freud's observation.

Before Zola's article appeared in 1866, Manet had left for Spain, anxious to get away from the insults to which he had been subjected because of *Olympia*. He traveled alone perhaps because "Spain [...] had haunted his dreams for so long,"[93] in the sense that he had to find out for himself what kind of bond tied him to these Spanish masters. Manet's voyage to Spain was partially motivated by his wish to find out who was at fault: Was he on the wrong track interpreting the traditional themes by the Spanish masters, as he had done in *Le Buveur d'absinthe*, *Le Vieux Musicien*, *Lola de Valence*, *Jeune Femme couchée en costume espagnol*, and *Le Chanteur espagnol*? Or was the public mistaken

---

91 Freud 1900: 314.

92 Freud 1905b: 32–33 (emphasis in the original). Freud's statement also evokes Jean-Michel Basquiat's use of words in his own paintings when he says: "I cross out the words to move them into the background a bit." Jean-Michel-Basquiat exhibition, Albertina Museum Vienna, 2022.

93 Duret, quoted in Courthion 1960: 57.

when it objected so violently to his works. We know from a letter Manet wrote to Fantin-Latour how pleased he was finally to study his predecessors directly and not from their reproductions: "Oh, what a pity you are not here; what pleasure it would have given you to see Velázquez, who alone is worth the whole journey," Manet writes, "He is the painter to beat all painters. He didn't astonish me, he enchanted me."[94]

During his voyage through Spain, Manet also made the acquaintance of Théodore Duret, a young businessman from the Charente who became an intimate friend of Manet and later on one of his first biographers. Through his association with the painter, Duret became so interested in art that he founded his own art journal, which was largely dedicated to reviews of the Impressionist movement. Curiously enough though, in 1870, Duret published an unfavorable article about Manet, which led the artist to challenge Duret to a duel. Fortunately, neither one was injured and they soon reconciled their differences.

Upon his return from Spain—from a search into his painterly past—Manet gradually recaptured his strength and again took up painting. Influenced by Baudelaire's advice not to despair about the critics' insults, Manet, perhaps in a gesture to his now deceased friend, mounted his own exhibition at the Pont d'Alma in 1867. Borrowing 28,000 Francs from his mother, he erected a shed adjacent to one built by Courbet,[95] in which he showed all the works rejected by the Selecting Committee of the Salon.

Although this private exhibition was largely ridiculed by the public, it did not provoke as much outrage as the Salon des Refusés had

---

94 Manet, dated Madrid, 1865; quoted in Courthion 1960: 14.

95 Gustave Courbet held an exhibition in a shed adjacent to Manet's at the Pont d'Alma. During their simultaneous exhibitions, Courbet often came to see how things were progressing with Manet, who quite in contrast to Courbet, was losing money. From other accounts we know that while Courbet and Manet respected each other's work, they did not cultivate a friendship as such. Courbet's influence upon Manet's works has often been underestimated, because their characters seemed to have little in common: Courbet was a radical socialist who preferred the countryside and ordinary people, whereas Manet was a bourgeois Republican who preferred the entertainment of a salon or the nightly discussion among painter friends at the Café Guerbois. Manet was always very elegantly attired, in contrast to Courbet, who dressed like a working man and who despised the affectations of the bourgeoisie.

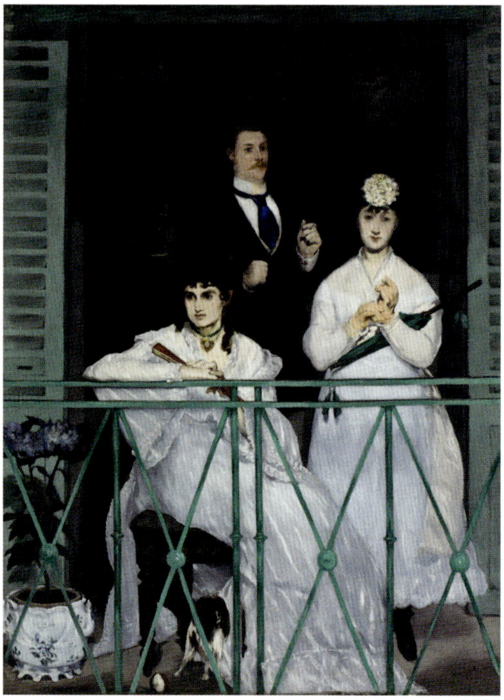

Plate 10:
Édouard Manet,
Le Balcon (1868–1869)

caused in 1864 when he showed *Le Déjeuner sur l'herbe*. It is possible that his assurance to the public—"Monsieur Manet has never wished to protest. On the contrary, the protest, entirely unexpected on his part, has been directed against himself"[96]—mitigated the officialdom's hostility towards Manet, and in turn made it possible for the painter to see an increasing number of his works accepted by the Salon. It was also in 1867 that Manet met Berthe Morisot, who soon became his favorite model and close friend. Fantin-Latour had introduced Berthe to Manet at the Louvre, and Manet was so taken by her appearance that he immediately asked permission to portray her. Manet captured her beauty in *Le Balcon* (1868–1869) **[Plate 10]**, where her aloof presence dominates the overall composition that the two other figures of Fanny Claus, a violinist, and Antoine Guillemet, a painter, merely function as props for her portrait. In a letter to her sister Edna, Berthe Morisot describes Manet's behavior at the opening of the Salon in 1869, where *Le Balcon* was exhibited for the first time:

> I don't have to tell you that one of the first things I did was to go to Room M. There I found Manet, with his hat on in bright sunlight, looking dazed. He begged me to go and see his painting, as he did not dare to move a step. I have never seen such an expressive face as his; he was laughing, then had a worried look, assuring everybody that his picture was very bad, and adding in the same breath that it would be a great success. I think he has a decidedly charming temperament, I like it very much.[97]

Le Balcon was one of the last paintings for which Manet positioned his models in a staged setting. For its layout he recreated the scene of

96 "Reasons for holding a private exhibition," 1867; quoted in Courthion 1960: 60.
97 Morisot, quoted in Rouart 1957: 30–31.

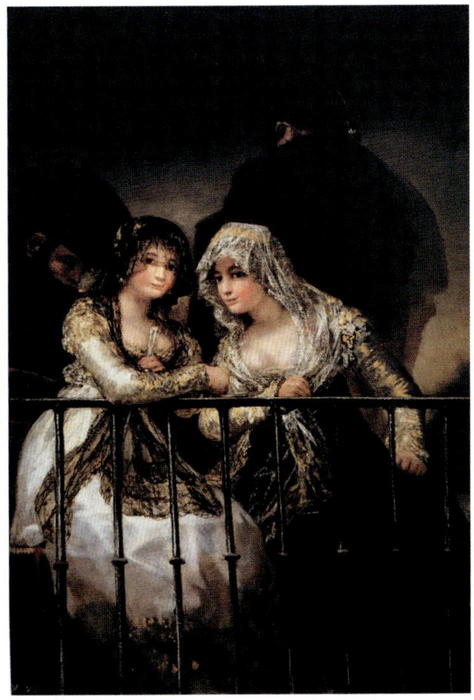

Plate 28:
Francisco de Goya,
Les Manolas au Balcon
(1808–1814)

Goya's *Les Manolas au Balcon* (1800–1814) [Plate 28]. This method of recreating themes from Old Masters and substituting contemporary models in them was largely abandoned by Manet after 1868. The subsequent portraits of Berthe Morisot no longer involve memories of Old Masters, but are simply modern depictions of a young Parisian woman in different settings and different moods. Manet's numerous portraits of Berthe Morisot, like *Le Repos* (1870–1871) [Plate 13], *Berthe Morisot au bouquet de violettes* (1872) [Plate 30], *Berthe Morisot en chapeau de deuil à long voile* and *Berthe Morisot à l'éventail* (1874) [Plate 31] recall Baudelaire's phrase "in the painter's soul there are just as many ideals as individuals, because a portrait is a model complicated by an artist."[98] While Victorine Meurent's "sculptural look"[99] constituted an ideal model for Manet's endeavors to link contemporary scenes like *Olympia* and *Le Déjeuner sur l'herbe* with icons from the artistic tradition, Berthe Morisot's figure relocated Manet's representations exclusively in the contemporary setting. Through Berthe Morisot, Manet also became ultimately acquainted with the painters of the Impressionist movement, whose techniques he would adopt after the siege of Paris in 1870/1871. In a sense, as model and friend, Berthe Morisot formed a link between Manet's past and future, and she was in part responsible for a change that occurred in Manet's works. From this perspective, one may understand the full meaning of Manet's proclamation that "Berthe brings me luck." In contrast to the muse-like Berthe, Eva Gonzalès, Manet's sole disciple, posed only once as a model for the painter. Berthe complained: "Manet lectures me, and holds up that eternal Mademoiselle Gonzalès as an example; she has poise, persever-

98 Baudelaire 1981: 81 (emphasis in the original).
99 According to Théodore Duret, Manet had been struck by Victorine Meurent's "original appearance and sculptural look" when he first met her in front of the Palais de Justice (see Courthion 1960: 53).

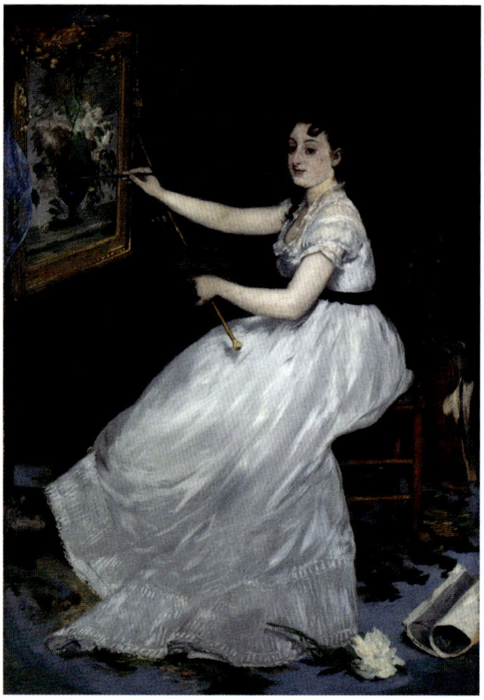

Plate 29:
Édouard Manet,
Portrait d' Eva Gonzalès
(1869–1870)

ance, she is able to carry an undertaking to a successful issue, whereas I am not capable of anything.[100]

Despite Manet's apparent criticism of Berthe Morisot's painting talents, a comparison of the *Portrait d'Eva Gonzalès* (1870) **[Plate 29]** with the portraits of Berthe Morisot reveals once again that Manet was more honest in his painterly depictions than in his words. Berthe Morisot realized the irony behind Manet's proclaimed preference for his disciple when she wrote to her sister: "As of now, all his admiration is concentrated on Mademoiselle Gonzalès, but her portrait does not progress; he says that he is at the fortieth sitting and that the head is again effaced. He is the first to laugh about it…"[101]

It was not unusual for Manet to have his models pose for up to forty or fifty sessions before their portraits were completed, a practice which often resulted in furious debates between the painter and the model, who could no longer bear to remain in the same pose or who did not have the time to spend entire months in Manet's atelier. Yet, in the case of Eva Gonzalès's portrait, it seems as if Manet himself acknowledged that his laborious attempts at portraying his favorite pupil betrayed his own ambiguous relationship to her. Manet depicts her in an awkward position, seated in front of an easel which holds a flower painting, stiffly holding a brush in her right hand and clumsily balancing a palette in her left, her head turned sideways, not exactly facing the painting on her easel, and instead staring out beyond the picture frame, perhaps at Manet himself. This arrangement is physically impossible. When compared to similar situations, such as Fantin-Latour's *Un atelier aux Batignolles* (in which Manet is shown while painting Zacharie Astruc), or Manet's *Claude Monet peignant*

---

100 See also Rouart 1957: 38.

101 Morisot, quoted Rouart 1957: 39.

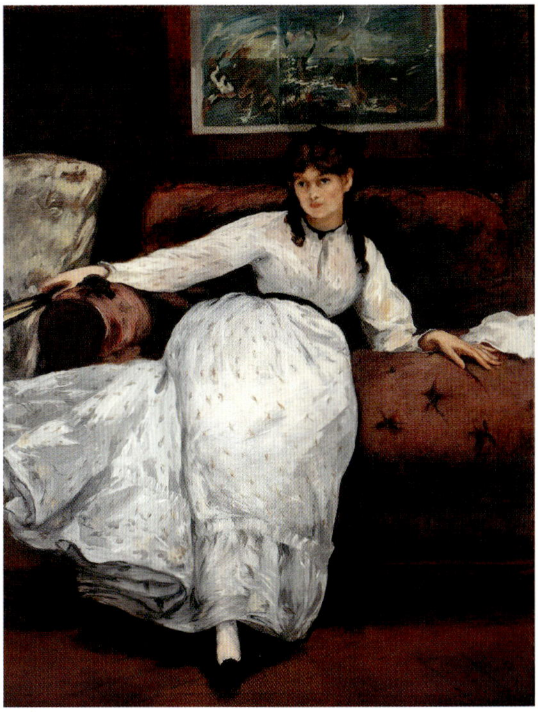

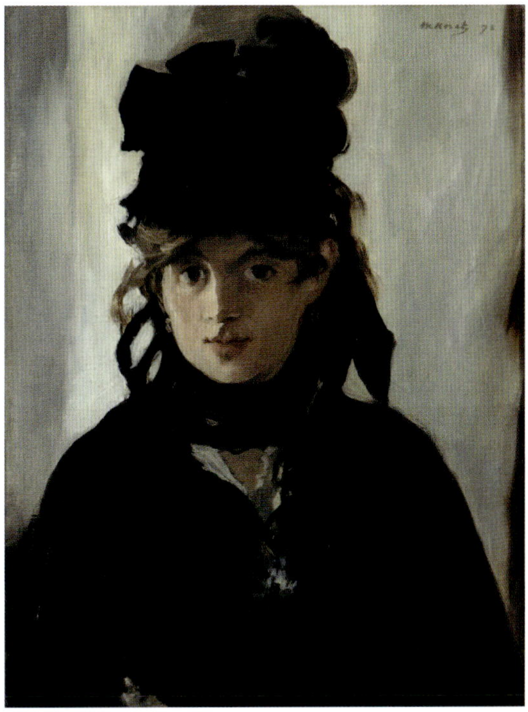

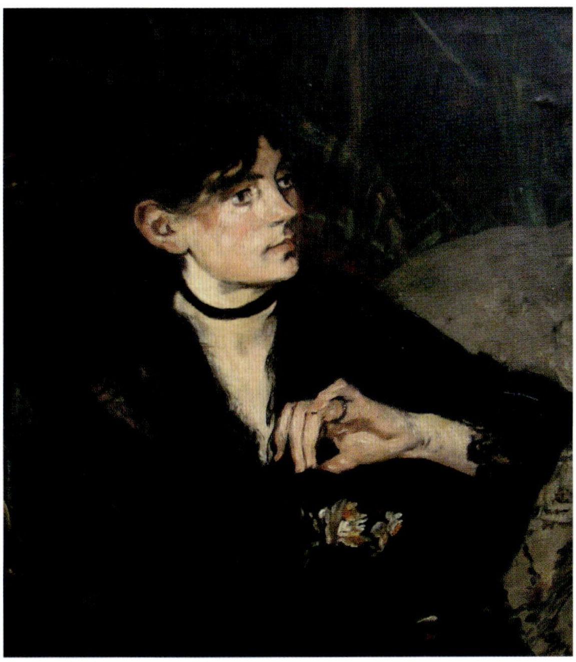

Plate 13:
Édouard Manet, *Le Repos* (1870/71)
Plate 30:
Édouard Manet, *Berthe Morisot au bouquet de violettes* (1872)
Plate 31:
Édouard Manet, *Berthe Morisot à l'éventail* (1874)

dans son atelier (which gives the impression that Monet is actually caught by surprise), Manet's *Portrait d'Eva Gonzalès* comes across as a staged scene and as somewhat contrived. Even if we assume that her gaze was not directed at the painter portraying her, but at the "original" model for the vase of flowers on her canvas, the woman's "unnatural" composure belies this idea. And yet, Manet intended to emphasize the fact that he was portraying a woman painter by including a painting portfolio leaning towards a chair, a rolled-up print lying on the floor, and a white flower which might have served as a model for the white flowers depicted in the painting on the easel.

What are we to make of this ambiguous portrayal of Manet's only known disciple? Contemporary opinion about this painting was divided. Mme. Morisot, for instance, thought that "Manet has never done anything as good as his portrait of Mademoiselle Gonzalès,"[102] whereas Laurent Pichat decried the painting in 1870 with the following words:

> Saints in the desert or delivered into the hands of their executioners are no more courageous than the young lady who has allowed Manet to represent her life-sized in a rather dirty white dress. And far from expressing her horror she laughs at the torture, she smiles in the midst of her filthiness [...]. She laughs and she paints![103]

Théodore Duret, a close friend of Manet, praised the harmony of the *Portrait d'Eva Gonzalès*, and stated:

> The prevailing tone of the whole work is in no way crude or shrill: Quite on the contrary, the white dress of the young lady harmonizes with the sky-blue carpet and the grey background of the painting, the pose is natural, the body full of movement, and [...] this facial type is at the least full of life and does not lack elegance.[104]

Duret's description could not be at greater variance from my own impression of this painting. In comparison with the portraits of Berthe Morisot as well as with the great number of Manet's female

102 Rouart 1957: 42.
103 Hamilton 1969: 143.
104 Hamilton 1969: 146.

portraits of the later 1870s, the Gonzalès portrait stands out for its crude execution. Her figure neither embodies the estranging quality with which Manet had imbued his mother in the *Portrait de Monsieur et Madame Auguste Manet*, or Victorine Meurent in *Olympia*, or Berthe Morisot in *Le Balcon*; nor does her image capture the intimate radiance of his sitter in *Berthe Morisot au bouquet de violettes*. For once, a hostile critic is correct when he writes that "[u]nable to draw carefully, he [Manet] paints dislocated figures awkwardly and painfully."[105] Although Chaumelin meant to criticize all of Manet's portraits, his description is justified regarding the *Portrait d'Eva Gonzalès*. I think that Manet unconsciously parodied his own techniques in this portrait. While the casual poses of his previous models only gradually transmit a psychological effect of "dislocation and awkwardness," Eva Gonzalès is indeed depicted in a dislocated and awkward position. In this portrait Manet had inserted the effect of his previous works into the content of his canvas, and thereby abolished the enigmatic effect so characteristic of his best works.

In a sense, the *Portrait d'Eva Gonzalès* demonstrates what the major canvases do not: it proves that the enigmatic quality of his sitters is not achieved by depicting physically distorted or awkwardly posed figures, but rather, by placing a convincingly "natural" figure into a dislocated or unexpected context and by problematizing the figure's relationship to the spectator's gaze. The *Portrait d'Eva Gonzalès* serves as an example of "how not to do it," and it thereby becomes a caricature of Manet's own painterly procedures. This parody is emphasized in the image of his student, whose painting within the painting depicts a trite version of Manet's own still-lifes. Indeed, her relationship to the painting on the easel appears to be rather haphazard, as if she were placed in front of the easel by the command of someone else and not by her own choice. Her submissive posture is perhaps meant as a symbolic representation of her infatuation with her teacher Manet. However, by thus placing herself at the service of the master, she basically deprived him of a foil against whom he could act, and as a result, he lost interest in her. Indeed, the conquest became little more than a

---

105 Marius Chaumelin in *La Presse*, June 23, 1870; quoted in Hamilton 1969: 143.

willful tour de force that he described as cumbersome, a burden. Just as he had once before used a portrait to subvert his apparent reverence for his supporter Émile Zola, here Manet used a similar ploy of ill-concealed ridicule on the very student he publicly claimed to cherish.

If we turn to Manet's various portraits of Berthe Morisot, the painter's responsiveness to her enigmatic beauty is strikingly evident. By capturing her in different moods—relaxed and thoughtful in *Le Repos*, sad and mourning her father's death in *Berthe Morisot en chapeau de deuil long voile* or coquettish and charming in *Berthe Morisot au bouquet de violettes*—, Manet embarked upon a series of visual attempts to woo this young woman who so inspired him. These variations on Berthe echo Freud's description of the central mechanism of creativity: "A strong experience in the present awakens in the creative writer a memory of an earlier experience (usually belonging to his childhood) from which there now proceeds a wish which finds its fulfilment in the creative work."[106]

While these canvases offer some insights into the relationship between the painter and his models, they shed little light on why Manet accepted Eva Gonzalès as apprentice, why he used her to provoke Berthe's jealousy, or why he subsequently distanced himself from Berthe herself. The only details we have is that the young woman was the daughter of Emmanuel Gonzalès, a prolific writer of popular novels and former President of the Société des Gens de Lettres. As the daughter of an influential man, she might have awakened Manet's hopes of being associated with someone who could further his career. Elsewhere it has been suggested that Manet had been immensely flattered by being pursued by a student who had previously taken lessons from Chaplin, an artist who was successful in Parisian society as "the emotional painter of hot-house beauties,"[107] and whom Manet despised for that very reason. It is revealing that both Eva Gonzalès and Berthe Morisot remained indirectly attached to Manet throughout his life. They both married late in life, a fact which caused a great deal of concern to Berthe Morisot's mother, who grew anxious that

106 Freud 1908: 151.

107 Courthion 1960: 64.

her youngest daughter would not be marriageable anymore. In 1879, Eva Gonzalès married the etcher Henri Guérard, a close friend of Manet's. In 1883, she bore a son and died a month after his birth, and five days after Manet's death. Similarly, Berthe Morisot remained linked to Manet by marrying his younger brother Eugène in 1874. After her marriage, Manet never used her as a model again, and the terms of their relationship remain obscure. However, from a letter to a friend which Berthe wrote a few days after Manet's death, we learn:

> I know, my dear friend, that you have understood how painful the spectacle of that terrible agony was for me. Édouard and I were friends for many, many years, and he is associated with all the memories of my youth; moreover, he was such an attractive personality, his mind was so young and alert, that it seemed that more than others he was beyond the power of death.[108]

Both women paid their own personal tribute to Manet by marrying men through whom a link to the artist was assured. After his studies of Berthe, Manet shifted his attention to portraits of women and men belonging to the high bourgeois society, situating them in "the ambiance of the world to which they belonged."[109] The portraits of Nina de Callias, Méry Laurent, Isabelle Lemonnier, Jeanne Demarsy and Irma Brunner are, as Manet once put it, not "the woman of the Second Empire, but [...] her successor. In my portraits, I don't pretend to sum up an epoch but I do claim to paint the unusual types."[110] Yet, by painting such unusual types as Nina de Callias, a nymphomaniac who entertained a salon for avant-garde artists, writers and musicians; or Méry Laurent, a former nude dancer who was to become the mistress of several important functionaries of Napoleon III's court, and later also of Manet, Manet did sum up an epoch which had become famous for its moral decadence and political bankruptcy. In 1870, with the outbreak of the Franco-Prussian War and the advance of the Prussian enemy to the walls of Paris, Manet, a patriot and staunch

108 Morisot, quoted in Rouart 1957: 117.
109 Huysmans, quoted in Courthion 1960: 90.
110 Manet, quoted in Courthion 1960: 9.

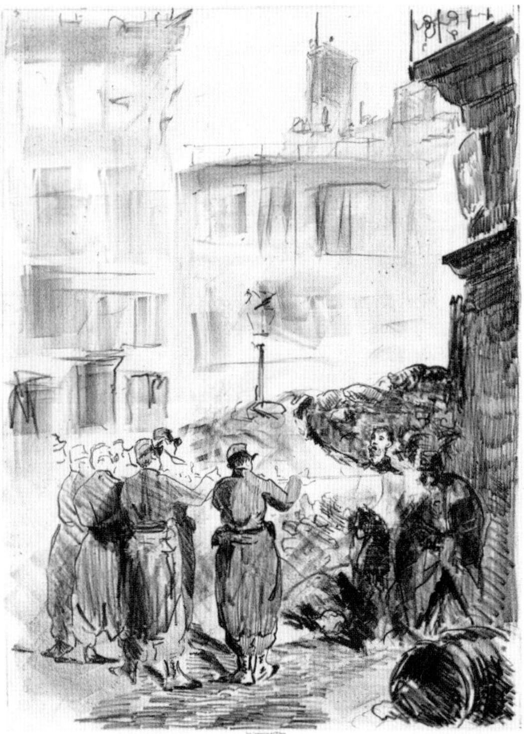

Plate 32: Édouard Manet, *La Barricade* (1871)

Republican, joined a corps of gunners chiefly recruited from artists and writers. In December 1870 he was summoned to the National Guard and promoted to the rank of lieutenant. Manet's two brothers stayed behind in Paris, whereas Manet's mother, his wife and young Léon were sent to a safe location in the French countryside. Among his painter friends, only Degas and Bazille fought the Prussians; the rest of his friends like Zola and the Impressionist painters either escaped to the countryside or took exile in England. The accounts of Manet's direct military involvements differ, depending upon which source of information one consults. According to Berthe Morisot, who was one of the few bourgeoise women remaining in Paris during the siege, "Manet spent his time during the siege changing his uniform. His brother writes us today that in Bordeaux he recounted a number of imaginary exploits."[111] Yet, judging from Manet's letters to Suzanne, one gains a different impression:

> Yesterday I was in the battle which took place between Le Bourget and Champigny. What a racket! However, it was all over very quickly. Shells passed over our heads from all sides. The result was satisfactory, according to this morning's proclamation made by Trochu.[112]

Up to 1870, little had been known about Manet's political beliefs, yet with the siege of Paris, a picture of Manet emerges which depicts him as a radical Republican, and admirer of Gambetta, and an antagonist of Napoleon III. Manet, who seems to have fluctuated between silent

---

111 Morisot quoted in Rouart 1957: 52.

112 December 2, 1870; quoted in Courthion 1960: 27.

depression and anxious tension during the first months of the war, became jubilant when on September 4 the Empire was dissolved and the Third Republic was proclaimed:

> Since 1868, when the censorship laws lightened, Manet had been attending political meetings organized by the Republican journalist Lissagray. [...] With his involvement in the radical Republican life of Paris, Manet predictably chose to remain there once the official declaration of the new republic was made.[113]

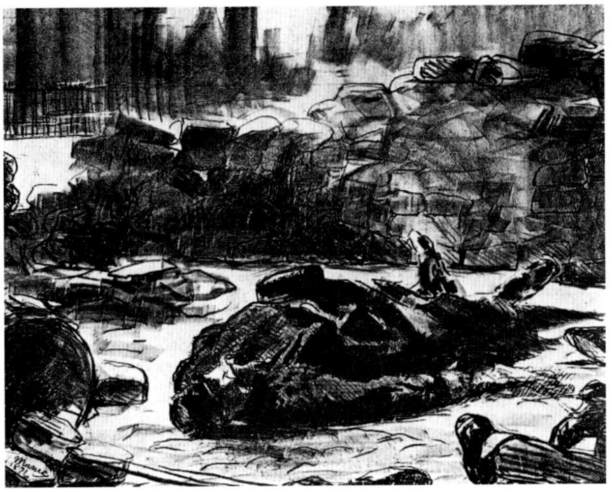

Plate 33:
Édouard Manet,
Guerre civile (1871)

Although he objected to Thiers's armistice with Bismarck in 1871, Manet left Paris to join his family when the Prussian siege of Paris ended. As a result, he did not participate in the civil war during the Commune in 1871, although he returned to Paris during the last and "bloodiest" week of the Commune, witnessing the cruel executions of the Communards by their fellow French compatriots. The fact that Manet was a mere witness, rather than an active participant in this bloody revolt, led Mme. Morisot to comment sarcastically in a letter to her daughter, Berthe:

> Tiburce [Berthe's father] has met two Communards, at this moment when they are all being shot... Manet and Degas! Even at this stage they are condemning the drastic measures used to repress them. I think they are insane, don't you?[114]

Manet did not conceal his sympathies for the Communards and commemorated their brutal slaughter in two drawings, *La Barricade* (1871) **[Plate 32]** and *Guerre civile* (1871) **[Plate 33]**. Although Manet had sided with the revolt of the Communards, he also realized that they

---

113 Ruggierro 1981: 28.
114 Rouart 1957: 63.

had committed atrocities during their three-month reign. In a letter to Berthe Morisot, he writes: "What terrible events, and how are we going to come out of this? Each one lays the blame on his neighbour, but to tell the truth all of us are responsible for what has happend."[115]

Yet, Manet remained faithful to the heroes of the Commune until the end of his life. In 1879, he painted the portrait of George Clemenceau, who had presided over Paris during the siege and the Commune as a joint mayor and who continued to represent the working-class district of Montmartre at the National Assembly and the Chamber of Deputies. In 1881, Manet portrayed Henri Rochefort, one of the most successful journalistic opponents of the Second Empire. During the siege and the Commune, Rochefort had served as a member of the Government of Defense and was elected to head the Barricades Committee during the siege. Arrested for his journalistic activities in 1874, Rochefort was sentenced to life imprisonment at a penal colony in New Caledonia. His dramatic escape, in which he was aided by Gambetta, was also commemorated by Manet in 1880, the year that a general amnesty for all Communards had been declared, allowing Rochefort to return to France from his exile. Manet would also have painted Gambetta if the latter had found the time to pose for him. This gallery of political figures in part illustrates Manet's changing perspective on his role as a painter. Instead of being the painter dedicated to illuminating the past and its undercurrents towards the present, Manet was now developing into a chronicler of the world around him. While the majority of his paintings were still executed in his atelier, where he recreated scenes he had observed outside, his later paintings evoke the impression of being composed directly in the public arena. Manet documented the world he was living in, the coffee-houses, restaurants, the opera, and the parks and streets of Paris, scenes which presented "the heroism of modern life." Manet was famous for cultivating his leisure activity as a *flâneur*—a man who with "skill and ease moves among the crowd."[116] For Manet, the crowd was not an antagonistic or repulsive element, but a group that fascinated

115 Rouart 1957: 64.
116 Benjamin 1978: 167.

him and served him as "a reservoir of electric energy,"[117] from which he retrieved the impressions he would later memorialize in his paintings. It was not uncommon for Manet to stop people in the street whose looks fascinated him. This is the way he met Victorine Meurent in 1862 in front of the Palace of Justice in Paris. Baudelaire describes the *flâneur* as being married to the crowd and needing the crowd as a bird needs air to live. For the perfect *flâneur*, for the passionate observer, it is an immense pleasure to choose his home in the crowd, in the fluctuating, in the movement, in the fleeting and in the moment. To be outside oneself and yet to feel at home, to see the world and yet to remain hidden from it, these are some of the small pleasures of these independent, passionate and important spirits, for whom language cannot find a correct definition. The observer is a prince who is especially in love with his incognito.[118] It was in the attire of a perfect dandy and *flâneur* that Fantin-Latour portrayed Manet in *Portrait d'Édouard Manet* [**Plate 34**], capturing an image of the painter as the quintessential *bon vivant* and womanizer whom Degas described as "so thoroughly bourgeois."[119]

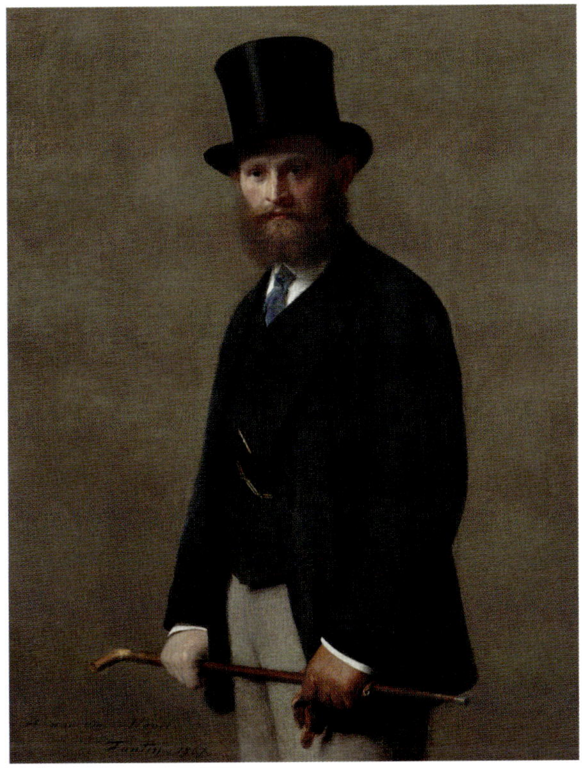

Plate 34:
Henri Fantin-Latour,
Portrait d'Édouard Manet
(1867)

---

117 Benjamin 1978: 175

118 See Baudelaire 1965: 9.

119 According to a conversation reported by Joseph de Vernet, Degas's scorn was boundless when Manet was awarded his first medal, the Légion d'Honneur. "D. took him to task, but his biting remarks did not put out Manet in the least, who ended by saying, 'My dear fellow, if there were no awards, I would not invent them, but as they do exist, you must take everything you can wherever possible. It is one stage passed and a weapon in your hand. [...] It's not my fault that I'm not decorated. I promise you I would be if I could, and I'll do everything I can to achieve it.' / 'Naturally,' D. interrupted angrily, shrugging his shoulders, 'It is not the first time I realize how thoroughly bourgeois you are.'" (quoted in Courthion 1960: 85).

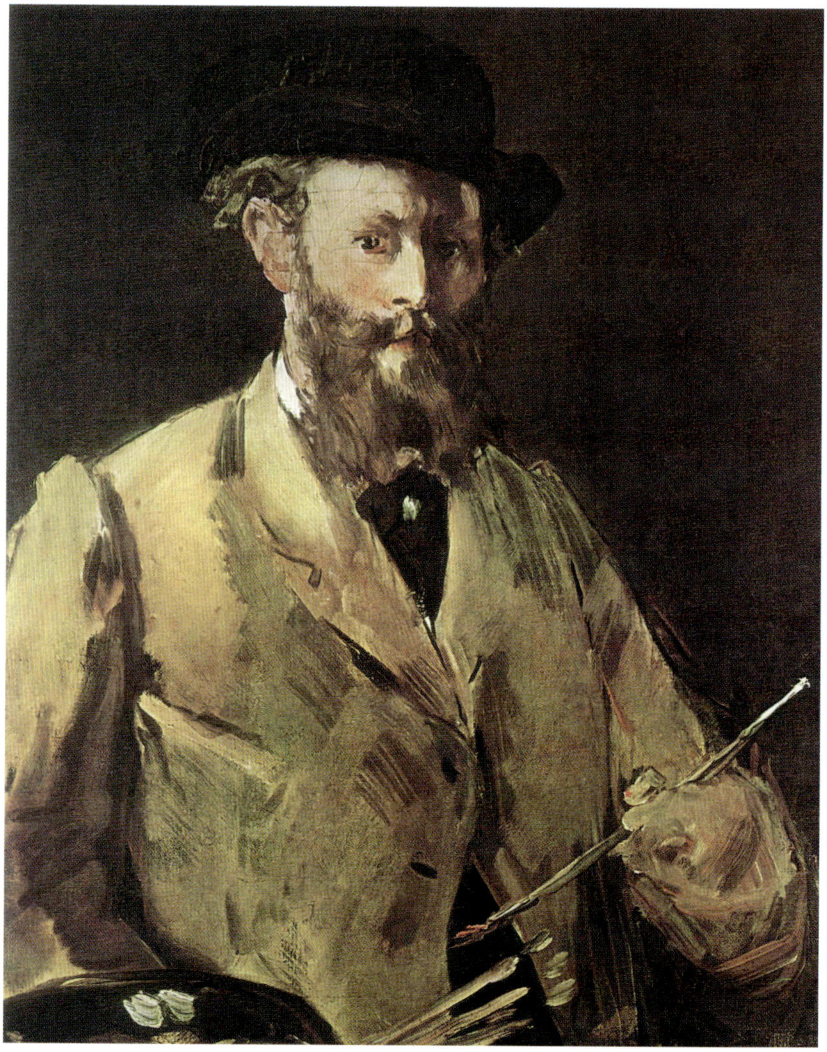

Plate 35:
Édouard Manet,
Autoportrait à la palette
(1878–1879)

How different is the portrait of Manet by Fantin-Latour when compared to Manet's self-portrait, *Autoportrait à la palette* (1878/1879) [**Plate 35**]. Here, the painter presents himself to the public at the height of his career in formal attire, complete with *chapeau melon*, facing the spectator with a melancholic, undeniably self-assured presence. The image of a dandy who "adores society and [...] found secret pleasure in the perfumed and glittering refinement of *soirées*"[120] is not part of

120 Zola 1867; quoted in Courthion 1960: 117 (emphasis in the original).

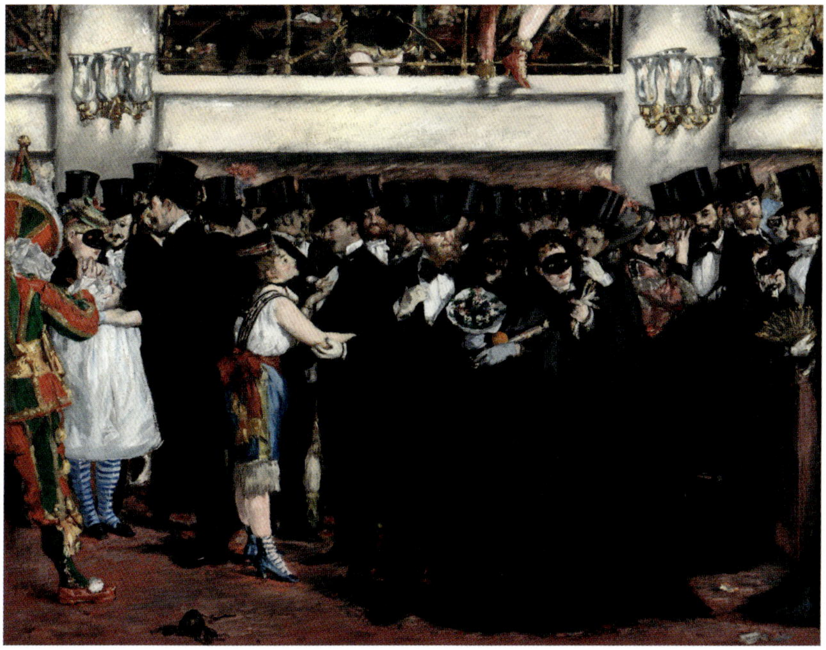

Plate 36:
Édouard Manet,
Bal masqué à l'opéra (1873)

Manet's own image of himself as a painter. Manet's self-portrait of 1879 is of particular importance to any biographical interpretation, since it is one of only two self-representations which Manet devised for the public eye. In previous paintings he had made his presence known, but only in concealed ways: either as a semi-concealed figure in *Le Vieux Musicien*, or disguised in a Rubenesque costume in *La Pêche*, or by substituting for himself the figures of his two brothers.[121] Moreover, his subtle but insistent presence had been continuously marked by the carefully chosen placing of his signature. "A great painter always knows where to sign his pictures, and he never signs twice in the same place."[122] Indeed, Manet never signed twice in the same place, and he chose places which betrayed his curious presence

121 Here I agree with George Mauner's observation that Manet had a "penchant for calling attention to himself in concealed but insistent ways: the semi-concealed portrait in *Le Vieux Musicien* and the disguised self-portrait in *La Pêche*; substitutions for himself in the persons of his brothers; the contrived and integrated placing of his signature." (Mauner 1975: 149).

122 George Moore, *Memoirs of my Dead Life*; quoted in Courthion 1960: 92.

within the painting. For *Olympia*, he chose to sign his name on the couch below the pillows on which her arm is placed, right on the spot where the sheets are tucked in. For his *Portrait d'Émile Zola*, he used Zola's pamphlet on Manet in lieu of a handwritten signature, concealing his first name by the pen which reveals only the first letter of his name (the same as Zola's). In the *Bal masqué à l'opéra* (1873) **[Plate 36]**, he signs his name on an opera program which casually lies on the ground. A similar device is used for his last major work, *Un Bar aux Folies Bergère*, where his signature appears on the label of a beer bottle. While the significance of Manet's integration of word and image will be discussed later in greater detail, at this point it is important only to note that before Manet had consistently chosen an unobtrusive and shrewd location to leave his autograph. Yet, once detected, his presence embodied the function of a witty commentator who deliberately played with the spectator's gaze. In *Autoportrait à la palette* **[Plate 35]**, however, Manet no longer tries to play hide-and-seek with his audience, and instead exposes himself directly. The self-assurance which Manet conveys through his posture is one of the signs which draws a reference to the equally self-assured and proud representation of Velázquez's *Las Meninas* (1656) **[Plate 37]**. A comparison of the appearances of these two painters reveals further similarities:

> The poses are clearly related, and the hand holding the brush in each case has lost all detail. Manet goes further than Velázquez here, blurring his hand beyond recognition, an indication of his interest in this device for fusing the brush with the hand used by the Spanish master.[123]

It is hardly surprising that Manet quoted Velázquez's self-representation in *Las Meninas* in his own self-portrait, since he had always esteemed the Spaniard as "the painter of all painters." By echoing Velázquez's works throughout his entire career, beginning with *Le Buveur d'absinthe* and ending with *Un Bar aux Folies Bergère*, as well as by using the Spaniard's masterpiece *Las Meninas* as a source for his own self-portrait, Manet confirmed the link which intimately connected

---

123 Mauner 1975: 149.

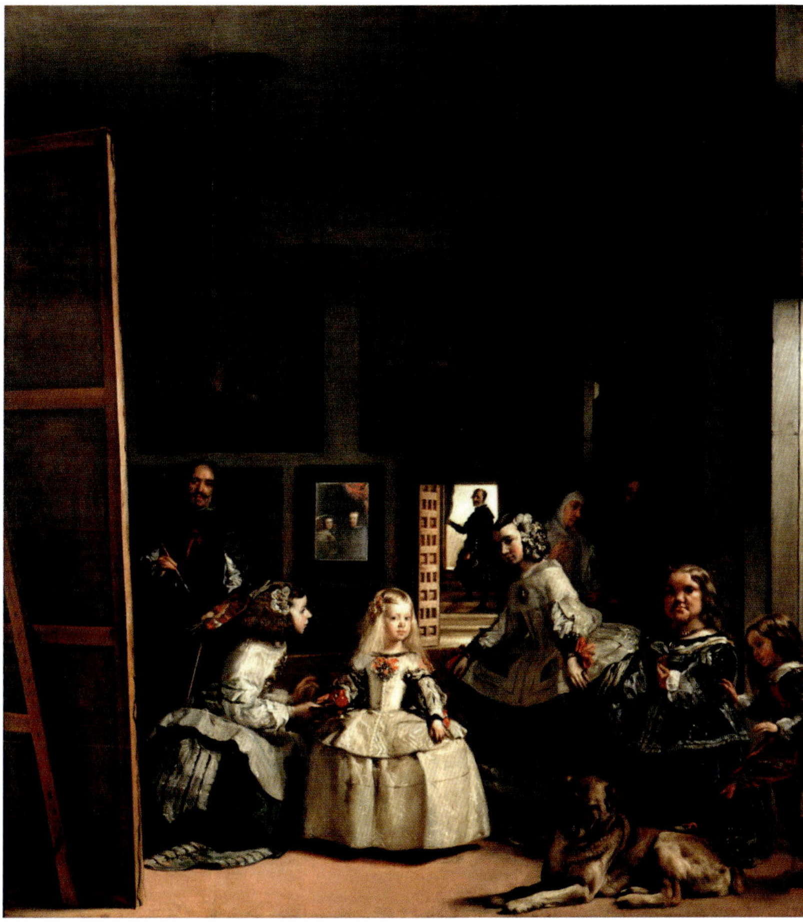

Plate 37: Diego Velázquez, *Las Meninas* (1656)

him to the great Spanish master. Postponing a detailed discussion of the relationship between the works of these two painters, let me single out one particular element that sums up their differences in a nutshell.

The artist in *Las Meninas* is studying the model he is portraying on a canvas that remains invisible to the spectator. The model caught in his scrutiny is the observer himself. However, as Michel Foucault argues, this exchange of gazes, is "a matter of pure reciprocity: we are looking at a picture in which the painter is in turn looking out at us."[124] This is not a simple matter, since the subject of the canvas

124 Foucault 1970/1973: 4.

within the canvas remains stubbornly invisible. The canvas from which the painter Velázquez steps back

> prevents the relation of these gazes from ever being discoverable or definitely established. The opaque fixity that it establishes on one side renders forever unstable the play of metamorphoses established in the centre between spectator and model. Because we can see only that reverse side, we do not know who we are, or what we are doing. Seen or seeing?[125]

Now, when we look at Manet's *Autoportrait à la palette* we might at first think that we are viewing a self-portrait in which we exchange looks with the artist represented. However, upon closer scrutiny we realize that we are seeing not only a painted self-representation, but the mirror-image itself. And the gaze of the artist is ambiguously fixed both on the spectator and on the mirror. Thus, the spectator is put in the same position as the mirror through which the artist fixed his own image. Although Velázquez made use of this same device, Manet dispensed with any expedients that might encourage the illusion that the artist was actually engaged in painting another picture, like the portrayal of the Spanish king's family in *Las Meninas*. In this seemingly simple self-portrait, Manet embodies the complex relationship of a represented reality mirrored and inverted in its own imaginary reality by including in his self-portrait the invisible mirror which makes his image left-handed. By condensing this mirrored image upon the artist himself, Manet directly challenges the position of the spectator, who now clearly emerges as the canvas's infinite subject and object, model and spectator. While Velázquez made the royal family the manifest subject of his painting, Manet directly addresses his patrons, namely, those observing his painting. With this direct appeal to the spectator, Manet not only underscored his dependency upon the model qua model—as he had often proclaimed—but also upon the model as spectator and consumer. Since the old system of royal or imperial patronage ceased to exist after Napoleon III, Manet was indeed dependent upon the multitude of spectators for approval

125 Foucault 1970/1973: 5.

and upon the occasional art critic for recognition, a more difficult position than that of a Velázquez, who was accountable solely to his patron King Philip IV, at whose court he lived and worked.

By confusing the source of his "original" model in the spectator's eyes by portraying his own mirror reflection—while creating the image as if he were portraying the spectator in front of the painted canvas—Manet subtly negated the generally accepted view of the authentic painter who represented things "as they are." In a sense, through his self-portrait Manet seems to say that instead "things are never what they seem," nor can the source of any depiction ever be reduced to one single phenomenon, an objectively certified external reality. On the contrary, these reproduced realities, these snapshots of life, can be understood only if the viewer remembers that reality itself involves continual re-interpretation, and that this interpreted recreation is in itself part of a system or discourse in which it assumes its own variable function.

Autoportrait à la palette recalls Foucault's assertion that the creative subject "must be stripped of its creative role and analysed as a complex and variable function of discourse,"[126] for no other painting illustrates so cogently the diverse functions Manet adopted throughout his career as painter, spectator, model, observer and observed, commentator, critic and subject of criticism, and lastly as a representative of the modern era for whom the contradictions and ambiguities of the age are centered within the individual, rather than between the individual and their external world.

In 1879, at the time of his self-portrait, Manet was already suffering from the first symptoms of *Locomotor ataxia*, which eventually led to his death in 1883. Taking his illness for rheumatism, Manet spent the following summers at the Bellevue hospital, where he would undergo various curative treatments. The fact that Manet mistook tertiary syphilis for his venereal rheumatism leads us back to the apparent family secret of Léon, the half-brother/godson constellation. While Manet was the bearer of a well-kept secret, in his death he was no longer able to maintain it as tightly, since he died of the same af-

---

126 Foucault 1977: 138.

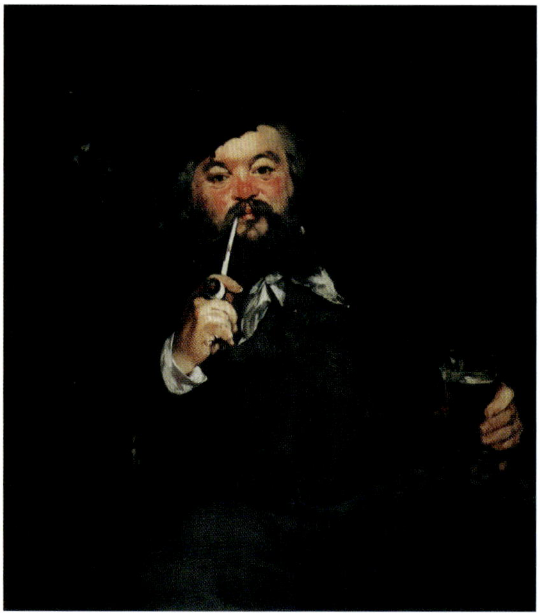

fliction as his father, namely syphilis. At the eleventh hour, a bond was struck between father and son, postmortem.

By 1879, Manet was still under attack from certain conservative critics—most notably Albert Wolff and Paul Mantz—as being a painter who had no talent and lacked imagination, who did not know how to draw; and even Manet's staunch defender Émile Zola changed his opinion.

> The Impressionists are, in my opinion, just exactly pioneers. At one time they put great hopes in Manet; but Manet seems to have exhausted himself through production. He is satisfied with unfinished work; he does not study nature with the passion of the truly creative. All these artists are too easily satisfied.[127]

Plate 38: Édouard Manet, *Le Bon Bock* (1873)

Although Zola tried to convince Manet that his article—which had appeared in a Russian journal—had been mistranslated and reviewed out of context in the French daily *Le Figaro*, it is generally believed that Zola's perplexity at Manet's new works was accurately represented in the French papers. At the same time, however, the list of his supporters had grown, including Stéphane Mallarmé, a most faithful friend and ardent advocate, whose translation of Edgar Allen Poe's "The Raven" was illustrated by Manet in 1875. Other critics, who had initially been hostile, were gradually hailing Manet as the originator of modern art. Manet even gained greater public support for two canvases, *Le Bon Bock* (1873) **[Plate 38]** in 1873, and *Portrait de M. Pertuiset, le chasseur de lions* in 1881. The former canvas depicts the engraver Émile Bellot sitting at a restaurant table enjoying a pipe and a mug of beer, a scene reminiscent of typical tavern scenes by Dutch masters. In comparison to his other portraits, *Le Bon Bock* stands out as being quite uncharacteristic of Manet's style because of its con-

127 Zola 1879, quoted in Hamilton 1969: 219.

ventional genre format and sentimental rendition. *Le Bon Bock* has been generally regarded as Manet's concession to public opinion. Perhaps exacerbated by an uninterrupted stream of criticism and motivated by financial concerns, Manet portrayed this beer-drinking, jovial character in a manner which he expected to please his audience. Curiously enough, it was the other, equally uncharacteristic canvas, the *Portrait de M. Pertuiset, le chasseur de lions* that finally won Manet the coveted "Chevalier de la Légion d'Honneur" title, which made him "hors concours," meaning that he could henceforth exhibit freely at the Salon, no matter what the jury thought of his paintings. However, this belated official recognition no longer served Manet's needs. He had only two more years to live, and by 1881, the financial benefits that usually accompanied an official decoration were no longer that crucial to Manet. Since the early seventies, his works had been sold at private galleries, most notably by the gallery of Durand-Ruel, who in 1871 had bought thirty works for 50,000 Francs (equivalent to over ten million Euro today). Private collectors, such as Théodore Duranty and Albert Hecht, also continued to purchase Manet's paintings. Yet, this official recognition might at least have fulfilled Manet's long-standing prediction: "I shall never exhibit in the stand next door; I shall enter the Salon by the main door."[128]

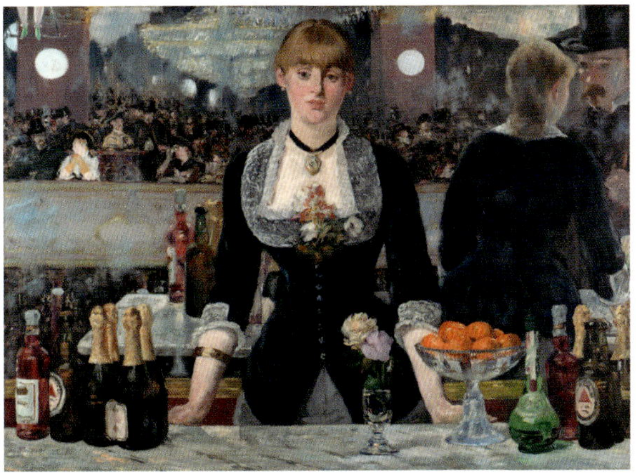

Plate 15:
Édouard Manet,
Un Bar aux Folies Bergère
(1881–1882)

During the last years of his life, Manet ceased to ally himself with Impressionism. Although his canvases, like *Argenteuil*, *Claude Monet peignant dans son atelier*, *Le Grand Canal à Venise*, *La Rue Mosnier aux Paveurs*, and *En bateau*, are testaments to Manet's Impressionist influence, even though his aims did not match those of the movement of Impressionism. Rather than conform to Impressionist theory and practice, he had taken from them whatever suited his own aspirations: freedom, the constant struggle against routine. For a short while—as

128 Manet, quoted in Schneider 1968: 110.

long as the improvisatory freshness that blossomed at L'Argenteuil lasted—, Manet went along with Claude Monet and his entourage. But as they increasingly resorted to *method*, Manet instinctively declined to follow. For him there could be no method as such, no scientific truth, no foolproof style: "Every time I paint, I throw myself into the water in order to learn how to swim."[129] He would not apply the Impressionist technique of nervous brushstrokes in outdoor settings, but in an atmosphere of glimmering artificial light, as exemplified in the nightclub scene of *Un Bar Folies aux Bergère* [**Plate 15**]. In his last masterpiece, Manet incorporates elements that trace numerous strands weaving through his entire oeuvre. Reminiscent of his first major work, *Le Buveur d'absinthe,* in its handling of the theme of the lonely figure and the consumption of alcohol—the bland expression of the barmaid reminiscent of the aloof gaze of Manet's mother, of Léon Leenhoff in *Le Déjeuner dans l'atelier*, and not least of Berthe Morisot in *Le Balcon*—, the solid massing and black outlines of the barmaid recalls *Olympia*, the Impressionist brushstrokes of the crowd echo the technique he employed in *La liseuse* (1879), and the mirrored and fragmented perspectives offer hints at his self-portrait, so that *Un Bar aux Folies Bergère* reverberates with the network of complex ideas which Manet had tried to express throughout his life. Completed in 1882, the *Un Bar aux Folies Bergère* was to be his last chef d'oeuvre. Manet was already too sick to go to the bar and paint the barmaid Suzon in place because walking had become too painful, especially climbing steps. Not giving in to the pain, Manet therefore had the bar counter rebuilt in his own studio and summoned the barmaid herself. He painted this superb last canvas in a seated position. In 1878/79 Manet began to feel

> [...] the consequences of his untreated tertiary syphilis [...], when he apparently experienced severe shooting pains in his legs. Chronic pain became an almost permanent condition after 1879. [...] Manet was suffering from *tabes dorsalis*, the degeneration of nerves in the dorsal column of his spinal cord, a primary symptom of which was *locomotor ataxia*.[130]

---

129 Manet, quoted in Schneider 1968: 111.

130 Bailey 2020.

In the end, Manet died of the same illness as his father, but in contrast to his father whose syphilis rendered him demented and paralyzed for the last three years of his life, Manet *fils* kept his wits and, despite tremendous pains, completed some of his most evocative works, including *Chez le père Lathuille* (1879) and *Un Bar aux Folies Bergère*. Toward the end of his life, at just fifty-one years of age, his left leg had to be amputated because of incurable gangrene. Ten days after this operation—performed at his home at 39, Rue de Saint-Pétersbourg—Édouard Manet passed away. The story has it that during the last days of his life the artist had developed phantom pains, and when Claude Monet came to visit, Manet insisted loudly that his friend not sit down where his leg was.

Over 1,500 people attended Manet's funeral at the Cimetière de Passy to bid their farewells. The poet Stéphane Mallarmé summed up his personal loss with pithy agility as follows: "For ten years, I have seen my dear Manet every day, whose absence now seems improbable."[131]

Manet the artist and person had affected many people throughout his life, he was the figure around whom the most celebrated artists of his time gathered to discuss life, art, and politics. But alongside his intellectual undertakings there was also his career as a painter, and it was through his work that he instigated some of the most intriguing and enduring dialogues with his contemporaries, both friends and fellow artists. It is to this artistic backstory that I will now turn my attention.

---

131 "Les relations de Manet et de Mallarmé furent immédiatement fréquentes: la proximité des ateliers successifs du peintre facilitait au poëte des visites qui devinrent quotidiennes, au retour du lycée Condorcet vers la rue de Rome; et en 1885, deux ans après la mort de Manet, il écrivait à Verlaine: 'J'ai, dix ans, vu tous les jours mon cher Manet, dont l'absence aujourd'hui me paraît invraisemblable.' Ce qui, aussi, daterait bien de 1873 leur première rencontre. Méry Laurent fut au centre de cette amitié." Note in the French edition of Stéphane Mallarmé: *Œuvre complètes,* Paris: Gallimard, 1951: 1620, p. 1620 ("The relations between Manet and Mallarmé were immediately frequent. The proximity of the painter's successive studios facilitated daily visits for the poet, on his way back from the Lycée Condorcet to the Rue de Rome; and in 1885, two years after Manet's death, he wrote to Verlaine: 'For ten years, I have seen my dear Manet every day, whose absence now seems improbable.' This too would date their first meeting to 1873. Méry Laurent was at the center of this friendship." [author's translation]).

Chapter III

PAINTING REMEMBRANCES: THE ROLE OF THE PAST IN MANET'S WORKS AND HIS USE OF APRÈS-COUP

Those who cannot remember the past
are condemned to repeat it.

George Santayana, *The Life of Reason*, 1905

Intelligent understanding of past history is
to some extent a lever for moving the present into
a certain kind of future.

John Dewey, *Logic – The Theory of Inquiry*, 1938

To my mind one does not put oneself in place of the past,
one only adds a new link.

Paul Cézanne, *Correspondence*, 1905

As we have seen in the previous chapter, a full understanding of Manet's works can be gained only by identifying the traditional motifs and themes Manet echoed in his paintings. *La Pêche* cannot be fully appreciated without recognizing its references to Rubens's *Château de Steen* (1635–1637) **[Plate 39]**, nor could *La Nymphe surprise* be adequately understood without a knowledge of its connections to Rubens's *Susanna and the Elders* and Rembrandt's *Susanna in the Bath*. To search for and relate traditional sources to Manet's paintings is not a novel approach. On the contrary, nearly every art history book or critical

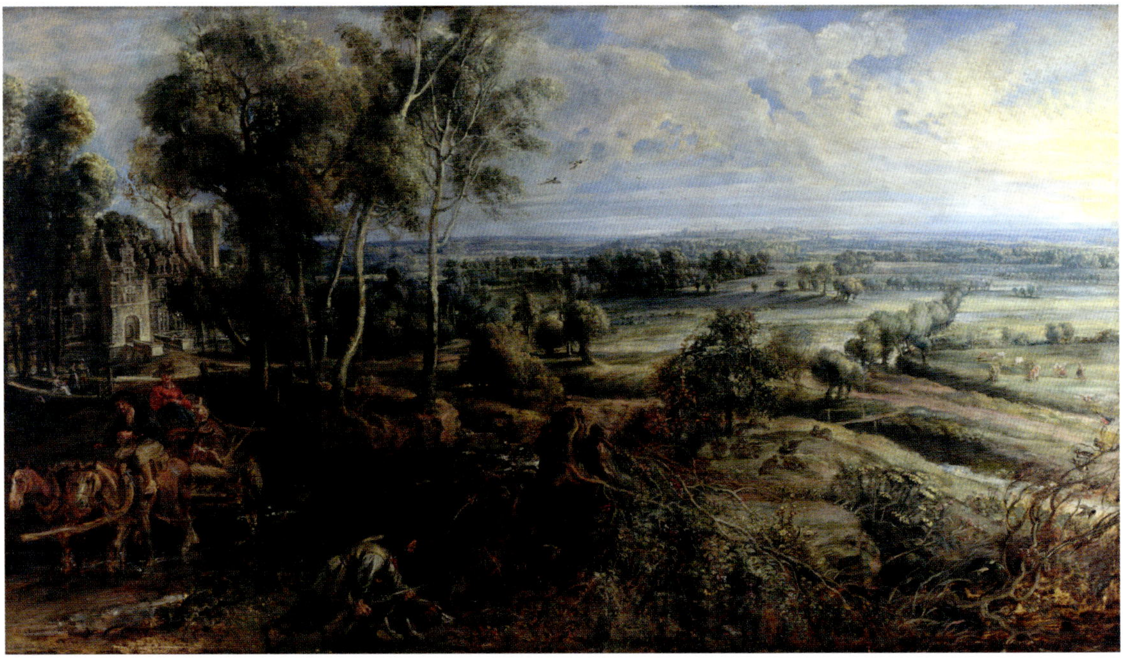

Plate 39: Peter Paul Rubens, *Château de Steen* (1635–1637)

essay on Manet diligently reminds the reader of the link between, for example, Manet's *Olympia* and Titian's *Venus of Urbino*, or of the association between *Le Déjeuner sur l'herbe* and Giorgione's/Titian's *Le Concert Champêtre*. Indeed, it has almost become impossible to think of Manet's *Olympia* or *Déjeuner* as paintings in their own right without mentally comparing their depictions to these earlier canvases. Almost no other painter has evoked such detailed research into his pictorial sources of the Old Masters as Manet has. Nearly every year, an essay or addendum is published that has found yet another new source for some or other work by Manet, or that refutes a source previously discovered by this or that critic.[1] The recognition, however, that Manet's canvases were deeply anchored in themes depicted by such artists as Velázquez, Goya, Rubens, Titian, Giorgione, Le Nain, Watteau, Courbet, and so

1 For further discussion, see Beatrice Farwell, *Manet's Nymphe Surprise* (1975); Theodore Reff, *Manet and Blanc's 'Histoire des Peintres'* (1970); and Françoise Cachin, "Introduction to the catalogue of the exhibition 'Manet (1832–1883)' at the Grand Palais, Paris, April–August, 1983.

on, was not shared by his contemporary critics, at least not to the same extent and not with the same understanding as it has been practiced by modern art critics. While T. J. Clark is correct when he states in his essay on *Olympia* that "only two critics talked at all of this relation to Titian's *Venus*; only twice, in other words, was it allowed that *Olympia* existed 'with reference to' the great tradition of European painting,"[2] it is often too readily assumed that Manet's public was scarcely aware of the painter's references to previous artists. For example, in an essay, Michael Fried argues that:

> The problem of the meaning of Manet's use of sources first arose in 1864, when the critic Ernest Chesneau spotted the painter's adaptation in his *Déjeuner sur l'herbe* [...] of a figure group from Marcantonio Raimondi's engraving after Raphael's *Judgment of Paris*. That same year, a more distinguished critic, Théophile Thoré, remarked in the course of a largely favorable review that Manet had "pastiched" Velázquez, Goya, and El Greco and called attention to certain striking similarities between Manet's art and the work of other old masters. Thereafter the topic was largely moot, until 1908, when the German art historian Gustav Pauli rediscovered the Marcantonio connection.[3]

While Fried is essentially correct in stating that the particular themes were not usually recognized by Manet's contemporary critics, he is simply wrong in his conclusion that contemporaries did not notice Manet's close association with Spanish masters such as Velázquez, El Greco, and Goya. Nor is it true that the subject remained closed after 1864, when Théophile Thoré-Bürger remarked on the striking similarities between the Spanish painters and Manet. Nineteenth-century critics were far from being ignorant; rather, their debate took a different form from that of modern art commentaries. Moreover, Manet's critics argued from a different ideological vantage point than today's art historians. It is oversimplifying to propose a strict division between Manet's contemporary audience—which largely failed to recognize his specific references to the traditional art—and the modern art critic.

---

2 Clark 1980: 26.
3 Fried 1984: 522.

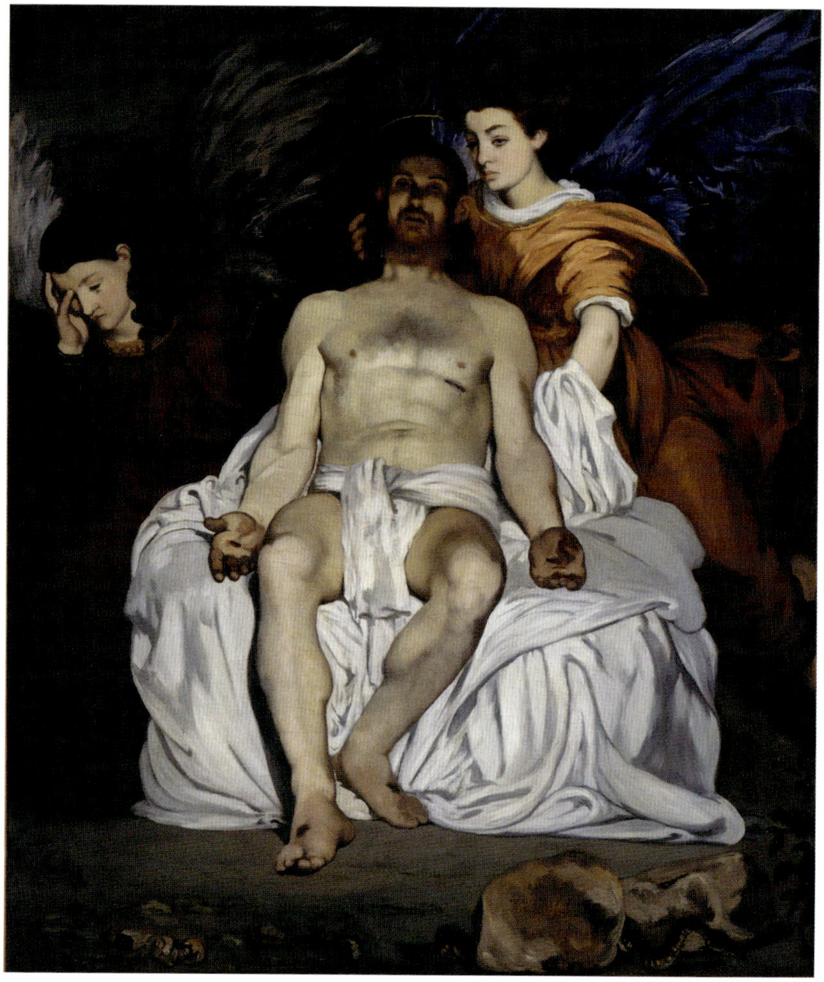

Plate 40: Édouard Manet, *Le Christ mort et les anges* (1864)

Such a supposition ignores the profound shifts that took place in the course of a century in the attitudes and ideological positions of the spectator vis-à-vis painting relationship and the history that helped shape these perceptions. Perceptions are, as we know, imbued with historical fluctuations and overlapping meanings, they always constitute an interpretative act. As Henri Bergson wrote, "Perception is never a mere contact of the mind with the object present; it is impregnated with memory-images which complete it as they interpret it."[4]

4 Bergson 1911: 170.

In contrast to the modern view that Manet re-interpreted the scenes of the past and molded them into contemporary images, the critics of the day accused him of plagiarism and technical inexperience whenever they pointed to his reliance upon the Spanish masters. It is true that while they rarely recognized the specific themes he borrowed, they were aware of his strong affinity with the traditional Masters and that he painted "in the style" of Velázquez, Goya, or El Greco. "He's a Velasquez of the boulevards, let us say, or a Spaniard of Paris..."[5] Or, as Courbet scathingly put it, "This young man shouldn't play the role of a Velazquez in front of us."[6] How serious these accusations were, is illustrated in the response of Manet's two most famous admirers. Charles Baudelaire vehemently defended Manet from Thoré-Bürger's allegations that the painter had slavishly imitated the Spanish Masters in *Le Christ mort et les anges* (1864) **[Plate 40]**. He writes:

> Monsieur Manet, who is credited with being mad and hot-tempered, is quite simply, a very loyal and unpretentious man, who does everything possible to behave rationally [...] The word *imitate* is not the right one. Monsieur Manet has never seen a Goya; Monsieur Manet has never seen an El Greco; Monsieur Manet has never seen the Galerie Pourtalès. This may seem incredible–but it is a fact.[7]

---

5 Hamilton 1969: 107.

6 Courbet, quoted in Courthion 1960: 45.

7 Baudelaire's letter to Thoré-Bürger continues as follows: "At the time when we were the happy owners of this marvelous Spanish Museum (which the stupid French Republic with its *improper* respect for property, has handed back to the Prince of Orléans), Monsieur Manet was serving on board of a ship. He has been told so often about his imitations of Goya that he is now making arrangements to see some Goya paintings. It's true, he has seen some Velazquez paintings–I don't know where. Do you doubt my word? Do you question the fact that astonishing parallels can exist in Nature? Very well! *I* am accused of imitating Edgar Poe! Do you know why I have so patiently studied Poe? Because he resembles *me*! The first time I opened a book by Poe I was astonished and delighted to find, not only plots dreamed-up by me, but whole phrases that I had composed, which *he* had written twenty years before. *Et nunc erudimini, vos qui judicates!* Don't be cross, but keep a happy memory of me in a corner of your heart. I'll thank you every time you try to be of service to Manet." (Baudelaire, quoted in Courthion 1960: 50–51 [emphasis in the original]).

Émile Zola took a more cautious and conciliatory approach towards the hostile critics when he explained that:

> He [Manet] has been reproached for imitating the Spanish painters. I agree that there is some resemblance in his early work to those masters. One is always someone's son. But ever since his *Le Déjeuner sur l'herbe* he seems to me to assert clearly this personality which I have tried briefly to explain and criticize.[8]

The different strategies these two writers took in defending their shared friend are significant. While Baudelaire vehemently denied the influence of the Spanish masters upon Manet's work on the basis of geographical constraints, Zola excused Manet's "imitation" and diagnosed it as a temporary malaise from which Manet had seemingly recovered by the time he painted *Le Déjeuner sur l'herbe*. Just how mistaken Zola's impression was, is of course clearly shown by the fact that *Le Déjeuner* comprises numerous references to the Italian masters, as well as to Courbet. However, as I will argue later, it was not the references per se which evoked the critic's outrage, but rather the fact that they were so strikingly Spanish that irritated contemporary aesthetic tastes. The debate about Manet's supposed imitations invokes Derrida's notion of mimesis and supplement. Rather than thinking in terms of an original and a copy, Derrida introduces the idea that imitation does not produce likeness but difference, and that each work of art constitutes a supplement to the one it references. Transposing what Derrida says about writing, one might say that every painting stands in a mimetic relation to another one, rendering terms like first or second, original and copy, or beginning and end obsolete. For Derrida, mimesis is a kind of productive force imbued in every painting, since every painting follows suit to another, and has been the product of a self-perpetuating genesis.[9] What makes the dispute about Manet's imitations so absurd, is the fact that the practice of imitating the Old Masters was a core requirement of the École des

---

8 Hamilton 1968: 96.

9 See Derrida 1976.

Beaux-Arts.[10] Interestingly enough, the antithetical positions held by Baudelaire and Zola set the general tone for the major art historical debates in the following years. In fact, to a certain extent, they are still alive today. On the one hand, we have the type of analysis which attempts to disprove Baudelaire's conviction that M. Manet had never seen a Velázquez, Goya or El Greco. By painstakingly chronicling the art journals and magazines of Manet's era, art historians have successfully proven that Manet had access to the works of all three through reproductions and lithographs available in France.[11] On the other hand, we have the formalist perspective engendered by Zola, who minimized the Spanish influence. He argued that Manet was not primarily interested in his subject matter per se, but used it only as a pretext for solving problems of form and color, which alone preoccupied him. In the twentieth century this view has been powerfully articulated by Georges Bataille, who still represents the most eminent theoretician of this formalist perspective.[12] However, a third critical position persisted into recent times, one which unknowingly echoed Manet's self-description to his intimates that he lacked imagination and thus had to resign himself to imitating the great masters. In 1932, the year of the first major retrospective of Manet's work in commemoration of the centenary of his birth, Germain Bazin argued that Manet did not possess the ability to compose, or was uninterested in the problems of composition, and therefore turned to traditional painting to avoid this issue altogether. It is easy to see how this viewpoint informed the formalist theory of Zola and later Bataille, since both exclusively emphasized the significance of color, form and tones, meaning the ideology of "pure painting," which is only a particular sub-set of the general conception of "art for art's sake."

---

10 See Schweiker 1988: 21–38.

11 See, for instance, Anne Coffin Hanson 1977, in particular her discussion of Manet's painting *Le Combat du Kearsarge et de l'Alabama* and *L'évasion de Rochefort* (121–127).

12 Georges Bataille's discussion of Manet's work is of course more astute and wide-ranging than Zola's passionate defense. In addition, it is important to remember that by 1955, a purely formalistic view of Manet's paintings was difficult to sustain since art historians had uncovered the wide array of traditional sources cited in Manet's works.

While one group of critics intensified their empirical research to confirm that Manet had indeed known his Spanish predecessors (but without analyzing the significance of his borrowings), another group discounted the sources of past motifs in favor of Manet's color composition. In addition, there was a small group that argued that Manet's reliance on the traditional sources was far from being an impediment or an act of plagiarism, but instead represented a necessary component of his artistic intention. Curiously enought, it was Zola who was the first to mention that "the Spanish masters gave […] to him [Manet] 'the Spanish accent with which he spoke for the first time'."[13] According to Jean Harris, Stéphane Mallarmé was the only contemporary writer to extend the metaphor of painting-as-language to account for Manet's use of past references:

> Learning from the techniques of past masters provides the young artist with a *vocabulary* and a manner of handling adaptable to his own artistic ends. The artist's dependence upon the past is viewed as performing a positive function in his education, Mallarmé says, by providing him with "friendly counsel in remedying the evils of his country and his time."[14]

Paul Jamot figures prominently among the small group who reinforced the position that the use of traditional sources did not constitute an impediment for Manet, nor a substitute for his own creative compositions. In the catalogue for the Manet exhibition of 1932, Jamot explains: "Manet has borrowed a lot. He has borrowed from the dead and from the living. It is a method only permitted to the strong for they know they don't risk compromising their originality."[15]

Jamot predated T. S. Eliot's famous phrase that the artist (in his case, the poet) has to "work the dead" and "wrest authority away from all those who have come before through a kind of imaginative and rhetorical violence, a kind of insurrection in the temple of culture."[16]

---

13 Hamilton 1969: 115.

14 Harris 1964: 560 (author's emphasis).

15 Jamot, quoted in Courthion 1960: 202.

16 Eliot, quoted in Hammer 2021.

Jamot was the only contemporary critic to recognize that Manet's "imitation" of the past represented an act of strength rather than an admission of weakness. Jamot's essay might have prepared the way for future students to look at Manet's extensive quotations from the Old Masters as a deliberate strategy—rather than as a remedial device. Yet, by the 1950s and '60s, art historians were still puzzled by Manet's intricate use of traditional sources, and they sought to solve this strange phenomenon by claiming that Manet used his sources either to identify with those painters he most cherished, or to compete with them.[17] It has never been made clear, however, why Manet should have felt the need to emulate or compete with the particular artists in question, nor why he would select certain themes over others as the vehicles of his admiration or his rivalry. The task of excavating the traditional sources for Manet's paintings has been relatively straightforward, though arduous, compared to the project of arriving at a coherent analysis of why and how and to what effect Manet chose to imbue his modern painting with such an array of traditional references.

It is all the more curious to note to what extent recipients of Manet's work neglected to consider the meanings embedded in Manet's citations from the past when T. S. Eliot, the famous British poet and master of quotations, refuted, like Manet, the linearity of time. In *Tradition and the Individual Talent*, Eliot writes:

> No poet, no artist of any art, has his complete meaning alone. His significance, his appreciation is the appreciation of his relation to the dead poets and artists. You cannot value him alone; you must set him, for contrast and comparison, among the dead. I mean this as a principle of aesthetic, not merely historical, criticism.[18]

The Canadian psychoanalyst Cecilia Taiana describes Eliot's concept of tradition with the following words:

> Eliot brings the dead and the living together through his use of quotations. He resignifies the past by inserting a piece of the past

17 For a more detailed discussion of this view, see Sandblad 1954.

18 Eliot 1919: 37.

> into the present, and we, as readers, retrospectively see the past from a new vertex of the present; Eliot thereby [*here I add, like Manet*] allows his precursors to shine a new light on what is here now.[19]

In dealing with clinical material, psychoanalysts are confronted with a similar task. They also first engage in the excavation of memories, and then attempt to arrive at a meaningful interpretation of those memories in light of the present situation. Thus, not unlike art historians, psychoanalysts are confronted with two notions of truth,

> [...] truth understood as the correct statement, the historical fact – only in need of discovery to be brought to the surface; and truth as the emergent, the construction of something that makes sense and that permits one to rely on it [...] [20]

Loch calls the one truth the historical truth and understands the second truth as "sense," and defines "sense" in Heideggerian terms: "'Meaning signifies the 'upon-which' [*das Woraufhin*] of the primary projection in terms of which something can be conceived in its possibility as that which it is."[21] From this vantage-point, one can argue that "the historical truth," which in terms of this discussion can be related to Manet's echoing of the art of the past, has been discovered, but that the "construction of something that makes sense" has not been attempted with nearly the same degree of insight.

Using Donald Spence's terminology, one may postulate that those art historians interested in locating the precise historical sources for Manet's paintings have largely failed to analyze how the artist's narrative truth has been shaped, and thus altered the historical truth of his quotations. In other words, they have considered Manet as an imitator of traditional masters and as a faithful chronicler of his time without noticing the potential tension in such a dual role, and without interpreting the constructive links Manet established through

---

19 Taiana 2022: 197 (author's emphasis).
20 Loch 1977: 220–221.
21 Heidegger 1962: 371.

his own renditions.[22] I know of only two exceptions to this situation: Michael Fried's article "Manet's Sources: Aspects of His Art 1859–1865," and George Mauner's book *Manet, Peintre-Philosophe* are both studies which attach a specific meaning to—and which discover a specific reason for—Manet's use of traditional sources. Michael Fried argues that the artist's enterprise constituted a deliberate attempt to establish the relation of his art to that of the "authentically French" tradition and through that association, a connection to the art of foreign schools. In Fried's words:

> [Manet] wished to go beyond the art of France to comprehend and in effect to subsume the painting of the other major national schools and, by doing so, to establish explicitly the internationalism or better, the *universality* of his own painting [...][23]

Conversely, George Mauner views Manet's works as a continuous struggle to unify opposites into a single principle: past and present, life and mortality, profane and sacred love, and so forth. Manet's specific quotations of Dutch and Spanish art are thought to accentuate the "homo duplex" theme in his own paintings. By means of a carefully arranged set of poses and formal relationships, through references made to familiar concepts by means of allusions to well-known artworks of the past, and finally, through the use of live models and a spontaneous, fresh technique, Manet communicates a complex and profound idea without violating his concept of the expressive means peculiar to painting.[24]

---

22 Donald Spence draws an analogy with painting when he distinguishes between the narrative and the historical truth in a patient's clinical discourse: "A good narrative explanation may be useful," he writes, "because it brings together disparate pieces of a patient's life in an appealing way, but what might be called its narrative truth may depend more on its aesthetic properties (which stem from matters of time and phrasing) than on its historical validity. [...] If we were able to know, by some kind of magic, which pieces of the narrative were historically false and could revise our narrative to leave them out, we might seriously jeopardize its aesthetic appeal, just as a painting might be seriously flawed by turning it into a strict representation of reality." (Spence 1982: 49).

23 Fried 1984: 526 (emphasis in the original).

24 See Mauner 1975: 78.

The studies of Fried and Mauner significantly advanced the general level of art-historical discussions about Manet's works, because they were the first to uncover a specific intention behind his quotations. And unlike other art-historians who had analyzed single paintings and their relationships to traditional works, both critics saw the ideas of "the authentic French tradition" and "human double nature" flowing through all those paintings that shared such striking similarities to Manet's predecessors. Of course, such a single-minded approach entails its own inherent limitations. In this instance, both Fried and Mauner risk so uncompromising a fascination with their arguments that their accounts tolerate no other interpretation. They are not open, that is, to questioning whether Manet was guided solely by his wish to be recognized as an authentic French painter, or entirely defined by his urge to represent variations of the *homo-duplex* theme, a theme that is to illustrate the divided nature of the human being. These two distinct interpretive strategies are proffered by Fried and Mauner without entering into a dialogue with one another.

I would argue that Manet's quotations from past sources cannot be reduced to a single theme, but that the themes emerging from his paraphrases can be more comprehensively understood if one first analyzes the process of his embodiment of references from previous works of art. It is interesting to note that even the most eminent art historians treat Manet's sources of the Old Masters as a unique phenomenon, just as if no other painter before Manet had so extensively quoted previous works. Yet, when one looks at the history of painting, one realizes how painters have quoted each other throughout the centuries; how Rubens's *The Garden of Love*, for example, quoted Titian's *Bacchanal*, and how the former's *Garden* was subsequently evoked in Watteau's *Pilgrimage to Cythera*. It is nonetheless true, however, that no other painter before Manet seems to have stimulated such a zealous quest for his "original" sources. The question that arises is: What was the reason that Manet was initially denounced for quoting from Velázquez, Goya, and El Greco, and why was he accused of plagiarism when the "imitation" of traditional art had hitherto been accepted as standard practice? What was it about these quotations that so unsettled succeeding generations of spectators and critics? How did Manet use these sources, how did he distort, adapt and transform them? What did Manet remember, and what did he aim to remind the spectator of?

In attempting to answer these questions, we must dare to explore how history interleaves with art and politics and with psychoanalysis—a procedure that may ultimately prove not to be too dissimilar from the one Manet pursued in his paintings, when he installed his contemporary figures in scenes from the past. The belief that unearthing past references would provide sufficient evidence to analyze Manet's use of traditional themes, which is analogous to the psychoanalysts' attempt to excavate repressed memories and reinsert them back into conscious life, is short-sighted and limited. They mistake a hermeneutic task for an empirical conquest, and, accordingly, restrict their work to helping the analysand uncover the past "as it really was."[25] By doing so, they fail to see that the process of remembrance is an interpretive act, one through which the individual attempts to construct a meaning for the subject's present condition through their new understanding of the past. This understanding of the past is a process which is constantly undergoing revisions and changes, it is not a fixed object that is sealed forever. Thus, it is not the retrieval of the factual past per se that can or should be attained, but the meaning(s) that the analysand is constructing around their past in relationship to their present and future, that constitutes the proper focus of psychoanalysis—just like clay that is gradually applied to the armature of an evolving sculpture. Freud himself contributed to this confusion and never developed a unified concept for the analytic value of recalling the past. On the one hand,

25 Margaret Mahler's developmental stage theory, which focuses on the infant's separation and individuation process from the mother, is—among many others—the most prominent psychoanalytic theory exhibiting this tendency. Linking adult psychopathological disturbances to specific developmental phases, Mahler attends to the history of actual childhood traumas, rather than to the adult's interpretive reconstructions around a given past event. Her analytic therapy emphasizes the search for developmental disturbances that are to be remedied through "emotionally corrective experiences". From its beginnings, psychoanalytic theory has been divided between emphasizing the past as an archeological find that needs to be unearthed, and an interpretive approach that views the past as formed by memories which are subject to unconscious interpretations, screened memories, and the interpretive and temporal process of après-coup/Nachträglichkeit.

he compared the analyst's task of reconstructing forgotten events to the archaeologist's restoration of excavated artifacts. From this vantage point, he believed that the adult's reconstructions of past events were equivalent to the actual thoughts and behaviors of their childhood. This view implied that memory was merely a process of registration, a process that may be overwhelmed by an excess of traumatic stimuli so that the psyche resorts to the mechanism of repression. Once the repression was lifted, the adult could regain access to their past.

However, in his essay "Screen Memories" Freud discovered as early as 1899, that "It may indeed be questioned whether we have any memories at all *from* our childhood: memories *relating to* our childhood may be all that we possess."[26] In other words, what we can analyze are the memories relating to our childhood, and not the factual content of what we recall from that period. Moreover, Freud discovered that memory, like the dream-work, is an activity that constantly selects, distorts, and constructs a meaning around the remembered events; it is not a conflict-free mechanism, but it itself subject to complex dynamics. Here, distortions are to be understood as *Entstellungen*—deformations—which represent ways within forbidden wishes can find new expressions. As Hans Loewald observes:

> Memory, however, does not simply enable us to hang on to the past in some way; it gives meaning to the present and helps to shape a future. [...] It is not merely a faculty of reviving or reproducing the past, nor is it simply the faculty of recording and retaining present but fleeting perceptions so that they may last in some other form. By virtue of memory, our experiences become connectable, are woven into a context, and extend into a past and a future.[27]

Yet, as Jed Sekoff has argued, Freud never resolved the conflict of whether "analysis devise[s] or retrieve[s] the past"; or whether "interpretation build[s] again what once existed in actuality", or whether "it re-construct[s] what was already a construction of phantasy: these are the kinds of questions psychoanalysis comes up against time and

26 Freud 1899: 322 (emphasis in the original).
27 Loewald 1976: 198.

again."[28] Freud's theory about *Nachträglichkeit*, to which I will come in a moment, complicated the debate about the functioning of memory even further. *Nachträglichkeit*, which is nowadays most commonly translated as "afterwardedness" or "retrospective modification" implies "the resignification of memories, a kind of reversal of 'the arrow of time.'"[29] In line with Freud's notion of *Nachträglichkeit*, T.S. Eliot remarks in 1920:

> [W]hat happens when a new work of art is created is something that happens simultaneously to all the works of art which preceded it. [...] The whole existing order must be, if ever so slightly, altered, and so the relations, proportions, values of each work of art towards the whole are readjusted [...]. Whoever has approved this idea of order [...] will not find it preposterous that the past should be altered by the present as much as the present is directed by the past, which preceded it.[30]

Freud's twofold model about memory mirrored the ambivalent stance philosophers and artists assumed at that time, who extensively debated the use and appropriation of the past and of tradition for their present time. The different strategies that painters, historians, and writers have devised in their dealings with memory also demonstrate that the past is susceptible not only to diverse interpretive methodologies, but can also be the servant of many different masters.

Each society tends to institute some form of ritual to commemorate past events. Dates such as the Fourth of July and the First of May have a different significance for every nation. Yet, in each case, the choice of when to celebrate national holidays is how nations interpret and use their past in a specific way. The aim is to cultivate and preserve the spirit of certain heroic events and instill in the peoples a sense of reverence for the deeds of the past. Yet, nations not only commemorate these events in order to preserve a sense of history, but—as demonstrated by the parades in front of the White House, the Bastille, or the Kremlin—they are simultaneously used by the

28 Sekoff 1982: 106.
29 House/Slotnick 2015: 685.
30 Eliot, quoted in Taiana 2022: 198.

respective governments as a means of validating their policies under the protective screen of a "historical consciousness."

In many cases, a certain view of the past is learned by rote and cherished blindly. This unquestioned version of national history serves as a refuge, an idealized world that shields the population from the conflicts of the present. It can also be used for didactic purposes, to instruct people about the good and the evil of the past. On the other hand, a critical understanding of history is often viewed as a dangerous tool, since it empowers people to situate their present predicament within a concrete historical context. To avoid the attendant risks of free access to the knowledge of history, totalitarian governments typically "white-out" past events which contest the present self-definition and challenge the official framing of national identity.[31] For those who either blindly revere their past or who deliberately suppress and deny parts of it, history is considered sacred, something that anchors identity and functions as a useful tool for propagandistic purposes. In both instances, the aleatory mechanisms of memory are artfully channeled into specific directions, manipulated, repurposed, or even erased. Where the remembrance of the past is turned into a ritual—for religious purposes or as a coercive didactic instrument typical of totalitarian societies—people are unable to use their past as a means of transformation, or as a means of situating and continuously reevaluating their present condition within a context of their past-history which extends into the future.[32]

We encounter similar phenomena in many psychoanalytic case studies. It was Freud who determined that hysterics did not suffer from organic dysfunctions, but "from reminiscences." Their symptoms, he asserted, were sites of remembrance, scars of thoughts, and

---

31 Here, I am thinking of Russia erasing every reference to Trotsky from the Russian history books since his defeat and subsequent murder by Stalin. Trotsky's figure was literally whited-out in photographs where he was standing next to Stalin. His role as a leader of the Red Army during the Civil War no longer exists for the post-World War-II generation because of the total erasure of Trotsky's accomplishments.

32 With the Ukrainian war, Russia has demonstrated once again that it can use, abuse and rewrite its history in order to justify its imperialist and destructive motive to invade a sovereign neighbor. Under the guise of needing to "denazify" Ukraine, and to liberate its citizens from genocide and humiliation, the supposed liberators act like the Nazis themselves, brutally destroying the very country they pronounced to liberate.

feelings too painful to be brought to the surface, and instead manifested themselves as bodily symptoms.

While the symptoms provided a temporary flight from the past, they also constituted a consistent reminder of this past: hysterics repress the past by concealing their conflictual thoughts behind less threatening ideas and through defense mechanisms, such as repression, denial, and conversion symptoms; more acutely disturbed individuals meanwhile repudiate their more disturbing thoughts from the psychical realm altogether. Although the memories of the traumatic events may not be entirely erased, any revisiting of those disturbing events is experienced as an intensely dangerous, if not life-threatening process. For this reason their defense mechanisms—such as splitting, denial, projective identification, and mania—are of a more severe and pathological nature. I do not intend to psychologize the way nations and their representatives deal with and construct their history, but I contend that one can learn from the psychoanalytic studies of memory which routes and detours memory can take to circumvent, confront, and adapt to conflicts. Like a neurotic individual who conceals disturbing ideas behind less threatening thoughts, at a wider level there have been moments in history when entrenched sacred ideas suddenly seemed obsolete, or at most contradictory to the emerging belief system. For instance, with the onset of the period of artistic production we now call the Renaissance, painters and sculptors sought new ways of imbuing human bodies with the kind of reverential attitude that had hitherto been the reserve of religious figures. Renaissance artists saw themselves confronted with the task of shifting the focus from staged supernatural events to more mundane, everyday situations, without making these appear trivial or incongruous. Conversely, during times where the change from one belief system to another was more abrupt and occasionally more violent, the preservation of the previous ideas and type of imagery was deemed threatening to the new system. Residues of the old system were expected to be eradicated. An example of the shift underway is the style of the Rococo, which expressed the luxury and playful lavishness that so characterized the reign of Louis XIV. The subsequent French Revolution provoked a violent reaction against any traces of the Rococo, and art in all its forms attempted a return to Classical Antiquity, and with it to the demand for linear forms, clear outlines, and muted contrasts in colors in a bid to abolish all traces of the former frivolity. Thus, in contrast to the Renaissance painters who reworked religious ideas into a new secular imagery, the French Neoclassicist painters had to repudiate their Rococo heritage and submit to the politico-aesthetic guidelines of the Académie and the incoming Revolutionary government.

As noted earlier, there is no single explanation for Manet's choice of quotes from the past in his works, nor can the stratified meanings therein be analyzed without a prior analysis of the memorial process he employed in weaving together these various associations. To examine the artist's remembrance of the past, we must locate his practice both within the larger context of the tradition of painting as a whole, and within the polemical environment out of which Manet's work itself grew. It is my contention that the psychoanalytic studies of memory can illuminate the different mechanisms of remembrance applied by painters, and, at the same time, they can bring into sharper focus the ideological processes served by these remembrances. In some sense, a painting functions like a sign whose meaning is to be interpreted by locating its position in the context and chain of surrounding paintings. Here, T. S. Eliot's theory of tradition comes to mind again, as he argues that a new idea must both preserve and transcend tradition. As Taiana notes:

> In Eliot's quotational style, tradition is superseded, at once both abolished and preserved—*Aufhebung* in Hegel's terminology, meaning "to lift up–retain–suppress"—, the quotation sublating the tradition by simultaneous affirmation and negation […].[33]

Ricoeur, in addition, made the following observation:

> This memory is treated as a construction "after the fact," cast back into childhood. It serves as a link to an entire series of "translations" which reveal nothing other than the capacity for substituting

33 Taiana 2022: 15.

> one for another the figures of fantasy, not to mention the dream, mythical, or literary modality of the figures.[34]

In his endeavor to understand the artistic heritage at his feet, and to define himself as a new link to this heritage, Manet quoted those masters who, like him, were trapped in the dilemma of transforming opposing worldviews into an imagery capable of harmonizing antithetical ideas. Manet found himself embroiled in the nineteenth-century crisis between modernity and the Classical/Romanticist tradition. The acceleration of the Industrial Revolution and the gradual decline of the Second Empire saw an intelligentsia calling for scientific, positivistic methods in the arts to truthfully represent the contemporary scene, without traditional mythologizing techniques, which idealized and falsified everyday reality. At the same time, however, this demand was opposed by a bourgeois public and a bourgeois emperor who enjoyed the enormous economic prosperity made possible by industrial and scientific advances,[35] but who mixed their reverence for science with a longing for the past glory of France. The bourgeois' self-divided stance of welcoming the prosperity and capitalism while longing for the stability of ancient institutions and classical heroes is one of the most common characteristics of the French middle class. As Emmanuel Berl remarked in his memoirs:

> I understood very quickly that the bourgeoisie was one thing and capitalism another. The capitalist wants to undertake, to earn, to expand his business, to change the world. Although he derives from the bourgeoisie, he is in no way in agreement with it. The French bourgeois [...] is much more afraid of losing what he has than of enriching himself, and if he wants to possess more, he hopes to do so more from a spirit of saving than through his imagination. For many years, the French bourgeois distrusted investments in industry and distrusts them even today. He wants social respect much more than wealth, which in any case he sees only as a means of obtaining that respect.[36]

---

34 Ricoeur 1976: 28.

35 Theodore Zeldin reports that during the Second Empire the income of the French industry rose by 73% and that of the French agriculture by 58%. See Zeldin 1973: 91.

36 Berl 1976: 167 (author's translation).

Elsewhere, the Hungarian art historian Arnold Hauser describes the bourgeois public as "the newly rich, who are wealthy enough to want to shine, but not old enough to shine without ostentation […]. They imitate Roman palaces and the castles on the Loire, Pompeian atriums, baroque salons […]."[37] Never in the history of art had the gap between the public's taste and the painters' output been as wide as it was during the period between 1830 and 1870. The values once shared between the public and the artists had collapsed: people now expected art to idealize and exalt their lifestyle, something that would transport them to a higher level. Instead, the avant-garde artists depicted the present reality in all its shades and configurations, good and bad. Manet's teacher, Thomas Couture, had articulated their conflict in his writings and seminars, but never succeeded in transferring his theories to his art, which instead of subverting bourgeois self-importance tended to substantiate their sense of grandiosity. Initially, it was Gustave Courbet (1819–1877) who openly broke with the Romanticist/Classical tradition. Single-handedly, Courbet deliberately violated all the rules determining what a historical painting was supposed to represent. Ingres, a staunch defender of Jacques-Louis David and leader of the Neoclassicist movement, reiterated those rules for nineteenth-century painting: modern painters would call themselves "history painters," and Courbet felt it essential to demolish this claim. "A history painter is one who represents heroic deeds, and such deeds are only to be found in the history of the Greeks and the Romans; and it is through them that the artist can display his skill in painting nudes and draperies […]."[38]

Unlike Couture—who, even if in a partially mocking manner, still used the conventions of historical paintings by portraying the Romans performing unheroic deeds—, Courbet abolished the Roman and Greek settings altogether. Instead, he went further and portrayed his contemporaries in natural settings and poses. Moreover, his preferred subjects no longer were the rich and prominent figures of his time, but the ordinary people of his day—the rag-pickers, peasants, and

37 Hauser 1959: 62–63.

38 Ingres, quoted in Letheve 1972: 63.

stonebreakers. In this way, as the most prominent representative of the French Realist School, Courbet clashed directly with the painters of the Académie, and with every painting he exhibited he challenged their corseted guidelines anew. He wholeheartedly embraced the Realist battle-cry "Il faut être de son temps!" ("You must be of your own time!"). Unlike the classical historical painters, such as David, Greuze, and Ingres—who portrayed historical events not as real actions, but as they might have transpired under the most idealized circumstances—, the duty of the Realists was to paint only what they personally had witnessed or experienced, "without any alteration and without any conventional response or aesthetic affectation."[39] Just how seriously they took their obligation can be deduced from their scrupulous notation of the minutest details in the scenes they represented. In their revolt against the traditional conventions of the Académie, the Realists even proclaimed that having no formal education was a positive asset for a painter. In order to depict ordinary life truthfully and sincerely, the Realist was advised to rid himself of all traditional aesthetic conventions and preconceptions, so as to keep his vision free from distortion of any kind. The art critic and novelist Champfleury described the difficult process of making a *tabula rasa* of his mind. In the preface to his 1852 *Contes domestiques*, he writes:

> What I see in my head descends into my pen, and becomes what I have seen. The method is simple, within anybody's reach. But how much time is necessary to get rid of memories, imitations, the milieu in which one lives, and to rediscover one's own nature.[40]

It is paradoxical that Courbet, the rebel who was so committed to eliminating the past and jettisoning the shackles of convention, ultimately produced an oeuvre redolent of these same conventions, whereas Manet's way of rebelling against conventions deliberately involved the past. Although Courbet engendered a vibrant new subject matter—, depicting ordinary people engaged in everyday

39 Nochlin 1971: 36.

40 Champfleury, quoted in Nochlin 1971: 38–39.

activities—he nonetheless continued to foster the moral virtues of traditional history painting. And although he radicalized the genre's subject matter and was keen not to sentimentalize the virtues of the common people, his paintings were still inscribed within a moralistic convention. By making the peasants, workers, and beggars the central subjects of his canvases, Courbet not only celebrated a return to Nature, but also exposed the hypocrisy of the glittering urban milieu, which sought its glory in Antiquity and ignored the virtues (and plight) of the oppressed. Notably, Courbet was so grounded in the Realist movement and so taken by his mission as a socialist artist that he never experienced the ambiguities and crises that Manet underwent. Courbet did not fall into the same nineteenth-century crisis between modernity and tradition as the one Manet found himself entangled in. Courbet did not use the past as a means of understanding the present, nor to illuminate the present within the past; instead, he reacted more radically to conventions by rebelling against them rather than by finding meaning in them. However, through this blatant rebellion against tradition, Courbet provided an important stepping stone for Manet's subsequent works.

Unlike Courbet, who could boldly attack the conventions of the French Académie and all that it stood for, Manet embarked upon a more cautious, yet, ultimately, more revolutionary path. Instead of openly rejecting all the mythological and allegorical subject matters, he first questioned what function they had served for the traditional painters. His journey through the traditional Masters opened up a dialogue with past artists who had drawn from ancient myths as a means of fusing religious imagery with secular ideas. Renaissance culture conveyed a greater awareness of the history of human achievements and rewrote its own history, no longer according to the scheme of divine salvation, but in terms of human historical events. This groundbreaking transition heralded a greater emphasis on the human figure, prompting artists to honor particular individuals for their achievements and portray them in their full secular dignity. Moreover, instead of divorcing the spiritual world from the natural world—and continuing to subject the latter to the former—the two realms were merged into one. Everyday reality could thus be imbued with spiritual

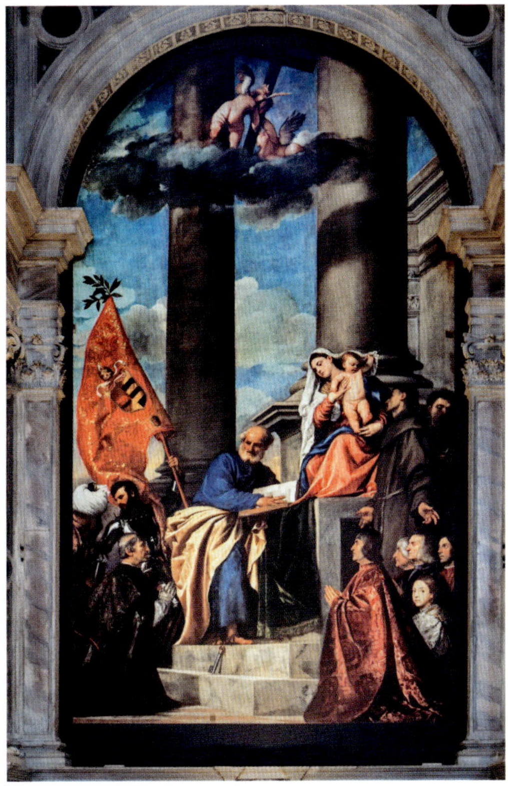

Plate 41: Titian, *Madonna with Saints and Members of the Pesaro Family* (1519–1526)

significance so that the physical universe below became the glowing reflection of the divine spirit above. This focal shift entailed a degree of *finesse*. How could artists celebrate human achievements without alienating the Church? How could they avoid the accusation of neo-paganism? The revival of Classical Antiquity during the Renaissance era addressed this quandary by providing writers and artists alike with a wide array of themes, within which they could address contemporary events. While the Classical forms had been largely divorced from the original Graeco-Roman content during the Middle Ages—whereby ancient myths were portrayed as allegories of Christian precepts for the instruction of the illiterate masses—the Renaissance scholars rejoined the Classical form and subject matter into an accessible whole. The new interchangeability of religious imagery that enabled artists to draw equally upon the iconography of the Virgin Mary and that of the goddess Venus, provided an enormous repertoire of possible associations between myth and religion. By the Late Renaissance, however, some of the characteristic poses derived from mythology were used to depict common individuals in the attitudes of pagan divinities. Curiously enough, this increased humanization of mythological themes did not eradicate the Christian imagery from which it had evolved: on the contrary, the Late Renaissance painter could simultaneously evoke the three different registers of religion, mythology, and everyday aristocratic reality, and play upon these interdependent associations. Titian, whom Manet quotes directly in *Olympia*, was a master at substituting and exchanging one symbolic language for another. Titian's *Madonna with Saints and Members of the Pesaro Family* (1519–1526) **[Plate 41]** illustrates how a painting can function both as homage to the Virgin and as a group portrait of one of the richest families of the Venetian Republic. The figures, young and old, kneeling at the side of the altar of the

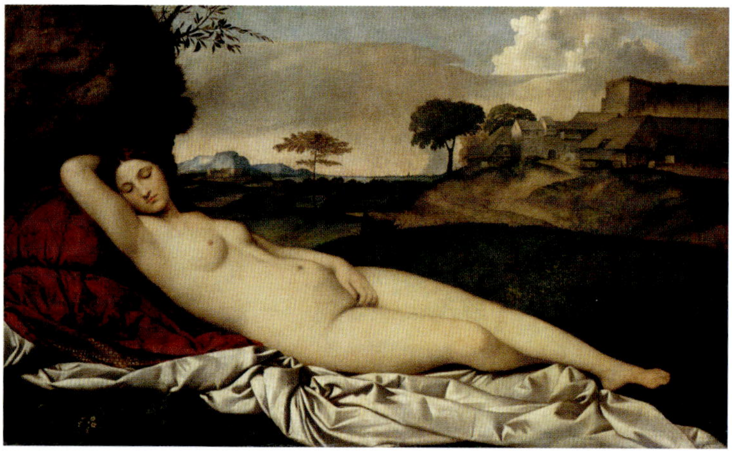

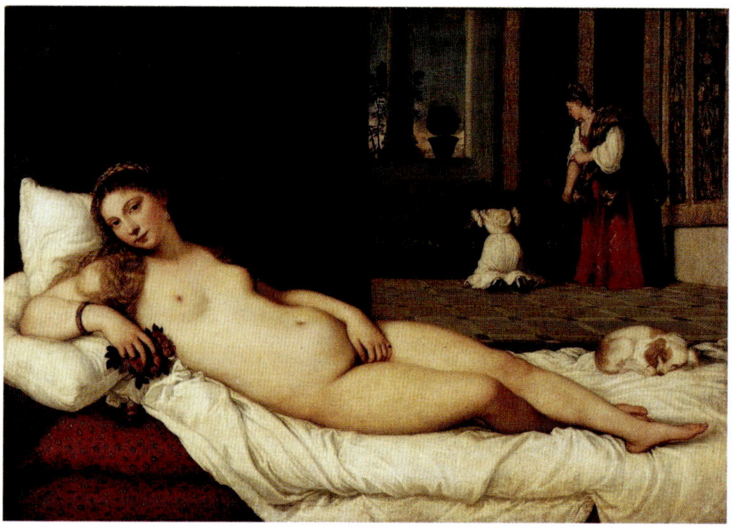

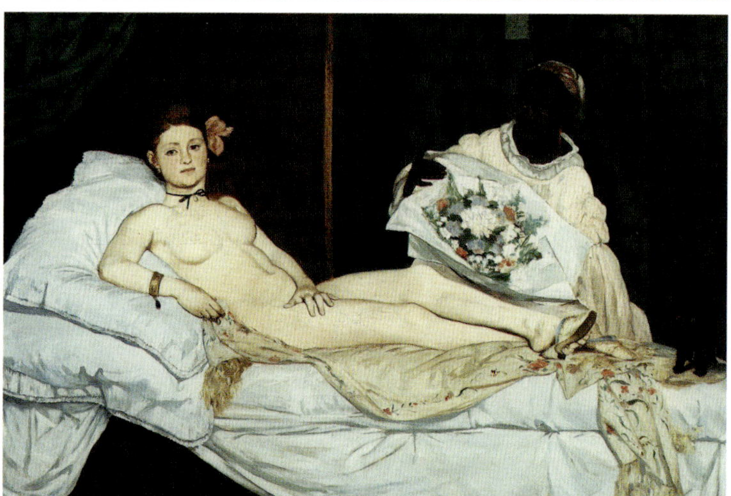

Madonna, are all members of the Pesaro family, Titian's patrons. Unlike medieval artists, who drew from the ancient repertory of poses, gestures and expressions and merely changed the identity of their sources, Titian could even transform a wealthy Venetian merchant into an Apostle, now, without being accused of blasphemy.

We should also note that Titian's barely disguised portrait is firmly grounded in details specific to the Venetian Republic (i.e., the banner bearing the family insignia) and the Pesaro family, one of whose members rather knowingly returns the gaze of the spectator. Never before were secular and human figures allowed to co-exist harmoniously together without offending the Christian faith. In his *Venus of Urbino,* Titian once again freely interleaves the religious and the human realms, responding to the commission of the young Guidobaldo, son of the future Duke of Urbino, to portray his mistress. The American art historian Theodore Reff reports the story that Titian's mistress, the Duchess of Este, persuaded the prince's lover to recline completely naked on a sofa, emulating the divine Venus. We cannot determine whether it was the model who inspired this pose, or if Titian intended to "domesticate" the celestial Venus as an earthly woman of the court. Any analysis of Manet's *Olympia* must take into account that Titian himself borrowed both overall composition and details from his teacher Giorgione, whose *Sleeping Venus* dates around 1510 **[Plate 42]**. If we compare Giorgione's supine figure with Titian's *Venus of Urbino* (1538) **[Plate 6]** and Manet's *Olympia* (1863) **[Plate 5]**, the striking variations of each artist's version of the same motif are keenly indicative of the changing attitudes of their day. In Giorgione's painting, Venus is depicted sleeping in a garden which, according to the Roman myth, was "the *numen* of gardens— gardens where food and herbs were grown as well as flowers."[41] The symbolism of fertility, figured in the icons of flowers, food and herbs, was also a symbolism that was attached to the Virgin Mary. "The medieval Mirror of Man's Salvation calls the Virgin the walled garden containing all fragrant spices and pleasant fruits whose door-keeper is the true God."[42] The

page 158:
Plate 42: Giorgione, *Sleeping Venus* (1510)
Plate 6: Titian, *Venus of Urbino* (1538)
Plate 5: Édouard Manet, *Olympia* (1863)

41 Stapleton 1978: 207 (emphasis in the original).
42 Stapleton 1978: 265.

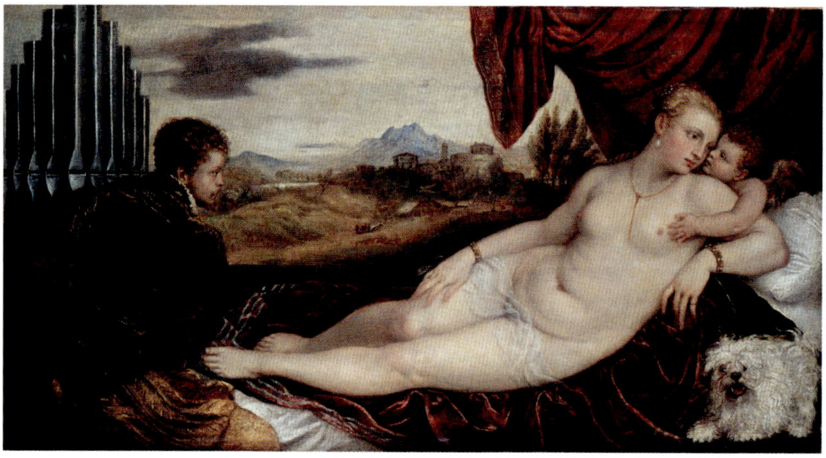

Plate 43: Titian, *Venus with the Organ Player* (1550)

impression one gathers is that Giorgione's Venus was secured under the benevolent gaze of God, so distant and peaceful does she seem to recline in the idyllic landscape. At any event, placing a classical Venus in a landscape was a novel approach which, as Fritz Saxl points out, showed "an inner incongruity of the parts." "Giorgione painted the sacred sleeping goddess lying like a beautiful marble which has by chance been brought into a modern landscape."[43] By disassociating the classical Venus from the landscape in which she looks like a stranger, Giorgione was perhaps one of the first artists to draw attention to the fact that it was the painter's liberty to bring together diverse elements that had hitherto been rigidly divided into separate categories. This, as we shall see subsequently, constitutes a characteristic of Manet's paintings in which themes and figures are brought together apparently at random, not because they are commonly linked, but because the artist wished to do so for his own purposes. The second striking element in the *Sleeping Venus* is the omission of the customary bystander. The "typical" Venus composition includes an Adonis or Cupid gazing in adoration, such as in Titian's *Venus with the Organ Player* (1550) **[Plate 43]**, whereas in the *Sleeping Venus,* it is the spectator who plays this role. While this Venus offers the spectator the visual delight of contemplating her nude marbled body, she denies

43 Saxl 1970: 85 + 78.

any direct exchange with her admirers. The omission of the conventional male voyeur—a role accorded to the spectator in this case—is a second feature that both Titian and Manet maintained in their re-interpretations of Giorgione's *Sleeping Venus*. Curiously enough, they also reiterated three particular details of striking incongruity in Giorgione's painting: first, he places his Venus upon a lavish white drapery—characteristic of Classical statuary—and lets her arm and head rest upon two pillows of an arresting crimson that suggests a decisively earthly origin. Furthermore, her left hand tenderly covers her pubis—a gesture known as "Venus pudica"—suggesting that this Venus is not merely a token of ethereal beauty, but instead a mortal, a woman like any other with feelings of both desire and modesty.

As noted earlier, both Titian and Manet preserved the overall composition and reclining pose of Giorgione's *Sleeping Venus*. But even more interestingly, they both paid particular attention to those three details which marked the crucial break between a mythological and a realist representation, between Venus's celestial and her earthly origins. Titian clearly understood Giorgione's implicit suggestion of a real figure elevated by an antique ideal and even carried it further in his *Venus of Urbino*. The title of the painting already suggests that this Venus is not an imaginary figure, but that she can be found living at the ducal palace of Urbino. Venus has been brought indoors, away from the numen of the garden, and is now firmly located in the midst of the splendor of the Urbino court. The idyllic realm whence she originated is alluded to in the scenery visible through the window. But instead of the hamlet in the background of Giorgione's *Sleeping Venus*, we see two female figures, possibly servants of the ducal household. And, of course, most strikingly, Venus is no longer asleep but awake, returning the gaze of her beholder. Unlike Giorgione's *Venus*, whose eroticism emerges from her innocent sleeping state, the Urbino *Venus* seems to entice the beholder, her left hand grazing her pubic region, the other clutching a bouquet of faded red roses. Titian has retained the red and white palette of Giorgione's drapery and pillow upon which the sleeping Venus rests, but now the arm formerly supporting her head is used to prop up her body so that it turns fully toward the light. In this way, Titian reiterates Giorgione's suggestion of Venus's earthly origins, but expands this device to include the interior of the Palazzo Ducale. Here, Venus is a tangible pleasure-object—not so much for the spectator as for the patron in whose house she resides. Like the imagined God in Giorgione's *Sleeping Venus*, here the woman's patron is noticeably out of the picture, yet Titian includes sufficient details to imply that this beautiful woman is the duke's chattel. The presence of the two maids, one holding a gown that her mistress has perhaps just removed, the other kneeling in front of a trunk possibly searching for other garments, are strong reminders of the opulence of Venus's surroundings. If the two maids were not so set apart from the central figure of the reclining Venus, one might think they were discreetly turning their backs on their mistress. However, the arrangement gives the impression that Titian composed these two figures as a separate scene, as if the maids were in a different room and unaware of their mistress's seductive pose vis-à-vis the painter, leaving the spectator the only one aware that these two scenes are related. One can almost imagine the heavy green curtain behind her being drawn aside to reveal Duke Guidobaldo's private domestic life.

While Giorgione's implied divine presence meant his Venus could be safely alone, Titian included two figures from the ducal household to ensure a safe distance between the spectator and the duke's mistress; the dozing dog at Venus's feet is presumed to symbolize fidelity in contrast to the cat in Manet's *Olympia* which so notoriously stood for a symbol of wild sexuality. Titian's artful transfer of sleep from Venus herself to the dog resting at her feet may also hint at Titian's fidelity to his teacher Giorgione. The fact that Titian's Venus was no longer asleep but an alive and an awake human being signals a small step in the gradual secularization process by which the aristocracy inexorably gained greater power, wealth, and influence over the Church. And at a certain point, the private Venuses of the aristocracy simply bypassed the censorship of the Church. More than three hundred years would pass before Manet recaptured the *Venus of Urbino* for modern times. That's not to say that before Manet, no other painter had referenced Titian's work, but no-one had so specifically traced his depiction to the Venetian master's reclining nude. Why, one may ask, did Manet choose this particular painting over Titian's numerous other works? Just as Vecellio had acknowledged the radical iconographic changes Giorgione had evoked in his *Sleeping Venus*, so, three centuries later, Manet understood the breakthrough Titian had accomplished by "privatizing" a mythological figure without erasing its underlying symbolic code.

Thanks to Titian's genius, the *Venus of Urbino* could exist simultaneously as a seductive young woman and as a goddess descending from Mount Olympus. Both Giorgione and his pupil Titian had released Venus from her narrative constrictions and presented her as an object of beauty, a delight to be contemplated, rather than a distant figure destined to illustrate a myth. Titian relocated the mythological figure to a natural everyday setting with such striking authority. This breakthrough enabled later painters—from the Renaissance to the Baroque—to experiment more freely, which ultimately led to the complete humanization of the mythological and religious themes. While Giorgione still modeled his Venus upon Classical sculpture, and Titian clothed his human Venus in a delicate haze, a century later, Rubens no longer used either of these techniques to invoke a mythological aura. In his work, the natural world and the past realm of Classical myth and religious themes had become fully intertwined, enabling him to situate contemporary figures in the poses of Roman gods or Christian prophets. Rubens's figures no longer illustrated a remote mythological theme; instead, they enacted scenes for the enchantment of the contemporary spectator. In this progressive development, Classical myth increasingly lost its didactic value and was used largely as a pretext for the celebration of the human form.

In *Olympia*, Manet not only evokes Titian's *Venus of Urbino*, but also subtly includes the changes that had followed Titian's crucial breakthrough. It is as if Manet was tracing his historical origins back through the three hundred intervening years. Here is a moment where we can observe how Manet "put the dead to work" (to use Eliot's metaphor); he did not use his primordial source of the *Venus of Urbino* as a simple predecessor, but instead actively attempted to unlock the concealed meanings in the Urbino canvas, making them accessible to the present spectator.[44] Manet is therefore careful to include first the three details that inspired Titian's representation of Giorgione's *Sleeping Venus*. Manet copies more faithfully from Titian than did Titian from Giorgione the red couch and the white drapes on which the Olympian Venus is recumbent. The manner in which the drapes cover the couch is almost exactly replicated in *Olympia*—except for the important difference that the drapes wrapped around the Urbino Venus have been transformed into ordinary bedsheets, a detail which was considered especially scandalous by Manet's audience. The elegant davenport upon which Titian's Venus reclines, enveloped in the sculptured drapes reminiscent of those garments worn by Roman gods, has become an ordinary velvet couch upon whose "dirty linen" the modern Olympia presents herself. The right arm—on which the Venus of Urbino leans her head—stiffly serves Olympia to prop up her body. What Giorgione and Titian had only intimated when they depicted Venus's left hand coyly covering her intimate parts is made explicit by Olympia's insistent gesture of partially hiding her genitalia while, at the same time, drawing attention towards them. "The hand is *shamelessly flexed*, it is *improper*, it is *in the form of a toad*, it is *dirty*, it is in a state of *contraction*. It comes to stand for the way Olympia's whole body is disobedient: the hand is the sign of the unyielding, the un-relaxed [...]."[45]

While Olympia knows what she possesses and to what she deliberately and firmly precludes access, the Venus of Urbino cannot claim that level of self-awareness, and therefore can only coyly conceal. She knows and does not know, since her gaze reveals what her hand barely hides. Like the sleeping dog at her feet, Titian's *Venus* can display her naked body trustfully and intimately to the eyes of her beholder, so securely is she enframed by the palace grounds for whose owner this portrait is intended. Moreover, the mythological conventions permit the young mistress to take up the position of Venus and to display within this fictitious frame her sensuous love, while repressing her sexuality.

---

44 See Taiana 2022 on Eliot: 203.

45 Clark 1980: 25 (emphasis in the original).

Conversely, Manet's Olympia makes no attempt to disguise her sexuality behind the pretension of a sensuous love. Her body is the site of carnal knowledge, and it is she who knows and controls what her naked body can arouse in the spectator. She does not seduce, she does not deceive. Even the cat knows that she is fully awake and conscious, as does the servant who fixes her gaze upon her recumbent mistress. The green curtain has finally fallen, captivating the spectator in Olympia's private boudoir. "No conventional generalizations of face or figure mitigated the disconcerting surprise of seeing a young modern woman in a situation few ladies and gentlemen could publicly acknowledge."[46]

In contrast to the Venus figure in the Urbino canvas, who reclines indolently on her davenport, at ease with her nudity, Manet's Olympia props herself up stiffly, tense and self-conscious in her nakedness. As many critics have observed, Olympia is not a nude, she is naked; her Japanese shawl and little slippers reveal that Olympia has undressed herself for the visual consumption by both her spectator outside the painting and her next customer inside the canvas, a figure whose presence is signaled by the bouquet of flowers held by her servant. While Titian securely enframes his Venus in the domestic interior of the Palazzo Ducale, Manet closes off the view, leaving the observer in suspension about the scene behind the green curtain. Whereas the symbolic "accessories," like the small bouquet of fading flowers, the waving curly hair, the bracelet and the one pearl earring heighten the sensual enticement in Titian's painting, the symbolism in *Olympia* is undermined and parodied by its overabundance. The black cat symbolizing female sexuality, promiscuity and evil powers, while the black servant (a popular nineteenth-century image of uninhibited and passionate love) and the orchid in her hair—a flower widely believed to excite lust and guarantee potency—oversaturate a painting which so openly displays what other paintings in the nineteenth century only alluded to through the use of such symbolic metaphors of eroticism. Meyer Schapiro's observation about *Le Déjeuner sur l'herbe* applies to *Olympia* as well: "Manet's

46 Hamilton 1969: 68.

painting does not simply translate Giorgione's and Raphael's imagery into modern clothes; the meaning of clothes and nakedness as signs has changed."[47] Thus, a comparison of Titian's *Venus of Urbino* with Manet's *Olympia* not only alerts the spectator to the painting's artistic origins, but it also points towards the multiplicity of meanings emanating from a depiction of a nude woman. A juxtaposition of the two paintings confronts spectators with the question of how they can be so charmed by the Venetian painting, yet be so disconcerted by the Parisian work, since the same basic subject matter is represented in both. How different is the mistress of a prince from a Parisian courtesan? Both are an item of property for others' delectation (including the viewer, male or female). The comparison compels us to re-evaluate not only the indignant response to *Olympia* but also the ready approval of the *Venus of Urbino*. Manet's reinterpretation of Titian's work forces contemporary spectators to see the Venetian Venus in a new light. The past is no longer conveniently buried and divorced from the present: Manet's new articulation of the subject has re-appropriated the painting for the contemporary audience. "Manet's strategy closely resembles the psychoanalytic task which also aims at not simply reviving unearthed buried memories, but at reviving exchanges with the past."[48]

This kind of re-articulation contains parallels to the process mentioned earlier, namely Freud's concept of *Nachträglichkeit*, which was somewhat inadequately translated by Alix Strachey as "deferred action." Over the last thirty years, the literature on *Nachträglichkeit* has gained considerable traction in psychoanalytic studies. It was Jacques Lacan who reclaimed the term from obscurity in the 1950s, and it was he who re-translated it as *après-coup*. By returning to Freud's original *Project* of 1895, in which he explains for the first time the dynamics of *Nachträglichkeit*, Lacan emphasizes the complex process of re-signification, of a retroactive modification in the human psyche. Freud's paper described a process whereby a traumatic event is not initially perceived as such until a later (deferred) experience

47 Schapiro 1978: 9.

48 See also Anzieu 1970: 70.

attaches a new meaning to the earlier event. In other words, the subject only *retroactively* interpreted the initial experience as traumatic when it had not experienced it as such during the initial occurrence. For instance, a child may not perceive the father's molestation as traumatic until she reaches adolescence, at which point she becomes aware of the sexual underpinnings of the earlier event only in retrospect. Put simply, the trauma only materializes retroactively. House explains this in the following way: "When memories, previously not seen in the light of sexuality, are abruptly endowed with the sexual knowledge that comes with puberty, it *may* result in repression and then the repressed content *may* create (return as) symptoms."[49] Basically, "[i]t's not what happened afterwards which is modified, but everything which went on before. We have a retroactive effect—*nachträglich*, as Freud calls it—specific to the structure of symbolic memory, in other words to the function of remembering."[50] The concept and use of *Nachträglichkeit* has evolved significantly over the last few decades and is now no longer associated so tightly with the experience of trauma. Instead, it has taken up an important place in the field of psychoanalysis as a concept that speaks against the linearity of time—the arrow of time—as opposed to Freud's other temporal model, his developmental stage theory. Meanwhile *Nachträglichkeit* has come to mean more the "recontextualization and re-signification" of memories.

Given its expanded signification, we may easily transfer the idea of *Nachträglichkeit* or *après-coup* to the method which Manet employed when he engaged the past with the present, transforming the spectator's perception of the present through their prior knowledge of the past. An exchange between the beautiful Venetian courtesan is revised with the now new impression of *Olympia*. The frank sexuality of Manet's reclining woman invests her Urbino counterpart with a new dynamic, she no longer serves as a locus of idealized titillation, instead, the implicit voyeurism of the *Venus of Urbino* is made explicit in *Olympia*, thereby unveiling the hypocrisy of bourgeois prudery.

---

49 House/Slotnick 2015: 689 (emphasis in the original).

50 Lacan 1955: 185 (emphasis in the original).

It was Jean Laplanche who further developed the idea of *Nachträglichkeit* by emphasizing the bi-directionality of the movement. *Nachträglichkeit* does not only reverse the arrow of time, but also points forwards and holds the past and present in a constant dialogue and movement. The past is no longer what it was, and the present is no longer the present, both are mutually transformed by one another at the same time.[51]

Comparing the *Venus of Urbino* against Manet's vision somewhat mitigates what Paul Valéry called "a sacred horror" in front of "the cold and naked *Olympia*, that monster of banal sensuality, ministered to by a negress."[52] This retroactive view of Titian's opus does not mean that the modern spectator might be held in a more enlightened position than a Renaissance viewer of the day, who might likewise have remarked upon the overt sensuality and sexuality of the Venetian beauty. Manet's reinterpretation of Titian was not intended to expose the Renaissance view as ignorant of the sexual overtones present in the *Venus of Urbino*.

On the contrary, to my mind Manet wanted to underscore the radical daring of Titian, who stretched the mythological framework to its limits by displaying the nude mistress of an Italian prince in the pose of the classical goddess Venus. Although we have no reliable records of the general reaction of contemporaries to the *Venus of Urbino*, it is evident that subsequent painters comprehended Titian's audacity, since many continued to explore, traverse, and ultimately condense the framework of mythological depictions. At the same time, Manet seems to willfully provoke his contemporaries to rethink Titian's painting, and thus provoke a direct confrontation with the *grandes machines* favored by the French bourgeoisie and the academic Salons. Now, the antiquated mythological allusions and representations of Classical subjects rife among the Académie's scions and acolytes seemed all the more ludicrous when compared with a genuine Renaissance work. Manet's remembrance of the *Venus of Urbino*—a work that had signaled the gradual decline of

51 For more detailed discussion see House/Slotnick 2015.

52 Valéry 1960: 109.

allegorical painting—underlined how moribund the mythological and religious schemata had become when it came to depiction the nineteenth-century society. This process of actively shifting between the present and the past, re-evaluating the past in light of the present and the present under the glare of the past, is what makes Manet the quintessential psychoanalytic painter.

As Karl Marx writes:

> Man makes his own history, but he does not make it out of the whole cloth; he does not make it out of conditions chosen by himself, but out of such as he finds close at hand. The tradition of all past generations weighs like an alp upon the brain of the living. At the very time when men appear engaged in revolutionizing things and themselves, in bringing about what never was before, at such very epochs of revolutionary crises do they anxiously conjure up into their service the spirits of the past, assume their names, their battle cries, their costumes to enact a new historic scene in such time-honored disguise and with such borrowed language.[53]

When all is said and done, the references to Giorgione's *Sleeping Venus* and Titian's *Venus of Urbino* do not complete the puzzle that is posed by *Olympia*.

A curious thing happens: once a quotation is found for Manet's painting, other pieces begin to fall into line—Rubens's *The Toilet of Venus*, Correggio's *Jupiter and Io*, Canova's *Pauline Bonaparte* (1805–1808) **[Plate 44]**, Ingres's *La Grande Odalisque* (1814) **[Plate 45]**, Goya's *La maja desnuda* (1797-1800) **[Plate 46]**, and not least Couture's *Les Romains de la décadence*—they are all drawn into the pattern of associations. In contrast to Michael Fried, who suggested that Manet's remembrance of traditional Masters was intended to establish his affiliation with the "authentic" French painting tradition and thereby demonstrate the "internationalism or, better, the *universality* of his own painting,"[54] I propose a different path, not so much to refute Fried's approach as to offer an alternative. I believe that Manet's use of citations from

---

53 Marx 1907: 5

54 Fried 1984: 526.

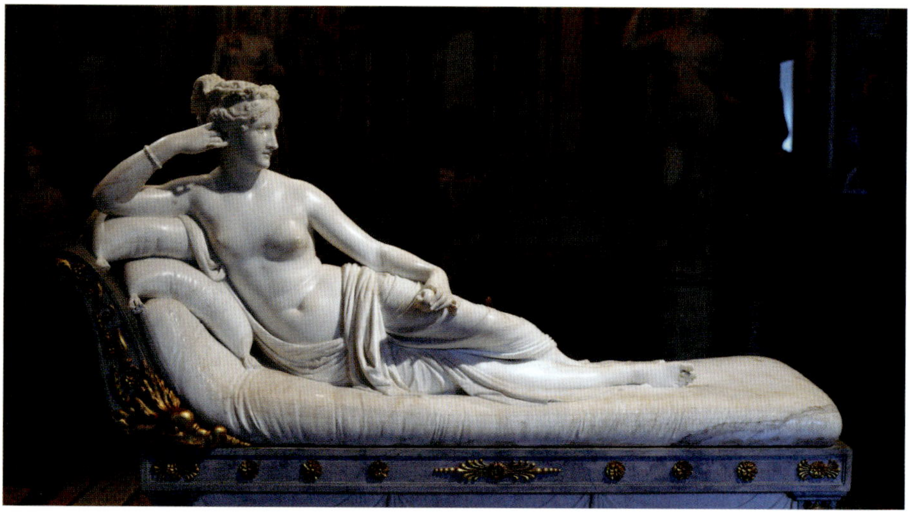

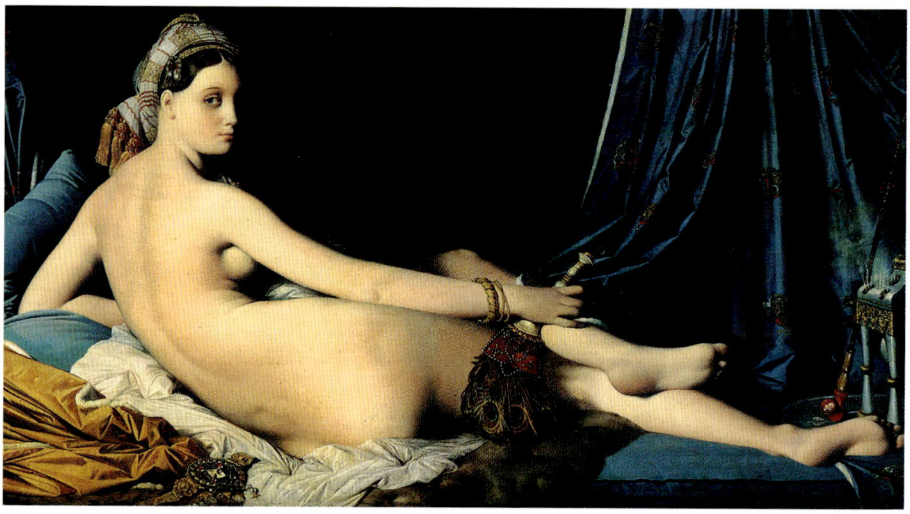

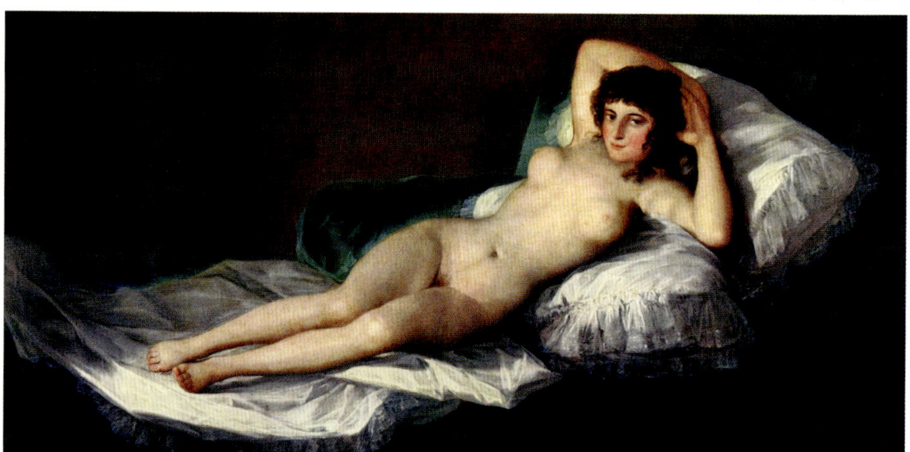

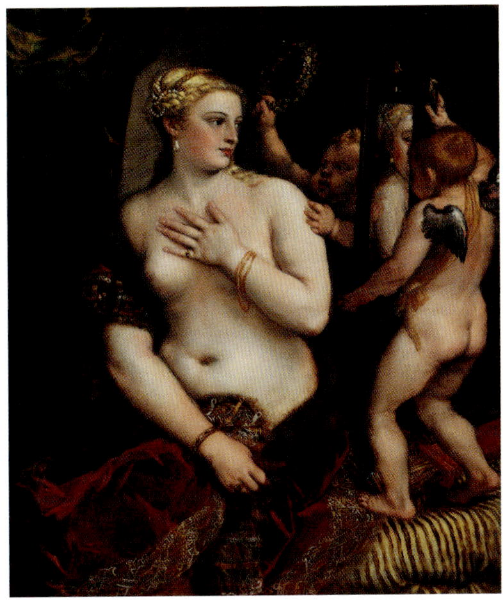

traditional painters served manifold purposes and was not based upon a single, overarching intention. His habit of referencing past works was aimed at restoring a memory process that had been repressed with the re-emergence of Classicism in the seventeenth century under Poussin, and again in the eighteenth century with the revival of Neoclassical art under Jean-Jacques David. Throughout the Renaissance and the Baroque, artists freely borrowed themes, compositions, details, gestures, and techniques from one another without ever being accused of plagiarism. Raphael had "absorbed" Michelangelo's style. Titian, as we have just seen borrowed themes and compositions from his teacher Giorgione. And Rubens quoted freely and frequently from Titian throughout his career. This practice of cross-referencing was widely accepted until the nineteenth and twentieth centuries, in part because the Renaissance and the Baroque painters were still bound by Christian iconography in illustrating episodes from the Old Testament, and by the Renaissance catalogues of gestures and poses deemed appropriate for depicting Classical myths. Therefore, painters had a more limited range of subject matter to transfer to the canvas. With the increasing wealth and power of the aristocracy and the merchant classes, however, the painter's scope of themes also expanded to encompass portraits of monarchs, courtiers, merchants, and famous cultural figures. As a result, the change in patronage exerted a direct influence upon the variety of themes considered permissible.

Plate 47:
Titian,
Venus with a Mirror
(1555–1560)

Throughout these historical changes, painters regarded their works as issuing from an evolutionary process in which artists attempted to understand how religious or mythological scenes could be contextualized in their own epoch. Of course, the painters would look to their predecessors to learn how they had resolved a particular task. If we compare, for instance, Titian's *Venus with a Mirror* (1555–1560) [**Plate 47**] with Rubens's *The Toilet of Venus* (1641–1615), we immediately notice how Rubens adapted the same theme to his own cultural environment.

page 170: **Plate 44:**
Antonio Canova,
Pauline Bonaparte
(1805–1808)
Plate 45:
Jean-Auguste-Dominique Ingres,
La Grande Odalisque
(1814)
Plate 46:
Francisco de Goya,
La maja desnuda
(1797–1800)

A Dutch model has taken the place of the Venetian beauty, and the two cupids have been transformed into a black servant and a male figure with wings. The dream-like intimacy of Titian's *Venus with a Mirror* has been reset into a stark naturalistic atmosphere in Rubens's painting. One consequence of this "domestication" of traditional iconography was the greater liberty given to the individual artists to insert their own idiosyncratic mark upon their paintings and to elicit a new range of emotional responses in the beholders, whether sanctioned or not by the religious or mythological precedents. However, with the triumph of Classicism, the mode of searching the world for resemblances and the aesthetic practice of finding inspiration in echoing the art of works by diverse masters and themes was abandoned:

> [...] it is Classical thought excluding resemblance as the fundamental experience and primary form of knowledge, denouncing it as a confused mixture that must be analysed in terms of identity, difference, measurement, and order. [...] comparison became a function of order; and, lastly, comparison ceased to fulfil the function of revealing how the world is ordered, since it was now accomplished according to the order laid down by thought, progressing naturally from the simple to the complex.[55]

This change in self-understanding of art history was signaled by Nicolas Poussin, the most famous representative of French Classicism. While Poussin was initially influenced by Titian's work and composed his paintings in a Venetian style which was playfully suggestive and sensuous, he gradually distanced himself from the Venetian school, arguing for a more disciplined and intellectual approach. He instituted the term "historical painting" and laid down the rules for this new order:

> The idea of beauty only descends into a subject matter if it is prepared with the minutest care. This preparation consists of three things: order, mode, and space or form. The order signifies the distance between parts, the mode is relative to quantity, and the form consists of lines and colors.[56]

---

55 Foucault 1973: 52 + 54.

56 Poussin, quoted in Hermann 1964: 171–172 (author's translation). "L'idée de beauté ne descend pas dans la matière qu'elle n'y soit préparée le plus possible.

In addition to such precise rules for the structure of a given work, Poussin also outlined the themes to be depicted by Classicist artists:

> The highest aim of painting [...] is to represent noble and serious human actions. These must be shown in a logical and orderly way—not as they really happened, but as they would have happened if nature were perfect. To this end, the artist must strive for the general and typical; appealing to the mind rather than the senses, he should suppress such trivialities as glowing color, and stress form and composition. In a good picture, the beholder must be able to "read" the exact emotions of each figure, and relate them to the given event.[57]

The views expounded by Poussin were later institutionalized by the Académie, which was founded by Colbert and Le Brun in 1666 and carried out Poussin's rationalistic extremes by devising methods for tabulating the merits of past and present artists. Artists of Antiquity received the highest marks, followed by Michelangelo, Raphael and their schools, who in turn were followed by Poussin and the Venetians, who overemphasized color; the Dutch and the Flemish, who violated both the rules of subject matter and of logical composition, were ranked lowest. This deliberate decision to institutionalize an ideal of Classical art channeled memory into precise and predetermined paths, thus severing the multiple associative paths upon which memory had embarked during Renaissance and Baroque. These strict categories forbade depictions of contemporary events, since only Roman and Greek heroic deeds were deemed worthy of illustration. After a century of emotional exaltation, art was brought back under the authority of moralistic thought.

> So signs are now set free from that teeming world throughout which the Renaissance had distributed them. They are lodged henceforth within the confines of representation, in the interstices of ideas, in that

---

Cette préparation consiste en trois choses: l'ordre, le mode et l'espèce ou forme. L'ordre signifie l'intervalle des parties, le mode est à la quantité, la forme consiste dans les lignes et les couleurs."

57 Janson 1973: 441.

life while incorporating elements of Classical mythology. The lightness and frivolity so characteristic of Watteau's work posited a direct denial of the rational and strict composition of the Poussinesque style. Instead of depicting noble, ancient deeds, Watteau captured scenes of elegant entertainments cherished by the French aristocratic society.

The work of Watteau signaled a shift in French art and society. After the death of Louis XIV, the aristocracy had moved out from beeing under the immediate surveillance of the royal court, leaving Versailles for Paris, where they in turn established their own private courts. The Rococo style incarnated the luxurious and frivolous life of the Parisian nobility, one that was also widely illustrated in the fanciful works of Jean-Honoré Fragonard. With the approach of the French Revolution, however, this style of painting was increasingly subject to stern criticism, or ignored entirely. Linked as it was to celebrating the aristocracy's worldview, Rococo art was despised by the Revolutionary aestheticians as epitomizing all the vices of the nobility against which the French bourgeoisie and proletariat had risen in 1789. Once again, it was the emotional exuberance and playfulness of a previous tradition against which the representatives of the Neoclassical school reacted. Jacques-Louis David, an ardent Republican, called for a return to morality and virtue, and what art could fulfill this idea more effectively than the monuments of Antiquity?

With the disintegration of the Ancien Régime, a passionate desire to erase the old forms erupted, and everything that served as a reminder of feudalism was violently rejected.

> The new doctrine disapproved of baroque and rococo as the art of the ephemeral, stimulating fleeting impressions according to the inconstant whim of fashion. The new view wanted architecture to become an art of permanence once more and wanted man to recognize in that permanence not only the authority of simple and eternal geometrical forms but also the edict of a mind that had left its own massive mark upon things and their duration in time.[62]

62 Starobinski 1982: 76.

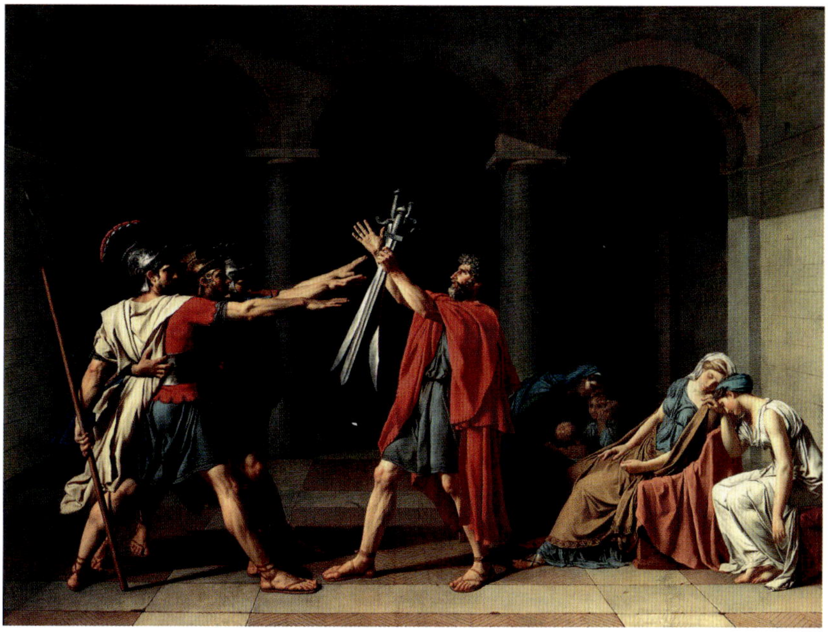

Plate 48:
Jacques-Louis David,
Oath of the Horatii (1784)

Both Poussin and David, a hundred years later, viewed the art of Antiquity as an exemplum to be copied, and as a source of inspiration and purification. Yet, while David utilized the art of Antiquity to lend permanence to the revolutionary ideas, Poussin simply draped the past over the present so that the latter was no longer visible. Whereas Poussin had disavowed his immediate predecessors and retreated into an imaginary realm of perfect forms, David did not repress the past of Baroque and Rococo: first he polemicized against it, and once his victory was assured, he proceeded as though the work of the artists belonging to those periods had never existed. With Poussin, the past was repudiated and denied, with David the mechanisms of repudiation and heroic idealization joined forces for the first time. While rejecting in the Baroque and Rococo, in truth David used a system of heroization akin to Renaissance techniques as a means of extoling the virtues of the French Revolution.

David's *Oath of the Horatii* (1784) **[Plate 48]**, for instance, depicts a scene in Rome in the early days of the Republic. In the presence of their father, the three Horatii swear to defend their fatherland. While David does not yet use living models to embody this scene and instead bases his figures on Roman statues, the message he wished to communicate through the *Oath of the Horatii* was clearly understood by his public. The terror and violence that had erupted after the Revolution threatened to alienate many of the very individuals who had helped shape the revolutionary movement. A symbol from the past was needed to exhort the citizens of the free Republic to remain loyal to their ideas.

> Some significant act was needed to mark the encounter between transient crowds and eternal principles, to seal the indissoluble bond which men contracted with one another [...]. An oath was such an act. It was a single act, a brief event, taking place in a fleeting moment [...].[63]

The return to Antiquity and the urge for a fresh beginning, for the rebirth of a new order, was transformed into nostalgia for the past. The past was not re-constructed to be transformed into what Loch calls "a livable future"; instead, it was re-enacted so that people began to live and think as if they were the late incarnations of Roman and Greek figures.[64] In other words, they became the Romans and Greeks of their time. David's *Madame Récamier* serves as a good example of an eighteenth-century woman who is portrayed as a Roman figure in the

---

63 Starobinski 1982: 101.

64 Jean Starobinski (1982) provides an excellent description of a "typical" Greek banquet given by a fashionable member of the Parisian society in 1788: "One day [in 1788] when I [Mme Vigée-Lebrun] had invited a dozen or fifteen people to come to that evening and hear a reading by the poet Lebrun, my brother, during my rest, read me a few pages from *The Travels of Anarcharsis*. When he came to the passage which describes a Greek dinner and explains how to make some of the sauces, he said, 'We ought to serve this to our guests tonight.' I at once sent for my cook and told her what I had in mind [...]. As I was expecting some very pretty women, I thought we would all dress up in Greek costume so as to give a surprise to M. de Vaudreuil and M. Botin, who weren't to arrive until ten o'clock. I could get all the clothes I needed from my studio, which was full of stuff I used to drape my models, and the comte de Parois, who lived in my house in the rue de Cléry, had a superb collection of Etruscan vases. [...] Then I put a big screen behind the chairs and covered it with a large drapery looped up at intervals as in the paintings of Poussin. [...] All was ready [...] when the first guest arrived [...]. All three ladies were metamorphosed into real Athenians." (Starobinski 1982: 270–271).

Pompeiian style. Modeling one's government and architecture after the Roman world vividly attests to the post-revolutionary desire to resurrect the vigor of Antiquity and the global puissance of the Roman Empire.

This enactment of Roman rituals brings to mind the observation Freud made in his paper *Remembering, Repeating and Working Through*: "[...] we may say that the patient does not *remember* anything of what he has forgotten and repressed, but *acts* it out. He reproduces it not as a memory but as an action; he *repeats* it, without, of course, knowing that he is repeating it."[65] Now, one may, of course, object that the Neoclassical period was fully conscious of the Classical traditions. Yet, I think that the memory of Antiquity served largely as an excuse for the institutionalization of Roman and Greek rituals, which were shrewdly manipulated by those who rose to power. Through the enactment of classical customs, people not only forgot the past but they also forgot the present and began to deceive themselves about the terror and the anarchy that were soon to disrupt their hopes for a republic. While I called the Neoclassicist's type of re-memorization fetishistic, I would describe its manner of remembering the past as mythical. Unlike historical reflection—which situates events within a temporal framework—, mythical thought sees the world governed by a series of timeless, permanent patterns and cycles. According to Mircea Eliade, a mythical man is not only "obliged to remember mythical history but also to *re-enact* a large part of it periodically. [...] by recollecting the myths, by re-enacting them, he is able to repeat what the Gods, the Heroes, or the Ancestors did *ab origine*."[66] Eliade adds that by knowing the myth one knows the "origin" of things and hence can control and manipulate them at will; this is not an "external," "abstract" knowledge but a knowledge that one actually "experiences" either by ceremoniously recounting the myth or by performing the ritual for which it is the justification.[67]

At this point let me restate the differences and similarities between a fetishistic and a mythological memorial process. We know

---

65 Freud 1914a: 150 (emphasis in the original).
66 Eliade 1963: 13 (emphasis in the original).
67 See Eliade 1963: 18–19.

from psychoanalytic studies that the fetishist engages in ritualistic behaviors. Whenever he is threatened by castration, he engages in a magical ritual by means of the chosen fetish, which serves to concretize the female phallus for him. He can appropriate it as his own and thereby salvage his potency. In other words, he first builds a myth of the female phallus, and then, in order to sustain this myth, he engages in the fetishistic ritual as "a token of triumph over the threat of castration and a protection against it."[68] From this vantage point, we can say that both the fetishistic and mythological processes of remembrance encompass the establishment of a myth and the need for a ritualized behavior in order to sustain the created myth. However, unlike the fetishist, who disavows the past and buries within it his ossified memories of the actual experience of his early trauma, the individual who engages in a mythological thought process conceals rather than repudiates the past. Now, within the context of comparing the French Classicist invocation of Antiquity with that of the Neoclassicists, we may say that Poussin simply repudiated his immediate past and acted as if the only art that existed for him was that of Antiquity. As I mentioned earlier, he imposed the past upon the present without adapting the present to the past. This process served, as a good example of the manner in which the fetishist remembers. In contrast, the Neoclassical movement actively manipulated the figures of the past to suit the needs of the contemporary situation. By carefully selecting features of Antiquity, a Napoleon could be linked with the glory of a young Caesar, a demagogue could be portrayed in the pose of a Greek Stoic philosopher, or Napoleon's sister could be sculptured as a nude in the guise of a Roman goddess, as in Canova's *Pauline Bonaparte*. The imagery of the Classical past thus served as a shield behind which the glories of Napoleon's victories could be compared favorably to those of Caesar. Between these two chains of images there seems to exist no gap, no ambiguity, the meaning produced is full and yet empty at the same time. As Roland Barthes remarks:

---

68 Freud 1927: 154.

> The meaning is *already* complete it postulates a kind of knowledge, a past, a memory, a comparative order of facts, ideas, decisions. When it becomes form, the meaning leaves its contingency behind; it empties itself, it becomes impoverished, history evaporates, only the letter remains. [...] However paradoxical it may seem, myth hides nothing: its function is to distort, not to make disappear.[69]

In other words, Napoleon is thrust into the role of a Roman emperor—but in order to maintain this distortion, the image of Caesar has to remain and stand side by side with that of the French emperor. In mythical thought (as opposed to historical thought), signification is already embedded in the myth, and, as Barthes points out, myth has a double function—it indicates and notifies, it makes events accessible, and yet it imposes their *meaning* upon us. Moreover, myth never becomes extinct; instead, it adapts itself to new social conditions and cultural formations. For this reason, myth lends itself so readily to all kinds of propagandistic purposes: It can function as a compilation of sacred and heroic stories that tell how the world came into existence; it highlights exemplary models for cultural rites and significant human actions, and it tells its stories in a coherent and memorable fashion.

In France, Neoclassical art continued to be championed by Jean-Auguste-Dominique Ingres, whose career spanned from 1780 to 1867. An avid defender of the art of his predecessor David, in the nineteenth century, Ingres was partly responsible for the revival of the old Poussin-Rubens conflict. In the opposite camp were the Romantics, who rejected the excessive artificiality of the Baroque but welcomed its exuberance and were especially receptive to Rubens's vision. Artists of the Romantic School strove to express ideals that spoke to the individual soul, ideals that lay beyond the bounds of logical discourse. For the Romantics, the individual sensibility was the sole faculty of aesthetic judgment and could not be circumscribed by the rigidly universal guidelines propounded by Poussin and his ilk. The Romantic artist was primarily concerned with personal liberty—with the individual's freedom to express their own inner vision and to choose among different styles from the past. Central to this idea

69 Barthes 1972: 117 + 121 (emphasis in the original).

was the emancipation from the dictatorial powers of the academies and the whims of patrons. The yoke of Classical Antiquity was broken decisively when the excavations of Pompeii and Herculaneum revealed that Greek and Roman art was not, as Johann Joachim Winkelmann had argued, constituted of masterpieces of "noble and quiet grandeur," but by works fraught with tension and a bent for garish decorations. In other words, Antiquity could no longer be seen as a purely ideal era, but as a period "of life more feverish if less noble, more colourful if less pure, than had previously been imagined. The obscurantism, superstition, viciousness and cruelty of the ancient world were only too clearly displayed."[70] However, the gradual demythologization of Antiquity's supposed nobility and perfection did not make the depiction of Classical themes any less attractive to the new breed of Roman artists. Instead, the Romantics began to link their own revolutionary spirit to that of Graeco-Roman scenes which encapsulated the violence, vitality, and decadence of pagan life.

> The distinction is similar to that between the Neo-classical artists' selection from Antiquity and the Romantics' attempt to retrieve a moment of the past. Both looked back, but in different ways and for different purposes. Attention had shifted from the eternal to the transient; from the merits of works of art which might assist in the creation of the 'true style', to the clues which buildings, paintings [...] might provide for the re-creation of the past which would extend knowledge of how people lived and felt in the first century [...].[71]

In addition to the Romantics' re-evaluation of Antiquity—and in part as a result of it—, the early nineteenth-century painters also rediscovered medieval, Renaissance, and Baroque art.

No earlier school of painting was shunned; instead, the different styles were freely intermixed and referenced, although the sources of these quotations were not as clearly defined as during the Renaissance. The enhanced status of the individual artist as a free-working creator shifted the emphasis from a "truthful" depiction of a mythological

---

70 Honour 1979: 211.

71 Honour 1979: 208–209.

scene to the originality of the conception of their own work of art. Historical painting also underwent changes. Instead of posing for Graeco-Roman sculptures, contemporary models were used to depict Classical tales, and the heroic actions were no longer limited to Classical times, but now covered events from contemporary history.

In his painting *The Raft of the Medusa* (1819), Géricault applied the grand scale typical of history painting to represent the sufferings of ordinary people, something that had hitherto been reserved for biblical scenes, the exploits of Greek and Roman heroes, or the deeds of political and military rulers. Here, instead of showing the survivors of the shipwrecked *Medusa* as heroes, they are visibly miserable and terrified at the mercy of the sea. Géricault's student Delacroix, the foremost representative of the Romantic spirit in painting, also chose tragic or heroic scenes of contemporary history as subjects for his history paintings. His *Scenes from the Massacre at Chios*, for instance, depicts the horrors suffered by the Greeks in their war of liberation against the Turks, while the famous *Liberty Leading the People* focused on the recent eruption of the July Revolution of 1830.

Memory unfettered from its bondage to an idealized Classical past—and allowed to follow the multiple and often circuitous paths into different art-historical epochs, subject matters and styles—sharpened the artists' historical awareness and allowed for new forms of expression. Examining their own genealogy, the painters found not so much a linear heritage leading back to Classical origins, but rather a complex path of development that exposed the frailty of reason, the inadequacy of theory, and the power of circumstances that contributed to shaping past events. In other words, neither the present nor the past offered firm bearings for their orientation. Everything was thrown into doubt, and no single approach seemed to provide a secure solution. Faced with this crisis, the Romantics turned their interests towards magical, exotic settings that offered viable loci in which to express their inner passions. "Any time but now, and any place but here" became the battle-cry of Romanticism. Thus, although they had started by rejecting the Neoclassicist enslavement to traditional mythology, the Romantics ultimately ended up equally bound to a nostalgic longing for exotic places and distant epochs. It was precisely the Romantics' melodramatization of ordinary events and their escape into exotic realms—such as the images from Delacroix's Moroccan travel diaries—to which the Realist school so bitterly objected. While the Romantics had detached themselves from contemporary life—painting exotic scenes in which the spectators could unravel their own dreams and fantasies and forget about their immediate situation—, the Realists purposely returned to the here-and-now. For them, in the wake of the 1848 revolution, depicting mythical figures and tragic heroes from exotic lands was no longer compatible with the urgency of the present. Abruptly, the present had made the past redundant, signaling a radical break with previous conventions and inaugurating a whole new approach to depicting the past in the present. The Realist movement did not take offense against the Romantic spirit, but campaigned against the French academic tradition, the "official" art, which represented a compromised fusion of the Classical School of Ingres and Romantic painting. The *juste milieu*, as this group of artists became to be known, were those painters "who steered a careful path between the moribund classicism of the school of David and the wild-eyed Romanticism of the more audacious younger artists."[72] Horace Vernet, a typical example of the "middle of the road tradition" and a frequent recipient of government commissions, formulated their perspective:

> [Painting] is caught between two doctors who are killing her: one is Classical and the other Romantic. The former is a dull fellow who is causing her to expire from listlessness and chill; the other is giving her such stimulants that the unfortunate lady is having attacks of madness […].[73]

The easy synthesis of these two styles produced an art that lacked both the vitality of Romanticism and the austerity of Neoclassicism. Zola compared the Art of the Salon to a candy shop where "mahogany Romans and Greeks and porcelain nymphs" seem like "the sweets of the fashionable artistic confectioners, sugar candy trees

72 Rosen/Zerner 1982b: 49.

73 Vernet, quoted in Boime 1980: 42.

and pastry houses, gingerbread gentlemen and ladies made of vanilla cream."[74] It was against this context of academic art that the Realists advocated the forgetting of the painterly tradition and techniques, and advised their disciples to record faithfully the natural world. With realism, a moment had arrived when no segment of the past tradition was deemed artistically useful or worthy of remembrance. Artists were seemingly independent of any obligations to the history of their craft and stood alone in their confrontation with the natural world. The mind's interpretive faculties were regarded as dangerous since they had invariably led the artists of the past into a fantastic and idealized representation of everyday reality. For this reason, Realism stressed the importance of a faithful and sincere copy of everyday life, an intention that could only be subverted if memory were permitted to intervene.

So far, we have seen how the remembrance of the past served different purposes throughout the centuries of painting. The tradition would have a liberating effect in the Renaissance, a transformative effect during the Baroque, a stifling force during Classicism, a propagandistic and manipulative effect during Classicism, and, finally, a disruptive and confusing effect upon the Romantic School. With the *juste milieu*, a period in French art when creative production was once again firmly regulated by a government-controlled Salon, the reliance on the past became a caricature of itself. Memory, which had once served "as a fulcrum around which contradictions emerge"[75] as in Titian's *Venus of Urbino*, had gradually become spoiled so that it provided only a false model of harmony for the Salon painters. As Hanna Segal described an analogous moment from the realm of the individual psyche, "when the world within us is destroyed, when it is dead and loveless, when our loved ones are in fragments [...] then we must re-create our world anew, reassemble the pieces, infuse life into dead fragments, re-create life."[76] Instead of recreating life, the painters of the *juste milieu* were resurrecting a dead past, a corpse that

---

74 Hamilton 1969: 86–87.

75 Sekoff 1982: iv.

76 Segal 1981: 190.

took on the form of an idealized object which was never resuscitated but artificially kept alive. The thick coats of bitumen smeared over the monumental historical and mythological canvases of official art were indicative of the massive repression of the realities of the present day. Once again, the past had become a fetishistic prop that could be invoked as a magical tool to ward off the complexities and crises of the industrial age. Perhaps, the Realists had no choice but to reject completely the act of remembrance. Manet once said: "Art is a circle, one is either inside or outside."[77] After the Revolution of 1848 and the emergence of an ever more diluted version of Neoclassicism as the official style under Napoleon III, it was time to break out of the circle, to stop the wheel of repetition. Yet, as with so many new beginnings which in time had proved only too ready to become assimilated into the old structures, so realism itself gradually crossed the line separating the outside from the inside of the circle and became another powerful link in the chain of the history of art.

***

77 Manet, quoted in Courthion 1960: 221.

> Memory works radially, that is to say with an enormous number of associations all leading to the same event. [...] There is never a single approach to something remembered. The remembered is not like a terminus at the end of a line. Numerous approaches or stimuli converge upon it and lead to it.
>
> John Berger, 2013

> As you know, I am working on the assumption
> that our psychical mechanism has come into being
> by a process of stratification:
> the material present in the form of memory-traces
> being subjected from time to time to a
> re-arrangement in accordance
> with fresh circumstances—to a re-transcription.
>
> Sigmund Freud, December 6, 1896,
> Letter 52 to Wilhelm Fliess

Édouard Manet emerged at a decisive moment in the history of art. Painting seemed to be at the crossroads between three distinct movements: One sought to erase memory, another to canonize a petrified and artificial version of memory which blocked the representation of the present, and a third, not yet fully developed, a modernism which in Baudelaire's opinion had become necessary if art was to continue producing significant works:

> The painter, the true painter for whom we are looking, will be he who can snatch its epic quality from the life of today and can make us see

> and understand, with brush or with pencil, how great and poetic we are in our cravats and our patent-leather boots.[78]

What method could work out these contradictory impulses? How could Manet define his own position vis-à-vis the past, incorporate his own relationship to the present and articulate a direction towards the future at the same time? It seems as if Manet chose a method that approximated his own definition of art as a circle, a method analogous to what Robert S. Steele calls interpretation's hermeneutic circle:

> The hermeneutic circle best captures the synchronic aspects of interpretation. We widen our understanding of a given time by broadening our interpretations so as to include more and more contemporary events. Synchronically, understanding widens in ever-growing concentric circles. We need an image that layers circles on top of one another in order to capture both the synchronic and diachronic dimensions. Such a figure is the 'hermeneutic spiral'. [...] The vertical dimension of the spiral represents time, with each new understanding being built upon and replacing an older circle of meaning. [...] While synchronic interpretation widens our understanding of contemporaneous material, diachronic interpretation situates the material in reference to past and future.[79]

Jean Laplanche also used the metaphor of a spiral when he explained the bi-directionality of *après-coup*. He writes:

> The work of a thought does not travel in a straight line like an arrow. It follows a movement I call "spiral" but that, in reality, is a helix. This means that the life of human beings, and especially the movement of their thought, is neither linear, constantly leaving one point to pass on to another, nor circular, constrained to repeat the same sequences. The movement of a spiral constantly distances itself from one pole, but at the same time, it is led to return again and again to points along the same vertical. Returning to a vertical, one is led to reconsider the same themes at another and higher level.[80]

---

78 Baudelaire 1981: 32.

79 Steele 1979: 393.

80 Laplanche, qoted in House 2017: 772–773.

Le Buveur d'absinthe, Manet's first painting exhibited at the Salon in 1859, illustrates how he interwove the synchronic and diachronic circles. At first sight, *Le Buveur d'absinthe* [Plate 11] portrays a rag-picker that Manet had met at the Louvre. Here, depicted on a grand scale, was a representative of the lower classes, one of the *Lumpenproletariat* who served as a stark reminder of the other side of the shiny and glorious sugar-coated nymphs of the *grandes machines*. Before Realism commenced, this kind of subject had passed under the radar as a social "sub-species" unworthy of pictorial representation by the Académie and the Salons. From this vantage point, Manet was clearly in accordance with the Realists' belief in the "ordinary" individual as the true hero of modern times. But in a way radically different from any Realist painter, with the *Buveur* Manet harked back to a memory that had been largely ignored by the entire French painting tradition. Although Couture was not alone in recommending Velázquez and Goya as models for his students, no other painter prior to Manet had alluded so blatantly to the great Spanish tradition. Velázquez, a contemporary of Poussin and Rubens, was never part of nor was he influenced by the Neoclassicist suppression of Baroque art. Instead of purging the excesses of Baroque by retreating to the virtuous tales of Antiquity, Velázquez had continued the Venetian tradition of naturalizing mythological compositions and rendered the mythological heroes in a decidedly more domestic, matter-of-fact style. As Ortega y Gassett had correctly observed, "Velasquez had turned myth around, instead of seducing the spectator into a world of fantasy, he had placed the world of fantasy into the realm of daily life."[81] In Velázquez, Manet found an artist who had already fathomed the principles that were now being hailed as a radical innovation by the Realist school. Like the Realists, Velázquez had asserted that he was not a man given to imagination, but an artist who painted only what he personally observed. Moreover, he could show how the realist portraits of ordinary and even aristocratic figures could transmit an aura of poetic mystery that hitherto was deemed attainable only through the representation of mythological, religious or Classical subjects.

81 Ortega y Gassett, quoted in Muller 1976: 76.

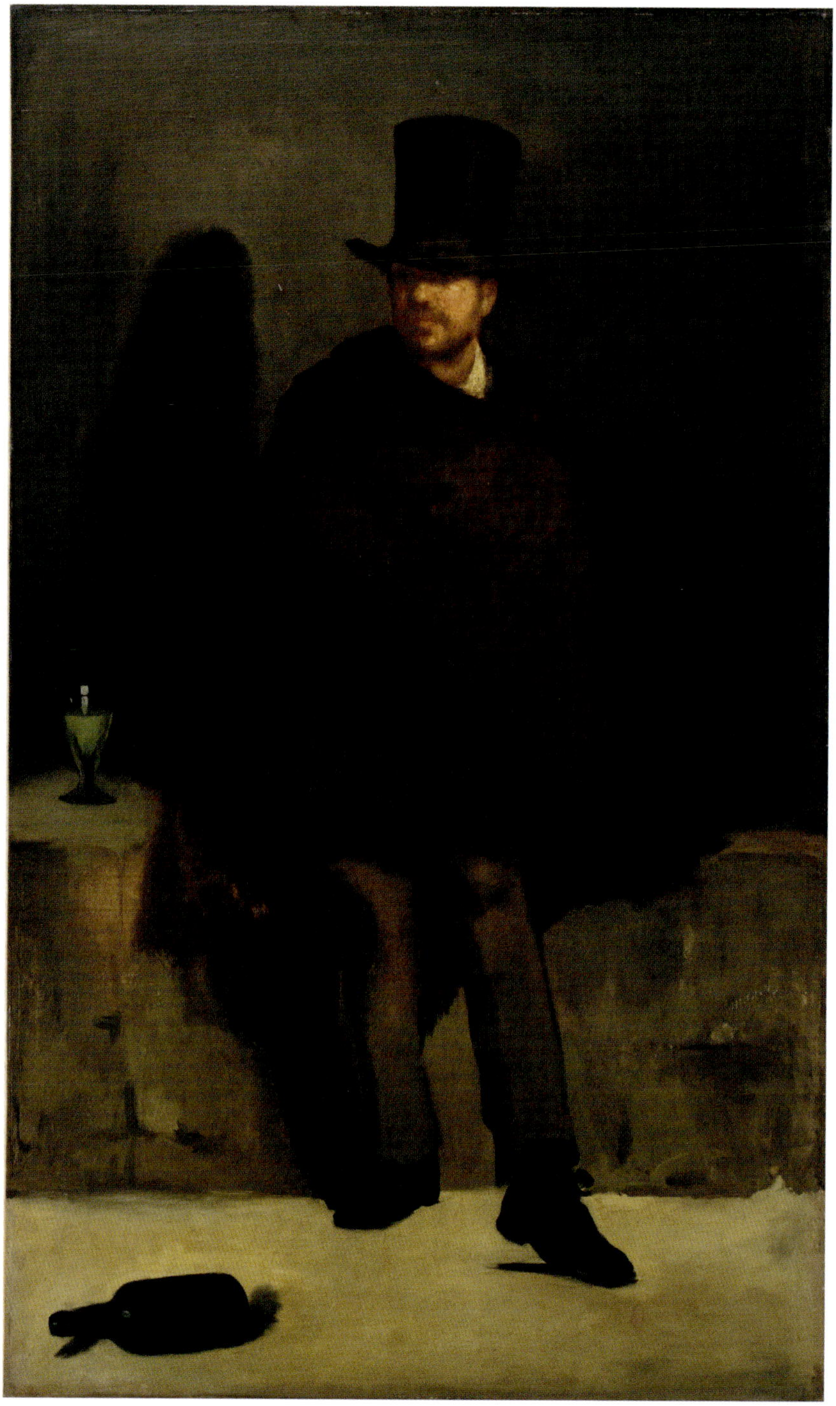

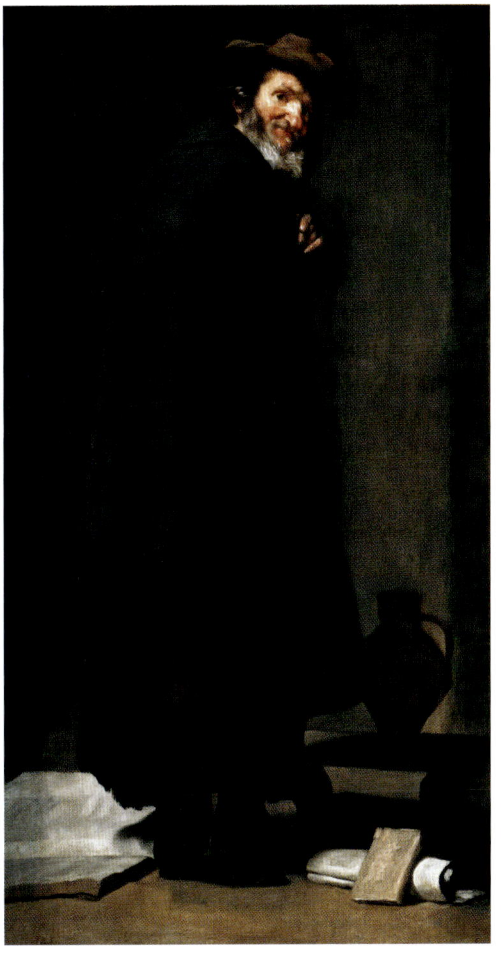

Plate 19:
Diego Velázquez,
Menippos (1640)

Whereas Titian had used narrative truth as a means of concealing historical truth (and Rubens had used historical fact as a pretext for narrative truth), Velázquez succeeded in placing both truths side by side, without either one rebutting the other. This crucial step also triggered a change in the relationship between painters and their spectators: from then on, it was no longer the painter who resolved the conflict between these two realities for the spectator, now it was up to the spectators themselves to work out this conflict in their confrontation with the canvas.

In this manner, we witness how the memory of Velázquez's *Menippos* [Plate 19] served different and often contradictory purposes. On the surface, *Le Buveur d'absinthe* appears as a recreation of Velázquez's philosopher, and with this particular approach Manet revived an aspect of the Renaissance tradition that had been forgotten. Although Manet's contemporaries faithfully copied Renaissance and Baroque paintings as part of their artistic training, they did not think of reinterpreting the traditional themes within a contemporary frame. Instead, they continued the French classicist tradition of representing an idealized world which bore no resemblance to the contemporary scene. If we did not know for certain that Manet had met the rag-picker Colardet at the Louvre, we might assume that he was imitating the Neo-classical technique of dressing contemporary subjects—like Napoleon or Mme Récamier—in the costume of a Classical philosopher in order to establish a connection with the Velázquez painting. Instead, it seems as if Manet used a technique which Freud described as the underlying mechanism of creativity:

> A strong experience in the present awakens in the creative writer a memory of an earlier experience (usually belonging to his childhood)

page 190: **Plate 11:**
Édouard Manet,
Le Buveur d'absinthe
(1859)

> from which there now proceeds a wish which finds its fulfilment in the creative work. The work itself exhibits elements of the recent provoking occasion as well as of the old memory.[82]

Perhaps Meyer Schapiro summarized the difference between the Neoclassical tradition and Manet most succinctly when he said that "Gérome [...] painted modern life in ancient costumes. Here Manet painted an ancient scene in a modern dress."[83] By the same token, Manet did not freeze his memory into a straight path, but let his memories travel freely through the past to capture those connections which seemed most characteristic of the figure or theme he wanted to paint. Freud himself used the metaphor of the artist when he described how dreaming utilized random impressions from the past and present:

> I believe, that is, that [indifferent impressions] are brought in to help in the formation of dream if they fit in appropriately with the ideational content derived from the dream's psychical sources, but otherwise not. They are treated like some cheap material always ready to hand, which is employed whenever it is needed, in contrast to precious material which itself prescribes the way in which it shall be employed. If, to take a simile, a patron of the arts brings an artist some rare stone [...] and asks him to create a work of art from it, then the size of the stone, its colors and markings help to decide what head or what scene shall be represented in it. Whereas in the case of a uniform and plentiful material such as marble or sandstone, the artist merely follows some idea that is present in his own mind.[84]

If Freud had added that the patron not only provided the precious stone but also the ideas according to which the artist was supposed to shape his image, he would have accurately described the difference between the Neoclassical painter's use of past imagery and that of Manet. Yet, Manet's remembrance of earlier painterly depictions differed in still one other aspect from French Neoclassicist art. Freud's text on "Jensen's Gradiva" may help us sharpen this distinction. At

---

82 Freud 1908: 151.
83 Schapiro 1978: 35.
84 Freud 1900: 237.

first sight, a strong resemblance seems to exist between Norbert Hanold's voyage to Pompeii to find the original of his Gradiva and Manet's search into the past to find the original of his contemporary rag-picker. Both are obsessed by "something of 'to-day' [...], a glimpse in the street [...] captured 'from the life'."[85] Like Manet, Hanold had to search for the images locked up behind the momentary glimpse of an object that completely took over his fantasies. And only at the moment when his fantasies coincided with the memories of the past did Hanold realize that the Gradiva he was searching for was Zoe Bertgang, his childhood love. As Hanold had to dig out the ruins of Pompeii to find the original of the relief, so Manet had to dig up the treasures of past art to find the original for his current strong impression of a contemporary scene or figure. But unlike Hanold, who is content once he locates the source of his obsession, Manet not merely restores a lost object, but constructs a new one out of the interplay between the current impression and a figure from a past painting. Manet does not make use of the traditional Masters to show how the past really was, instead he creates a present image by re-interpreting it in the light of the past, thereby modifying his understanding of that past according to its present utility. Hence, it is important not to focus exclusively upon Manet's memory from Velázquez, but on the ways in which his work relates to the Spanish painter. As with the interpretation of dreams and jokes, in our analysis of Manet's innovations, we have to concentrate upon "the relations between the manifest content of dreams and the latent dream-thoughts, and [we must trace out] the processes by which the latter have been changed into the former."[86] Thus, we need to examine the artwork like a dream-work or a joke-work, where different and often contradictory sources, impressions, ideas, and memories are combined into a unified picture. The artist also uses the mechanisms of condensation, displacement, and indirect representation to almagamate the various emotional and thematic strands into a single image. Yet, the dream and the joke are forced to condense and displace images and words

85 Freud 1907: 11.
86 Freud 1900: 277.

not only for the sake of representability or brevity, but also because they are subject to the laws of censorship. These laws, as the word "censor" itself shows, operate as much in the public, social sphere as in the internal individual psyche. Manet, whose work was produced under Napoleon III's strict censorship code, was certainly aware of both forms of constraint.

In the context of analyzing Manet's sources, I think that Freud's thoughts in the text *Jokes and their Relations to the Unconscious* will prove ultimately more helpful than *The Interpretation of Dreams*. Although both works are intimately related (since Freud used the same technique to interpret dreams and jokes), the joke resembles the artwork much more since it is a public and social product which wants to be understood in and through its disguises. But this is not the only grounds for interpreting Manet's works within the context of Freud's paper on jokes. It so happens that Manet himself chose the medium of the joke to express his ideas through his paintings. Manet was like the writer whom Freud in *The Interpretation of Dreams* described as a man who

> must [...] aware of the censorship, and on its account he must soften and distort the expression of his opinion. According to the strength and sensitiveness of the censorship he finds himself compelled either merely to refrain from certain forms of attack, or to speak in allusions in place of direct references, or he must conceal his objectionable pronouncement beneath some apparently innocent disguise [...].[87]

Manet, like Freud's joker, was not a man who could resist criticizing his milieu, but he was unwilling to attack openly the government and the society. As we have seen in the previous chapter, his bourgeois upbringing neither permitted nor even tempted Manet to become an outspoken rebel like Courbet, nor a declared satirist like Daumier. He was much more inclined to speak in allusions and to conceal his pronouncements in innocent disguises. This, of course, raises the question of why he was actually so unsuccessful a joker, since he never ceased to be the target of public outcry and rarely had his paintings

87 Freud 1900: 142.

accepted by the Salon. In some instances, the disguises proved to be too thin, as we will see. In other instances, what he hoped to disguise remained hidden, yet, the very material he chose as means of concealment raised other objections on their own account. In *Le Buveur d'absinthe*, for example, Manet employs the mechanism of condensation. In the figure of the alcoholic, he condenses the image of a lower-class subject, who lives on the fringes of society, with that of a Classical satirist, as depicted by Velázquez in the painting of Menippos. *Le Buveur d'absinthe* has become the modern Menippos, one whose satiric impulses can be expressed only in an intoxicated state. In this, he resembles one of Manet's chief literary sources for the painting: Baudelaire's "Le Vin des Chiffonniers," with its image of the drunkard who imagines himself the emperor of the night,

> One comes upon a shaking ragman, who
> Staggers against the walls, as poets do,
> And disregardful of policemen's spies,
> Pours from his heart some glorious enterprise.[88]

In the figure of Ratapoil, "the great Napoleonic hustler, the 'hand-to-mouth demagogue […]', old soldier, ex-crook […]",[89] Daumier had already used the image of a rag-picker as a satiric vehicle. Baudelaire himself was influenced by Daumier's paintings and caricatures when he composed "Le Vin des chiffonniers," in which he contrasts the double life of the rag-picker as outcast during the day and as the night's "drunken pariah [who] rules at last, in fantasy and isolation."[90] By using this poem as one source for *Le Buveur d'absinthe*, Manet traced a genealogy from Velázquez to Daumier and Baudelaire to his own work. Yet, the quotation of a past figure not only served to establish a linkage to the Spanish Master, but was used for two contradictory purposes: on the one hand, the allusion to a traditional

88 Baudelaire 1998: 217; "On voit un chiffonnier qui vient, hochant la tête, / Butant, et se cognant aux murs comme un poète, / Et, sans prendre souci des mouchards, ses sujets, / Épanche tout son cœur en glorieux projets."
89 Clark 1973: 105.
90 Clark 1973: 163.

style was thought to mitigate the sharpness of his social commentary. After all, what could be offensive about a re-interpretation of a Spanish Menippos previously executed under the eyes of the Spanish king. The wretchedness of this figure was "embellished" once it was transposed into the style of an acknowledged Old Master. Yet, Manet mocked his own imitation of the Neoclassical technique by linking *Le Buveur d'absinthe* to a work as peculiar as *Menippos*, whose theme only substantiated the satirical comment that Manet seemingly wanted to disguise in the first place. This technique of masking a thing only to unmask it in other ways, corresponds to the process of "unification," which "is clearly analogous to condensation by compression into the same words."[91] Freud compares unification with the peculiarly negative relation present between jokes and riddles, according to which "one conceals what the other exhibits."[92] The technique of unification is part of the mechanisms of joke-work since it binds "into a unity [...] several ideas which are in fact alien to one another both in their internal content and in the nexus to which they belong."[93] However, unification also makes use of the displacement technique by presenting "us with a façade, in which a striking parade of logical thinking was exhibited; and we learnt from analysing it [an example of a joke] that this logic was used to conceal a piece of faulty reasoning—namely, a displacement of the train of thought."[94]

What Manet concealed under the apparent logic of painting a lower-class subject in the spirit of French Realism was a critique of that same movement. By placing *Le Buveur d'absinthe* in a position similar to that of Velázquez's *Menippos*, Manet undermined the Realists' claim that they had made a radical break from traditional painting. With Velázquez, Manet could cite a painter of the Baroque who had struggled with problems similar to those confronted by the French Realists. Moreover, in quoting Velázquez, he demonstrated that "truthful and sincere" depictions of everyday life can appear as

91 Freud 1905b: 66–67.
92 Freud 1905b: 67.
93 Freud 1905b: 11.
94 Freud 1905b: 56.

truthful even when they are taken from a fictitious reality like the realm of painting. The Realists' belief that an unmediated reality could be depicted objectively was mocked by Manet's ability to fuse into one image a representation of an actual contemporary subject and one of a traditional fictional figure. Although the Realists had begun to explore the non-mimetic aspects of painting by abolishing the system of perspective and calling the spectator's attention to the "reality" of the canvas—in and of itself a factor of distortion—, Manet extended that concept in *Le Buveur d'absinthe*. Like Courbet, he would paint his figure on a flat surface, but, unlike the "master-realist," Manet would also include obvious mistakes in his painting, such as the "shadow" of the absinthe drinker, which is merely a dark patch on the wall that does not correspond to the outline of the figure.[95] His positioning is entirely illogical: while his right leg indicates a seated position, his left leg suggests an upright one. The curious stance of the left leg is further underscored by the rag-picker's wearing a right shoe on his left foot. This imbalance of the figure is obscured by the shapeless brown coat, but judging by the discordant position of the two legs we can assume that beneath the coat the man's body is in disarray, that his left side does not correspond to the right, and that no "real" human being could both sit and stand leaning against a wall at the same time. Yet, in painting, this fiction can be realized, since the reality of a canvas does not coincide with the reality of the natural world.

In Velázquez's time, the conflict resided between a mythological/religious and a realist depiction of the human figure. With Manet, the conflict had shifted to the question of man's inner and outer nature, and the disembodied representation of the *Le Buveur d'absinthe* attempts to capture this estranged relationship between man and his own being. The sense of irrationality, isolation and despair emanating from *Le Buveur* also testifies to the influence of Baudelaire's poetry upon Manet. Yet, even here, Manet speaks in two voices, since on the one hand, he accentuates the poetic source of his painting and on the other hand he employs a technique that seems to violate Baudelaire's

95 Manet would use this same device in one of his last paintings, *Un Bar aux Folies Bergère* [**Plate 15**].

entire notion of modern painting. While Baudelaire lamented that the Salon painters were easily satisfied with the imitation of the Old Masters, he also believed that the perception of a new work must trigger or activate an endlessly expressive sequence of memories of earlier works; but, he thought, not only must those memories not be allowed to overwhelm or otherwise displace that perception, they must remain below the threshold of conscious awareness, investing the present with the aura and significance of memory without for a moment appearing on its stage.[96]

Clearly, Manet fulfills the former condition but not the latter, since his figures actually seem to announce their appearance on stage, and are not in the least inclined to remain below the threshold of the viewer's awareness. Indeed, as we will see in a moment, in *Le Vieux Musicien* quotations seem to fulfill no other role than to appear on-stage as actors from memory. Yet, before discussing *Le Vieux Musicien*, it is helpful to clarify one issue. We have seen thus far how Manet used quotations from traditional artists simultaneously to illuminate and obscure his intentions. The reactions of Courbet and Baudelaire may, however, reveal that even Manet's most hidden intentions were in fact understood by both men, if only subconsciously. Courbet's cynical remark that Manet should not play Velázquez in front of us, seems to indicate his awareness of Manet's implicit critique of the Realist movement. Possibly offended by Manet's suggestion that French Realism did not offer a genuine alternative, but only was a continuation of the Spanish Baroque, Courbet attempted to counter that charge by turning the argument around and denouncing Manet's affiliation with Velázquez as merely an affectation. Conversely, Baudelaire was anxious to validate his own theories of modern art. From his standpoint, a deliberate quotation from a traditional painting inevitably overshadowed the painter's own style. If, however, that style was clearly recognizable despite the painting's resemblance to an older work, the resemblance could only be the result of a coincidence and not of a deliberate effort. Seeing his own theory being invalidated by Manet's works, Baudelaire had no other

---

96 See Fried 1984: 521.

recourse but to insist that his friend had never seen the works of the Spanish painters.

With *Le Vieux Musicien* (1862) **[Plate 14]** Manet modified his technique of quoting earlier sources. Previously, he had faithfully adhered to the overall composition of only one traditional painting; but in *Le Vieux Musicien*, Manet quoted more freely from a variety of sources. The general composition is borrowed largely from Velázquez's *Los Borrachos* (1626–1628) **[Plate 49]**, Antoine Le Nain's *Le vieux joueur de flageolet* and Louis Le Nain's *La Halte du cavalier* (1640) **[Plate 50]**, but the individual figures reference paintings by Watteau, Schlesinger, Le Nain, and a Classical sculptor. No attempt is made to situate these figures in a modern context, and there is no sense that "a strong experience in the present" had awakened the memory of an earlier experience. Instead, Manet made use of another mechanism that had already appeared in *Le Buveur d'absinthe*, but which he would accentuate increasingly in his subsequent works: "Might we not say that every child at play behaves like a *creative writer*, in that he creates a world of his own, or, rather re-arranges the things of his world in a new way which pleases him?"[97] In *Le Vieux Musicien*, Manet assumes the role of a director who uses his models as actors on a stage: he gives various parts of different performers, including that of the musician, modeled on Watteau's *Gilles* (or *Pierrot*); a little boy styled after Velázquez's *The Water Carrier of Seville*; a little girl holding a baby, modeled after Schlesinger's *L'Enfant volé*, the *Turk* or *Ahasuerus*, the *Wandering Jew*; modeled after Rembrandt's *The Mocking of Christ*; and lastly, *Le Buveur d'absinthe* based upon his own earlier canvas. Yet, the actors do not relate to each other; they are frozen in the positions Manet directed them to take. No story unfolds between these characters, nor can a particular meaning be attached to their grouping. The painting strikes us as a bravura showpiece—but we cannot be certain of what. Michael Fried interprets this showpiece as Manet's desire to draw "a deep connection" between Watteau and Le Nain, two French painters whose works had been repressed during the Neoclassicist revival. By grouping them in a Spanish composition,

---

97 Freud 1908: 143–144 (author's emphasis).

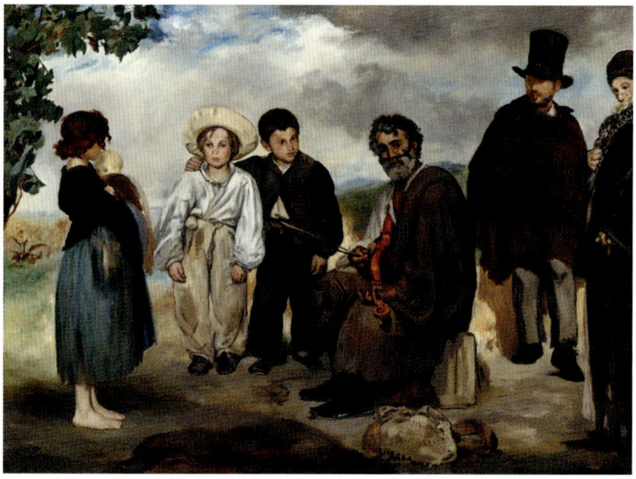

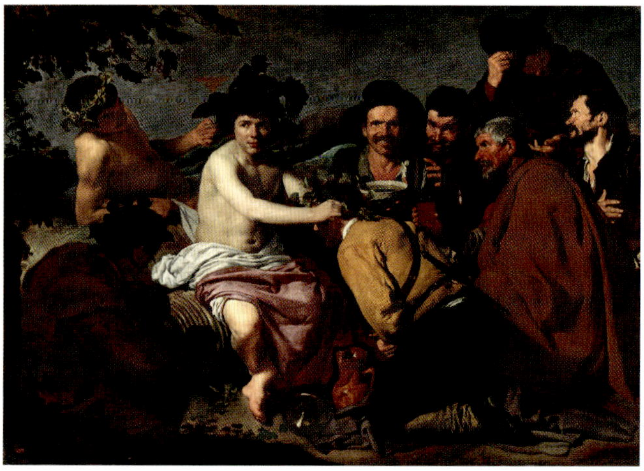

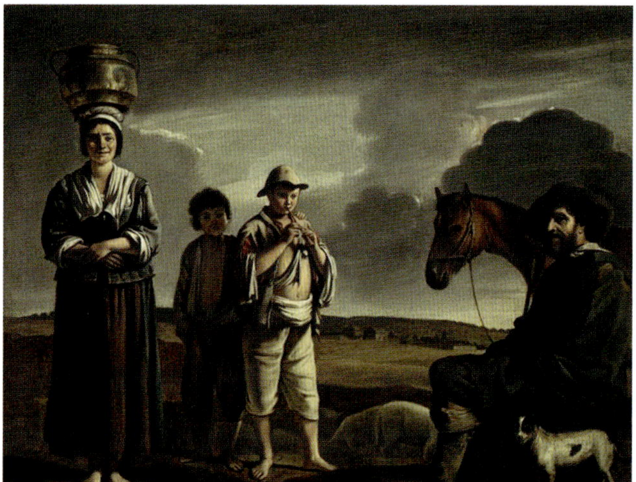

Manet could trace his own lineage from Velázquez to Le Nain and Watteau and could demonstrate how all three are intimately related to one another in their personal conception of artistic expression.

From a very different perspective, George Mauner locates a theme linking these isolated characters by assuming that each figure symbolizes life's double nature and that together they represent the various stages of life. The little Pierrot figure recalls the dark and bright sides of life, a blend of laughter and terror; Ahasuerus unites the themes of life and death, of youth being restored on the brink of death, and so forth. The theme of regeneration and renewal of life is given greater precision by the portrayal of Chrysippus, a philosopher who systematized the Stoic doctrine that "[t]he universe, [...] at the end of each of a never-ending series of cycles, is absorbed into the divine fire, and then starts on a fresh course exactly reproducing its predecessor."[98] Although each believes his "reading" to be the only correct one, their arguments do not even contradict one another since they are directed to such different aspects of the painting. Unwillingly, however, they both point to the ambiguous nature of Manet's practice, his pictorializing of themes and artistic principles that can never be deciphered into a single, unidirectional proposition. I believe that more than any other painting *Le Vieux Musicien* constitutes a didactic piece. In this painting, Manet shows the various tenets of his method and comes closest to exposing his own philosophy of painting. Manet takes on the role of analyst who dissects the different parts of the dream or joke to understand by what techniques they were formed. By detaching his figures from their varoius contexts and assembling them in a different order, Manet accentuates the importance of play for the creation of a work. Like the joke, which is a play on words and which produces a "playful judgment," painting is a play with images executed under the direction of the artist. And like the dreamer, Manet is "an actor who at his own will plays the parts of madmen and philosophers, of executioners and their victims, of dwarfs and giants, of demons and angels."[99]

page 200: **Plate 14:**
Édouard Manet,
Le Vieux Musicien (1862)
Plate 49:
Diego Velázquez,
Los Borrachos (1626–1628)
Plate 50:
Louis Le Nain,
Le Halte du cavalier (1640)

98 Oxford Companion to Classical Literature, 1959: 407.

99 Freud 1900: 60.

Unlike George Mauner, who reckons that Manet was primarily interested in the depiction of the individual's double nature, I believe that Manet's chief concern was not to make a general statement about human nature. Rather than serving as a vehicle for some unchanging truth, for Manet the subject itself changes depending upon the position in which it is placed. Therefore, different interpretations are produced according to the *positioning*, and not because the figures themselves bear some inner truth. Manet exemplifies this by displacing the absinthe drinker from his initial context into *Le Vieux Musicien*. Within this new frame, the absinthe drinker no longer only represents the rag-picker Colardet, but is turned into a fictional character, a model and the painter's own past. From being a subject observed by others, in *Le Vieux Musicien,* the absinthe drinker becomes the spectator. It is possible that, in reaction to the public's misunderstanding of how he had employed the figures of traditional painters in his works, Manet was now doing the same with figures from his *own* paintings. This way, the critics could hardly accuse Manet of imitating himself, and therefore would be compelled to acknowledge that he was no slavish copyist. Manet wished, instead, to emphasize the complex interconnections between the imaginary and the material world, between the realm of painting with its own codes and conventions and the external world with its distinct laws and regulations. By quoting a figure from his own works, Manet was also recalling the Renaissance and Baroque traditions whereby painters would regularly rework their own compositions, such as Titian did with *Venus with the Organ Player*, and *Venus and Cupid with a Lute Player*. Yet this practice had gained a different meaning as soon as the painter ceased to illustrate mythological tales. The same Venus can be shown in different narratives, but when a figure previously regarded as a "sincere" portrait of a Parisian figure turns into a fictional character, the two realms of material and imaginary reality are combined, leaving the spectator in a state of confusion. Manet's inclusion of *Le Pierrot* modeled after Watteau's *Gilles/Pierrot* (1719) **[Plate 51]** echoes the same theme. Watteau had also depicted the Pierrot character as someone intermingling social and theatrical life, blurring reality with fantasy, and as such he was in the unique position of challeng-

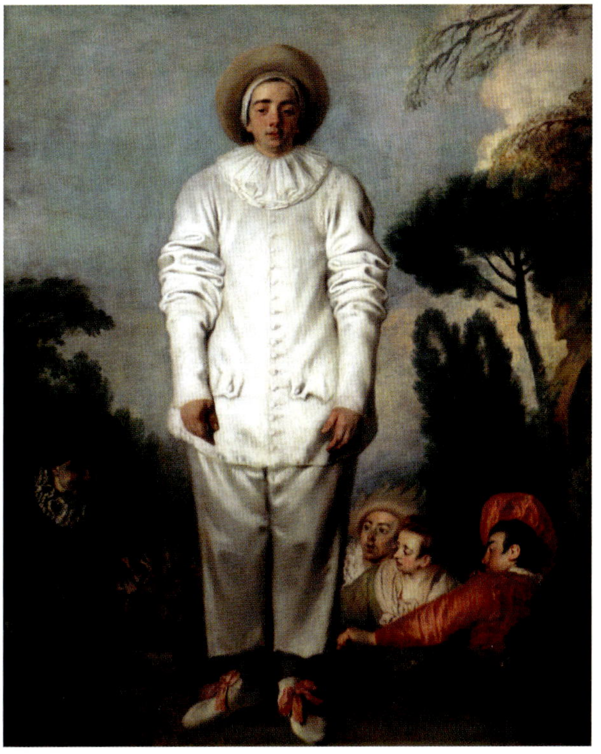

Plate 51:
Antoine Watteau,
Gilles/Pierrot (1719)

ing societal hierarchies and traditions. I think that Manet had found a modern Menippos in the figure of *Le Buveur d'absinthe* who was echoing *Gilles's (Pierrot's)* iridescent and irreverent character. Both served as models for Manet's own ambition to blur the boundaries between reality and fantasy. In *Le Vieux Musicien* he assembles six figures who resemble "real" people—since they were drawn from living models—but who are also fragments from the fictional reality of painting. With the mechanism of displacement or—as Roman Jacobson defined it—a *synecdoche*, Manet allows each figure to stand for the whole of the quoted source. In other words, the memory of Velázquez's *Water Carrier* is preserved in the little boy embracing the Pierrot figure, who in turn stands for the whole of Watteau's *Gilles*. The spectators are simultaneously inscribed within two languages, between which they can playfully shift back and forth. In *Le Vieux Musicien*, Manet toys with the confines of painting, and discovers that, just as "[...] the realm of jokes knows no boundaries,"[100] except the formal laws, painting can liberally dovetail realms traditionally considered distinct. In an era in which history was canonized as scientific truth, one in which Courbet, a student of positivism, could declare that "painting is an essentially *concrete* art and can only consist of the presentation of *real and existing things*,"[101] Manet's intentional fusion of the fictional realm with the material world provides a powerful counter-example. While Mauner reads the entire painting as a symbolic representation of life's never-ending cycle, he fails to understand how this Stoic concept—for him embodied by the

100 Freud 1900: 176.
101 Nochlin 1987: 23 (emphasis in the original).

old musician—instead represents Manet's fundamental theory of art. As mentioned earlier, Manet had described art as a circular movement within which ideas are constantly revised, and this is precisely what he accomplishes figure by figure in *Le Vieux Musicien*. It is as if each figure constitutes one word of the large vocabulary of painting, a word which is rearranged and combined with others to form new constructions and new meanings. The endless pliability of pictorial images is also an inherent characteristic of words, fundamental to the joke-work. Freud observed that "Words are plastic material with which one can do all kinds of things. They are words which, when used in certain connections, have lost their original full meaning, but which regain it in other connections."[102]

Like the joker who can play upon the double meaning of words, establish sense in nonsense, condense contradictory ideas into one unified concept, and reestablish the forgotten meaning of a word, Manet lays out these techniques in an almost didactic manner in *Le Vieux Musicien*. It is as if Manet were once and for all releating to the spectator the basic rules of his technique, which he would use more playfully in his subsequent canvases.

With *Le Déjeuner sur l'herbe* and *Olympia*, Manet expanded his vocabulary to include the pictorial language of such Venetian painters as Giorgione and Titian (but also Raphael from Urbino). Unlike the Spanish masters he had quoted from, these Italian masters, though revered by the Académie, were precisely those sources which still remained obscure to the public. Moreover, with the inclusion of the Venetian references, Manet's satire changed direction: he no longer concealed his "dissent" behind some harmless disguise and instead made his protest so blatant that the public never suspected some hidden design and took everything at face value. To understand this change in technique, we have to comprehend what it meant for an artist in the nineteenth century to quote so freely from the Venetian painterly tradition. When Manet made his references to the Spanish masters, he was quoting artists who had fallen out of favor with the Académie; and, as outsiders, they were largely deemed to be eccen-

102 Freud 1905b: 34.

trics. For the Académie their status evidently corresponded with the common conviction of Manet as a rebel at war with the *juste milieu*. Conversely, the Italian painters belonged inside the accepted circle and, as a consequence, were regularly copied by the painters of the Académie. Indeed, the practice of copying the Old Masters constituted its core curriculum, and while this routine had always been taught as a means of analyzing *disegno* and color composition, for the Académie it served another purpose as well. As the late Albert Boime pointed out: "The copy, together with its model, furnished a convenient test for discovering potential talent and for encouraging the loyalty of artists to the institutional system."[103] The artist's skills and loyalty were judged on the degree of their reproduction of the original, whereas a truly interpretive copy was rejected as a "commonplace industry."[104] Perhaps unsurprisingly, those painters who proved their loyalty to the academic system were rewarded with generous government commissions, while those who took more liberties in copying a masterwork found themselves ostracized. In this sense, the Académie embodied the suffocating patronage and favoritism system that was endemic under Napoleon III's regime. In his shrewd parody of the basic pedagogical technique of the Académie, Manet parodied the corrupt politics of this system. His mockery was such that he painted *Le Déjeuner sur l'herbe* in the same year that Alexandre Cabanel, a prominent member of the Académie, exhibited a nearly "perfect" copy of Giorgione's/Titian's *Le Concert Champêtre*. This form of mockery reminds one of what Freud wrote about tendentious jokes which "are especially favored in order to make aggressiveness or criticism possible against persons in exalted positions who claim to exercise authority. The joke then represents a rebellion against that authority, a liberation from its pressure."[105] However, it seems as if Manet was not content to subvert the Académie's emphasis on copying-as-education by means of a witty counter-example, since the very camouflage he selected—an obscene joke—ultimately raised far more objections than would an

103 Boime 1970: 11.
104 Boime 1970: 43.
105 Freud 1905b: 105.

open critique of academic practices. Yet, his provocation does not involve the formal techniques of allusion, "that is, replacement by something small, something remotely connected, which the hearer reconstructs in his imagination into a complete and straightforward obscenity."[106] Instead, it presented in plain sight everything that was to be seen: an undressed woman in the company of two elegantly attired gentlemen serenely gathered at a picnic outdoors. Moreover, the naked woman does not toy with the viewer's libido through coy appeals to her nakedness. On the contrary, her unabashed composure quashes any obscene implications. For Freud, such nakedness would normally elicit advances that the wooer would expect no resistance from. Despite the evidence, Manet's (male) public was torn between arousal and outrage towards this conflicting vision of "indecent exposure." As Etienne notes: "A commonplace woman of the demimonde, as naked as can be, shamelessly lolls between two dandies dressed to the teeth. […] This is a young man's practical joke, a shameful open sore not worth exhibiting this way…"[107]

Manet did nothing to mitigate the prospective scandal he knew would ensue. He even carefully arranged in full view the garments the seated nude had removed for the portrait. He also made clear that he himself had been a witness to such a scene. In 1862, during a day at the Seine in Argenteuil, Manet and his friend Antonin Proust had watched two women bathing in the river, and Manet suddenly exclaimed:

> 'It seems,' he said to me, 'that I've got to paint a nude. Very well! I'll do'em one. When we were working at the atelier, I copied a picture of some women by Giorgione—the women with the musicians—but it's too black, that picture—the background's too strong. I would like to re-do it and make it translucent, using models like those people we see over there.'[108]

This episode not only reveals how profoundly the traditional arts had shaped Manet's vision of the present, but it also raises the im-

106 Freud 1905b: 100.
107 Hamilton 1969: 45.
108 Proust, quoted in Courthion 1960: 6.

portant question of why Manet never publicly announced these sources, namely, Giorgione's/Titian's *Le Concert Champêtre* (1509) [Plate 4], and Marcantonio Raimondi's engraving *Judgment of Paris* (1510–1520) [Plate 52] after Raphael to his audience. Any concession Manet might have found to citing directly Giorgione's/Titian's painting—where an almost identical situation had been treated in terms of early sixteenth-century Venice—was ruled out by the artist's reticence. I think Manet's silence about his quotations from past works remains a puzzle even today and cannot be satisfactorily resolved. Several answers come up, but they are unconvincing. We might surmise that Manet began to despair of his audience's continual misunderstanding of his references to traditional painters. And the insistent charge of plagiarism continued, no matter how distinctly modern his technique was. Anticipating a similar accusation against *Le Déjeuner sur l'herbe*, for this new work Manet decided to disguise his quotations more thoroughly than before. That said, one may well argue that Manet also wished to keep the best jokes to himself. Had he disclosed the literalness with which he had "copied" the Venetian masters, he would have made a public issue of his contempt for the Académie, which had awarded their highest decoration to Alexandre Cabanel's garish depiction of *La Naissance de Vénus* (1863) [Plate 53] at the 1863 Paris Salon, the same year that *Le Déjeuner sur l'herbe* (1863) [Plate 3] was rejected (and, notably, Manet's demythologizing *Olympia* received a similar opprobrium two years later). Ultimately, it is also likely that by 1863, Manet had gained such confidence in his ability to speak simultaneously in the language of the past and the present and to capture the epic quality of the transitory nature of his own era, that he no longer felt obliged to emphasize his memories from the past. In short, diachronically speaking, Manet's paintings were securely situated in reference to the past, and he had reached the point at which he thought it necessary to emphasize the synchronic, contemporaneous aspects of his interpretations. Perhaps he had learned from Couture's highly praised *Les Romains de la décadence* of 1847 (a year before the Revolution) that an indirect allusion to the decadence of French society was blithely misunderstood by the public, who had applauded a work intended as a *direct criticism* of their

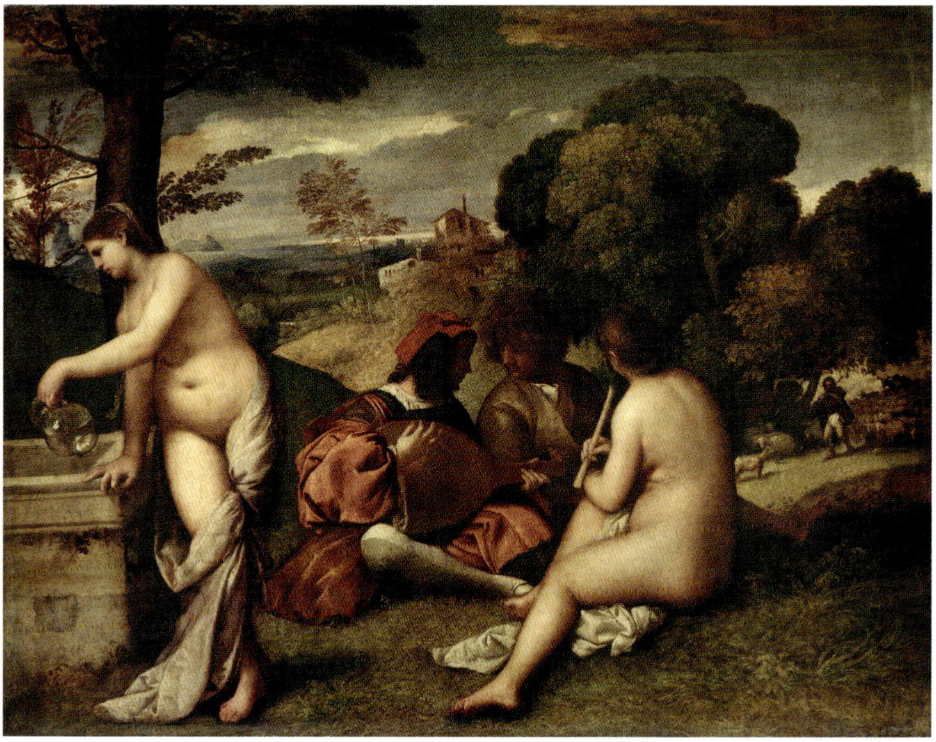

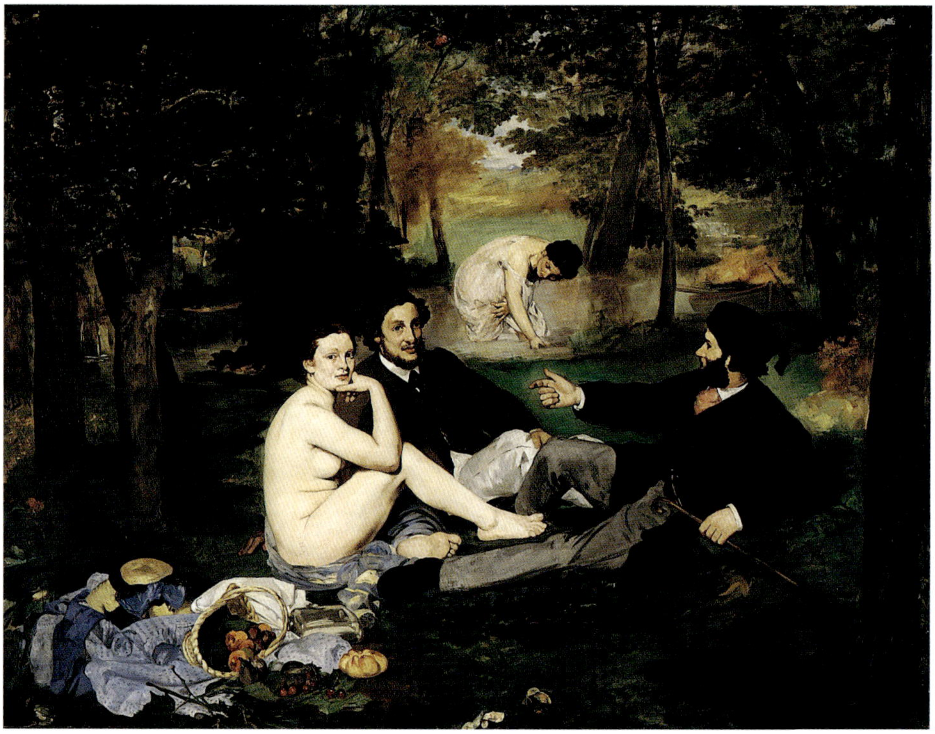

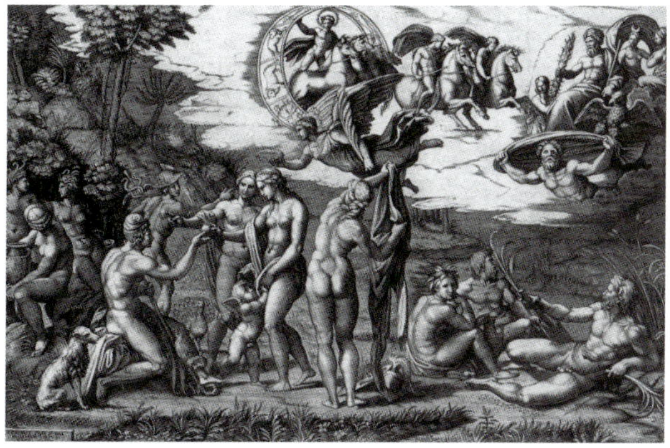

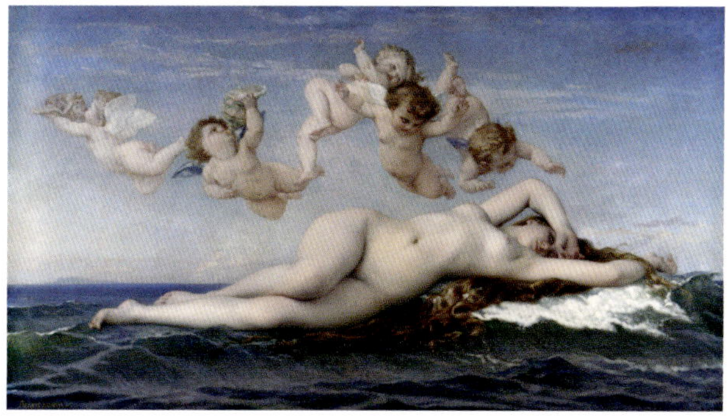

mores. Therefore, instead of lecturing to his public, Manet painted a scene in a matter-of-fact style, as an actual witness of an event on the outskirts of the Parisian metropolis. Believing that this approach might unmask the pretentious attitudes and ambitions of the bourgeois public of his day, Manet encountered precisely the opposite reaction. Instead of feeling challenged by Manet's depiction of a bourgeois gathering at the Seine, the public scoffed at his efforts and made him a target of ridicule. Suddently, the roles of joke-teller and listener were reversed: despite aiming to divest himself of his aggressive impulses, Manet's irony met with public hostility. As Manet had torn down the façade—or at least refused to spell it out—the public could hide behind their own façades and pretend to be indignant at Manet's presumed indecency. It was not until 1867, the year he painted *L'Exécution de Maximilien*, that Manet again employed as complicated techniques as he had used in *Le Buveur d'absinthe* and *Le Vieux Musicien*.

Plate 52: Marcantonio Raimondi, *Judgment of Paris* (1510–1520)
Plate 53: Alexandre Cabanel, *La Naissance de Vénus* (1863)

In the hierarchy of themes established by the Académie and the Salons, History Painting still possessed its traditional pre-eminence in the middle of the century. As Antonin Proust recounts about his friend Manet:

> To him 'historical painter' was the most insulting term of abuse that could be addressed to any artist. He had the greatest contempt for painters who shut themselves up with models, costumes, lay figures and all the other accessories which result in lifeless pictures, when out of doors there were so many vital things to be done.[109]

page 208:
Plate 4: Giorgione/Titian, *Le Concert Champêtre* (1509)
Plate 3: Édouard Manet, *Le Déjeuner sur l'herbe* (1863)

109 Proust, quoted in Courthion 1960: 5.

History Painting per se was not anathema to Manet, but the works of the contemporary history painters were contemptible to him. The execution of Ferdinand Maximilian Joseph, archduke of Austria and emperor of Mexico, on June 19, 1867, provided Manet with a unique historical event to show how this antiquated genre could be reappropriated to suit the contemporary political situation. Manet's acute ability to frame the present in the language of the past proved not only a means of sharpening his sarcasm toward society and the art world, but it also served as a powerful form of political indictment. How deeply Manet's interest in the creation of a modern genre of historical painting was, is perhaps documented in the fact that over a period of two years, he painted five versions of *L'Exécution de Maximilien* (1868–1869) **[Plate 54]**. When Manet conceived his own canvases, he had in mind Goya's *The Third of May 1808* (1814) **[Plate 55]**, a painting that depicted the execution of a Spanish soldier by Napoleonic troops. Manet's *Exécution* preserves the arrangement of the firing squad on the right, aiming their rifles at the victims to the left. We know how scrupulously Manet researched the actual details of the execution of Maximilian by assembling all the available news articles and photographs and getting models to reconstruct the execution scene in his studio. This re-enactment is particularly significant in as much as Manet dressed the firing squad in French uniforms instead of Mexican ones. This "mistake" was of course intentional, since it both denounced the real culprit, namely Napoleon III, who was indirectly responsible for Maximilian's death. And at the same time, it established a direct link to the Napoleonic soldiers in Goya's depiction. Like his uncle Napoleon I, who had promised to liberate Spain and had broken his word by turning a liberation into a bloody occupation, Napoleon III had promised Maximilian the support of the French army to fight the Mexican Republicans under Benito Juárez. Napoleon notoriously jettisoned the Austrian duke as soon as the illusion of an easy victory in Mexico was shattered. By then, his army was needed at home in France to counter the threat of the Prussian assault. By borrowing the composition of Goya's *The Third of May*, Manet not only brought into focus his own painterly genealogy, but ingeniously created a visual link endorsing the historical roots

page 211: **Plate 54:** Édouard Manet, *L'Exécution de Maximilien* (1868–1869)
Plate 55: Francisco de Goya, *The Third of May 1808* (1814)
Plate 48: Jacques-Louis David, *Oath of the Horatii* (1784)

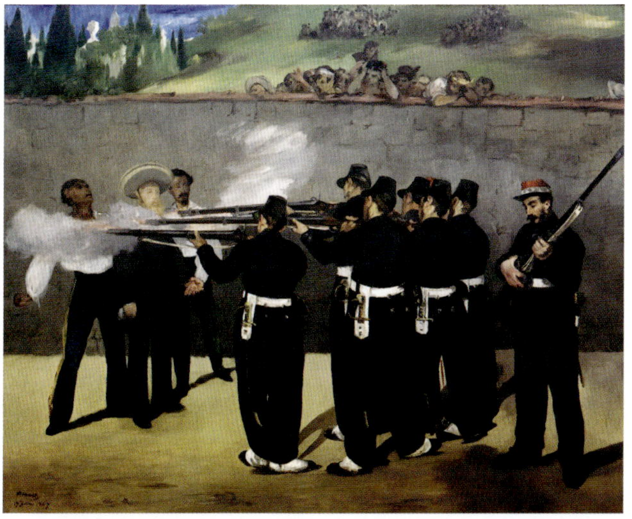

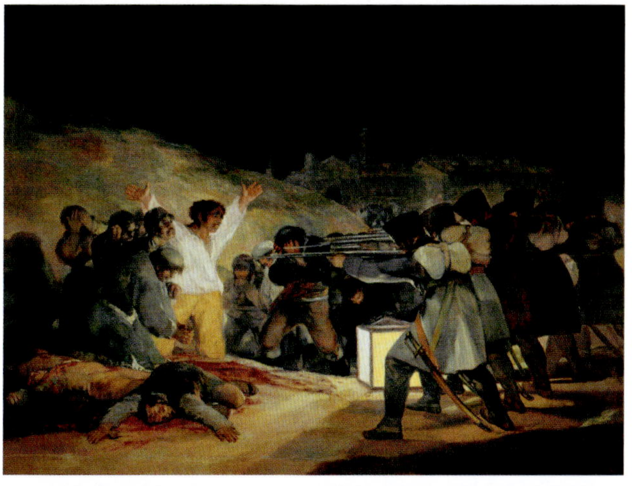

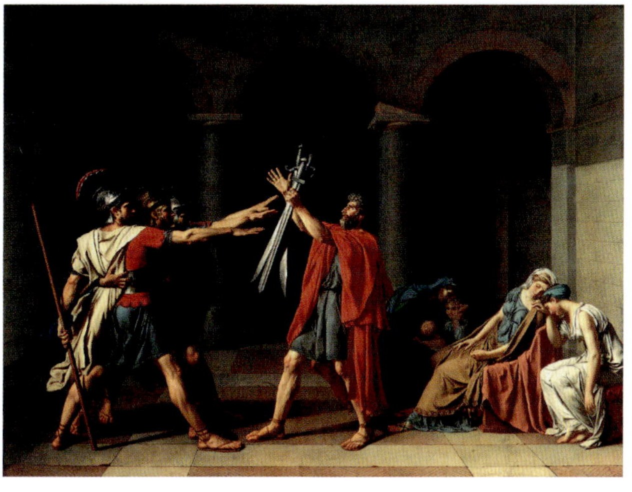

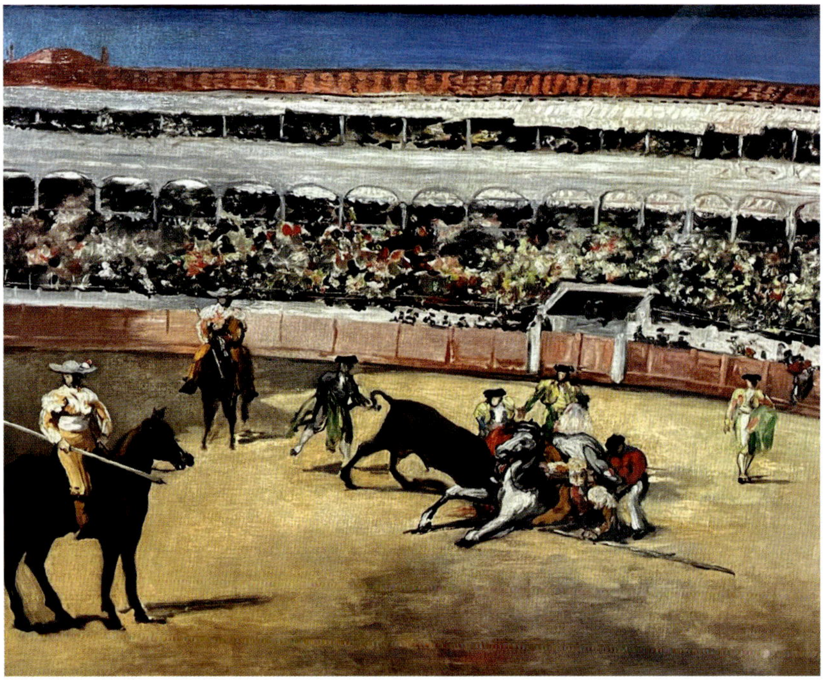

Plate 56:
Édouard Manet,
Combat de taureaux
(1865–1866)

between the two very distinct Bonaparte regimes. One of Napoleon III's aspirations was to restore the Empire, a goal that required persuading his country that his uncle Napoleon I's foreign policy was driven by purely defensive aims. Manet's striking pictorial parallels between the sacrifice of the innocent archduke by Napoleon III and the earlier murder of a defenseless Spanish soldier by Napoleon I underscores the brutally destructive aspects of the declared "defensive" policy. While Manet preserved the overall composition of Goya's painting, he avoided imbuing his canvas with the same sense of horror that permeates *The Third of May*. Instead, the spectator is struck by Manet's dispassionate and laconic depiction of the execution. This sense of secretarial detachment is heightened by the soldier on the right, who cleans his rifle with an air of routine, and by the crowd witnessing the event with passing curiosity. There is none of the horror of Goya's depiction of the event. This sense of the spectacle as "entertainment" is by no means accidental: Manet had already used the idea in *Combat de taureaux* (1865–1866) **[Plate 56]**. By transferring the mood of the crowd in the bullfight to the one of the execution of the archduke, Manet construes parallels between the execution of a hapless puppet of the French monarch and the slaughter of an innocent animal in an arena. This analogy between the bullfight and the execution can be expanded when we consider that in Manet's view, Maximilian himself never posed a political threat but was executed because the Mexican people required a concrete representation of the defeat and humiliation of the French imperial forces.

Several critics have remarked that the painting makes no attempt to evoke a Mexican setting, an omission particularly striking given that Manet had previously painted a great many Hispanic subjects. In the present case, it is only through this indirect reference to the bullfight painting and his quotations of Goya that Manet locates the work at all. By omitting any reference to the setting, Manet was implying that the execution was not done at the Mexican government's instigation, but instead was a consequence of Napoleon III's blundering foreign policies. The practice of omission constitutes one of the central mechanisms of Freud's theory about the joke-work. Omission forms part of an allusion. "What is omitted has been replaced by an inference, which then leads back to what has been omitted, in the form of an allusion [...]."[110] The fact that Manet represents the Mexican soldiers in the uniform of their opponents, is a blatant accusation of culpability. Here again, Manet uses heavy irony, a characteristic of the embittered joker. Mauner and Nochlin have argued that Manet refused to imbue his painting with any sense of tragedy because he was interested primarily in the moment of death as a mere visual and physical fact. Death is treated simply as a process that "must be described in all its trivial detail to convey a sense of actuality."[111] Manet's dry depiction of Maximilian's execution certainly reconfirmed his affiliations with the principles of Realism, which postulated that any event—no matter how tragic or banal—should be represented with a rightful degree of accuracy. However, I believe that Manet's dispassionate approach underscored his characteristic ironic undertone. In short, the artist was less interested in embroiling emotions (as the Romantic historical

110 Freud 1905b: 78.
111 Nochlin 1971: 66.

painters had done), but instead preferred to appeal to the viewer's intellectual judgment. In this sense, Manet followed Poussin's doctrine of addressing the mind and not the senses.

At the same time, *L'Exécution de Maximilien* offered a sort of counter-statement to Poussin's definition of Historical Painting. Manet's work exposed the ignoble deed of a coward and irresponsible French emperor and a pathetic Habsburg archduke, a degenerate with romantic illusions of "rescuing" the Mexican people from barbarism and poverty. Furthermore, his record of this despicable act eschews the canons of Classicism: in an orderly sequence the beholder is invited "to 'read' the exact emotions of each figure," as Poussin would have it.[112] Actually, if we follow closely the direction of the squad's rifles, we notice that they do not aim at the three targets, but shoot right past them. And although the victim on the left, General Mejía, appears to have been hit, he does not crumple with signs of impending death, but merely leans back stiffly. The proximity between the victims and the firing squad prompts another conundrum: which are the six rifles reportedly directed at the targets, we can see only three, so close as to almost touch the archduke and the two generals.

This peculiar intimacy between aggressors and victims confounds our ability to read the emotions of each figure. In contrast to Goya, who unfurls a narrative—progressing from the blood-encrusted victims already hit, to the men about to fall—Manet eschews the rules of causality and continuity. By omitting these logical connections and referring us to Goya's *The Third of May*, Manet obliges us to piece together the events ourselves. With this gesture Manet also subverts the role of the History Painter, whose traditional duty was to pictorialize a virtuous theme and to convey a sense of immutable morality to his audience.

Another quotation from the past is incorporated into *L'Exécution de Maximilien* which combines, in one stroke, an indictment of Bonapartist politics and the type of History Painting that had fostered the original myth of Napoleonic grandeur. We know that Goya was influenced in his conception of the *The Third of May* by

---

112 Janson 1973: 441.

Jacques-Louis David's *Le Serment des Horaces*, also known as *Oath of the Horatii* (1784) **[Plate 48]**. "Undoubtedly Goya was familiar with engravings and drawings made after this painting, which as an image of patriotic dedication exerted and continued to exert a tremendous impact on the European mind."[113] In *The Third of May*, Goya reverses the position of the three warriors, who pledge their moral commitment to the fatherland, and the father as a representative of the State from the left to the right side of the canvas. The warriors become the firing squad and the State becomes the Spanish soldiers to be executed. Initially inspired by the French revolutionary spirit himself, Goya now experienced the bitter fruits and obverse side of French patriotism. The consequences of the sacred oath to the French state were now directly felt by the Spanish people. The guns were turned at them—not to join the fight, but to slay them. For Manet, of course, the Davidian quotation gained yet another meaning. Making cross-references between Goya's *The Third of May* and David's *Oath of the Horatii*, Manet places Maximilian and the two generals, all allies of Napoleon III, in the position of David's three warriors, and the Mexican firing squad assumes the place of David's Horatii, namely, of the State. Through this memory of David's painting, Manet unravels the entire story behind the execution of Maximilian. Because the Austrian archduke had remained faithful to Napoleon III's mission and had not escaped from Mexico along with the rest of the French army, he was ultimately gunned down by the State that had sent him there in the first place. In other words, he was sacrificed for his moral commitment to the French monarch. Through the Davidian quotation, Manet could express his most fierce anti-Napoleonic sentiments.

The way these traditional references unfold in *L'Exécution de Maximilien* graphically illustrates how the psychoanalytic interpretation of a dream proceeds. When a patient reports a dream, the analyst inquires about the separate elements within the dream and listens to the various associations. He never loses sight of the initial story as the analysand's diachronic and synchronic narrative cycles become ever

---

113 Brush 1981: 43.

more elaborate, until they merge again into a single configuration. It is in the gap between the dream content, in this case *L'Exécution de Maximilien*, and the dream thoughts, in this case the various quotations from the past, the contemporary political event, and the distortion of the figures in the painting, that we can disentangle the various meanings. Yet, again it is valuable to remember that we will never excavate the "real" story behind the painting, a fact which is strikingly illustrated by Manet's complex rendition of the execution of Maximilian.

According to M.I. Finley, myth presents "concrete facts, but these facts [are] completely detached; they [are] linked neither with what went on before nor with what comes after."[114] Essentially, Manet's characteristic strategy was to employ a customary mythical staging to represent instead the modernity of his time; in other words, to find a purely painterly means of representing a dialectic between myth and history. Canvases like *Le Buveur d'absinthe* or *Le Vieux Musicien* or *Le Fifre* reveal no particular clues about their historical epoch. These paintings stand in contrast to later canvases like *Le Balcon*, *Chez le père Lathuille*, or *Un Bar aux Folies Bergère* where the theme and depiction leave no doubt that these are truly modern Parisian characters, arrested in the fleeting moment. In *Le Déjeuner sur l'herbe* and *Olympia*, Manet complicates the dialectic of the relationship between history and myth by arranging his models in a mythological scene and inviting his audience to give free rein to their own thoughts and fantasies. Yet, the stark immediate presence of the nude in *Le Déjeuner sur l'herbe* and *Olympia* counteracts the spectators' desire to complete their own story. One is constantly reminded that this is not a mythological representation, but an actual depiction of a living nude or practicing courtesan. However, with *L'Exécution de Maximilien*, Manet develops this strategy in yet another and still more subtly polemical direction. By referencing Goya's *The Third of May*, Manet bases one real event upon another. Yet, by taking Goya and David as models for his own interpretation, he distances and mythologizes the actual political moment of Maximilian's death in 1867. Consequently, the spectator

114 Finley 1965: 285.

remains trapped between fiction and reality, even while knowing that the painting represents a historical event.

Critics generally agree that with the beginning of the 1870s, Manet ceased to echo the works of traditional artists (as if the artist stopped the process of remembrance at the age of thirty-eight). The influence of the Impressionist movement is usually considered to be the main reason for this change of technique. While, admittedly, the references to his predecessors are no longer so explicit nor so specific to the canonic tradition, the quotations in his later paintings are more often than not to his own canvases. After having convincingly established that the past could neither be ignored nor forgotten—but used as a fulcrum for opening up contradictions in the present—Manet could now borrow from his own representations and embody them in his later works. Looking at Manet's oeuvre as a whole, we discover that a story gradually unfolds, a story that begins with *Le Buveur d'absinthe* and ends with *Un Bar aux Folies Bergère*. In these, his first and his last canvas, we detect a similar loneliness and alienation emanating from the two principal isolated figures. Both deal with the theme of alcohol, the one in his solitary existence, the other in a crowded bar. One is the consumer and the other a victim of consumption made socially acceptable by the elegance of the setting and the costumes. The memory of the destitute absinthe drinker evoked by the melancholic barmaid at the Folies Bergère reminds us that not even this glittering and fashionable meeting place can mask the desolation and callousness of modern urban life.

Other echoes continue to be heard in Manet's later works, including, for example, *Bal masqué a l'opéra* (1873) and *La Musique aux Tuileries* (1862) or between the position of *La Dame aux éventails* (1874) and *Olympia* (1863). A certain similarity can be detected as well between *Le Repos* (1870–1871), which portrays Berthe Morisot, and *La Maîtresse de Baudelaire alongée* (1862), the painting which depicts Jeanne Duval, Baudelaire's mistress. On occasion, certain emblems which Manet omitted in his re-castings of traditional paintings find their way back into his later works. The little dog resting at the feet of the *Venus of Urbino*, which Manet had replaced with the notorious cat in *Olympia*, reemerges on the lap of Victorine Meurent in *Le Chemin de fer* (1873)

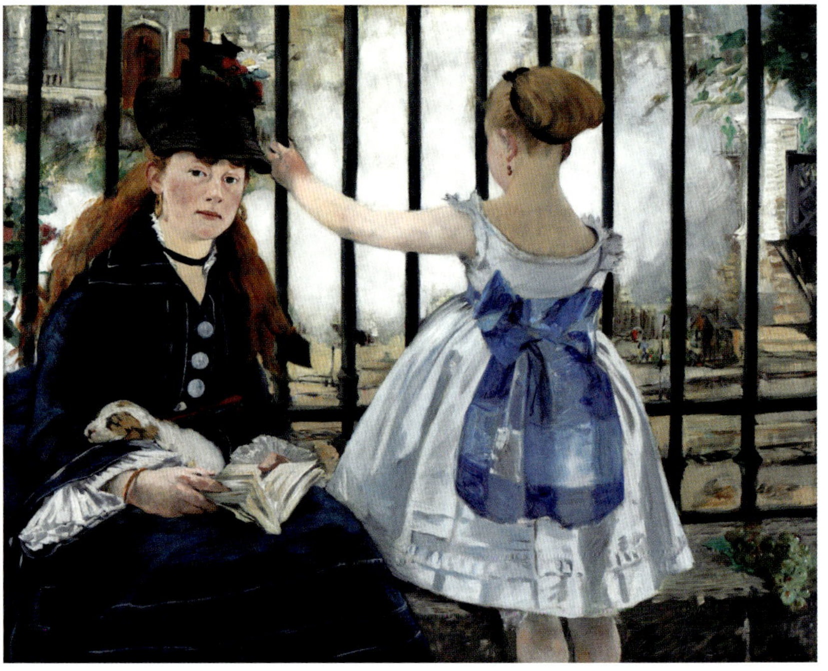

Plate 57:
Édouard Manet,
Le Chemin de fer (1873)

[Plate 57]. By reconnecting Titian's image of the dog with his own model for *Olympia*, Manet wanted to summon up once more a cherished icon, and perhaps show how his own young Venus had aged over the ten years separating the creation of *Olympia* (1863) and *Le Chemin de fer*. The passage of time has turned the young seductive *Olympia* into a well-proportioned middle-aged woman in whose company the wild and sensuous cat no longer seems appropriate. The sleeping dog not only mirrors Venus's waning sexual provocativeness, but it also pays tribute to Victorine Meurent's faithfulness to the artist who made her image a *cause célèbre*. These few examples document that Manet was far from forgetting the traditional artworks, but continued to interpret them through his own recreations. Manet remained true to his position that the ever-recurring, fundamental themes of life do not lose significance in their passage through different historical epochs; for him, the lens through which they are perceived is what may alter their meanings. In one important aspect, however, Manet's quotations did change: they no longer served primarily as a disguise for his critical comments vis-à-vis society. For instance, Nina de

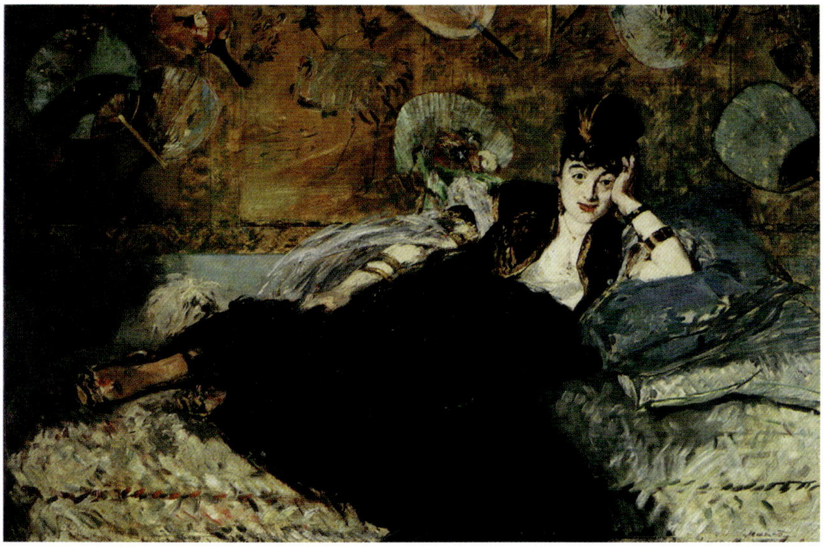

Plate 58:
Édouard Manet,
La Dame aux éventails
(1873)

Callias was no longer situated in the mythological frame of a quondam the renowned courtesan of the French bourgeois society, *Venus of Urbino*. The similarity of her reclining position in *La Dame aux éventails* (1873) **[Plate 58]** was now sufficient to evoke the memory of *Olympia*, at least to those familiar with Manet's works.

The reason why these contemporary figures could now be more openly displayed may be that in 1868, Napoleon III had eased the censorship rules, which in turn paved the way for a more liberal political and social environment. Following the Commune in 1870/1871, Manet, a staunch Republican, had found in Gambetta a politician who satisfied his political ideals and who was about to reorganize the corrupt system of the Académie. Under these changing political circumstances, Manet had perhaps lost a significant opponent against whom he could direct his attacks in such eloquent disguises. And at the same time, Manet had found his own idiom, since his contemporary language had by then been sufficiently saturated by the past. As of 1870, he could speak with more confidence, and also with more self-irony.

The disappearance of the black outline surrounding his figures in the paintings of the 1860s may symbolize Manet's altered position as well. Some critics have argued that its absence after the 1870s signals Manet's final disengagement from Couture's influ-

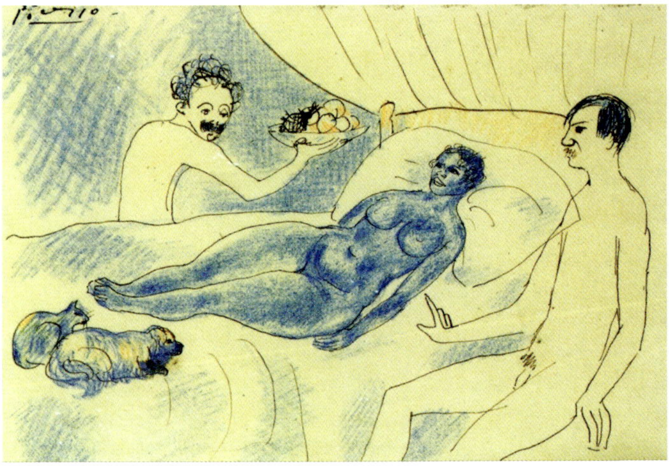

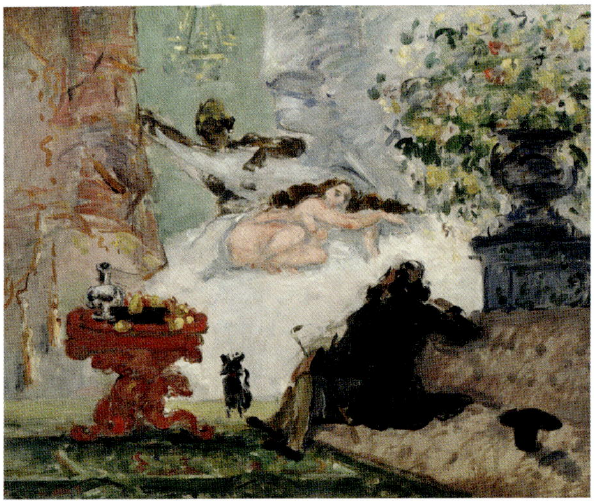

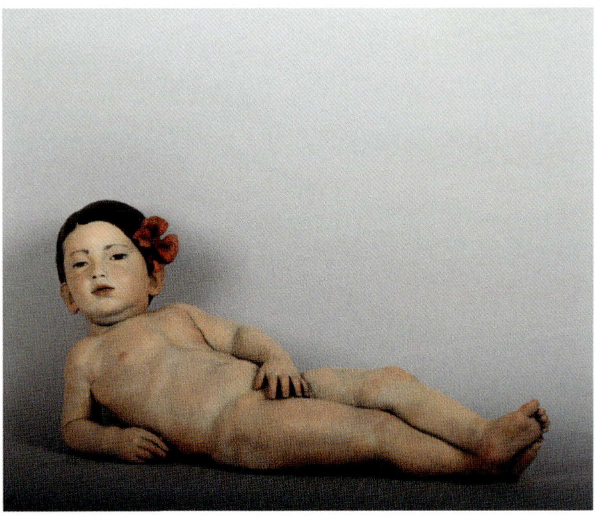

Plate 59:
Pablo Picasso,
A Parody of Manet's Olympia with Junyer and Picasso (1902)
Plate 60:
Paul Cezanne,
A Modern Olympia,
(1873–1874)
Plate 61:
Judy Fox, *Olympia*
(1996/2001)

ence, since his teacher had used the device as a means of emphasizing the figures' expressive contours. But the black outline may also have been a symbolic reminder of the barrier between what was permissible to say and what was forbidden. Yet, despite this change, Manet's remembrances were still as playful and polemical as in the early 1860s. From contemporary caricatures of Manet's works in the magazine *Cham* to Cézanne's *A Modern Olympia* (1873–1874) **[Plate 60]** to Picasso's *Parody of Olympia* (1902) **[Plate 59]** to Magritte's humorous reinterpretation of *Le Balcon* (1950) **[Plate 62]**, and finally to Judy Fox's most recent depiction of *Olympia* (1996/2001) **[Plate 61]**, Manet continued to inspire the wit of his artistic successors. Yet, even more importantly, he knew how to interweave his memories of traditional paintings with those of his present, thereby preparing a path for future generations to link more candidly and forcefully the past with the present and the present with the past. Fried underscores this achievement when he states: "[...] no painter since Manet has been faced with the need to secure the connectedness of his art to that of the distant past, to the enterprise of the Old Masters. With Manet's paintings of the first half of the sixties, that simply and without notice disappeared as a problem for painting."[115] Until the end of his lifetime, Manet paid tribute to the meaning of his own name, as one of his contemporary admirers pointed out to him: "*manet et manebit*,"[116] which means in Latin, "He remains and will remain."

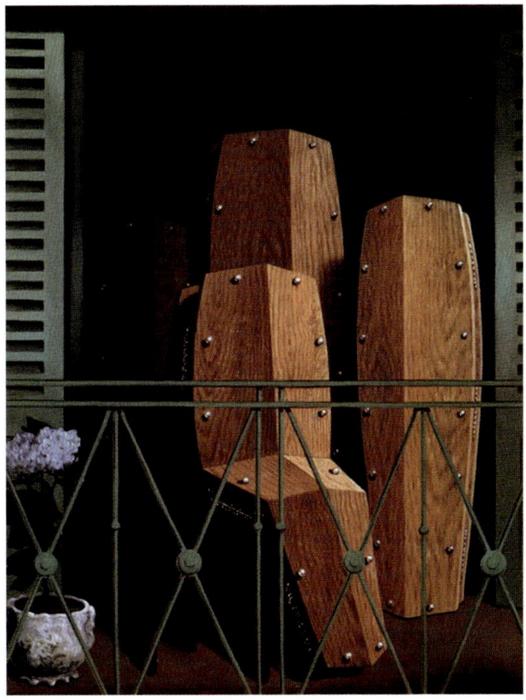

Plate 62:
René Magritte,
Le Balcon de Manet (1950)

115 Fried 1969: 66.
116 Malassis, quoted in Courthion 1960: 78 (emphasis in the original).

Chapter IV

REVERSING THE GAZE ON ITS BEHOLDERS

L'homme y passe à travers des forêts de symboles
Qui l'observent avec des regards familiers.[1]

"Correspondances," Charles Baudelaire, 1857

But looking at someone carries the implicit expectation
that our look will be returned by the object of our gaze.
Where this expectation is met (which, in the case of
thought processes, can apply equally to the look of the eye
of the mind and to a glance pure and simple),
there is an experience of the aura to the fullest extent.

Walter Benjamin, *Illuminations*, 1955

One of the most strikingly enigmatic characteristics of Manet's paintings is the manner in which he captured the uncanny way his figures stare out of the pictures. Although it is not unusual for painted figures to confront their audience, Manet's figures are particularly unsettling, as they compel us to return their gaze. We are caused to feel that we too are being observed. In his day, Manet's critics rarely sought an explanation for this feature in the works themselves, but instead referred to the painter's own physical characteristics for an explanation. In personal descriptions of Manet, both friends and critics frequently remarked upon his "keen" glance and upon his

1 "Man wends his way through forests of symbols. / Which look at him with their familiar glances." (From Benjamin, *Illuminations*).

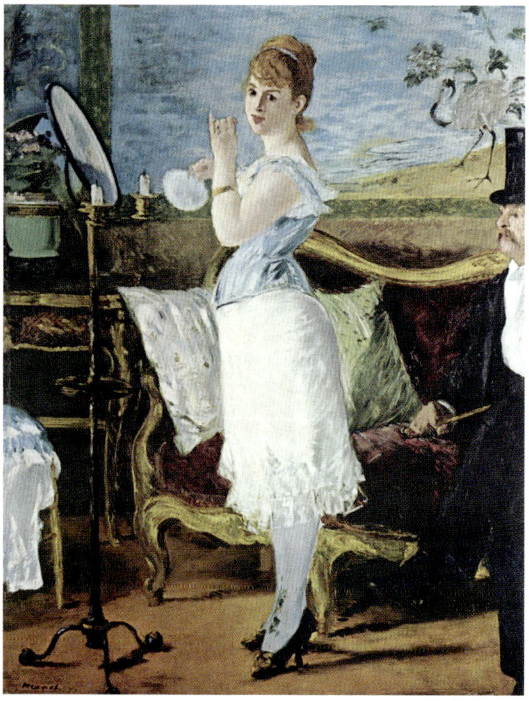

Plate 63:
Édouard Manet,
Nana (1877)

"small but very mobile" eyes.[2] Edmond Bazire detected a distinct vivacity, while Émile Zola described the artist's stare as obstinate and exacting. In an era in which public behavior became "a matter of observation, of passive participation, of a certain kind of voyeurism,"[3] it is hardly surprising that Manet's admirers and detractors alike attributed a certain significance to Manet's powers of observation. The journalist-critic Théophile Thoré-Bürger asserted that Manet saw very well indeed. "He paints what he sees, as he sees it, and he sees truly."[4] Conversely, his more hostile critics sought to limit the enigmatic quality of his painted figures by demystifying the man's own vision. Meanwhile, Louis Leroy, an art critic writing for the satirical magazine *Charivari* believed that

> Manet must suffer from an acute affliction of the retina. Nature couldn't appear this way without an aberration of the optic nerve. I hope the artist will have his eyes examined by a good oculist. More than that, I earnestly urge his family to take pains to prevent him, when he is cured, from seeing the paintings he produced during his illness. He would suffer too much if he saw them.[5]

Elsewhere, Albert Wolff—another unfavorable art critic—opined that the intimacy and detachment simultaneously embodied in Manet's figures lay in the fact that "[a]s a painter he has an eye but

---

2 See *Memoirs of Antonin Proust*, quoted in Courthion (1960: 39); see also Jacques de Biez's description: "Piercingly alert eyes, rather narrow and deep-set, lent a warmth to the trenchant remarks—where every shaft struck home—which fell from his delicate and expressive lips." (de Biez, quoted in Courthion 1960: 45).

3 Sennett 1977: 27.

4 Hamilton 1969: 125.

5 Leroy, quoted in Hamilton 1969: 55.

no soul."[6] While the examination of Manet's vision ultimately cannot help us to decipher *Olympia's* knowing glare, or the provocative gaze of *Nana* (1877) **[Plate 63]**, there is nonetheless one personal incident in Manet's life that may shed light upon the frigid, intimidating stare he bestowed upon his figures.

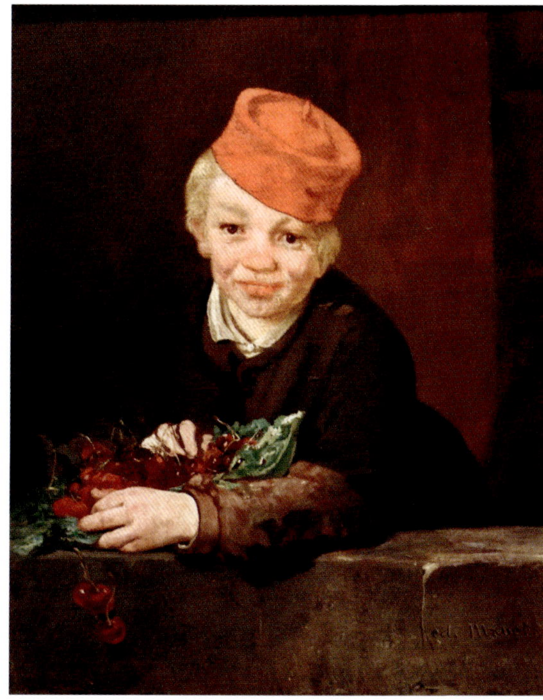

Plate 64:
Édouard Manet,
L'Enfant aux cerises (1858)

It is important to realize that Manet never recounted this incident himself and that it has survived only through the poeticized account narrated by his friend, Charles Baudelaire. In the prose poem "La Corde," Baudelaire tells the story of a young boy named Alexandre, who had posed for Manet's *L'Enfant aux cérises* (1858) **[Plate 64]**. He was a poor urchin taken in by Manet to help clean the brushes and palette. One day, when Manet returned to his studio, he found the young boy had hanged himself:

> [...] his convulsed head had dropped onto his shoulder, his face was a swollen mass and his eyes were wide open and fixed in a icy stare, making me think at first he was still alive. [...] Now I had to get back to work, redouble my application, ease from my mind the corpse whose ghost was wearing me down with its wide stare.[7]

Although we cannot know whether Baudelaire accurately recounts Manet's reaction to the suicide of his apprentice, or construed it based on his own impressions of Manet's account, it is tempting to argue that Manet did indeed attempt to recapture the young Alexandre's

---

6 Wolff, quoted in Hamilton 1969: 196.

7 Baudelaire 2023: 64–65; "[S]a tête était penchée convulsivement sur une épaule; son visage, boursouflé, et ses yeux, tout grands ouverts avec une fixité effrayante, me causèrent d'abord l'illusion de la vie. [...] Il ne me restait plus qu'à me remettre au travail, plus vivement encore que d'habitude, pour chasser peu à peu ce petit cadavre qui hantait les replis de mon cerveau, et dont le fantôme me fatiguait de ses grands yeux fixes." (Baudelaire 1962: 149–151).

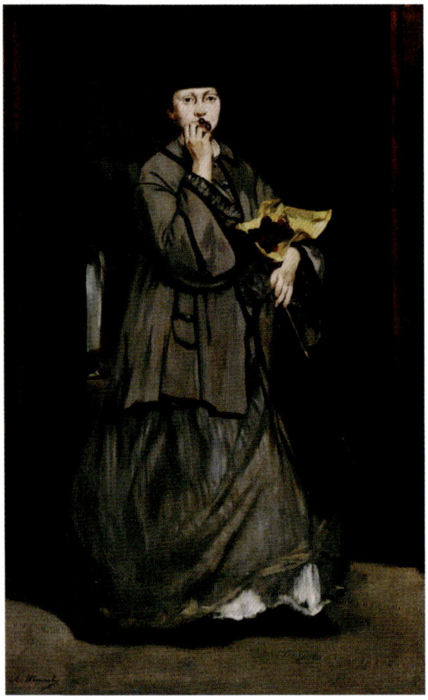

Plate 16: Édouard Manet, *La Chanteuse de rue* (1862)

petrifying stare in figures like *Le Pierrot*, *Le Vieux Musicien*, *Le Fifre*, or even the young dandy (Léon) in *Le Déjeuner dans l'atelier.* It is also tempting to believe that Manet was haunted by this horrible experience and used his paintings as a means of making the kid come to life again: perhaps the disturbing stare in the dead boy's eyes inspired Manet to give "an illusion of life" throughout his later canvases. A semblance of life permeates works such as *La Chanteuse de rue* [**Plate 16**], *Olympia*, and *Un Bar aux Folies Bergère*, giving the spectator the impression that these figures might step out of the frame at any moment and join the viewer. Manet's apparent wish to "ease from my mind the corpse" brings to mind Hanna Segal's words that "when the world within us is destroyed [...], we must recreate our world anew, reassemble the pieces, infuse life into dead fragments, recreate life."[8] Perhaps because Manet was a man of images and not of words, he never outwardly mourned the urchin's death and instead used his brush to work through the loss and sense of horror at discovering the lifeless body in his studio. By endowing his figures with a similar quality of cool detachment, freeze-framing them as it were, Manet situated both himself and the spectator in the same position he was forced to adopt when he discovered Alexandre and could not revive him.

The viewer's position vis-à-vis a painting had not always been as unsettling as in Manet's works. Historically, painters had either drawn spectators into the canvas, precisely in order to make them forget their position as spectators, or they had kept them at a distance by structuring the work as a pure picture *qua* picture, namely, an object to be looked at. Manet, however, simultaneously accomplished a peculiar intimacy and a harsh distance between his figures and their onlookers. Just how novel the challenge of so direct an address to the spectator was at the time becomes clear when we consider

---

8 Segal 1981: 190.

Diderot's indications, whereby the artist is urged to banish the idea of a viewer altogether:

> If, when one makes a painting, one supposes beholders, everything is lost. The painter leaves his canvas, just as the actor who speaks to the audience steps down from the stage. In supposing that there is no one else in the world except the personages of the painting, Van Dyck's painting is sublime. Now this is a supposition that must always be made.[9]

Diderot argued that for a painting to be a convincing representation of reality, the viewer's emotional absorption in the painting can be secured only if the figures portrayed are perceived to be so entirely caught up in the drama represented that they preclude the presence of an onlooker. In other words, for him the figures' actions and expressions should portray "natural signs of intention or emotion," and not "impostures aimed at the beholder."[10] Even in portraits of single figures, Diderot demanded that the painter represent them in a state of absorbed unselfconsciousness that preempted the very idea of an onlooker (bar the painter himself). As Fried argues: "Diderot's conception of painting rested ultimately upon the supreme fiction that the beholder did not exist, that he was not really there, standing before the canvas [...]."[11]

However, this paradigm of excluding a putative future public in order to capture their attention became increasingly problematic in the late eighteenth and nineteenth century.

Indeed, gradually, the very opposite became the norm of the Romantics, whose gigantic canvases depicted dramatic situations in an entirely theatrical and staged manner, thereby acknowledging outright that the scenes were orchestrated precisely for the benefit of the viewer.

With the emergence of the Realist movement, painters were once again engaged in the task of de-theatricalizing the relationship between a canvas and its public. However, instead of seeking to negate

9 Diderot, quoted in Fried 1980: 148.
10 Fried 1978: 112.
11 Fried 1978: 113.

the spectator's existence, artists such as Courbet attempted to restructure the painting/beholder relationship by absorbing the spectator "in a new, almost corporeal way."[12] Courbet's paintings do not shut the spectator out, nor do they totally engulf him by means of the represented dramatic action. Instead, Courbet placed his figures so close to the pictorial surface that the viewers could no longer consider themselves "outside" the scene as such, but were virtually compelled to merge with the figures represented. Fried argues that Courbet's "essential impulse seems to have been to eliminate all sense of mutual confrontation between subject and beholder."[13] He concludes his essay on Courbet with the observation that:

> In Édouard Manet's seminal masterpieces of the first half of the 1860s, Courbet's enterprise is reversed in almost all aspect. Most important, Manet seems intuitively to have recognized that Courbet's attempt to abolish the very possibility of spectatordom was doomed in every instance to (ontological not artistic) failure [...] and that it was therefore necessary to establish the beholder's presence abstractly—to build into the painting the separateness, distancedness and mutual facing that I have associated with the painting-beholder relationship [...] in order that the worst consequences of the theatricalization of that relationship be averted.[14]

Instead of de-theatricalizing the realm of painting, Manet placed his figures right back onstage. In this way, his model Victorine Meurent could personify the naked woman in both *Le Déjeuner sur l'herbe* and *Olympia,* or be dressed up in a Spanish costume in *Mlle V. en costume d'espada* (1862) **[Plate 65]**. Yet, her frozen posture and hollow gaze reveal her distance from the role she is required to assume. Manet provided the role, but left it up to the spectator to complete the scenario.[15] By

---

12 Fried 1978: 119.

13 Fried 1978: 121.

14 Fried 1978: 121.

15 From Baudelaire's long poem *La Corde*, we can gain some insight into Manet's own conceptualization of how he staged his portraits and scenes: "In the backwater in which I live, where vast areas of grass still separate the buildings, I often used to see a child, whose keen roguish expression beguiled me more than any other. He posed more

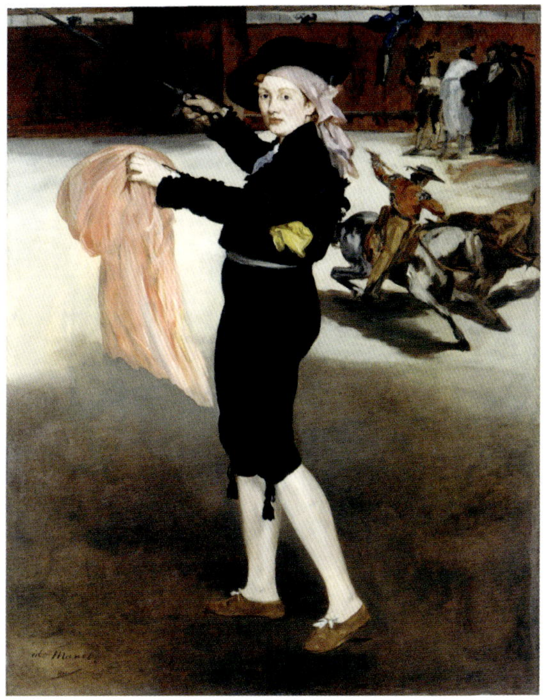

Plate 65:
Édouard Manet,
Mlle V. en costume d'espada
(1862)

simultaneously affirming the fictitious and staged reality of the painted figure and insisting upon the active participation of the spectators to "complete" the scene with their imagination, Manet succeeded in dismantling the mimetic intentionality expected of painting as a faithful representation of real life, while demystifying the presumed absence of a viewing public. In this way, Courbet's system of drawing the observer into the canvas was subverted, detachment was re-established, and figures and observers were caught in a mutual face-off. Furthermore, Manet never lets his models forget that they are impersonating the role of an Other, caught in a fiction, as it were; nor does he permit the spectators to forget their due position outside of the canvas. In this respect, Manet's works share certain significant characteristics of the Brechtian theater.

Like Manet's painted figures Olympia, Nana, or Berthe Morisot in *Le Balcon* the Brechtian actor is not supposed to impersonate a character, but to narrate the actions of another person:

> To illustrate these actions and to make them fully understood by the audience he goes through the motions the character made, imitates the tone of his voice, repeats his facial expression, but only to the extent of *quoting* them. The Brechtian style of acting is acting in quotation marks.[16]

---

than once for me. Sometimes I turned him into a little vagabond, sometimes an angel, sometimes a mythological *amorino*. I made him carry the vagabond's violin, the crown of thorns and the nails of the Passion, and the torch of Eros." (Baudelaire, quoted in Courthion 1960: 145). It is interesting to note that the first portrait Manet painted of Victorine Meurent was an intimate and beautiful study of her face, reminiscent of Vermeer's *Girl with a Pearl Earring* **[Plate 66]**. It was as if Manet presented Victorine first in person before he dressed her in different roles, see *Portrait of Victorine Meurent* **[Plate 67]**.

16 Esslin 1971: 137 (emphasis in the original).

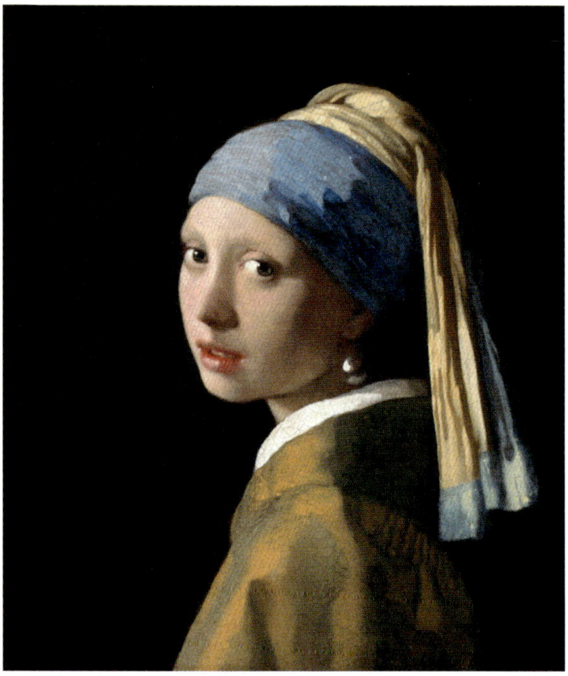

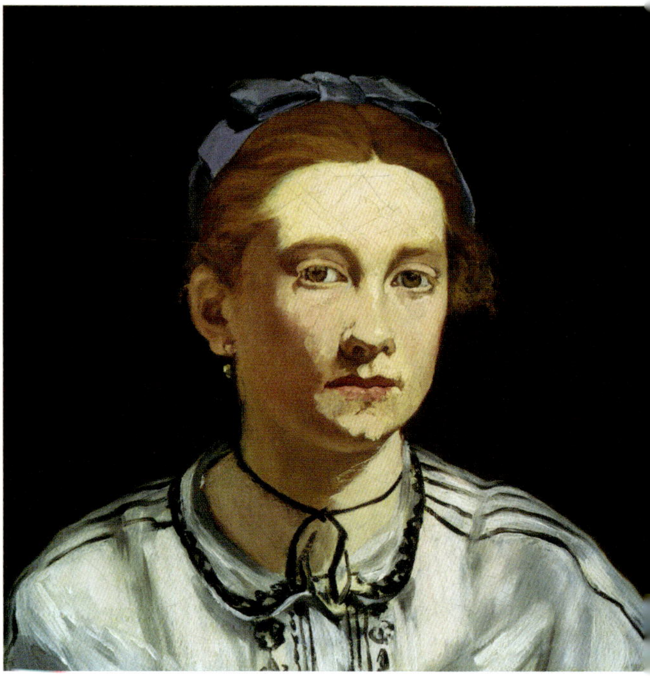

Plate 66: Johannes Vermeer, *Girl with a Pearl Earring* (1665)
Plate 67: Édouard Manet, *Portrait de Victorine Meurent* (1862)

In the previous chapter we discussed how Manet's works referenced the works of traditional artists in an attempt to re-interpret and re-contextualize their imagery, adapting it for his own age. However, as we can now see, his citations from the past also served as a means of creating a distance within his figures, between the roles they were adopting and their own characters. Brecht demanded from his performers that they never forgot who they were in real life, nor allowed others to forget that the actors were not the real protagonists of the drama, but merely the individuals enacting it. "The character who is being shown and the actor who demonstrates him remain clearly differentiated."[17] Although the gap between the projected figures and the model impersonating them is not so clearly demarcated in Manet's work (for whom the possibility of ambiguity offered a constant technical and emotional resource), it is evident that such bold ventures as the re-staging of Titian's *Venus of Urbino* with Victorine Meurent as *Olympia* served as an important device to generate the

---

17 Esslin 1971: 137.

self-estranging pose he attempted to invoke. Instead of forging an artificial distance between his viewers and his painting by negating their presence, he established a scenario within which he instructed his model not to forget that she was engaged in an impersonation, thereby succeeding in painting precisely what he saw before him. The result is the model Victorine's aloofness from the role she was adopting, towards her spectators. Even in paintings in which Manet did not deliberately recreate a composition from an Old Master, he would rarely portray figures as he observed them in a street or a café (unlike Renoir and Degas, for instance). Instead, he would generally use his favorite models—or in rare instances, the actual person who had caught his attention—and re-stage the observed scene in his atelier. While this method was partly caused by the technical difficulties of capturing the instant—Manet is known to have been a notoriously slow painter—it also helped to sustain the staged and alienated effect his earlier, cautious reworkings of traditional paintings had so deliberately produced. Put differently, Manet sincerely depicted nature as it was, but his work passed through distinct intermediary stages: via the reproductions of the works he quoted and through the roles adopted by his models to embody modern scenes of typical Parisian life. Perhaps Manet's exasperated claim that he was unable to finish a painting if his model failed to show up may be interpreted from yet another perspective: without her reliable attendance, Manet may have felt unable to recapture the innate tensions that arose in each sitting between the model and the role she performed for Manet's depiction.

Another device the epic theater used to keep the audience in an atmosphere of estrangement and at a distance from the action presented on stage was the use of undisguised physical props.

To dispel any illusion of reality, Brecht insisted that the sources of light and the bare materials of the stage remain visible to the audience.

> … and make
> My curtain half-high, don't seal off the stage!
> Leaning back in his chair, let the spectator
> Be aware of busy preparations, made for him
> Cunningly; he sees a tinfoil moon

Float down, or a tiled roof
Being carried in; do not show him too much,
But show him something! And let him notice
That you are not wizards,
Friends, but workers ...[18]

By declining to apply a "*fini/finish*" to his paintings, Manet was insisting—in a manner analogous to Brecht's—upon openly acknowledging the presence of brush and paint in the creation of the work at hand. Instead, the standard *fini* technique delivered a polished and homogeneous surface that had become the hallmark of an accomplished painting. "It cleans up, rubs out traces of the real work, erases the evidence of the brush strokes, glosses over the rough edges of the forms, fills in the broken lines, hides the fact that the picture is a real object made out of paint."[19] Manet's decision not to apply this finish to his paintings left visible evidence of his labor, increasing "the impression of reality given by what is represented. By emphasizing the painting as representation, the artist confirms the existence of what is behind the representation."[20] Ultimately, Manet's audience rejected a number of his paintings because to them, these works looked like sketches and were not adequately finished. "He [Manet] begins and does not finish; as soon as his paintings have reached a certain point, he leaves them incomplete."[21] This critic's complaint was not just about the lack of *fini*, but to his mind, Manet's works never seemed completed and revealed a pervasive sense of emptiness and indifference. In a sense, Manet's refusal to apply a "finish" to his paintings mirrored the formal structure of his works, which never seemed "complete" without the beholder's direct engagement with the work. The *fini* had also been "associated with the qualities of probity, assiduity, professional conscience—and also discretion."[22] The purpose of "finishing" a painting was to assure the critic and the

18 Bertolt Brecht, "Die Vorhänge," *Schriften zum Theater*, p. 260; quoted in Esslin 1971: 143.
19 Rosen/Zerner, 1976: 33.
20 Rosen/Zerner 1976: 34.
21 Francion, quoted in Hamilton 1969: 191.
22 Rosen/Zerner 1976: 33.

purchaser that the artist knew his trade and had indeed labored to earn his pay. Since Manet refused to "complete" his works, both from a compositional and a technical point of view, the spectators were not given any conventional methods by which they could assess the artist's talents, that is, they could not even detect how much labor had gone into such shocking canvases as *Olympia* or *Nana*.

While Manet's technical methods curiously anticipated the Brechtian theories of creating an estranging effect (*Verfremdungseffekt*)—of alienating the audience from the action performed on the stage—, in one essential point Manet differed from the German playwright. Brecht had claimed that the audience must be completely impeded from identifying with the characters on the stage. He believed that the audience would resist any kind of identification with the performers as long as a separate existence could be strictly maintained between the performance and its onlookers. However, as Martin Esslin correctly observes:

> In his rejection of identification between audience and characters Brecht comes into conflict with the fundamental concept of psychology that regards processes of identification as the basic mechanism by which one human being communicates with another. Without identification and empathy each person would be irrevocably imprisoned within himself. [...] In practice, he [Brecht] succeeded at best merely in reducing to some extent the emotional identification of the audience with his characters.[23]

Rather than seeking to abolish the process of identification, and with more subtlety than Brecht, Manet employed the principles of the *Verfremdungseffekt* to render the spectator uneasily aware of his unconscious wish to identify with the painted figures on the canvas. Unlike traditional painters who relied upon—but never explicitly acknowledged—the identificatory process of the spectator and composed their paintings accordingly, Manet drew attention to the methods by which he attempted to lure his spectators into his canvases. As noted previously, Manet deliberately emphasized both his position as

---

23 Esslin 1971: 148–149.

a painter intending certain aesthetic effects and his link to the spectator as the recipient and object of these intentions. Lacan describes the relationship between the painter and spectator as "a play of *trompe l'œil*."[24] However, instead of deceiving the spectator into accepting the illusory world of the painted canvas as an unmediated representation of the natural world, Manet draws his audience into the painting by generating an absence, a missing element, a gap that the spectator feels compelled to fill. Yet, just when the viewer attempts to occupy this empty space, the painted figure bars access and redirects the viewer to his original position as an outsider, standing before the painting.

Though Diderot's comment was intended as a harsh criticism—that a painter whose composition presupposes the existence of an audience is like an actor who steps out of his role to address the audience—it closely describes the effect Manet sought to achieve regarding the spectator and the "theatrical" arena of the canvas. In this sense, Winnicott's concept of the *transitional space* offers a helpful tool for a visual illustration of the identificatory process that unfolds between the beholder and the image beheld. Let us imagine the gap between a Manet canvas and its beholder as an intangible circle that he weaves around these two positions, and let us call the volume between the painted canvas, the painter, and the viewer the potential or transitional space. Unlike traditional painters, who wanted their spectators to step inside and occupy that sphere, Manet conjures up a playful dance whereby the spectator is induced to cross the threshold of perception, shuttling back and forth: now observer, now participant. In this way, Manet invites the beholder from outside into the frame, but he also ensures that they cannot lose themselves inside the circle created. Although this device allows us to bridge the gap and merge with the scene depicted, we also realize that either way we will never have full access to the painting before our eyes. This constant evocation of a response to the canvas leaves us searching for the fulfillment of our own needs and constitutes an entirely new approach to the problem of arresting our attention. By luring the spectators into the painting and involving them in a canny interplay of presence and absence, Manet

---

24 Lacan 1978: 103.

no longer needed to deceive them about their position or create an illusory "natural" world on the canvas because he "simply" incorporated their imagined presence in the work of art itself.

So far, I have used the analogy of the Brechtian theater to explain Manet's dramatization of the relationship between artist, model, and spectator in his oeuvre. To some degree, this mechanism echoes Freud's detailed analysis of his emotional engagement with Michelangelo's statue of *Moses*, which he encountered while touring Rome. Although such a "theatrical" interpretation provides a useful model for analyzing artistic strategies—from Michelangelo's representation of Moses to Manet's "alienation effect"—, we must bear in mind that what we are discussing is the static realm that is the wordless inscape of painting.

Accordingly, our next question must be how and by what means did Manet succeed in bringing about his *Verfremdungseffekt*, considering that he had far fewer technical resources available to him than a stage director has. How could Manet hold his audience at this critical distance without the resources of language, music, and live actors? My answer lies in his complex compositions of painted figures who do not exchange looks with each other, but instead gaze vacantly at or *through* their spectators, or fix them directly with a penetrating stare. In order to comprehend the circuit of desire and reciprocal need for recognition that is set in motion by these gazes that incite such reactions, we first have to remember the psychological significance of the act of looking itself, and the vicissitudes this activity entails.[25]

***

25 The difference between looking and seeing is a subtle one, since looking indicates a direct contact of the eye into a particular direction, it is connected with sight, with vision. One can call a spectator an onlooker, but not a "seer" or "on-seer." To *see* suggests a more contemplative stance that involves time and internal reflection. When you *see*, you become aware of something by using your eyes; when you *look*, the contact is more immediate and directional. Voyeurism is more linked with looking. See also Otto Fenichel, *Schautrieb und Identifizierung* (1935). (Compare also with the comment by Jasper Johns: "he considers the flags and targets similar because 'they're both things which are seen and not looked at [...]'", in: Crichton 1994: 30).

Psychoanalysis is properly that which reveals both the one and the Other to be simply mirages.

Anthony Wilden, 1968

Seeing, as Freud observed, "is ultimately derived from touching. Visual impressions remain the most frequent pathway along which libidinal excitation is aroused […]."[26] During the first year of life, children explore their environment primarily by incorporating the objects in the surrounding world through their eyes. The children's pleasure of viewing the world around them is one of the most rudimentary drives and occurs before the infants are aware of their separateness from others. Although the scopophilic drive is auto-erotic, it already has an object in the infant's own body.

According to Freud, it is only by a process of comparison that the object of one's own body is exchanged for an analogous part of someone else's. Freud posits that the desire to look at others is bound up with the curiosity about one's own sexual organs, and later about another person's genitals, usually those of the opposite sex.

> A desire to see the organs peculiar to each sex exposed is one of the original components of our libido. It may itself be a substitute for something earlier and go back to a hypothetical primary desire to touch the sexual parts. […] The libido for looking and touching is present in everyone in two forms, active and passive, male and female; and, according to the preponderance of the sexual character, one form or the other predominates.[27]

26 Freud 1905a: 156.
27 Freud 1905b: 98.

Both Little Hans's desire to see his parents' "widdlers," and the Rat Man's "burning and tormenting curiosity to see the female body,"[28] are examples of the infant's intense desire to see and grasp the function of the sexual organs, as well as the difference between the female and male genitalia. If the sexual aim of looking is not sufficiently repressed and sublimated into more socially adapted behaviors, the pleasure in looking—scopophilia—can develop into a perversion: "[...] *(a)* if it is restricted exclusively to the genitals, or *(b)* if it is connected with the overriding of disgust [...], or *(c)* if, instead of being *preparatory* to the normal sexual aim, it supplants it."[29] Scopophilia is usually accompanied by sadistic impulses, whereby the subject wants to see something in order to destroy it. "Often looking itself is unconsciously thought of as a substitute for destroying ('I did not destroy it; I merely looked at it')."[30] Exhibitionism, on the other hand, is the desire to be looked at, hence a passive impulse. In Freud's view, both the active and passive forms of this perversion can be traced back to the child's early castration anxieties, during which he needs to look and confirm that his genitalia have not been cut off; or, when he exposes his penis, to gain reassurance through the reaction of others that he has one. The exhibitionist act is performed as a kind of magical gesture whereby "the exhibition of a penis is thought of as a magical means of achieving a situation in which the attacked girls can display the very same thing, that is, a penis and not a female organ."[31] Thus, the desire to be looked at not only serves as a means of reassuring oneself of the existence of one's penis, but also as a means of denying that the woman has been castrated. It is not difficult to see how the sexual and omnipotent

---

28 Freud 1909b: 160.

29 Freud 1905a: 157.

30 Fenichel 1972: 71. Looking can have the symbolic equivalent of eating and of destroying. I want what the otherone has, and if I eat it and thereby destroy it, I make sure that the other cannot have it. The wish to destroy is closely linked to envy. By destroying or harming the other, I make sure that s/he is damaged and no longer attractive. In the Kleinian tradition, envy is closely linked to the death drive, one wants to destroy the good object that satisfies, not the bad object that frustrates. For further discussion, see Elizabeth Bott Spillius (1993), "Varieties of envious experience", *International Journal of Psychoanalysis*, 74: 1199–1212.

31 Fenichel 1971: 345.

qualities associated with *looking* are closely linked to the castration complex, since looking unconsciously comprises the desire to devour and/or to destroy the other object, whereas being *looked at* conceals the desire to be reassured against castration fears. Because of the close relationship to the castration complex, eyes have often functioned as an upward displacement for the penis. As Freud observes:

> [...] the fear of damaging or losing one's eyes is a terrible one in children. Many adults retain their apprehensiveness in this respect, and no physical injury is so much dreaded by them as an injury to the eye. [...] A study of dreams, phantasies and myths has taught us that anxiety about one's eyes, the fear of going blind, is often enough a substitute for the dread of being castrated. The self-blinding of the mythical criminal, Oedipus, was simply a mitigated form of the punishment of castration.[32]

In addition to the Oedipus myth, such tales as that of Lady Godiva, of King Lear, and of Tiresias, as well as E.T.A. Hoffmann's story of "The Sandman" (all cited by Freud himself) testify to the powerful and fearful qualities associated with the activity of looking, and the mixture of pride and shame of being observed. However, besides the sexual components of looking and the symbolic identity of eyes and genitals, looking is also manifested as a powerful and potentially harmful activity, because it is through the look that individuals construct their own self-image and gain a perception of themselves, long before they conceive of themselves through words. It is through the infants' looking at themselves or at the mother holding them in front of the mirror that they come to recognize their own appearance, visually. As Merleau-Ponty observes:

> Until the moment when the specular image arises, the child's body is a strongly felt but confused reality. To recognize his image in the mirror is for him to learn that *there can be a viewpoint taken on him.* Hitherto he has never seen himself. [...] By means of the image in the mirror he becomes capable of being a spectator of himself.[33]

---

32 Freud 1919: 231.

33 Merleau-Ponty 1964: 136 (emphasis in the original).

According to Jacques Lacan, the infants enter the mirror stage at six months when they begin to recognize their own image in the mirror. This visual recognition is usually accompanied by an intense feeling of joy which the children express by their laughter and eagerness to play with the image perceived in the mirror. The children want to touch the mirror and look behind it to see whether they can grasp the reflection that gives them such pleasure. Lacan identifies the children's jubilation about their initial self-recognition as a sign of the fundamental mis-recognition in which the children—who do not yet possess complete motor coordination—identify with a specular image that promises a unified body. The children, therefore, misconstrue themselves through their own image, a reflection which represents a physical integrity that the children have not yet achieved. Hence the great pleasure at discovering that their body is all in one part, rather than a series of fragmented pieces. Captured and fascinated by their own image, the children are trying out movements they perceive in the mirror and reduplicate the image inside and outside themselves, constantly repeating the seduction which they experience in the mirror movements. Regardless of whether this projective identification arises from the children seeing their own reflection, or from the mother holding a child in front of the mirror, the image in the mirror always remains an Other, an alien body with which the children identify, thus mistaking the Other for themselves and themselves for the Other. What is true for the children's body, is also true for the Other's body. The children feel that they are inside the Other's body, just as they feel themselves to be in their visual image.

As Laura Mulvey points out:

> […] the image recognized is conceived as the reflected body of the self, but its misrecognition as superior projects this body outside itself as an ideal ego, the alienated subject, which, re-introjected it as an ego ideal, gives rise to the future generation of identification with others.[34]

---

34 Mulvey 1975: 9–10.

In other words, the child identifies with an image, either of itself or of the Other, and is thereby alienated and objectified from its true being since its self-definition is based upon a pure reflection or upon the being of a different person. The child identifies with a superior image of itself or of the other person, the ideal ego, or what Lacan calls the *moi* (the accusative case of 'I')—an alienated *moi*:

> On this immediate lived *me* there is superimposed a constructed *me*, a me that is visible at a distance, an imaginary *me* [...]. Henceforth the child's attention is captured by this "*me* above the *me*" or "this me before the *me*." [...] Finally, this alienation of the immediate *me*, its "confiscation" for the benefit of the *me* that is visible in the mirror, already outlines what will be the "confiscation" of the subject by the others who look at him.[35]

Thus, it is through the look of the Other that the subject comes into being as an object; he is delivered to himself through the gaze in the mirror that captures his attention. The child wants to become what it perceives in the mirror: the ideal image of itself. Yet, what it introjects is also experienced as an alien body which can take the form of a persecutory agent, rather than an ideal image because the gaze is always mediated through an Other. The child therefore sets up an internal rivalry within itself, constantly attempting to recapture the original of its mirror image. The tension between the projected image and the re-introjected image gives rise to a never-ending state of attraction and alienation which constitutes the erotic and aggressive relationship between the subject, his self-image and the image of the Other: "Since it is through the Other that the subject comes to being, he is constantly threatened by the possibility of being supplanted or annihilated by the Other."[36]

This imaginary identification of the child with the image of an Other is an identification grounded entirely in the visual realm, since the child has not yet acquired language in and through which it can represent itself to the Other. According to Lacan, this identification with

---

35 Merleau-Ponty 1964: 137 (emphasis in the original).

36 Aniel 1984: 116.

an ideal image remains the primary model for all later identifications, even after the child enters the symbolic realm constituted by language. Once the child enters that realm it has to repress the imaginary dual relationship to the Other, with whom it desired to fuse. The child has to recognize that its ideal image is merely a reflection and that the Other is a separate person with whom it cannot merge. In Lacanian terms, the imaginary, specular relationship to the Other is shattered by the intervention of the Father, who represents the Law. Prior to the awareness of a tertiary structure, the child had the illusion that its being was entirely constituted in the Other, and that it could become what the Other desired it to be. According to Lacan, the child wants to become what is lacking in the mother, namely a phallus. At the same time, the child is also the object of the mother's desire, and in order to satisfy her desire, the child identifies with the mother's original wish to have a phallus. In other words, the mother desires the child to complete and "fill up" her lack. However, with the father's intervention, the child has to acknowledge that it cannot have the phallus that the father has, and it is also forced to recognize that the mother does not have a phallus, and that she herself lives her own "lack."

> [T]he child must renounce the omnipotence of his desire and accept a Law of limitation; he must assume his lack. Through the paternal metaphor, the child names his desire and renounces it. His true desire [to become the object of his mother's desire, i.e., the phallus] and the multiple phantasmatic forms it took are pushed back into the unconscious. This is the primal repression which determines accession to language [...].[37]

Instead of the spectral image—the look of the other—which delivered the subject to himself, now it is language that mediates the subject to himself. Through language, subjectivity is restored to the alienated or objectified subject (the *moi*-me)—it is given a name and is taught to refer to itself as "I," a pure representative and formal signifier. The acquisition of language therefore increases the subject's estrangement from the Other—through whom he was

---

37 Lemaire 1977: 87.

constituted—since verbal tools create the illusion that the subject possesses a private identity, when in truth it was already identified and shaped by the discourse of the Other.

However, the imaginary identification by which the child equates itself with the ideal image proffered by the Other forms the primordial identificatory structure that underlies all subsequent acts of identification, and it does not cease to function once the subject has entered the symbolic realm. Rather, it continues to co-exist with the new demands of the Symbolic order. There is extensive literature on how myths, poetry and folk beliefs attach to a visual idea and desire to merge with it, while fearing it might destroy them. Take, for instance, the classical belief that a pregnant woman's intense contemplation of a given image could produce in her womb the image of that desired representation. Malebranche tells the story of a pregnant woman who

> [...] having attended too carefully to the portrait of Saint Pius on the feast of his canonization, gave birth to a child who looked exactly like the representation of the saint. [...] this child strongly resembled the tableau after which its mother had formed it by the power of her imagination.[38]

Another story, told by Ambroise Paré, "reports the birth of a fur-covered girl whose mother had spied from her bed a picture of John the Baptist in animal skins."[39] Along the same lines, myths and poems have often given expression to the individual's desire to have the painted image come to life. For instance, in the most celebrated of all such tales, Pygmalion, King of Cyprus, fell in love with the statue of a beautiful girl he had carved. Upon praying to Venus to be granted a wife like the statue he had created, the beautiful image came to life, embraced by Pygmalion. How strongly the representation of a figure can inspire love and passion in the individual is further evidenced in Wagner's opera "The Flying Dutchman," where Senta renounces all earthly pleasures and sacrifices her life to absolve the mysterious Flying Dutchman, whom she knows only through his portrait. In a

38 Malebranche, quoted in Huet 1983: 73.

39 Huet 1983: 73.

scene where Eric desperately tries to win her back, Senta clings to the picture of the Flying Dutchman, whose image gives her the needed strength to remain faithful to her desire to join the Dutchman in his death throes. This tale exemplifies how love, passion and truth have often been associated with sight and with the transparent force of a pictorial representation.

Phrases, such as "love at first sight," and "looking one in the eye," or "seeing the light", all refer back to the powerful impression the look of the Other exerts upon the individual. At the same time, the look which can inspire passion or establish truth can also be the one that destroys the individual. In an exchange of fairness, for instance, people see eye to eye; or in confrontations, they outstare each other to assert their dominance, or they hide behind dark spectacles because they fear that the looks of others will "kill" them. The belief in the evil eye is still a prevalent superstition where people suspect harmful intentions behind the menacing look of the Other. The fascination with and horror of Medusa, whose stare was used by the Greek hero Perseus to turn his enemies into stone, is also a theme that has attracted many poets, from Classical Antiquity to Goethe and Baudelaire, including Freud, who wrote a short essay about Medusa's head.[40]

40 In Goethe's *Faust,* Mephistopheles says to Faust on Walpurgis night: "Laß das nur stehn! dabei wird's niemand wohl. / Es ist ein Zauberbild, ist leblos, ein Idol. / Ihm zu begegnen ist nicht gut: / Vom starren Blick erstarrt des Menschen Blut, / Und er wird fast in Stein verkehrt / Von der Meduse hast du ja gehört." (Goethe 1970: 122) ("Let the thing be! All thence have evil drawn: / It is a magic shape, a lifeless eidolon. / Such to encounter is not good: / Their blank, set stare benumbs the human blood, / And one is almost turned to stone. / Medusa's tale to thee is known." [Goethe 1900: 224]) In *Hymne à la Beauté*, Baudelaire writes: "Viens-tu du ciel profond ou sors-tu de l'abîme, / O Beauté? ton regard, infernal et divin, / Verse confusément le bienfait et le crime [...]." (Baudelaire 1961: 28) ("O Beauty! do you visit from the sky / Or the abyss? infernal and divine / Your gaze bestows both kindnesses and crimes [...]." [Baudelaire 1998: 45]). Sigmund Freud refers twice to the Medusa legend in *The Infantile genital organization* (1923: 144), and in *New Introductory Lectures on Psychoanalysis* (1933: 24). In 1940, his little-known essay *Medusa's Head* was posthumously published, see S.E. Volume XVIII (1920–1922). For further references to the theme of the Medusa legend, see Praz 1970.

These few examples from mythology, literature, and folklore demonstrate how the gaze of the Other—be it alive or represented on canvas—can exert a powerful fascination upon the spectator, who can be entirely taken over by the beauty of the image, or completely undone by the terrifying effect of the represented figure.

It is my contention that these two reactions can be traced back to the mirror stage in which the child identifies itself through the image of the Other. Although a painting cannot be equated with a mirror (the traditional understanding of art as a mirror held up to the world, notwithstanding), the spectators nonetheless relate to a painting in much the same way as they do to a mirror. In the painting, they seeks a representation of themselves, desiring and awaiting the image they have projected into the painting to be re-introjected from the figure(s) represented on the canvas. While painters before Manet relied upon the spectators' phantasmagoric identification with and the desire for the painted figures—and composed their paintings accordingly—, Manet questions and explores the spectators' projected desire and confronts them with it. As a result, the spectators are always caught in the curious position of engaging in a fictive dual relationship with the figures represented on the canvas, while at the same time being acutely aware of the impossibility of this exchange. The enigmatic effect of Manet's approach lies partly in his having recognized this process at some unconscious level, which he then employed as a constituent element of his entire oeuvre.

***

> If I exist for the other person, I do so through his gaze […]. Consequently my fundamental relation to the other person is determined by the permanent possibility of being seen by him. The gaze of the other self reveals to me not only that I am an object to him, but also that the other self is a subject.
>
> Alfred Stern, 1967

> It is thus necessary to have recourse to the gaze of another, which is not without danger, that of having a vision of oneself absorbed within an alienated image.
>
> Jean-Luc Nancy, 1977

> Il y a des femmes qui inspirent l'envie de les vaincre et de jouir d'elles; mais celle-ci donne le désir de mourir lentement sous son regard.[41]
>
> Charles Baudelaire, "Le Désir de peindre," 1863

Olympia's celebrated gaze serves as the most instructive example of the complicated process between the painted figure who lures the spectator into the canvas, and, at the same time, entraps him in his voyeuristic activity. *Olympia* (1863) **[Plate 5]** lies on her divan for the gaze of another who is off-stage, as it were. Each figure in the canvas only serves to accentuate the display of her body, which is adorned like

41 "There are women who inspire the wish to conquer and enjoy them; this one, though, stirs the desire to die slowly, her eyes on you. (Baudelaire 2023: 151).

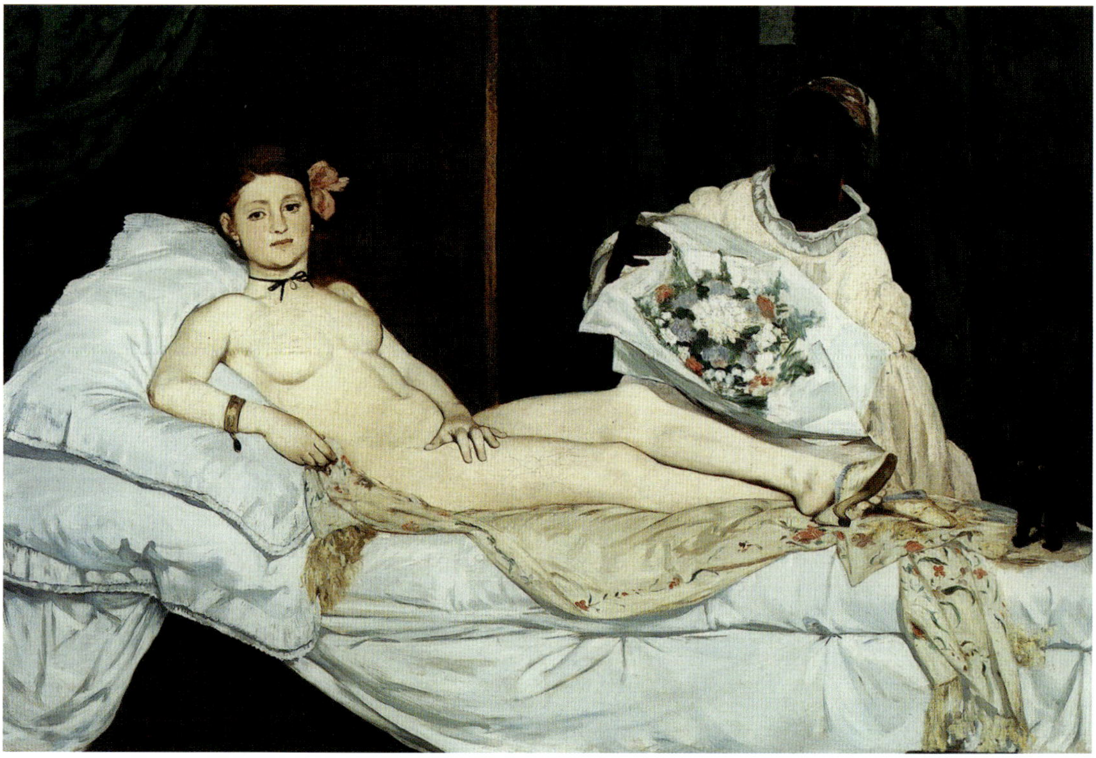

Plate 5:
Édouard Manet, *Olympia* (1863)

an item of merchandise. Reminiscent of the retail policies of Paris's first department store, "Le Bon Marché," Olympia is put on display like some factory-produced commodity whose appeal is increased by garbing her with assorted exotic objects. As Sennett observes:

> A buyer was stimulated when he or she was presented with objects whose existence seemed fleeting, and whose nature was veiled by associations out of the context of normal use. [...] making a pot "attractive" by placing it in a replica of a Moorish harem in the store window, these retailers diverted buyers, first, from thinking about how or even how well the objects were made, and second, about their own roles as buyers."[42]

The subject's exquisite jewelry, her oriental shawl, the bouquet of flowers held by the black servant, and the black cat, all of these are embellishments that enhance the woman's market value, and temporarily allow her next client to forget that she is up for sale only, not for love. For an instant Olympia entices the spectator into the belief that s/he is the only privileged beholder of her marbled body. It is as if her somewhat aloof gaze from the canvas appoints a precise place for her invisible and absent admirer, metaphorically marking the presence of his anticipated gaze and introducing it into the circuit of desire. In this way, her artfully arranged availability arouses us to possess and fill this empty place she has assigned her admirer(s). And yet, our access to Olympia is barred. The cat at her feet arching its back looks defiantly back at us, while the servant is so entirely absorbed in her carefully prepared "creation" that she provides no access either. The scene is set, and we are left to guess what lies behind the lush green drapes, through which a small opening offers a glimpse into her boudoir. The sense of expectation is signaled by the bouquet of flowers arranged in white silk papers, presumably sent in advance by the next client. The imminent entry of this rival both heightens

42 Sennet 1977: 145. Olympia's exoticism also entails references to the work of Ingres and Delacroix, who both chose exotic settings to depict sexually overt and depraved scenes. In their paintings, the exoticism functioned as a façade behind which the two painters could safely reveal the eroticism of their figures; see Ingres's *Odalisque* or Delacroix's *The Women of Algiers in their Harem.*

beholders. When Théophile Gautier complains that "*Olympia* can be understood from no point of view,"[51] I think it worthwhile to interpret his comment literally, as a sign of Manet's consummate artistic skill and psychological acumen. Indeed, the spectators are granted no single point of view, no central position has been reserved for them. No matter from which standpoint they attempt to apprehend the figure before them, this "tamed tiger" (*tigre dompté*) fearlessly relegates them as subordinate to *her* gaze. It is she—the painted objectified image—that objectifies and immobilizes the viewers, reminding them of their own self-alienating condition. Before her, the admirer is denied the illusion of omnipotence, and the roles are reversed: her candid glare defuses any desire she may have aroused, leaving her onlookers with a momentary thrill of voyeuristic pleasure. Lacan remarks that "The world is all-seeing, but it is not exhibitionistic—it does not provoke our gaze. When it begins to provoke our gaze, the feeling of strangeness begins too" (Lacan 1978: 75). In front of *Olympia*, that feeling of strangeness is intermingled with a sense of humiliation, shame and powerlessness when the viewers feel exposed in their scopophilic desires.

How does Manet's *Olympia* simultaneously evoke and castrate the spectator's desire? Might there be a pact between castration and desire as there is a pact between culture and barbarity, according to Freud (see Freud 1930). As Laura Mulvey observes:

> [I]n psychoanalytic terms, the female figure poses a deeper problem. She also connotes something that the look continually circles around but disavows: her lack of a penis, implying a threat of castration and hence unpleasure. Ultimately, the meaning of woman is sexual difference, the absence of the penis as visually ascertainable, the material evidence on which is based the castration complex essential for the organisation of entrance to the symbolic order and the law of the

51 Gautier, quoted in Hamilton 1969: 75. For Borges, the most compelling problem is metaphysical in nature, "the contradiction of time that passes and the identity that endures." (Johnson 2012: 25) He adds: "Time is the substance I am made of. Time is a river which sweeps me along,but I am the river; it is a tiger which destroys me, but I am the tiger; it is a fire which consumes me, but I am the fire. The world, unfortunately, is real; I, unfortunately, am Borges." (Borges 1964: 234).

> father. Thus the woman as icon, displayed for the gaze and enjoyment of men, the active controllers of the look, always threatens to evoke the anxiety it originally signified.[52]

The idea that the female body both incites desire and poses a threat of castration is captured in Manet's composition of Victorine Meurent as Olympia.

> As many observers have noted, the thin black ribbon around Olympia's neck divides her into two: a head that frontally addresses the viewer, and a body that may be made available to the right client.[53]

This internal division between head and body is reiterated in her hand gestures, with the left hand defiantly concealing her sexual parts and her right hand gently touching the oriental shawl that caresses her body. Similarly, her languid and dispassionate look is in contrast to the still and controlled posture of her body. Manet has painted this *Olympia* as a self-aware and self-controlling figure, in which one part of her body denies what the other offers. Olympia does not openly flaunt her "lack," she conceals it; rather than make the absence evident, she artfully alludes to it. With Olympia, Manet has created a figure who represents both the imaginary and symbolic realms. On the one hand she invites the spectators to immerse themselves in an imaginary relationship with her, whereby they can pretend that they are what Olympia desires them to be—in other words, they can fantasize that they complete or repair her lack. On the other hand, Olympia intervenes and destroys this imaginary bond by signaling to her admirers that she belongs to no one, that she cannot be completed by anyone inside or outside the canvas. By acknowledging her own lack, she forces the spectators outside the canvas to accept their separateness.

Manet uses several ideas and techniques to incorporate this fundamental lack within the canvas before it emerges as a dynamic

---

52 Mulvey 1975: 13.
53 Bargelow 1980: 12.

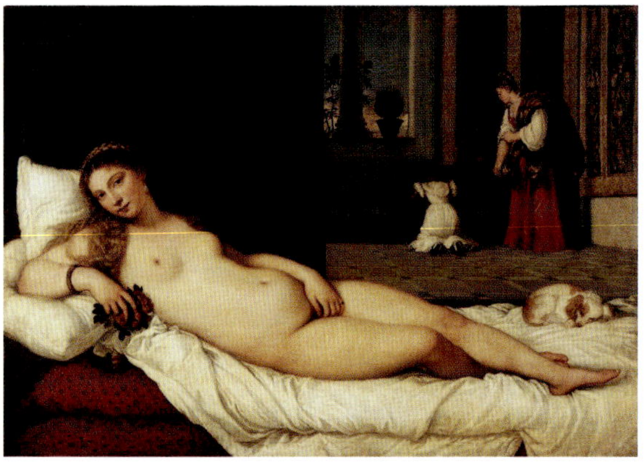
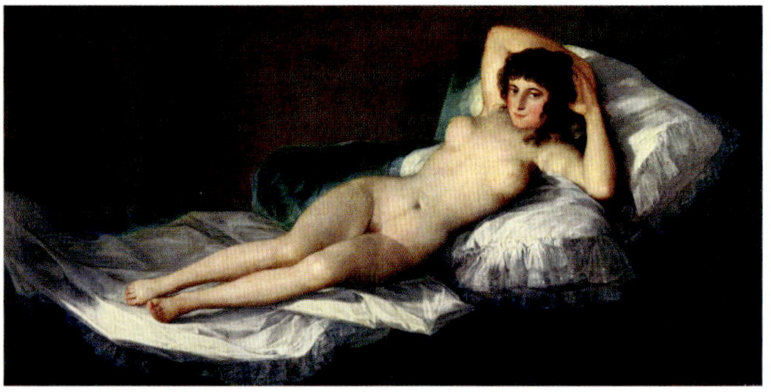
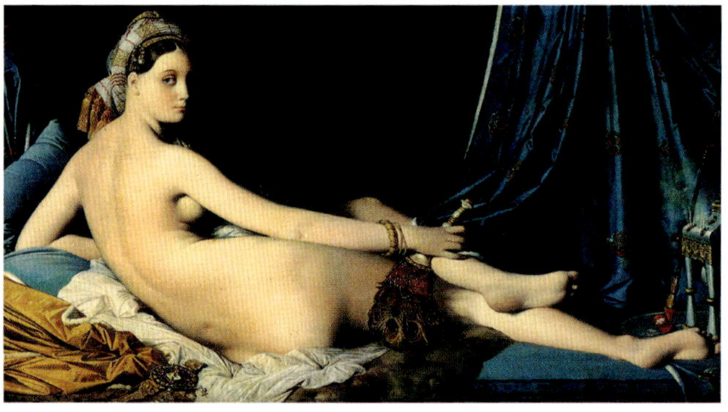
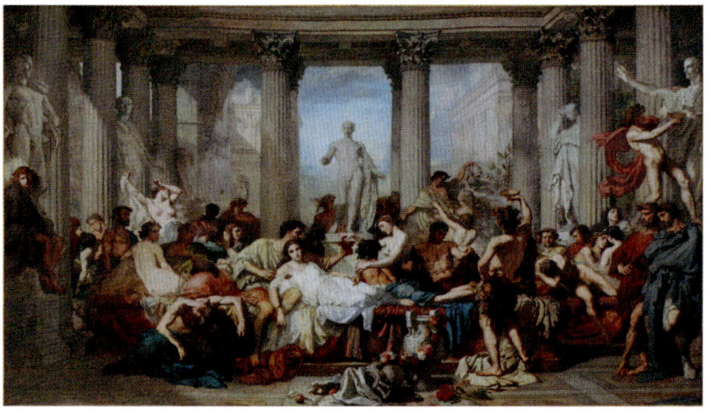

between the painted figure and the spectators. Firstly, the contrived and stiff pose of Olympia implies that this body does not belong to the person portrayed: Victorine Meurent plays at the role of being Olympia, but is not fully embodied by it. Secondly, Olympia does not represent herself, but is already depicted as a representation of prior depictions of which Titian's *Venus of Urbino*, Goya's *Maja*, Ingres's *Odalisque*, and Couture's *Les Romains de la décadence* are only the most celebrated examples. By incorporating such unmistakable references to previous depictions of Venus figures, Manet made sure the spectators realized that this *Olympia* was not a unique object of desire, but rather a substitution for earlier enticing odalisques. In this sense, one might argue that Olympia crystallizes the nature of desire, since at the moment that the spectator is caught in the allusion of naming her, she eludes any classification or single meaning and instead reveals an endless succession of possible references which can never be grasped in their entirety. D.N. Rodowick describes this chain of yearning as a circular path

> […] carved out by the absence, the loss, of the most archaic objects of satisfaction. The irretrievability of this lost object, and the anguish it supposes, is in a sense displaced by assigning the articulation of desire to a movement of repetition and difference in which a temporary satisfaction is achieved in the search for possible representatives or replacements for this loss. To call this movement a circuit is thus to imply a progress which is simultaneously a return, signifying in the presence of an imaginary object of satisfaction the condition of absence in which the whole movement is begun again.[54]

Perhaps when he created Olympia, Manet was on a similar path of loss, anguish and the search for representations. As a painter, Manet occupied the three-fold role of the stage-director, creator, *and* spectator of the scenes he portrayed. The slowness of the very process of painting placed him in an analogously deceptive position to that of the observers who imagine themselves—albeit only fleetingly—as possessors of the enticing figure on display. Yet, once the paint has

page 254:
Plate 6: Titian, *Venus of Urbino* (1538)
Plate 46: Francisco de Goya, *La maja desnuda* (1797–1800)
Plate 45: Jean-Auguste-Dominique Ingres, *La Grande Odalisque* (1814)
Plate 17: Thomas Couture, *Les Romains de la décadence* (1847)

54 Rodowick 1980: 85.

dried, Olympia remains a fictional, unobtainable creation as much to the painter as to the ordinary spectator. The only trace of the artist's presence is in his signature, which is neatly inscribed along the base of the crimson velvet of the divan beneath Olympia's supine body, perhaps intending to claim some privileged relationship with the model, while equally endorsing the audience's distance from the woman, the staged scene, and the painting itself. Since the painter himself is ultimately an onlooker like any other, the only mark of his passing remains his signature. By leaving his signature on Olympia's bed sheet, Manet signed off his own creation, submitting himself to the order of the Symbolic in which he can be known to others only in terms of his own representation.

In the depiction of a courtesan, or—as Zola called her—a "fille publique", Manet had of course found a symbolic figure who belonged to everybody, yet who could be *possessed* by nobody. A prostitute's relationship to society is based on a transaction: she is available to those who can afford her. Her body—or *product*—is offered to males who, by paying for her services to satisfy their desire, are in turn objectified, becoming anonymous and interchangeable customers. Today's lover is followed by another tomorrow.[55] And yet, as we have observed so frequently throughout Manet's works, any single definition of *Olympia*—no matter how ambiguous in and of itself—would never exhaust her full significance. As Norman Bryson observes:

> The image of *Olympia* refuses to settle in any legible middle ground between the discourses of the Odalisque and of the Prostitute: it is committed exactly to equivocation, to the equal voicing of both positions; and it know its entire conception is aware in advance, that this stubborn commitment means that it will not be read through the existing codes, that it cannot flow smoothly through the existing discursive circuits [...].[56]

---

55 I have paraphrased this expression from Raymond Bargelow's perceptive essay on Manet, *Role, Emotion and Power in Manet, A Sartrean Examination* (1980: 20, unpublished paper).

56 Bryson 1983: 147.

Although Manet had treated the theme of the prostitute before in *Le Déjeuner sur l'herbe* and was to do so again in *Nana, Olympia* remains his most powerful statement about the self-alienation of the modern subject. In *Olympia,* Manet not only succeeded in portraying a figure who emblematized the subject as an objectified being, but he also created a paradigmatic model of the essential process by which a subject becomes the object of the Other. We have seen how Manet, by foreshortening the distance between *Olympia* and her audience and by flattening its content up against the two-dimensional surface of the canvas, forced his spectators into a direct confrontation with the painted figure. By leaving them no choice but to enter the painted scene, Manet implicates them as participants in the depicted spectacle. Using Freud's three-stage model of identification from his essay "A Child is Being Beaten" (1919), we can see how Manet has inducted the spectators (subject) into the canvas, thereby subverting their passive role as mere onlookers. Once the beholders become part of the beheld image, they are compelled to realize that they are not the "missing" object completing the scenario. Faced with this powerlessness, the spectators find themselves in the demoralizing role of being merely one of a series of clients; moreover, Olympia's dismissive gaze warns them that the object of their desire will forever elude them. This awareness, which is felt more than seen through her indifference, confirms that she is not something they could ever grasp or claim as their own. Lastly, one element in *Olympia* that is rarely noted by art critics—but which articulates the theme of the Other as a permanent condition of the constitution of the Self—is the class/race relationship between the concubine and her servant.

Contemplating their relationship to one another, I am reminded of the Hegelian dialectic between slave and master, where the slave is the truth of the master; it is only through the presence of her servant that Olympia gains the status of mistress. Sartre observes that it was Hegel's brilliant intuition "to make me depend on the Other *in my being*. I am, he said, a being for-itself which is for-itself only through another."[57] How dependent Olympia's being is upon

---

57 Sartre 1968: 321 (emphasis in the original).

the presence of the servant holding the flowers becomes clearer if we try to imagine for a moment that the black servant is blotted out. Without her, Olympia's relationship to her spectators is abruptly transformed: she no longer forms part of a communicative nexus with her servant and has only the viewers to contend with, thereby granting them a far greater degree of intimacy and appropriation. Left thus in solitude, she would join her famous predecessors, the traditional nudes who seductively and unambiguously gaze at their imagined suitors. While the Black servant is generally seen to lend an air of "exotic" eroticism to the painting—the cat mirroring her presence—scant attention has been given to her role as an Other, through whose gaze Olympia is being further objectified in her reclining position. Ultimately, the spectator's awareness of Olympia's seemingly smug detachment is augmented by the presence of the servant: as much as this desirable white concubine is unattainable, so is her status. We might well ask ourselves what the servant's perception of Olympia is, and I believe the key lies in the bouquet of flowers that the maid is holding. As we have seen, the bouquet functions as a metonymy for the absent client, standing in for him, hinting at the possibility that Olympia will soon be possessed by some anonymous individual. However, the flowers also function as a metaphor for the merchandized and brazenly displayed Olympia herself. Like the bouquet, Olympia has been artfully arranged and enveloped in white linen. The arrangement is not designed to last, however: like the flowers, Olympia will wither once her client has left, only to be replaced by a new decorative orchestration. Showing the same care with which the flowers have been selected, the servant displays her mistress as an enticement for the next customer. It is only when the servant has satisfactorily packaged her "fruit" that Olympia is ready to be plucked again. In my discussion of the spectators' efforts to appropriate for themselves the empty space Olympia has seemingly marked out for them, I deliberately did not include the possibility that they might try to gain access by putting themselves in the place of the servant. Yet, now we can see that even in this imaginary identification with the servant, the viewer is once again relocated in the position of the Other. Instead of becoming the recipient of her desire, the spectators are subjected to the role of the servant—or mere "supplant" of her desire.

The Black maid has only very recently gained notoriety in her own right, both for reasons of her ethnicity and—as I have already noted—for the central position she assumes in *Olympia*. With Denise Murrell's work and subsequent exhibition first in New York in 2018 and then in Paris in 2019, called *Posing Modernity*,[58] Murrell is one of the first writers drawing attention to the figure of Laure, the model for the Black servant: "The maid figure embodies the overlooked interracial aspect of Manet's artistic milieu."[59] The author cites T. J. Clark's awkward response about this flagrant omission as he admits to having told a friend: "For God's sake! You've written about the white woman on the bed for fifty pages and more, and hardly mentioned the black woman alongside her!" Murrell notes further that

> Clark implies an ideological "blindness" in art history that justifies giving only nominal attention to the black maid because, as a servant, she is perceived to be in an immutable and natural role, and therefore expected, unworthy of notice; this perception deflects full attention to the prostitute because of the shock of her perceived "unnatural circumstances".[60]

Murrell's research reveals that Manet most probably met Laure through his friend Baudelaire, who had been in a tumultuous relationship with Jeanne Duval, a renowned actress of mixed race. Manet's Laure lived near his studio in the 9th arrondissement, and he had portrayed her earlier in 1863, shortly before he asked her to model for *Olympia*. In this painting, each model poses in a role emblematic

---

58 The exhibition, both in New York and then Paris, illustrates the changing representation of the Black female figure that has been central to the development of modernism, from Édouard Manet's *Olympia* to the present. Besides *Olympia,* other works with Black models are represented, painted by Frédéric Bazille, Edgar Degas, Nader, and Jean-Baptiste Carpeaux. "Through these works, the exhibition brings to light little-known connections between the avant-garde circles of 19th-century Paris and the post-abolition community of free black Parisians […]." (2019, Wallach Art Gallery, Columbia University).

59 Murrell 2018: 2.

60 Murrell 2018: 3.

of modern Parisian life: Victorine [Meurent] as the unsentimental prostitute who was rapidly replacing the referential Renaissance-style courtesan; and Laure as a representation of the changing racial composition of the Parisian working class. Consistent with my analysis of the relationship between the white prostitute Olympia and the Black maid Laure, Murrell also argues that

> Manet's revisionary depiction presented the black maid as a second focal point and site of disruptive modernity. [...] The greater equivalence between the two figures in *Olympia* sets up a counterbalancing relationship between them in purely formal terms—the maid's blackness is heightened by the prostitute's whiteness—and vice-versa with the effect [...] of transferring a racially charged connotation of uncleanliness and illicit sexuality from the black maid to the white prostitute.[61]

Therefore, by painting Laure in her own right—not just as a subservient maid to Olympia but as an equal focal point to Olympia's display—, Manet also revised the inferior position typically given to a Black subject.

The maid's stance and gaze vis-à-vis Olympia also provides access to how a woman might look at the supine figure. Recently, questions regularly arise about the female vs. the male gaze, and while such distinctions were not expressed during Manet's era (since the public in the Salons was primarily thought to be male), today we should pose the question of a female gaze, even retroactively, or après-coup, *nachträglich*. Through the maid's caring, attentive, yet detached gaze at her mistress, a kind of complicity can be subsumed that suggests a common knowledge about the business in which both are engaged. Laure is eager to provide the best possible presentation of her mistress, and Olympia has introjected Laure's unswerving attention and service to her so that she need not return her servant's gaze. Between the two female protagonists there is no need to provoke or to scandalize their situation; instead, the two female figures relate in a quiet, unquestioned and self-evident harmony towards one another.

61 Murrell 2018: 54–55.

I would argue that the canvas *Olympia* was primarily painted for a male audience, to whom the concubine had something to show, to both conceal and reveal. She was in the position of power vis-à-vis the male spectator, whereas the female spectator was taken for granted: for her, Olympia represented a common, secret and intimate knowledge of the female position in society.

In *Le Déjeuner sur l'herbe* [**Plate 3**], Manet had addressed a theme similar to the one in *Olympia*: a nude woman gazing out at her spectators. Like the supine Olympia, this woman's primary relationship is with the eyes of her beholder outside the painting, rather than with the other figures she shares the canvas with. Moreover, her gaze, like that of Olympia, reveals her "inner" awareness of being exposed to an infinite number of anonymous and interchangeable spectators, and, like Olympia, she is in complete control of how the audience contemplates her image. In other words, she does not simply give herself to being passively consumed by the looks of the Other, but stubbornly resists this appropriation. In this case, however, her gaze engages the viewer in a different relationship from that of Olympia, a difference that is manifested in the public's diverse reactions to both paintings. Both, as we know, shocked the public. Yet, while *Le Déjeuner sur l'herbe* was unanimously rejected by the Salon and exhibited only at the Refusés, *Olympia* was accepted, but it hung in a remote gallery so high up that nobody could really see it properly. As one of Manet's contemporary critics commented:

> You had seen Manet's *Venus with the Cat* flaunting her wan nudity on the stairs. Public censure chased her from that place of honor. One found the wretched woman again, when one did find her, at a height where even the worst daubs had never been hung, above the huge door of the last room, where you scarcely knew whether you were looking at a parcel of nude flesh or a bundle of laundry.[62]

Thus, paralleling the process evoked by Olympia's gaze vis-à-vis the spectator, the Salon was initially seduced into accepting "her" invitation. Yet, once they had to return Olympia's gaze and be confronted

---

62 Clarétie, quoted in Hamilton 1969: 73.

with her Medusan stare, they chose to turn away rather than to face being humiliated as one of "her" rejected admirers. In contrast to *Olympia, Le Déjeuner sur l'herbe* never produced such entangled desires or ambiguous reactions. The depicted scene of two women, one thinly wrapped in a veil, the other entirely nude, at a country picnic in the company of two fully clothed men, decidedly violated the public's notion of decorum. As George Heard Hamilton recounts:

> There is a story to the effect that Napoleon III confirmed the government's attitude for an obsequious press and bewildered public when, upon visiting the Salon, he paused before *Le Bain* for several minutes and then, without a word, turned away with a gesture indicating that he considered the painting an offense against public morality.[63]

In *Le Déjeuner sur l'herbe*, the naked woman openly violates the social codes by exposing herself to the well-dressed audience inside and outside the canvas. She addresses her spectators in their public roles, giving them free rein to protest *her* immoral behavior. In *Olympia*, the offense is of a different nature, since it is not public decorum per se that is violated, but rather the strict separation between private and public realms that is being subverted. By publicizing a strictly private—though well-known and frequently practiced— trade, Olympia exposes the duplicitous stance of the respectable public man who privately engages in decadent affairs. In *Le Déjeuner sur l'herbe,* the spectators can safely point their fingers at the nude woman and loudly pronounce their disapproval. In *Olympia,* the finger is pointed at them, and, feeling exposed by her, they can escape Olympia's penetrating look only by removing her from their sight. While Olympia merely implicates her spectators as her private customers, the nude in *Le Déjeuner sur l'herbe* openly addresses the audience as public voyeurs. Unlike Olympia, who defiantly displays her body to the eyes of her beholders, the nude woman in *Le Déjeuner sur l'herbe* exhibits her body confidently and freely. She knows that she is being looked at by anonymous spectators and she seemingly takes pleasure and pride in the spectacle she creates and the reaction she provokes in her beholders.

63 Hamilton 1969: 44.

Lemoine-Luccioni observed about the female exhibitionist, who by "offering herself thus to the gaze, in showing herself, following the sequence: seeing, seeing herself, showing herself, being seen, the girl [...] provokes the Other into an encounter and a response which gives her pleasure."[64] In contrast to the male exhibitionist who exposes his genitals to reassure himself against the fear of castration, the female exhibitionist has no object she fears to lose and therefore she is not dependent upon the reassurance of her onlookers. Her exhibitionism is in part motivated by a wish for revenge: by displaying her female beauty and charm—which may serve the unconscious purpose of humiliating men—she makes them in thrall to her and dependent upon what they formerly despised or feared. In *Le Déjeuner sur l'herbe*, the nude woman is not merely an object of the spectators' gaze, she is also a voyeur of their own act of looking. She derives as much pleasure from exhibiting her nude body and provoking a shocked response in her spectators as she does from looking at the spectators and watching their reaction. She exerts as much control over the beholders in making them an object of her gaze as she does over the object she exposes. Unlike Olympia, whose body is divided into two parts, where her controlling gaze withholds what her lower body exposes, Victorine Meurent's naked body in *Le Déjeuner sur l'herbe* reveals no sign of an internal split. She is simultaneously a voyeur and an exhibitionist, one who exerts equal control in both the passive position of being looked at and the active position of observing her audience. In the nude of *Le Déjeuner sur l'herbe,* Manet has created a sublime image of a narcissistic woman who resists any attempt to be subordinated to the consumption of the Other. Her image in *Le Déjeuner* recalls Freud's characterization of the narcissistic woman, whom he describes as having

> [...] the greatest fascination for men, not only for aesthetic reasons, since as a rule they are most beautiful, but also because of a combination of interesting psychological factors. For it seems very evident that another person's narcissism has a great attraction for those who have

---

64 Lemoine-Luccioni 1987: 70.

> renounced part of their own narcissism and are in search of object-love. The charm of a child lies to a great extent in his narcissism, his self-contentment and inaccessibility, just as does the charm of certain animals which seem not to concern themselves about us, such as cats and the large beasts of prey. [...] It is as if we envied them for maintaining a blissful state of mind—an unassailable libidinal position which we ourselves have since abandoned.[65]

It is the nude's lack of shame, her calm confidence and provocative and engaging look which make her appear self-sufficient and blissfully removed from the recognition of the Other. She gives the impression of not needing confirmation from the eyes of the Other, but assuredly anticipates her appeal for him. Unlike Olympia, who addresses the spectators as potential customers to fill or complete the empty space she has marked out for them, the nude in *Le Déjeuner sur l'herbe* seems to be self-contained, having no need for the spectators' imaginary presence within the canvas nor for their approval outside the frame. In *Being and Nothingness* (*L'être et le néant*, 1943) Sartre argues that the Other's look is a necessary condition for the individual's awareness of their own objectivity. He says: "Thus the look has set us on the track of our being-for-others and has revealed to us the indubitable existence of this Other for whom we are."[66] However, the nude of *Le Déjeuner sur l'herbe* uses the Other as a mere reflection of her own idealized image. Typical for the narcissistic personality, the nude is primarily in love with herself and uses the spectator simply as an object which reflects her own triumphant image back to her. In a sense, the characteristic roles of the spectator vis-à-vis the painted figure are reversed in *Le Déjeuner sur l'herbe*: instead of assuming the position of the desired object—as the traditional nude does—the nude adopts the role of the desiring subject who exploits the spectator for her own gratification. From clinical studies of standard and pathological narcissism, we know that the typical narcissist tends to evoke an angry response in the Other, because he treats them as a mere extension of himself. He uses the Other to fulfill his narcissistic needs, however,

---

65 Freud 1914c: 98.
66 Sartre 1968: 376.

once the other no longer fulfills this function, he is discarded. With this dynamic in mind, it is my contention that the outrage over *Le Déjeuner sur l'herbe* was to some extent driven by an unconscious feeling that the public had served as a mere extension of the nude woman's self-satisfied appeal. The viewers' own narcissistic sense of being the central, privileged spectator in front of a painting had been upended by her all-knowing look: before the viewers could articulate their rightful indignation, their response was preempted by Victorine Meurent's look of bemused insouciance. Her composure and challenging gaze forestalled any illusion of outside influence, since she made clear her indifference to the public's disapproving glance.

Yet, (out)rage is not the only prevalent reaction towards the representation of an omnipotent, self-assured female figure. Envy is another typical reaction of the narcissist, the urge to become part of this idealized image. "[T]rue envy," Lacan observes, "the envy that makes the subject pale before the image of completeness closed upon itself, before the idea that the *petit a*, the separated *a* from which he is hanging, may be for another the possession that gives satisfaction, *Befriedigung*."[67] It is the nude's aura of superiority in *Le Déjeuner sur l'herbe* that anchors the spectator's rapt attention. Marcel Proust's description of his first encounter with Albertine and her friends in the "petite bande" at Balbec illustrates this dynamic most vividly:

> [T]he supposition that I might some day be the friend of one or other of these girls, that their eyes, whose incomprehensible gaze struck me now and again, playing upon me unawares, like the play of sunlight upon a wall, might ever, by a miraculous alchemy, allow to interpenetrate among their ineffable particles the idea of my existence, some affection for my person, that I myself might someday take my place among them in the evolution of their course by the sea's edge—that supposition appeared to me to contain within it a contradiction as insoluble as if, standing before some classical frieze or a fresco representing a procession, I had believed it possible for me, the spectator, to take my place, beloved of them, among the godlike hierophants.[68]

---

67 Lacan 1978: 116 (emphasis in the original).

68 Proust 1924: 131–132.

Similar to Marcel's wish "to take my place, beloved of them, among the godlike hierophants," the spectators standing before the *Le Déjeuner sur l'herbe* seek to enter the canvas and swap places with the figures grouped around the unattainable nude. In their fantasy, they have three options: the man pointing his finger at the nude; the man seated behind her gazing into an empty space; and the woman bending down in the water averting her gaze from the spectacle in front of her. But it seems as if none of these three positions promises a closer access to the naked woman than the one already occupied by the spectator outside the painting. The man seated closest to the undressed Victorine Meurent stares ahead of himself into an empty space, suggesting no connection with her. His vacant stare, coming from directly behind her, serves primarily as a prop to accentuate her provocative gaze at the spectator. By the same token, his physical proximity to her only underscores her unattainability, since she seems to be entirely unaffected by his bodily presence. The man on the right side looking and pointing at her assumes a similar position to the one taken by the servant in *Olympia*. And like the servant, his function is to display this woman in her full nudity. Similarly, just as the bouquet held by the servant in *Olympia*—which serves as a displacement for Olympia's offered body—so the clothes, fruits and basket carefully laid out in front of Victorine Meurent are a displacement for the exhibitionistic quality of her nakedness. In particular, the half-empty basket, turned over on its side with the luscious apples, pears, cherries and brioche spilling out, mirrors the outline of Meurent's body. Seated upright, with her right leg pulled up, her right arm resting on her knee, and her head comfortably held in her right hand, staring out at the spectator, she reveals only one half of her body, barring a full view of her breasts and genitalia. The still life (in French *nature morte*—"dead nature") of the clothes and fruit is also a metaphor for the erotic, yet static and almost frozen quality of the nude's body.

Critics have wondered about the precise direction of the hand of the gentleman on the right, which points at the nude. Upon closer scrutiny, we can see that while the half-bent index finger points forward and left toward the seated nude, the thumb points toward the bather in the background. George Mauner is one of the few critics who has examined the gentleman's curious gesture, and he argues that the thematic unity achieved by this double indication ties together the spiritual/pure side (represented by the bather) with the evil/profane side of woman (represented by the nude).[69] I would like to suggest a different reading of the man's double-edged gesture. By pointing to these two female figures in a single gesture, the spectator is encouraged to make a comparison between a classically decorous nude, thinly veiled and averting her gaze from the spectator, and a modern one, undressed and openly staring at the viewer. Unlike the nude sitting between the two fully-clothed gentlemen, the bather assumes the traditional role of a nude, passively submitting her body to the viewers, and coyly avoiding any eye contact with them. Shuttling their gaze between these two figures, the viewers become aware of the different attitudes they assume towards a woman who passively presents herself as an object of male delight, and a woman who actively challenges the viewers' scopophilic desire. The bather is also the one figure who has undergone the fewest changes from her "original" position in Giorgione's/Titian's *Le Concert Champêtre.* Like Giorgione's/Titian's woman at the well, who is also partially draped, the bather in Manet's painting is set apart from the group of the two dressed gentlemen and the other nude woman. Like Giorgione's/Titian's figure, she is entirely absorbed in her pursuits, taking no notice of the activity between the other three figures. However, Manet has displaced the isolated woman from the front of the picture-plane to the back, a move that may mirror his intention of showing the classically draped woman as a figure of the past and the unclad woman as a figure of the present. The other compositional change Manet

---

69 George Mauner argues that the bathing woman is modeled after the figure of St. John in Raphael's *The Miraculous Draught of Fishes*, and that she is symbolically linked with the bird hovering above her. The association to the Christian pictorial source and the symbolic link to the bird, which is emblematic for the soul and spirit, represent the sacred theme in the painting. Conversely, Victorine Meurent's figure is modeled after a pagan source, i. e., Raimondi's *The Judgment of Paris*, and is therefore symbolically linked with the frog crouching to the left of her figure, symbolizing "lif's fleeting pleasures" and man's "insatiable desire" after "earthly goods" (Mauner, 1975: 28) and representing the decadent and profane nature of man. (For a more detailed discussion, see Mauner 1975: 7–45.)

undertook in his re-interpretation of Giorgione's/Titian's *Le Concert Champêtre* was to turn the nude woman listening to the music of the two shepherds around, so that she now faces the spectator. As a consequence, she is no longer the figure excluded by the company of the two men, but she has become the one who excludes them. In *Le Déjeuner sur l'herbe*, the two smartly-attired men are not engaged in a shared activity—as they are in Giorgione's/Titian's musical concert—but they seem almost accidentally grouped together, apparently ignoring each other's presence. Ultimately, it is the spectators who engage most closely with the nude, since among those "present" they are the only ones to which she pays any attention. However, like the three figures within the canvas, the viewers end up as merely a prop that endorses her domineering, self-sufficient presence. The notion that the viewers are the main focus of her attention—and indeed it was for their benefit that she poses undressed—is further underscored by her unwavering gaze toward her beholders. Because no matter where the viewers position themselves in front of the large canvas, her eyes follow them, ironically duplicating the convention in classical depictions of saintly figures whose eyes followed the worshipers as they moved in front of the painting.[70] Borrowing this technique from the classical painters, Manet perversely endowed the nude with an equally potent aura as that of a saint. The Christian artists were given the task of familiarizing the illiterate masses with the Bible stories by illustrating them. Each story had to be told impressively and believably, so that the faithful came to learn its message and thus become devotees.

Equally important was the concept that God the Almighty was an omniscient, all-seeing being aware of every thought and deed of his subjects.

---

70 The idea that the saint's eyes follow the spectator around the room was suggested to me by Professor Thomas Rosenmeyer who had kindly agreed to read my manuscript. He told me that it was common practice with Italian tourist guides to point towards the eyes of the painted saints and tell the gallery visitors how the saints' eyes were following them across the room. For a similar description, see also Robert Waelder, *Psychoanalytic Avenues to Art* (1965: 78).

> The spectacle of the world, in this sense, appears to us as all-seeing. This is the phantasy to be found in the Platonic perspective of an absolute being to whom is transferred the quality of being all-seeing. At the very level of the phenomenal experience of contemplation, this allseeing aspect is to be found in the satisfaction of a woman who knows that she is being looked at […].[71]

It is this all-seeing and all-knowing aspect of the nude's gaze in *Le Déjeuner sur l'herbe*—in conjunction with her expression of self-satisfaction—which evokes such an uncanny feeling in the spectator: the scrutiny is reversed.

A similar satisfied awareness of being observed can be seen in *Nana* (1877) **[Plate 63]**, painted fourteen years after *Olympia* and *Le Déjeuner sur l'herbe*. A family resemblance exists among these three paintings, and yet, each produces a different effect upon the spectator. Both *Olympia* and *Nana* represent a young courtesan in her boudoir. While the former exhibits her naked body to the eyes of the spectator, the latter is seen completing her toilette in the presence of an elderly gentleman in evening clothes, half of whose figure is cut off by the frame of the picture. Nana has momentarily interrupted her preening to look back at her admirer, who is therefore implicated as a third, invisible participant in the scene. Although Nana's name evokes associations to her literary counterpart, it is Olympia who more closely embodies Zola's account of a cynical courtesan who destroys the men attracted to her. This Nana instead gives the impression of a young and care-free *cocotte* who derives as much pleasure from dressing up as she does from showing herself off to her admirers, on whom she casts a fleeting glance. In this regard, she shares certain characteristics with the nude of *Le Déjeuner sur l'herbe*. Like her, Nana conveys a certain degree of pleasure in being watched; both the nude and Nana appear to be at ease with their bodies and essentially in love with themselves; each ignores her male company, giving in preference to those standing before the painting. In both canvases, the man (in *Le Déjeuner sur l'herbe*, the gentleman on the left, behind the nude) stares out blankly into empty space, betraying no intimate connection to

---

71 Lacan 1978: 75.

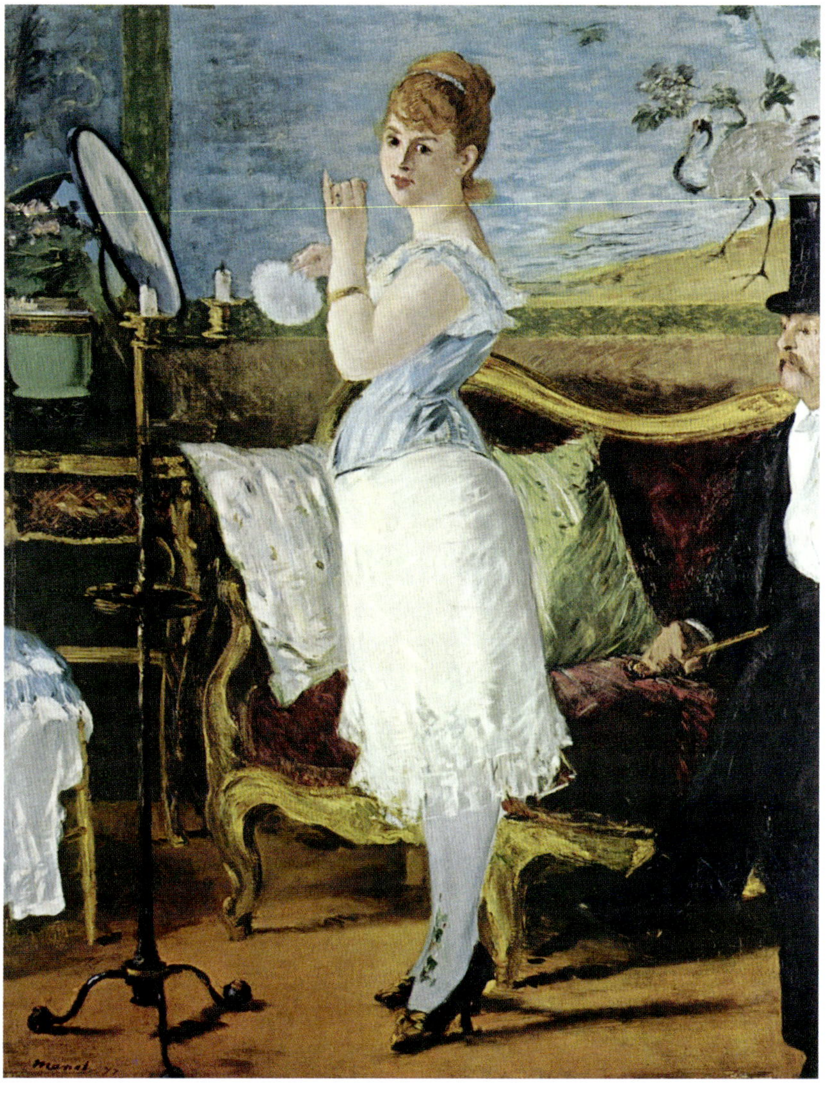

Plate 63:
Édouard Manet,
Nana (1877)

the central figure. In both instances, the male figure(s) seems to have succumbed to the objectifying force of the woman's stare.

While Manet directly implicated the spectator as a potential customer in *Olympia*, he included a definite place for the viewer's identificatory process in *Nana.* In other words, Manet has already mapped out the trajectory of the viewers' desire once they begin to return Nana's curious glance. Like the elderly gentleman who is seated on the red couch, the viewer will be displaced by Nana's enticing look and eventually disappear from her field of vision. At first, however, the spectator seems not to get entrapped by Nana's gaze, since she creates the illusion of having interrupted her toilette and forgotten her companion in order to focus her attention upon her beholder outside the canvas. Yet, at the moment the spectators have been seduced by Nana's gaze, their relationship to her grows more complex. As Lacan points out:

> The painter gives something to the person who must stand in front of his painting which, in part, at least, of the painting, might be summed up thus—*You want to see? Well, take a look at this!* He gives something for the eye to feed on, but he invites the person to whom this picture is presented to lay down his gaze there as one lays down one's weapons. [...] Something is given not so much to the gaze as to the eye, something that involves the abandonment, the *laying down*, of the gaze.[72]

For Lacan, the gaze is a marker of *lack*, similar to the phallus, which constitutes the central signifier of desire. The gaze contains within itself desire, or as Lacan describes it, the "petit objet a," the object that mediates the subject's desire for the desire of the Other, and thereby signals to the subject that their desire is always grounded in and through the eyes of the Other. At the moment that the observers recognize themselves as a desiring subject, they have to assume their *lack*, namely, they must acknowledge that their desire is not located within themselves but outside their desiring self, and thereby remains distant and unobtainable. Returning to *Nana*, we can say that from the moment the viewers apprehend their gaze, they adapt themselves to what her gaze elicits and recognize their status as only the object of her desire. Yet, in a way similar to the subjects' desire to capture their reflection in the mirror as an object to whom "the specular image lends its clothes,"[73] the viewers have to realize that Nana's gaze involves a trap: what they most wish to see is not what Nana presents to them. As an exotic object, Nana already determined

---

72 Lacan 1978: 101 (emphasis in the original).

73 "It is to the object that cannot be grasped in the mirror that the specular image lends its clothes." (Lacan 1977: 316).

the beholder's erotic project, anticipating and temporarily postponing the knowledge that what she represents would necessarily call forth the spectators' own absence and consequent disillusionment. The viewers have to acknowledge that it is not for them alone that she has turned her head, but for the anonymous audience imagined by Manet.

Not only must the spectators admit that they have been manipulated and ensnared by Nana's gaze, but that their own desire was revealed to them through the Other. Put differently, the desire invoked by *Nana* was not so much a yearning *for* her as a desire represented *through* her. In their attempt to capture this elusive object, the viewers notice that it will always elude their grasp. As Lacan notes: "This picture is simply what any picture is, a trap for the gaze. In any picture, it is precisely in seeking the gaze in each of its points that you will see it disappear."[74] Thus, from every angle, whether for the prospective client inside the canvas or the viewer shut outside, the desire Nana elicits remains unattainable. The top-hatted gentleman not only serves as a symbol for the multiple incarnations of Nana's desire, but also as a reminder that desire, fueled by its own insufficiency, generates an infinite number of attempts on the part of the beholders to recapture it for themselves. Like the fictional Count Muffat of Zola's novel—possibly represented in Manet's painting—the viewers return to Nana as an ideal object whose lack inspires them to ever more strenuous attempts to win what is beyond their grasp. The nature of desire is such that it generates its own desire, since it is the yearning for the missing object that constantly refuels itself.

Although a similar circuit of desire is evoked by Olympia and by the nude's look in *Le Déjeuner sur l'herbe*, Nana's look does not strike the viewer as the petrifying gaze of the fatally seductive Olympia, nor as the triumphantly unyielding gaze of the nude in the picnic scene. Instead, her rapport with her onlooker is more playful and less menacing than that of her two predecessors. The question then is how Manet manages to create a different dynamic in *Nana* while maintaining a similar movement of desire. It is executed in a different style than the two earlier paintings, which were modeled after the works

---

74 Lacan 1978: 89.

of Old Masters. *Nana* was painted during Manet's Impressionist phase and presented as a frank study of contemporary life similar to Impressionist canvases of women and men in public gathering places. The palette is lighter and the brush-strokes are more fleetingly and freely applied than in Manet's earlier works. Now the figures are no longer compressed against a flat background, instead they are arranged in an airy depth. Yet, beyond these radical stylistic changes, Manet has also altered the relationship between the central female and male figure, an alteration that produces a different dynamic between the viewer and the image represented. At first sight, it seems as if the figure of Count Muffat is a mere accessory to Nana's dominant presence, similar in function to that of the males in *Le Déjeuner sur l'herbe*. Upon closer examination, however, it becomes clear that the count signals more than the objectifying force of Nana's look, since his stare also mirrors what Nana represents for him. If we look closely into the mirror in front of Nana, the count's shadowy reflection can be discerned. Thus, although Nana does not yield to the look of her beholder and sustains his desiring gaze as if she merely objectified him as an aspect of her desire, in the Muffat figure we can see that Nana herself is also vulnerable to objectification by the Other. Nana and her client can be imagined in a mirroring relationship in which each one relates to the other through their specular representations. Nana not only contemplates an ideal image of herself but also conforms to the Other as he sees her. Similarly, Muffat is caught in the mirror image as he is seen through Nana's eyes. Their looks meet in the mirror, where each confronts the other in their alienated representations. Unlike the nude in *Le Déjeuner sur l'herbe*, whom I have described as a narcissistic figure, sustaining her desire by her insistent and provocative look, Nana—although evincing a similar pleasure at being the focus of attention—does not strike us as a "narcissistically intact" figure. While the nude of *Le Déjeuner sur l'herbe* objectifies the viewers without revealing herself to them, Nana seeks the look of the Other in whom she can reflect her own ideal image. In a sense, she seems to be more dependent upon the acknowledging gaze of the Other, the mirror, the elderly gentleman, and the viewer, and ready to adapt to it. She does not exhibit herself but masquerades in the

their gaze behind masks. Yet, because of Manet's ingenious cut-off point, the viewers are nonetheless implied as potential recipients of their hidden sexual pleasures. Stéphane Mallarmé remarked about Manet's technique that the "artist has discovered a new 'manner of cutting down pictures' so that the frame has 'all the charm of a merely fanciful boundary, such as that which is embraced at one glance of a scene framed in by the hands."[77] By the same token, the viewer is given a variety of models with which to identify. While the faces in the crowd represent men recognizable as members of the Parisian elite, the assemblage of hats behind them serves to evoke the identificatory process "whereby the subject assimilates an aspect, property or attribute of the other and is transformed, wholly or partially, after the model the other provides."[78]

How important it was for Manet to implicate the viewers in this spectacle, instead of leaving them as passive observers outside of the painting, is revealed in his elaborate effort to depict accurately the way the men in the crowd wore their hats. His friend Duret reports:

> He (Manet) was anxious to secure a variety of types and to ensure that each one should preserve his characteristic individuality of feature and bearing. Thus the fact that the men are seen wearing their hats in all sorts of different ways was not the result of a fantastic design, but simply of literal observation. He would say to them, "How do you ordinarily wear your hat—naturally, when you are not troubling about your appearance? Good!—well, put it on quite casually; just like that."[79]

As in his earlier compositions, here Manet was again mapping out the path of the viewers' unconscious desire to identify, namely, to take the place of the Other, with the figures depicted in this scene. Similarly, Manet included three figures two women concealed behind a mask and a man, on the right side of the painting, who stare out at the viewer looking at the crowd. Ironically, it is Manet himself, dressed up as one of the gentlemen of the night, who confronts the viewer.

---

77 Mallarmé, quoted in Harris 1964: 561.
78 Laplanche/Pontalis 1973: 205.
79 Duret 1910: 68–69.

By including himself as a participant in this painted spectacle, Manet visualizes a dizzying intermixture of realities. "The author [...] can present himself only in painting—and this painting is at once its own original as well as the mask of the original, which is concealed at two removes behind the portrait."[80] While Manet's presence is only implicit in *Olympia*, *Le Déjeuner sur l'herbe* and *Nana*, he introduces his fictive self-representation directly in *Bal masqué à l'opéra.* Manet is both author and product, seer and seen, actual spectator and fictive spectator, recipient of the spectator's gaze and fictive respondent to his gaze. Analogous to Freud's description of the identificatory process in "A Child is Being Beaten," in this work Manet changes from the author to the object and then to the spectator, with the curious twist that he also becomes the imagined spectator in the second phase (the second phase being the phase where the author of the fantasy changes into the object of the fantasy). The painter thus constitutes a curious double through whom the spectators retrace their identificatory desire and by whom they are at the same time reminded of their wish to exchange their position as spectators with the participants of the spectacle.

As I mentioned in the second chapter, Manet chose to sign his name on the opera-ticket casually lying on the ground almost directly in front of his self-portrait. It is tempting to ask why Manet chose to inscribe himself twice (through his name and through his physical representation) in such a playful manner in this painting. Looking back at the criteria Diderot had established for the eighteenth-century painting, *Bal masqué à l'opéra* appropriates most faithfully Diderot's principle that the figures within the painting must be portrayed as being entirely absorbed in their activities and states of mind. Perhaps *Bal masqué à l'opéra* enacts a deliberate witticism at such rules, and Manet used two different kinds of self-representation, that of his image and that of his name, to subvert this traditional "law" of painting. In an attempt to play with and expose the fallacies of submitting the creation of art to fixed rules, Manet inserted other devices reminiscent of the Old Masters and earlier paintings of his own. I began my

80 Nancy 1977: 18.

discussion of *Bal masqué à l'opéra* with the theme of the mask as an emblem of the subjects' desire simultaneously to hide and show what they expose to the other. The mask, Jean-Luc Nancy writes, "does not hide the subject as much as it does his shame."[81] Clearly, a woman's gaze hidden behind a mask does not reveal her own desire to the man, nor does it reflect the woman's shame once her desire has been recognized by the Other and returned in equal fashion. The woman has no need to avoid the man's gaze once she knows that she has become the object of his desire. Shame, as Sartre observes, "is shame of *self*; it is the *recognition* of the fact that I *am* indeed that object which the Other is looking at and judging. I can be ashamed only as my freedom escapes me in order to become a *given* object."[82] Thus, at the moment that the woman becomes aware of her objecthood through the gaze of the Other, she lays down her gaze because she feels exposed in her helpless state, which signals that her identity has a foundation outside of herself. However, behind a mask the woman cannot only conceal this self-awareness and feel free to sustain the man's desiring look, but she is also able to approach the Other with her selfhood disguised. In other words, she approaches men in her objecthood. As a result, the man is deprived of his role as the intermediary, as the one whose look determines the Other as an object. It is precisely for this reason that the woman feels more uninhibited behind the mask, since the Other cannot exercise his freedom to turn the woman into an object for himself. Because, as Sartre explains: "[…] the Other does not constitute me as an object for myself but *for him*. […] Later, he argues that "In fact it [the Other] reveals to me only the Other as-subject, a transcending presence to the world and the real condition of my being-as-object."[83] While the man cannot see who hides behind the mask, he knows that he is fully watched by this unknown Other whose imagined look turns him into an object for her. Thus, the roles are reversed: the man, whose look traditionally confers objecthood upon the woman, is now the one who is captured by the hidden eyes of an

81 Nancy 1977: 33.

82 Sartre 1968: 350.

83 Sartre 1968: 367 + 368 (emphasis in the original).

enigmatic Other. And yet, it is precisely this strangeness of the hidden Other which enhances the man's desire to conquer the disguised woman and win from her the "truth" of her sexuality.

What I have described thus far about the function of the mask and the ensuing dynamic between the masked subject and the unmasked spectator participant is a structure which Manet succeeded in producing in *Olympia* and *Le Déjeuner sur l'herbe* without the device of the mask. In both paintings, Manet represented a female figure who looks at her spectators as if she was wearing a mask, since like a woman behind a mask, the nudes in both earlier canvases resist the viewers' curious look and stare squarely back at them. Like the women in *Bal masqué à l'opéra* who offer themselves without revealing their identity, Olympia displays her body yet without revealing herself. She remains strangely mysterious behind her gaze, despite her complete physical exposure. Like the womens' eyes behind a mask, Olympia's and the nude's look in *Le Déjeuner sur l'herbe* appear to see out beyond the frame of the painting, and it is their imagined look which delivers the spectators (qua subject) to themselves (qua object), since he is forced to apprehend himself as a seen object. Unable to ascertain from where they are being looked at and to whom the look belongs, the viewers feel exposed as an object which is looked at from all sides. Recognizing her mysterious presence as an Other, for whom they are a helpless and dependent being, the spectators have to resign themselves to the powerlessness of their desiring position. In *Bal masqué à l'opéra,* Manet formed a theme that playfully illustrated the relationship between the seen viewer and the seeing but enigmatic object/subject within the painting, one which he had previously created between the actual viewer and the painting. A vague memory of *Olympia* and *Le Déjeuner sur l'herbe* is evoked in *Bal masqué à l'opéra* in form of the bouquet and the fruit held by the central masked female figure. These two emblems, which earlier had metaphorized the exhibitionistic quality of the two infamous nudes, emphasize the striking contrast between a socially sanctioned erotic commerce and one that aroused public indignation when it was openly depicted.

Before turning this discussion to an entirely different group of paintings, one in which the figures do not directly gaze at the spectators but overlook their presence, it is useful to recall once more Freud's analysis of the joke, especially the tendentious joke, which is relevant to the spectators' relationship with the artwork. Similar to a painting which embodies the artist-model-spectator relationship, the tendentious joke requires three positions to fulfill its aims successfully:

1) the joker himself
2) the object on whom the sexual or hostile impulses are directed
3) the object for whose pleasure the joke is recounted.

Smut, Freud asserts, involves the "exposure of the sexually different person to whom it is directed."[84] When the object of desire resists the sexual advances of the first person, the joke-teller, he takes his revenge and makes the woman the object of obscenities in which "the sadistic components of the sexual drives" are mobilized. Yet, for the obscene joke to be completed, the first person needs the audience of a third person who replaces the second as object for the first: "So that gradually, in place of the woman, the onlooker, now the listener, becomes the person to whom the smut is addressed."[85]

Consequently, the pleasure of the joke-teller will be mediated by and dependent upon the reaction of the third person. As Jeffrey Mehlman argues:

> This third person soon acquires the greatest importance in the development of smut. [...] With the transition from a dual to a triangular configuration, the loss of the object is consolidated. The joke is consummated when the woman leaves the room. The center of gravity of the interaction has shifted from the second to the third [...] term. But that third term [...] is less a term (a person) than a symbolic circuit, a structure of exchange which happens secondarily to find support or incarnation in an additional person.[86]

84 Freud 1905b: 98.
85 Freud 1905b: 99.
86 Mehlman 1975: 449.

The structure of a tendentious joke is marked both by the absence of the desired object and by the transformation of erotic into aggressive impulses. Thus, we can see how the listener, the third person, is invited as an ally to master the loss of the unattained object of desire. In a sense, the engagement of the third person within the structure of the tendentious joke parallels the child's acquisition of language in the Fort/Da Game, where the child substitutes words for the loss of the loved object. As Steven Neale points out:

> The third person emerges, again, as the site of the symbolic […] and the Law. […] If the disordering and reordering process is such as to reiterate or renew socially established discourses, meanings, modes and structures of signification, then the laughter of the third person can be seen as resulting from the re-inscription of the Law, as resulting from the re-stabilization of the subject.[87]

In Chapter I we saw how Manet might be considered the joke-teller who wished to possess the model represented in *Olympia*. I argued that it was not the physical model, Victorine Meurent, that he desired, but his phantasmagoric creation Olympia. Recognizing that this representation of a desired figure cannot be possessed, the painter also faces a loss. At the moment that desire can be named, or represented in a painting, it eludes the desirer, since it is the nature of desire that it cannot be satisfied. In order to overcome the loss, the second figure, the object of desire, is transformed into an exposed object, an object that is supposedly available to all, but ultimately accessible to none. The viewer/third person becomes simultaneously the painter's ally and adversary. On the one hand, the painter uses the spectator as an ally to mediate his loss, and on the other hand, he uses him as a figure through whom he can vicariously experience his own sadistic impulses, since the spectator will not get any closer to the desired object than the painter himself.

Throughout my discussion of *Olympia*, *Le Déjeuner sur l'herbe* and *Nana* we have seen how Manet included the presence of the spectator to complete the scenario. Yet, time and again, the public's reaction

87 Neale 1981: 40.

demonstrated that Manet's works were never properly understood and instead provoked an indignant rejection. The indignation did not seem to be a matter of unintelligibility, since his audience understood only too well what Manet represented on the canvas. Nor did his audience fail to understand that they were required to play an active part in the composition of Manet's works, as a contemporary critic's review clearly proves: "Through sheer incompetence Manet doesn't finish what he begins, and he must credit the spectator with a generous dose of good will to *add mentally what is lacking in his painting.*"[88]

Advancing the analogy between a successful dirty joke and a successful painting, it appears that Manet had cast the spectators into an uncomfortable position in which they did not want to be placed. Unlike Degas, for instance, who invited his spectators to spy on his female figures, Manet positioned his viewers into more interactive roles—such as the implicit client or rejected admirer. Given this premise, we can see how Manet's intentional miscasting contributed to the unsuccessful reception of his works. Moreover, Manet did not seem to construct a proper facade behind which he could hide the erotic and hostile elements of the scene depicted. Indeed, it appears as if Manet actively eliminated the facade in order to heighten the eroticism and hostility of his subject matter and to bring the spectator face to face with such figures as Olympia, the nude of *Le Déjeuner sur l'herbe* and *Nana*, who unashamedly lure the viewers into their orbit, and then just as abruptly eject them. In addition, Manet violated another crucial principle that would otherwise have assured a benevolent response to his work. In "Jokes and Their Relation to the Unconscious," Freud emphasizes the important role of the woman's shame and embarrassment at hearing the sexually provocative speech of the joke-teller, who is excited by her. The woman is thought to be incapable of tolerating undisguised sexuality and is expected, therefore, to resist the joke-teller's sexual advances. "The woman's inflexibility is therefore the first condition for the development of smut, although, to be sure, it seems merely to imply a postpone-

---

88 Porcheron, quoted in Hamilton 1969: 196–197 (author's emphasis).

ment and does not indicate that further efforts will be in vain."[89] However, in the case of a woman who quickly shows her readiness to the male wooer, "the obscene speech has a short life; it yields at once to a sexual action."[90] Of course, the apparent sexual readiness of Olympia, the picnicking nude, and Nana did not allow for the spectators' transition to direct sexual actions. Instead, they drove them to hostile outbursts which were motivated in part by the female figure's dominant placement in the picture. In these three paintings, Manet represented a female who knows no shame or embarrassment about being the object of the onlooker's lust. Neither will she leave the room and disappear when the joker/painter announces his sexual desire for her in the presence of other admirers. As a result, she cannot be transformed into an object of exposition, but instead she exposes the spectators' futile attempts to possess her. In the end, it is not the second figure, the woman, who is the butt of the joke, but the onlooker. By the same token, the position of the third person, generally thought of as the site of the symbolic and the Law, is also inverted. The viewers are no longer the ones who re-inscribe the Law, but they become active participants in the rearrangement and destabilization of the Law. The stability of the symbolic code is shattered because the secondary object refuses to acquiesce in her position: she is at once the violator and the upholder of the Law. From a different viewpoint, we can also characterize the position that Olympia, the nude in *Le Déjeuner sur l'herbe* and *Nana* occupy as the locus of what Lacan defined as "*jouissance*."

Jouissance is that pleasure that cannot be talked about, that defies the boundaries of the symbolic code. *Jouissance* can only be seen; it is, as Lacan observes, written over the woman's body. In contrast, the male's sexual *jouissance* is phallic. He does not derive sexual pleasure through the woman's body but through and in relation to the phallus. According to Lacan, the sexual relationship between a woman and a man is never symmetrical, but is always mediated through a third: the phallus. In other words, the phallus signifies both the cause of

---

89 Freud 1905b: 99.

90 Freud 1905b: 99.

and the obstacle to *jouissance*, since the male can never fully enjoy the woman's body except through his own organ. The woman, on the other hand, is also caught up in the phallic *jouissance* but she always has "something more," precisely this *jouissance*. Unlike men, who are alienated from their object of desire (the phallus has its own life and cannot be controlled), the woman does not have a separate and visible organ through which she experiences *jouissance*. Since her sexual parts are hidden even to herself, within her own body, the woman cannot talk about the pleasure that she experiences from within herself. And yet, because she has a supplementary *jouissance*, she poses a threat to the phallic order precisely by being self-sufficient and independent of the Other.[91] As my analysis of *Le Déjeuner sur l'herbe* has shown, the nude in the foreground clearly occupies the role of the woman who exposes feminine *jouissance*. Though she can exhibit her whole body and be seen freely by the spectator, she can keep her *jouissance* a secret, a secret that narcissistically gratifies her and that underscores the enigmatic power radiating from her whole body. In this context, the woman as a represented (i. e., exposed and secondary) object remains independent, both of the painter who created her and of the spectator who beholds her. Olympia, Nana and the nude of *Le Déjeuner sur l'herbe* exercise a control over themselves: they escape the tyranny of both the author's and the spectator's position and in the end constitute a relatively autonomous identity for themselves.

***

91 For further discussions of Lacan's concept of *jouissance*, see Lacan 1975, Heath 1973, Wolff Bernstein 2007 & 2012.

The Other's look tells me, as does the image in the mirror,
that I am *also* that being who is limited to a point in space,
that I am that visible "stand-in" [*doublure*] in whom
I would recognize only with difficulty the lived *me*.

Maurice Merleau-Ponty, 1964

I am not simply that punctiform being located at the
geometrical point from which the perspective is grasped.
No doubt, in the depths metral of my eye,
the picture is painted. The picture, certainly, is in my eye.
But I am not in the picture.

Jacques Lacan, 1978

In *Le Déjeuner dans l'atelier*, *Le Balcon*, and *Un Bar aux Folies Bergère* Manet developed a different technique, not consciously of course, to challenge the spectator's self-awareness vis-à-vis his paintings. Instead of depicting figures who look squarely at the spectator, like Olympia or the nude in *Le Déjeuner sur l'herbe*, these new creations ignore the spectator's gaze altogether. They literally face no one, neither the spectator nor any other figure in the painting; they refuse to return their gaze, leaving the viewer searching for the focus of the figure's contemplation. In contrast to Degas's figures, for instance, who are caught in positions where they seem unaware of any spectator, who thus assumes the pleasurable stance of the unobserved voyeur, Manet's figures are undoubtedly aware of being looked at by the viewer, but they do not return the viewer's look. In contrast to Manet's earlier paintings, in which the figures lock eyes with the spectator, they now look out in the public's direction, while intentionally avoiding an exchange of gaze. In *Le Déjeuner dans l'atelier*

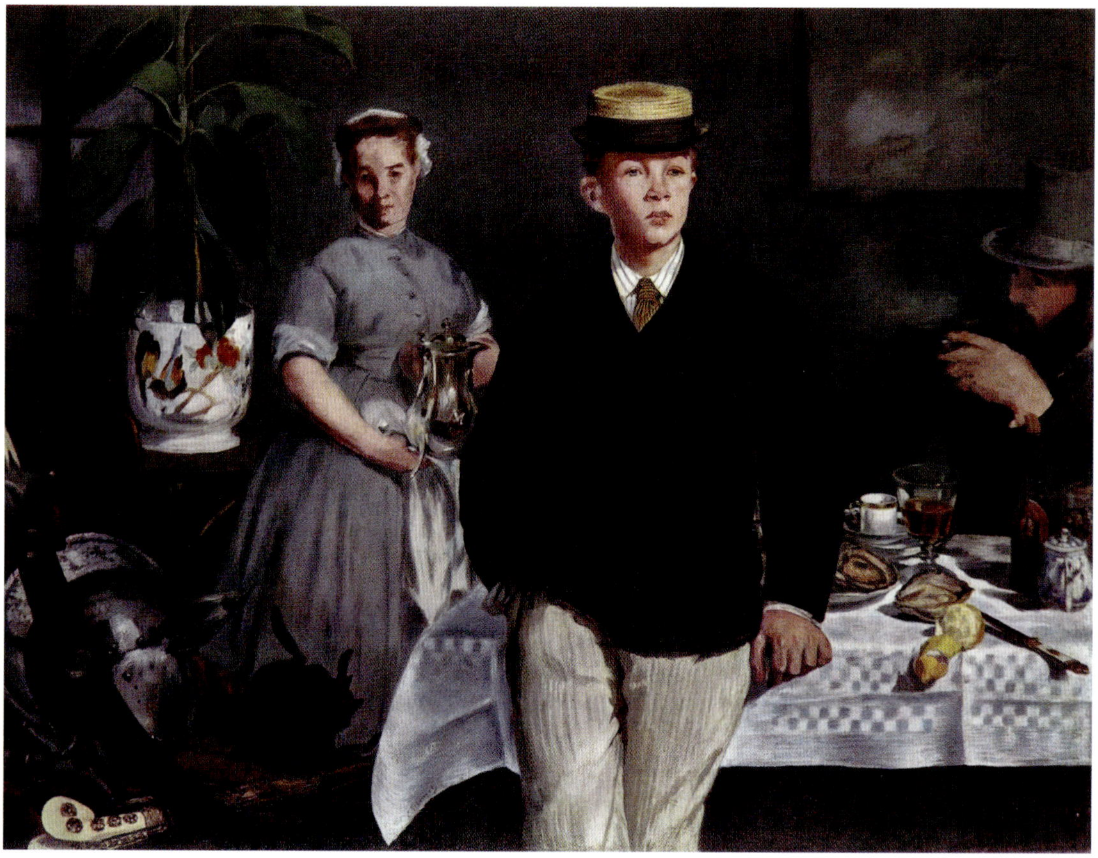

Plate 2:
Édouard Manet, *Le Déjeuner dans l'atelier* (1868)

[Plate 2], for example, we have three figures, a boy in the foreground looking straight out above the head of the spectator, leaving the focus of his eyes uncertain; a man to the right of the boy, smoking a cigar, sending his glance sideways to an unseen object, and a woman to the left of the boy, holding a coffee pot, ambiguously facing either the boy or the spectator. Upon closer examination, we discover that each figure is painted from a different perspective, and that none of the planes on which they are positioned ever meets at a central point. A diagram of this triad of gazes would look as follows:

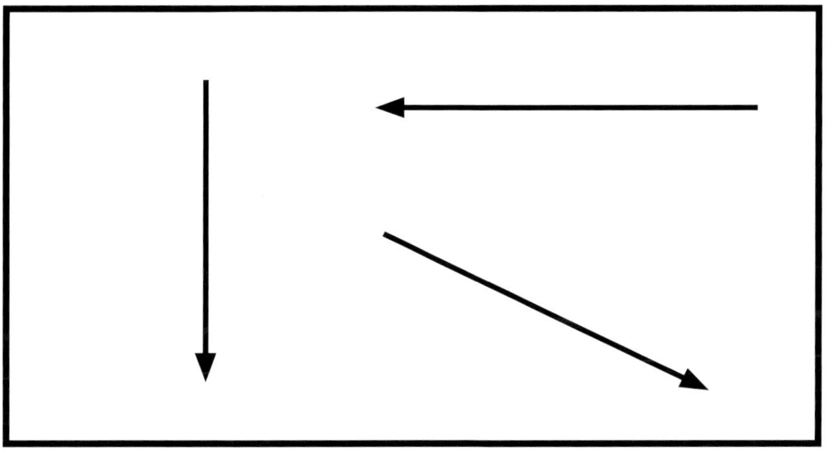

The expected intimacy of this "family luncheon" is strangely converted into a scene of utter isolation, fixing the figures in the painting, as well as the viewer, into a frozen and alienating position. Interestingly, *Le Déjeuner dans l'atelier* does not appear as a scene in which the figures are entirely disconnected from each other—at least not at first sight. Unlike *Olympia* or *Le Déjeuner sur l'herbe*, where the central female figure initially seems to invite the spectators to participate in the scene she has opened up for them, the tableau in *Le Déjeuner dans l'atelier* appears to illustrate what its title promises, namely, a lunch in the painter's studio. Put differently, Manet appears to recount a story to his audience. Yet, the closer we look at the painting, the more the seemingly coherent elements fall apart. Gradually, as Théophile Gautier's reaction to *Le Déjeuner dans l'atelier* illustrates, the story makes no sense:

> In the *Luncheon*, the figure of the fop leaning against the table is very true to type, in attitude and costume. The servant and the bearded man leaning on his elbow who are seen in the background are rather delicate in tone. But why this armor on the table? Is it a luncheon which follows or which precedes a duel? We don't know.[92]

It is not just the weaponry on the chair that belies the peaceful domestic scene of a family breakfast: the figures themselves reveal an inner discordance. It is unclear whether the young man is sitting or standing, has stopped in his tracks, or is most likely leaning back against the edge of the breakfast table. The melancholy of his expression is in stark contrast to his somewhat languid pose.

> Movement in these paintings is not given by the development of momentousness but by arrest [...] the figures are static, their actions on hold. The static pose of the figures in these scenes—as in other portraits by Manet—corresponds to the quiet assemblage of objects in a "nature morte." The pose exhibits but does not portray the human being. Portraits become still-lives and signatures of an aesthetic objectification.[93]

One may even argue that the still-life arrangement on the table—the lemon and oysters, the glass of wine and the sugar bowl, along with the plant pot on the left—expresses a greater vivacity than the figures themselves. Each object within the painting is assigned a specific placement in the composition, and each of them points in a different direction—the knife on the table, the sword on the chair—all of them seem to refuse to be forced into a unified arrangement. Violating every aspect of the Aristotelian laws of unity, Manet pictorially developed "devices to stress *casual,* not causal relationships. That is,

92 Quoted in Hamilton 1969: 134.

93 "Bewegung ist in diesen Bildern nicht in der Entwicklung von Momentaneität gegeben, sondern in deren Arretierung. [...] die Figuren sind statisch, als Pose gefaßt. Die statische Pose der Menschen in den Szenen der Figurenbilder und in den Porträts von Manet korrespondiert mit dem stillen Beieinander der Dinge im ‚Nature morte'. Die Pose stellt die Menschen aus, nicht dar. Porträts werden zu Stilleben, zu Signaturen einer ‚ästhetischen Verdinglichung' [...]." (Growe 1983, 173–174, author's translation).

relationships subject to, resulting from, or occurring by chance."[94] The longer the viewer contemplates this breakfast scene—at first seemingly domestic—the more he realizes how many disconcerting and contradictory entanglements Manet has managed to condense within the painting. In *Déjeuner dans l'atelier*, the picture frame acquires a different meaning from that of *Nana* or *Bal masqué*. Instead of emphasizing that the fictive reality extends beyond the formal boundaries, the frame now functions as a container, as a means of curbing the confusion within the painting and the disorientation it evokes.

Where are the viewers to consider thiemselves located in front of this painting? How are they supposed to react to these static, isolated figures? Paradoxically, they feel drawn into this painting, not because they are implicated as an imagined presence, but because they might be the only ones able to unite these estranged, disconnected figures and assemble their disparate gazes. The viewers are tempted to believe that it is up to them to restore order in this incoherent scene and mentally rearrange the characters so that they might comprise a meaningful "story." However, no matter which direction the viewers choose to follow—Manet has mapped out several paths—they encounter an impasse. Even the chair on the left, which might encourage the spectators' participation within the depicted scene, spurns their presence, thanks to the cat and heavy armor already occupying the space. As a result, the narrow space in which the three figures are entrapped leaves no opening for the viewers and forces them to remain as isolated and estranged in front of the painting as the figures before them. It is interesting to note how Manet used two cutting objects—the knife on the table and the sword on the chair—to project the viewers' gaze into the canvas. The symbolism of this gesture is in itself highly provocative. At least four interpretations are plausible, all of which are pertinent to the underlying meaning of *Le Déjeuner dans l'atelier*:

1) Manet wished to suggest that the viewers' eyes would pierce the canvas and slice the figures into separate elements; 2) he reckoned

94 Austin 1981: 55 (emphasis in the original).

that piecing together the painting's disparate elements would be futile; 3) he aimed to accentuate the chilling effect exerted by the painting as a whole, thereby encouraging the spectators' alienation, while the depicted figures likewise seem to be borrowed from other pictures and reassembled in the new context.[95] 4) Manet hints at the riddle of his family by portraying Léon Koëlla Leenhoff—his godson and alleged half-brother—standing between a Dutch-looking maid, his mother Suzanne Leenhoff, and a well-dressed man, looking across the canvas as if he is part of a triadic construction that he seems to ignore (a possible allusion to Manet's father's refusal to acknowledge Leon's paternity). Given the abundant recent literature about Suzanne Leenhoff's affair with Manet's father Auguste, *Le Déjeuner dans l'atelier*, painted six years after Auguste's death, appears to be the most revealing, yet mysterious depiction of this intricate family affair. A closer inspection reveals the following details, summarized by Joachim Kaak, former director of the Pinakothek in Munich, with the following words:

> [T]he assembled items in this picture confront the spectator with an unsolved puzzle. The left-overs from a meal, oysters and a peeled lemon, in addition to an already made coffee, port-wine, a half-smoked cigarette, the hot chocolate in the hands of the maid and, finally, a still-life of weapons on the chair with a cat which cleans itself: the classical unity of place, time and action did not want to cohere. The painting refuses to be legible, it remains fascinating, enigmatic, challenging.[96]

---

95 Different critics have characterized Manet's figures as "cut-outs," as figures cut out from the background; forinstance, Émile Cardon decried Manet's *Portrait dans le rôle de Hamlet* as "one of those crudely carved puppets from a marionette theater, whose limbs are dislocated, twisted, and badly attached." (Quoted in Hamilton 1969: 203). Paul Mantz commented upon *Le Fifre:* "The idea that there is a real atmosphere behind bodies or that they are surrounded by air does not enter Manet's head. He remains faithful to the good old makers of playing cards. 'Le Fifre', an amusing specimen of primitive illustration, is like a Jack of Diamonds, stuck on a door." (Quoted in Courthion 1960: 173).

96 Kaak 2016: 61 (author's translation).

Despite recent efforts to get "behind" the canvas via infra-red X-ray technology which revealed a large window behind the painting within the picture, confirming that this luncheon was actually staged in Manet's atelier in Boulogne-sur-Mer, the assembly of left-overs unfinished items and abandoned props, such as the sword Léon had worn in *L'Enfant à l'épée* (1861), the helmet worn by one of the soldiers in *Jésus insulté par les soldats* (1865) and of course the notorious cat from *Olympia* (1863), which now cleans itself and avoids eye contact, all elements shun the reconstruction of a unified tale. Everything points towards "unfinished business." Is Léon leaving or staying? What's the peeled lemon for? Who will finish the cigarette? Who will drink the wine? Everything is held in suspension, in a state of unknowing, which may be a metaphor for Léon's confusion, growing up with this contrived tale that his mother was his sister, and therefore his grandparents his actual parents. One small potential clue is found on the silver pitcher held by the Dutch-looking maid. It is, as Leslie Park (2012) remarked, where Manet signed the painting with the letter "M," possibly analogous to *La Pêche* (1861), in which Manet found another hidden way to bestow the correct family name upon the boy: not Leenhoff but Manet.

With *Le Balcon* [**Plate 10**], the spectator is left in an equally precarious position as in front of *Le Déjeuner dans l'atelier*. Confused by the three figures who seem to be suspended between motion and repose, the spectator is motivated to place the two women and the man on the balcony into a meaningful context. Yet, as Castagnary's reaction reveals, the three figures resist being subsumed into a coherent narrative account:

> Just as Manet assembles, for the mere pleasure of astonishing, objects which should be mutually incompatible, in the same fashion he arranges his people at random without any reason or meaning for the composition. [...] On the *Balcony* I see two women, one of whom is very young. Are they sisters? Is this a mother and daughter? I don't know. And then one has seated herself apparently just to enjoy the view of the street; the other is putting on her gloves as if she were about to leave. This contradictory attitude bewilders me.[97]

97 Castagnary, quoted in Hamilton 1969: 138.

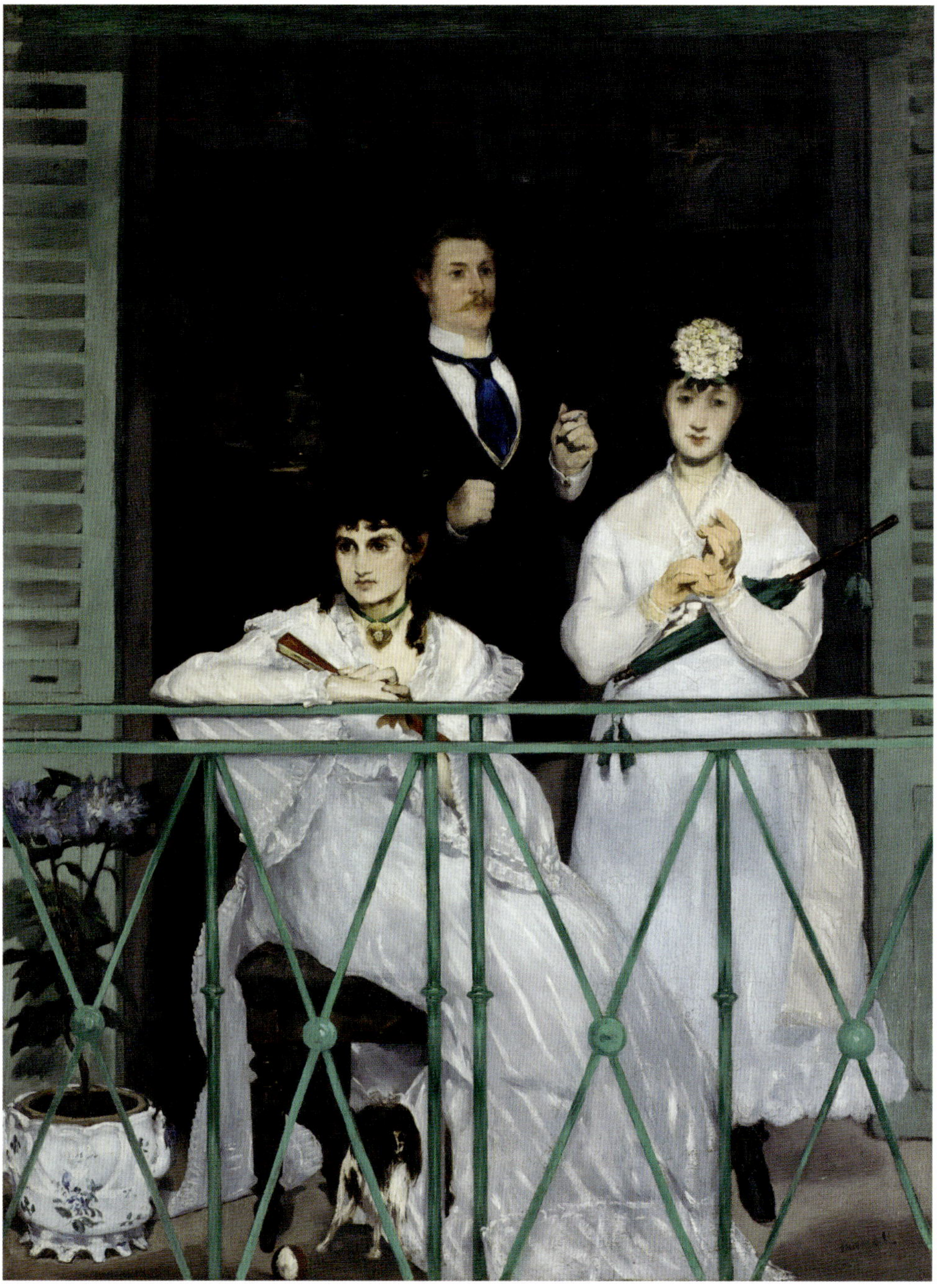

Plate 10:
Édouard Manet, *Le Balcon* (1868–1869)

By placing the figures behind the green railing—Berthe Morisot on the left, Fanny Claus on the right, and the elegantly dressed gentleman in the middle (impersonated by Antoine Guillemet)—Manet situates the spectators both in the position of the crowd surveyed by the group on the balcony, and of the observer of the scene as a whole.[98] As a consequence, the viewers constantly oscillate between the two roles: the one who sees and the one who is seen. Upon closer examination, however, the viewers notice that Morisot and Guillemet are looking beyond them, not *at* them as such. Indeed, Morisot is so absorbed in her thoughts, that she barely seems to notice the imaginary crowd below, nor the beholder who contemplates her from the street. She appears to be suspended between the two positions of the one who sees and the one who is beeing seen, a factor that accentuates her enigmatic attitude. The elegant gentleman behind her appears to be more static and frozen in his position, vacantly staring in an unspecified direction. Fanny Claus, the only figure who squarely faces the spectators, assumes a locus similar to that of the maid holding the coffee pot in *Le Déjeuner dans l'atelier*, leaving the viewers uncertain about the intent of her concerned look. Evidently—as in *Le Déjeuner dans l'atelier*—each figure seems isolated in his/her own world and strangely detached from the others.

> Trapped in the narrowing gap, the figures of Manet's pictures become flattened, disoriented, as in the strange, masterful *Balcony*. [...] This muteness, this refusal of human figures to be meaningful, was one of the problems that scandalized Manet's time—and still sometimes troubles ours.[99]

In contrast to *Olympia*, *Le Déjeuner sur l'herbe* and *Nana*, whose figures directly engage the spectators' fantasies, yet prohibit them to

---

98 The green railing serves as a powerful device to keep the spectator at a distance. It is as if Manet, as a spectator, saw himself barred from joining the trio on the balcony. It is interesting to note that spectators, even nowadays, invariably keep at a greater distance when they gaze upon *Le Balcon* than when they look at other paintings by Manet. The wall in *L'Exécution de Maximilien* and the counter in *Un Bar aux Folies Bergère* serve similar functions as the green railing in *Le Balcon.*
99 Schneider 1968: 60.

become absorbed and lost in their fictive reality, the characters in *Le Déjeuner dans l'atelier* and *Le Balcon* neither negate nor confirm the spectators' existence. They are curiously posed in a staged setting, yet they don't seem to know what roles they are enacting, nor to whom they are presenting themselves. Instead of ignoring or including the spectators, these figures intentionally overlook their beholders, leaving them searching for the gaze that acknowledges their presence:

> Thus self-consciousness is basically "acknowledgment" by another person; and our being-for-others is a necessary condition for the development of our self-consciousness, our being-for-ourselves. [...] Since I am an object only in so far as I exist for the other person, I have to obtain from that other person the acknowledgment of my being. The other person is the mediator between me and myself. "[...] I acknowledge that I am as the other sees me."[100]

While Olympia and Nana had at least addressed their onlookers as customers and the nude of *Le Déjeuner sur l'herbe* as potential voyeurs, the figures of *Le Déjeuner dans l'atelier* and *Le Balcon* avoid granting the spectators any specified role, no matter how objectionable that might be. They radically challenge the spectators' fundamental need to be recognized by the Other and to use the Other for their own reflection. Unlike the Salon painters of the eighteenth century, who created a "supreme fiction of the beholder's nonexistence" (Fried 1980: 113), Manet did not pretend that the spectator was not present, but rather that

> [...] the painting has a separate, but just as distinct and active reality as the viewer's own physical reality. Thus, when we are engaged more directly by the confrontational figures, his sheer presence and his just peculiar enough engagement from the other figures forces us to recognize the reality of the painted surface in an abrupt manner.[101]

In a sense, no matter which technique Manet employs, whether he directly addresses the spectators or intentionally overlooks them, he always insists upon their active participation vis-à-vis his works.

---

100 Stern 1967: 116.
101 Reid 1981: 79.

Manet never leaves the spectators in a comfortably passive role where they can forget their surroundings and let themselves be engulfed entirely by the fictive reality. The viewers' fantasies are never permitted to wander for long, since they are continuously forced to reflect upon themselves in order to subject themselves to the Other in order to grasp an image of themselves. Even where the spectators' position seems to have been "forgotten" or discounted, the viewers cannot simply leave and ignore the impact of the powerful figures of *Le Déjeuner dans l'atelier* and *Le Balcon.* Paradoxically, by realizing that their need for recognition in the gaze of the Other has been frustrated, the spectators become all the more acutely aware of their need to be acknowledged by the painted presence. From this vantage point, the dynamic Manet engenders between the spectator and *Le Déjeuner dans l'atelier* or *Le Balcon* can be compared to the relationship that the analyst establishes towards the patient:

> But the principal technical innovation was the removal of the therapist from the hysteric's field of vision, so that she was forced to make herself heard and was no longer before a real spectator in whose eyes she might find the desire that she sought. The patient was constrained to see through her own words her own internal divisions and find in the analytic mirror her own image.[102]

As we know from the previous chapter, *Le Balcon* is the last painting in which Manet quoted very broadly from the work of an Old Master. For this reason, it represents an important turning point in Manet's artistic development. In subsequent works, Manet turned his attention to documenting daily life in the city, he observed scenes in the coffee-houses, bars, salons, at the racetrack, and at the beach. He virtually eliminated the staged effect of his depicted scenes, and cast his figures in more natural and casual postures. This development was due in part to his adoption of Impressionist techniques of rendering forms and light, bestowing a more fleeting, temporary effect upon his chosen subjects. I believe that this change in Manet's career was also brought about by his fascination with Berthe Morisot, the woman

---

102 Major 1974: 387.

he portrayed for the first time in *Le Balcon*. In Morisot he had found a figure who exerted from within herself the enigmatic effect Manet had until then strived to establish on his own. As a consequence, his relationship to the model, the work, and the spectator underwent a dramatic change. In front of a figure who had captivated his own desires and phantasies so strongly, Manet had lost the control he had exerted so powerfully upon the spectator's presence before. Instead of mapping out an empty space for the spectator's imaginary presence, Manet now appears to be absorbed in overcoming the distance separating himself from Berthe Morisot. In front of her, he abandons the role of the stage director and exchanges it for that of the spectator, thereby submitting himself to the very object who captured his imagination. This transformation of the object also engendered a shift in Manet's creative aims. The painting no longer served as an Other through whom Manet marked out an alienating relationship between spectacle and spectator. Now, it became an instrument through which he attempted to captivate and possess this mysterious object of his desire. In other words, the painting was not created to underscore the distance that separated the spectator from a fantasized and desired object, but to narrow the distance that the desired object maintained towards the painter himself. In his various studies of Berthe Morisot, Manet eliminated all the devices that previously had given his representations their detached and enigmatic quality. Instead, Manet seemed dedicated to pursuing Berthe Morisot and depicting her in the various moods and states that so fascinated him. Instead of casting his models in a selection of disguises in order to enhance the distance between his painted objects and the spectator, he uses the portraits of Berthe Morisot as a way of tearing off her masks and of approximating whatever was hidden behind them. By painting Morisot in various poses, Manet hoped to unveil the mystery which separated him from her. Thus, we may argue that through her, Manet had been led to a different approach to painting. A painting could serve as more than a physical entity through which the artist might gain control of the spectator's presence and through which he could put to play the viewer's identificatory desires. At this point, it seems that Manet now felt that painting could also serve as a means of gaining access to a mysterious figure.[103] Significantly, once Manet used his art as a means of appropriating the subject before him, his paintings exerted a less alienating effect upon the spectator. In this way, portraits of society women like Nina de Callias, Méry Laurent, and Jeanne Demarsy become intimate character studies, not enigmatic puzzles from the realms of fantasy. Manet does not portray these public women in stiff and detached poses, but only attempts to capture an intimate glimpse of them. Yet, despite Manet's refusal to stage these contemporary public personalities in scenes from the past, in their actual realization on the canvas they essentially remain as unyielding and obscure as his earlier figures. However, because they are set in familiar, contemporary surroundings like the bars, cafes and salons of the Parisian metropolis, the spectator does not experience these figures as strange and distant as *Olympia* or the nude in *Le Déjeuner sur l'herbe.*

In the scenes portraying society women, famous politicians, and fellow artists, the public was confronted with their own outlook on life, with figures who were strangely isolated in their own familiar settings. The spectacles Manet had once staged according to models from Old Masters had become the daily sights of modern society—lonely women in bars and cafes, detached from themselves and from one another. Richard Sennett describes the change that had transformed a lively crowd into a silent assemblage in which people were afraid of socializing with each other for fear of revealing too much of their inner thoughts and emotions:

> In 1750, Parisians and Londoners conceived of their families as private domains. The manners, speech, and dress of the great world began to feel inappropriate within the intimacy of the home. One hundred and twenty-five years later, this divorce between the home and the great world had, in theory, become absolute. [...] Because silence created isolation, the public/private distinction would not hold as a pair of opposites. The silent spectator with no one in particular to watch,

103 See Manet's various studies of Berthe Morisot *Le Balcon* (1869), *Le Repos* (1870), *Berthe Morisot au bouquet de violettes* (1872), *Portrait de Berthe Morisot en chapeau de deuil à long voile* (1874), and *Berthe Morisot à l'éventail* (1874).

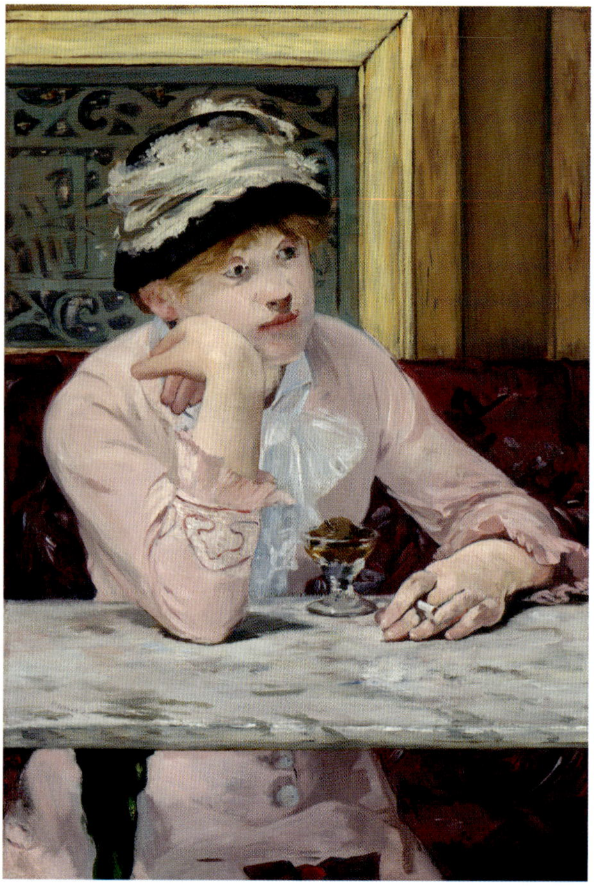

shielded by his right to be left alone, could now also be absolutely lost in his own thoughts, his daydreams [...]. One escaped from the family parlor to the club or cafe for this privacy. Silence therefore superimposed public and private imagery. Silence made it possible to be both visible to others and isolated from them.[104]

And yet, the public of Manet's era, as well as ours today, passes by these paintings as they pass by crowds in the street. To the modern eye, *Au Café*, *La Prune* (1878) **[Plate 68]**, or *La Liseuse* are interesting character studies of late nineteenth-century Parisian society; they represent "slices of life," through which we can gain an insight into the passive isolation of the modern subject lost in a large crowd. Yet, they do not halt us, they do not engage us in the same manner as did *Olympia* or *Le Balcon*. The reason for the spectator's different attitude in front of *La Prune, La Liseuse,* or the various portraits of society figures, lies in the fact that Manet had put aside his technique of making the spectator's identificatory process a constitutive part of the composition. The viewers can contemplate these detached figures at leisure without feeling implicated as the ones from whom these figures are alienated. In fact, the viewers are tempted to recognize themselves in the isolated figures represented on the canvas; they passively allow themselves to be "appropriated," to be seen, without involving the spectators in a process that questions their desire to become part of their reality.[105]

Plate 68:
Édouard Manet,
La Prune, (1878)

104 Sennet 1977: 217.

105 *Le Bon Bock* offers one of the most extreme examples of Manet's diverse constructions of the spectator's relationship to the figures on the canvas. I believe that

It was not until his last painting, *Un Bar aux Folies Bergère* [Plate 15] that Manet effectively combined his old technique of staging his subjects in "distant roles" with his more recent preoccupation with portraying contemporary subjects as he had observed them, isolated in their natural environment. In his first creative period, Manet had cast his figures into roles devoid of any coherent meaning, as in *Le Déjeuner sur l'herbe* or *Le Déjeuner dans l'atelier*. But in the barmaid of *Un Bar aux Folies Bergère*, he had found a subject supposedly engaged in a meaningful context, but who, upon closer examination, was as divided and detached from her surroundings as the dandy in *Le Déjeuner dans l'atelier*, or as Berthe Morisot in *Le Balcon*. Thus, Manet found a way of fusing the contrived detachment reminiscent of *Olympia* or *Le Fifre* [Plate 25] with the "natural" alienation as he observed it in his contemporary world. Yet, like the figures of *Le Balcon* and *Le Déjeuner dans l'atelier*—who affirm their detachment from their onlookers by averting their gaze—, the barmaid stares directly out at us, enigmatically. In this way, Manet invites us to imagine ourselves as a customer approaching the bar to order a drink. For her, we are just one of an endless series of customers, from whom she is ready to take any order. The uncanny trick Manet brings into play here is to confound the observer with the one observed. On what side of the counter are the spectators to imagine themselves? Are they part of the crowd mirrored in the background, where an asymmetrical reflection of the barmaid suggests a customer engaged in a conversation with her? Or are we peering into the framed canvas where

---

the great success Manet achieved with *Le Bon Bock* was in part due to the unquestioning relationship he set up between the jovial beer drinker and the viewer. The distance so characteristic of his earlier paintings is summarily eliminated in *Le Bon Bock* who seemingly invites his observers to join him for a glass of beer. In addition to the quotation of scenes by Dutch masters of the seventeenth century, *Le Bon Bock* is strongly reminiscent of the eighteenth-century genre espoused by Greuze, whereby the spectator is induced to be moved by representations of simple and common figure(s) and family scenes. It was precisely this sentimental reading of *Le Bon Bock* that contributed to the work's widely favorable reception, exemplified in Paul Mantz's observation: "What he [Manet] has also discovered is the perfect truth of an attitude, the representation of a typical personality. He has expressed a moment which resumes a whole lifetime." (Quoted in Hamilton 1969: 169).

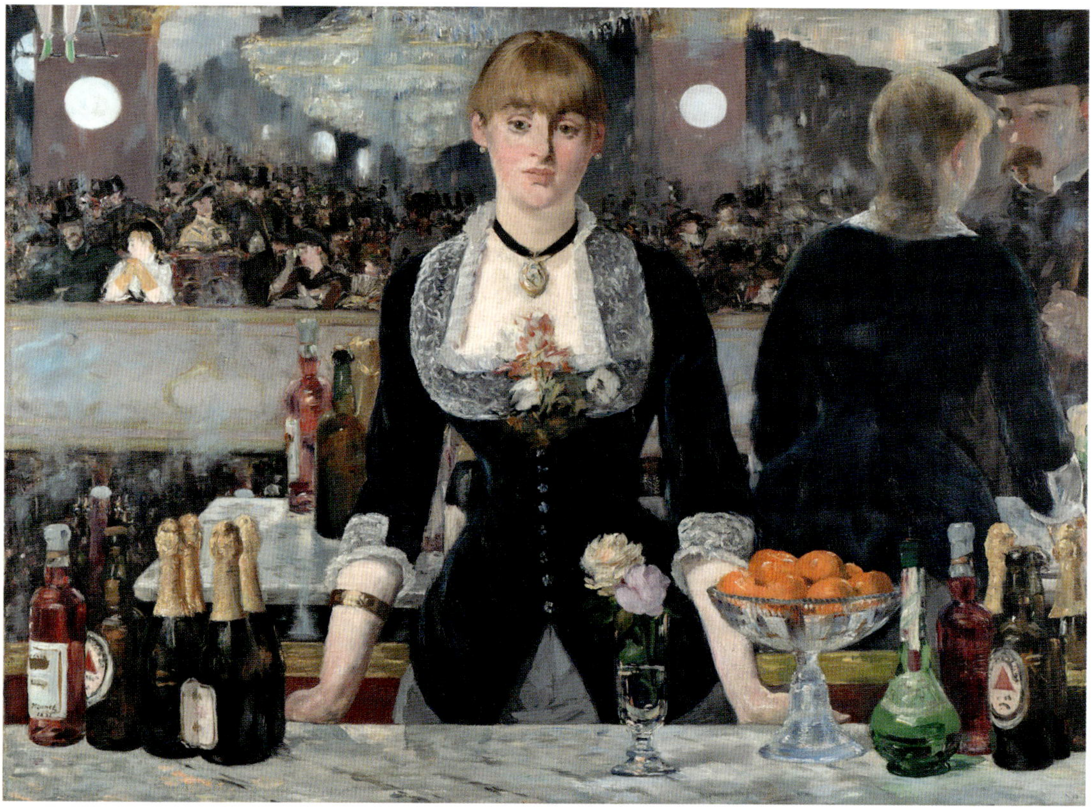

Plate 15:
Édouard Manet,
Un Bar aux Folies Bergère (1881–1882)

the scene is physically positioned? The deeper we attempt to locate ourselves in this glittering spectacle, the more we get lost amid the dizzying, overlapping specular realities. Every path that promises an opening merely reveals another false trail: what we perceive in front of us does not correspond to what we observe in the mirrored background. In addition to the distorted reflection of the barmaid—which seems to represent an extraneous figure rather than her view from behind—the bottles on the counter do not match those in the reflection, their arrangement simply does not correspond. Furthermore, though the front edge of the counter extends along the bottom from one edge of the picture frame to the other, in the reflection it is visibly shorter. We are also induced to assume that the crowd is on the balcony (as seen in the mirror), but this creates further conflicts of perspective between the barmaid, the customer, and the balcony in the rear. Furthermore, a second downstairs hall is visible below the balcony, and another one above, as suggested by the dangling green feet of a trapezist in the upper left corner.

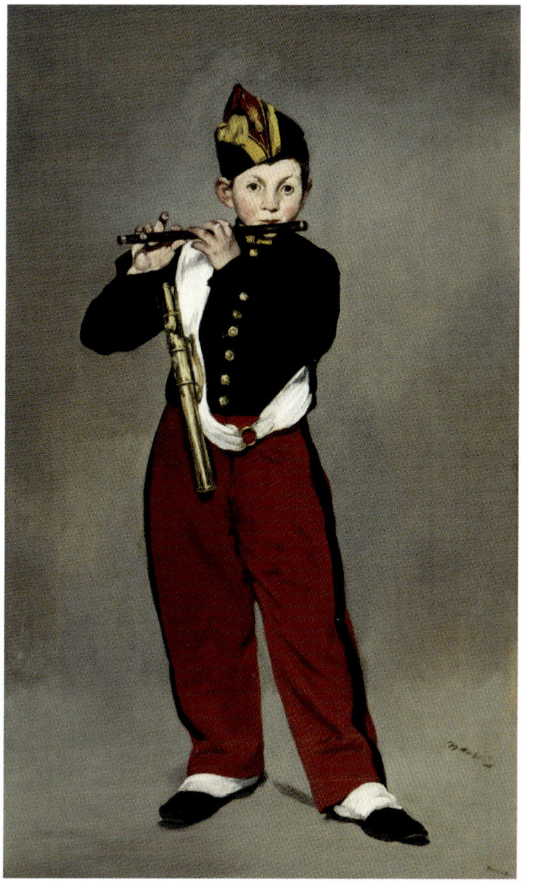

Plate 25:
Édouard Manet,
Le Fifre (1866)

Basically, in this single painting Manet has superimposed five different perspectives, all of which are anchored by the central figure of the barmaid. And yet, her centrality itself is so fragmented that we struggle to assemble the different segments into a unified whole. Everything defies our accepted perceptions, yet somehow all these dissonant narratives cohere. For Manet it was not enough to simply re-create actual figures whom he had observed. Instead, he wished to demonstrate that the representations could be further divided and reflected into still other representations of themselves. In *Un Bar aux Folies Bergère,* Manet represented a scene within a scene, a fabrication within a fictive realm.

Because Manet included such obvious incongruities in the reflection of the bar, he deliberately created an ambignity as to whether the spectator was confronted with a mirrored reality, or whether the mirrored realm constituted a distinctly separate domain.

> The fact that the mirror does not really reflect the phenomenal world as it should but, in effect, contains another and different one, should be enough [...] to make Manet's purpose clear to us. The mirror [...] represents another dimension, the other half, the complement to the other reality, in this case the actual barmaid.[106]

However, rather than simply constituting a complement to the other reality, Manet seems to imply that the mirrored reality was, as Merleau-Ponty points out, "a quasi-presence," a presence that is mysteriously but distantly inhabited by the person who is reflected in it. By the same token, Manet seems to have thought of a painting not merely as a reflection of an actual scene or figure, but an independent entity which, like the planes visible in a mirror reflection, cannot be grasped by either the image reflected in it or by the figure standing in front of it. Instead, it serves as a screen that can mediate between two realities but cannot absorb either one.

Unlike the stares of Olympia, Nana, or the nude in *Le Déjeuner sur l'herbe*—which designated the spectator as one of their costumers or eager voyeurs—, the barmaid's vacant gaze seems to pass right through us, defying our attempts to accommodate ourselves towards her look. What she presents to us is different from what we see, since we can discern her inverted mirror image behind her. Looking at the barmaid, one is reminded of Lacan's saying: "When, in love, I solicit a look, what is profoundly unsatisfying and always missing is that—*you never look at me from the place from which I see you.* Conversely, *what I look at is never what I wish to see.*"[107] In *Un Bar aux Folies Bergère,* Manet finally played out the imaginary path he had hitherto invited his viewers to complete. In contrast to *Olympia* or *Nana*, in which Manet set up relationships which were to be completed by the viewer's

---

106 Mauner 1975: 161.

107 Lacan 1978: 103 (emphasis in the original).

participation, in *Un Bar aux Folies Bergère* he demonstrates how each "completion" or "supplementation" is recontextualized into a network of fictive realities in which every new discovery simply unveils yet another unexpected possibility. Behind the barmaid on her right is her reflection, behind which the world of the spectator is revealed, behind which we perceive a crowd whose attention is directed to a spectacle invisible to us. Moreover, the suspended legs of the trapezist suggest that this glittering world extends beyond the frame, implying that an infinite variety of realities can still be imagined. The arbitrary physical frame of the painting is the only limit Manet establishes to contain the spectator's manifold imaginary "walks."

Returning for a moment to Freud's restaging of Michelangelo's *Moses* sculpture in Rome, we remember the sad moment in which he realizes that his attempt to complete the scene in his imagination was brought to a sudden halt by the awareness that "[n]othing of the kind happened. [...] and I was obliged to realize that something was represented here that could stay without change."[108] Similarly, the spectators in front of *Un Bar aux Folies Bergère* have to recognize that their wish to constitute themselves in the gaze of the barmaid is founded entirely in their imagination. Her aloof look—reminiscent of the detached gaze of Manet's mother's in *Portrait de Monsieur et Madame Auguste Manet* (1860) **[Plate 12]** [109]—reveals that she is not really seeing the spectator, but that she is the object through whom the spectator's fantasies are transcended.

Positioned between the counter and the mirror, she not only functions as the concrete connection between the realms within the painting, but also between the physical spectator and the fictive domain of the painting. Yet, even in her centrality as the reference point through whom these part-realities are channeled, she is divided within herself, one part being projected outward and another one backward to the client depicted in the canvas. What the spectators have fantasized as

---

108 Freud 1914b: 220–221.

109 At an exhibition of Manet's works, I overheard a guide saying that the necklace worn by the barmaid belonged to Manet's mother, and was used as a significant prop in *Un Bar aux Folies Bergère*—reminiscent of Olympia's necklace.

a unified figure—through whom they could grasp their own idealized image—, emerges as a subject who is herself fragmented into parts. Unlike Olympia's steady detached gaze, which suggests a firm control over her own multiple identities (prostitute, Venus, model, etc.), the barmaid displays her infinite fractured divisibility. Her languid, somewhat melancholic look not only hides the fatigue she feels from the attention required to perform her job, but also symbolizes the exhaustion of constituting this passive Other upon whom the actual and fictive spectators seek to ground their object-ness. She is weary of being consumed by others as an object like the ones she is offering to her clients at the counter. In contrast to the nude of *Le Déjeuner sur l'herbe,* whose gaze triumphs over the spectator's desire to grasp her, the barmaid submits herself to the visual consumption by the spectator's eyes. Like Olympia, the barmaid lures the spectator into assuming control of her image; yet, unlike Olympia—who ultimately arrests the spectator's phantasmagoric desires by her steady detached gaze—, the barmaid undermines the spectators' desires by not being in possession of her own image. Her image is so distorted and so infinitely divisible in the various reflections that the spectators no longer know what image they wish to possess. Through her, the spectators are forced to see that her image is no more than a combination of paint upon canvas—that this figure acts upon them like a vacuum. As a result, we are again thrust back to our own isolated position in which we must realize that our subjectivity is based on the fundamental misrecognition of taking ourselves as an Other, and the Other as a guarantor of our identity.

***

Throughout this discussion we have seen how Manet used various methods to seduce his audience into an active role *qua* beholder, and how he integrated an awareness of that role into the creative act itself. His consistent manipulation of the spectator's presence in front of the painting is due in part to Manet's ambition to paint not merely his own world, but his problematic relation to it. As Fried argues:

> But Manet's desire to make the estranging quality of self-awareness an essential part of the content of his work [...] has an important consequence: namely, that self-awareness in *this* particular situation necessarily entails the awareness that what one is looking at, is after all, merely a painting. And this awareness *too* must be made an essential part of the work itself. That is, there must be no question but that the painter *intended* it to be felt; and if necessary the spectator must be *compelled* to feel it.[110]

However, the role the painter assigned to his audience was anything but comfortable: according to some, Manet forced his viewer "to add mentally what is lacking in his painting,"[111] but the outrage of Manet's early public made it clear that they disliked being manipulated by the image on the canvas before them. They would not yield to this invitation, instead they retaliated and criticized Manet for his "inability to finish" his work. Reluctant to comply with the part they were invited to play, Manet's contemporaries redirected their irritation and found fault with the painter instead.

If we look back through tradition, we can see that no other painter had challenged his audience in quite the same fashion. Artists usually endorsed the privileged position of their spectators, who were either induced to appoint themselves as judges or passive admirers of the work before them. Manet's innovation was to disrupt this one-sided relationship which had fictionalized the spectator as a unified being by situating the painting in the position of the one who apprehends the spectator as an object who is in turn apprehended by the figures in the painting. He had devised a unique and disconcerting parity between viewer and viewed, since the interaction between the painted figures and their audience constantly fluctuates, rendering the two positions interchangeable. Of course, in those paintings where the figures avert their gaze, this binary relationship is less obvious. Although these paintings were created for contemplation, the viewer's Otherness as an outsider is also put into question— figures like the youth (Léon) in *Le Déjeuner dans l'atelier* or Berthe Morisot in *Le Balcon* patently

110 Fried 1965: 49 (emphasis in the original).

111 Porcheron, quoted in Hamilton 1969: 197.

ignore their supposed audience. Furthermore, the device whereby the painting becomes the "object" for the Other through which the viewers grasp awareness of themselves as observers, is equally precarious since they are no longer *seen,* but instead they are literally overlooked. As a result, the onlookers are confounded and unable to comprehend a scenario that does not only lend meaning to the figures assembled in the painting, but also reconfirms their own position as the Other, the outsider to whom the figures address their gaze.

In a peculiar sense, defining a painting, rather than a specific person, as an Other comes closest to the Sartrean and Lacanian definition of the Other. When Lacan, for example, talks about the Other in whom the subjects seek their self-recognition and in whom they locate their desire, what he has in mind is the Absolute Other Subject, the Almighty Father, the all-knowing and all-seeing God. Although the "real" God is "seen" only through pictorial representations, a painted God remains unchangeably visible and present. Like Olympia's gaze and that of the nude in *Le Déjeuner sur l'herbe*, God's eye remains fixed unwaveringly upon the beholder. While spectators can move elsewhere, close their eyes or change the viewing angle, the disconcerting look of Olympia and the barmaid's melancholic gaze always remain the same. The paranoic structure of subjectivity—in which the individuals invariably mistake their image for themselves and therefore identify with an alien body—is intensified before an immobile, all-seeing figure whose state the spectator cannot affect or alter by any means except by destroying it. And yet, throughout this entire process, the viewers have the paradoxical knowledge that they are the only ones who see—since Olympia, Nana, or the barmaid, who are no more than painted constructions upon canvas, cannot see but only absorb the spectator's own animating gaze. Yet, as Freud's scenario in front of the Moses sculpture revealed, it makes little difference for the subjects' identificatory process whether they desire to assimilate the attributes of a real or an imaginary Other, whether, that is, they constitute themselves as an object in the real or in the painted gaze of the Other.[112]

---

112 In "Seminar 5: 1919–1992, August Strindberg (1849–1912) and Martti Si-

As Jean-Luc Nancy writes:

> [T]he gaze sees nothing. Neither the one painted on the canvas nor that of the painter behind the canvas can see. They only appear to see. But to appear to see, or to *appear to oneself to see* is the necessary and sufficient condition upon which may be established the luminous evidence of cogito. [...] *Videor* [Latin for]: I seem, I appear, I am seen. I appear to myself in that I am seen—and I am seen as appearing to see. The *videor* guarantees the cogito, for it attests to the only presence into which even the most radical doubt cannot make a breach: *videor* endures, even at the height of phantasmagoria and illusion.[113]

Put in psychoanalytic terms, we may say that the look of the observing parent is internalized by the child as its own gaze upon itself, a gaze that it can recall even in the absence of its mother. It is through the parents' gaze that the child constitutes its own image, and while their look may communicate concern, love, and protection, it can also convey anger, hatred, and punishment. When alone, the child can recreate their look and imagine itself through the eyes of the other, this is an ability that is called the subject's "observing ego." Hence, it does not matter whether the subjects perceive the gaze

irala (1922–2008)", Françoise Davoine and Jean-Max Gaudillière vividly describe August Strindberg's mad wanderings through Paris after he had been left by his young wife and daughter. Strindberg was "assailed by the same social humiliations buried in his family's past [...]. No doctor understood his condition."(96) Strindberg had lost touch with social reality and it was in part only through the frequent visits of a "white marble *medaillon* in the Montparnasse cemetery," that an image of an Other could manifest itself which spoke to him. Strindberg had been completely isolated and lost in a delusional world before he could find access again to a symbolic realm through an exchange with a sculptured *medaillon* in his neighborhood. The contact with an Other—even a dead or immobile Other—brings Strindberg back to, what Davoine calls "the cut-out part of himself." The place of a symbolic Other, be it an institution, a person, a political party, or a painting, offers the possibility of an exchange which allows for a thinking process to unfold. Without an Other, one risks being mired in a self-delusional process. For a more detailed discussion, see Davoine/Gaudillière 2021: 95–121.

113 Nancy 1977: 20.

of a real or an imagined Other, their internalized representation of the Other's look serves as a reference for their self-understanding.

At the beginning of this chapter I raised the question of how Manet managed to establish the enigmatic bond between his works and the audience, despite the absence of language and of living performers. I believe that the artist intuited the powerful influence of the Imaginary upon his viewers' thoughts and feelings. The total, immediate and instantaneous effects of visual representations on the spectator parallel the experiences of early infancy, when impressions, thoughts, and ideas are not yet transposed into verbal constructs. Hence, the spectators' silent perusal of a painted image may resituate them in the Imaginary realm, a realm in which words cannot yet translate emotional states into abstract concepts. Thus, the cold stare of an Olympia, the seductive glance of a Nana, the aloof gaze of a young dandy, or the empty look of a barmaid, all they become visual experiences that relocate the spectators in the pre-oedipal realm, in which they imagined themselves the desire of the Other, and in which they determined their own image by the look of the Other projected onto them.

We know that the Imaginary, or pre-oedipal register, does not cease to exist when the child enters into the oedipal phase or the Symbolic realm; instead, it coexists as a second language side by side with the later phases. It is Manet's significant, yet probably entirely intuitive insight into the unconscious process of the Imaginary—and his skillful manipulation of the subjects' constant desire to locate themselves in the representation of the Other—that continues to lend his works such a powerful, mysterious, and enduring quality.

Conclusion

> [...] up until now we have looked at the text as a species of fruit with a kernel (an apricot, for example), the flesh being the form and the pit being the content, it would be better to see it as an onion, a construction of layers (or levels, or systems) whose body contains, finally, no heart, no kernel, no secret, no irreducible principle, nothing except the infinity of its own envelopes—which envelop nothing other than the unity of its own surfaces.
>
> Roland Barthes, "Style and Its Image," 1971

In my opinion, Barthes's argument that a text does not contain an "inherent kernel of truth" that can be revealed through an analysis of the layers enveloping this truth, is equally valid for a painting. This fact is reminiscent of the conclusion that Freud states in "The Interpretation of Dreams," namely that a dream analysis might never be completed in full, and that the analysis of any dream is as interminable as the "cure" itself. To my mind, the "interpretation" of a work of art can likewise never generate an exhaustive account of its multiple layered meanings. And in the case of Manet's paintings, I have tried to show that my analysis remains open-ended and inevitably incomplete, which is why I invite the reader and viewer to generate their own meanings of what they observe in Manet's works. His paintings do not prescribe a singular and fixed meaning; instead, they challenge the spectators not only to redefine themselves, but to invest the paintings with their own ideas and emotions. For this reason, I did not want to fall into the lure of offering another master key to "unlock" the unique truth of Manet's works. It seemed more fruitful to use the theory of psychoanalysis as a way of interpreting Manet's paintings from the various "levels of systems of meanings," in order to provide a variety of perspectives through which the elusive

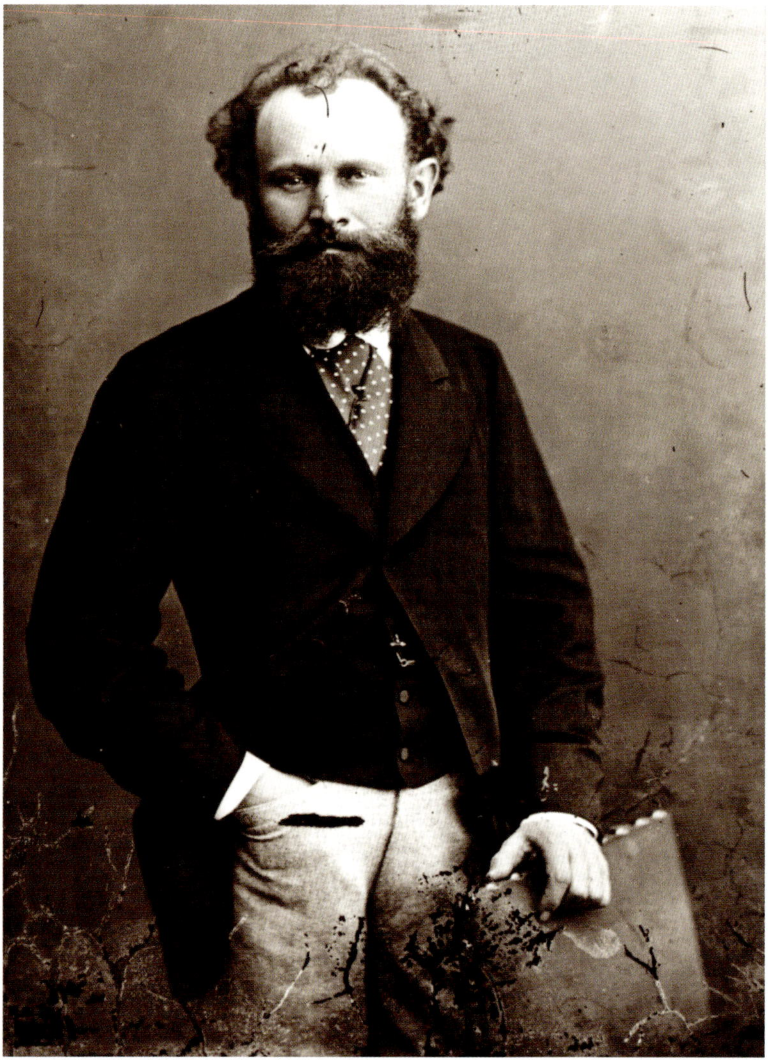

Plate 69: Nadar, *Portrait of Édouard Manet* (1874)

quality of these extraordinary canvases could be grasped with more conceptual rigor. The majority of psychoanalytic discussions of art tend to restrict their study of a painting to a psycho-biographic and psycho-pathological account of the life of the artists themselves and not of their works. I prefer to show how a psychoanalytic approach can offer an in-depth analysis of a wide range of paintings with greater subtlety.

Le Déjeuner sur l'herbe, for instance, could have been analyzed simply as a representation of Manet's divided interest in two women: his wife-to-be Suzanne Leenhoff, whom he casts in the virtuous traditional and "chaste" role of the partially veiled nude; and his young model Victorine Meurent, whom he places in the position of a provocatively self-exhibiting nude. To my mind, the painting is Manet's attempt to rework his painterly heritage—starting with Giorgione's/Titian's *Le Concert Champêtre*—and this legacy to his own day and age. Moreover, *Le Déjeuner sur l'herbe* offers a prism through which Manet addresses and challenges the spectator's identificatory desires with the figures on the canvas. In this way, I have intended to explain how Manet used his personal circumstances and wove them into well-known paintings by the Old Masters in order to expiate his own urges, thoughts and relationships. That said, Manet never lost sight of his audience. He chose to involve them as active participants, inviting them in the scenes he depicted. In contrast to a psycho-biographic account, which restricts its attention to the painter's personal history, I have shown how these three levels—the personal, the historical, and the identificatory—cannot be separated from one another in any serious psychoanalytic study of a work of art.

In my discussion of Édouard Manet, I have largely revised the standard methods applied for an artist's psycho-biographic account. Rather than re-excavating details about Manet's early childhood experiences, I have carefully studied the rather scant biographic information available about him and matched it alongside the paintings in which he represented relatives and friends, who were either the source of this biographical information, or who played a significant role in Manet's life. My analysis of those paintings in which he depicted these key people only reconfirmed the standard biographic data. However, the more I delved into certain canvases, the more their fascinating undercurrents surfaced, leading me to conclude that, deliberately or unconsciously, the artist revealed himself through his painterly output, rather than through any verbal expressions. For example, a careful examination of *Portrait d'Émile Zola* shows how the novelist, whom Manet openly praised, was instead someone he privately derided: two sides of the same coin, one opinion expressed in public, the other encrypted in the portrait. Similarly, regarding Manet's relationship with his parents—about whom significant information is scarce—the manner in which he depicted them in an early work closely matches the way he would subsequently portray figures who played an important part in his life: as dispassionate and remote. The same holds true for the portrait of his mother, and later Léon Koëlla-Leenhoff—his son (or, more likely, his half-brother), whom he officially acknowledged as a "godson." Likewise, Berthe Morisot, the woman he was strongly attracted to, but who became his sister-in-law and not his mistress. Admittedly, a causal relationship between these three occurrences is pure speculation, and this is merely one of several possible interpretations for the seemingly aloof and estranged mood that Manet repeatedly ascribed to his figures.

The psychological portrait of Manet that gradually emerged in the course of my inquiry was not determined by any a priori schemata, but surfaced from the artist's own personal observations, coupled with anecdotes reported by friends and relatives. Added to this information were investigations into the sociological, political and historical accounts of the era in which Manet grew up and shaped his life and work. This contextual overview allowed me to explore the symbolic milieu in which Manet depicted his figures, and, more specifically, the icons with which he associated the relatives and friends who became the objects of his inquiry, the metaphors he adopted to condense these figures into a single image, and which metonymies he employed to lend meaning to them, relying on the assumption that his contemporary public would view his works with some background knowledge of the Old Masters he referenced. He laid the groundwork and left his audience to piece together the message. He offered a societal mirror, which for many generated acute discomfort, their action being scorn and even public indignation. Moreover, the temporal sequence in which he painted his works sheds considerable light upon the artist's changing concepts of the depicted figures and upon his own evolving concerns and reflections. While remaining provisional, my psycho-biographic procedure is modeled after Freud's dream-analysis, in which, like the art-work, "the dream-work is under some kind of necessity to combine all the sources which have acted as stimuli for the dream into a single unity in the dream itself."[1] However, instead of imposing "the task of interpretation upon the dreamer himself,"[2] in a pictorial analysis, it is the critic-beholder to whom the task of interpreting the artist's work is assigned, and by the same token, it is that critic's task to explore all the diverse sources and stimuli which have been incorporated into the painting. The collection of all the reliable material available—including the texts of the artist's literary friends, from whom Manet frequently borrowed themes and descriptions—lent substance to my interpretation of his works from the psychoanalytic point of view, and at the same time, it reduced the risk of producing yet another highly speculative and arbitrary account of the artist's personality.

In addition to altering the traditional psycho-biographic method, I have sought to develop a psychoanalytic pictorial analysis centered upon the interpretation of the artistic "object" as a separate entity in its own right, rather than on its status as a kind of "higher-order symptom" of the artist's presumed neuroses. In his essay "Creative Writers and Day-Dreaming" (1908), Freud observed that the process of creation could be visualized as

> A strong experience in the present [which] awakens in the creative writer a memory of an earlier experience (usually belonging to his childhood) from which there now proceeds a wish which finds its fulfilment in the creative work. The work itself exhibits elements of the recent provoking occasion as well as of the old memory.[3]

---

1 Freud 1900: 179.

2 Freud 1900: 98.

3 Freud 1908: 151.

Manet's frequent and deliberate borrowings of specific themes, figures, motifs and compositions from the Old Masters—compositions that he then reinterpreted in a manner appropriate to his own milieu—convinced me that certain strong experiences in the present could evoke a memory from a given artist's mental and emotional experience of masterpieces that had been instrumental in the artist's career, as readily as such images might prompt specific recollections from their childhood or youth. Equating the traditional sources, Manet wove into his paintings memories of the past, and I aimed to explain how the process of remembrance is an *interpretive* act, one through which the artist—much like the analysand—attempts to construct meaning for his/her present condition through their new understanding of the past. The memorial process is an active one, a process that constantly undergoes revisions and changes—it is anything but fossilized, or sealed off from new openings. In other words, Manet did not simply *imitate* the Old Masters: he *reinterpreted* their works in order both to understand his own artistic genealogy and to consolidate meaning around his painterly past and fathom how that related to the present and future.

Consequently, it is not sufficient merely to adopt conventional art-historical methods to assess the paintings that Manet "quoted." We need to examine which works he chose for his process of reinscription, and, likewise, what specific methods he employed to transform those traditional themes into scenes of modern-life.

With all this in mind, I was also finally able to put to rest the idea that Manet was either imitating or copying the Old Masters to prove to a critical audience his allegiances and painterly ideals. And although he was apparently averse to obliging his spectators to ponder his paintings, his diligent choice of citations strongly suggests an acute awareness of the interdependence and interaction between past and present. "The notion that the present modifies the past as much as the past modifies the present is very familiar to us psychoanalysts […]. It is at the centre of Freud's understanding of the psyche and the core of our praxis."[4] In sum, during this research Freud's concept

4 Taiana 2021: 14.

of *Nachträglichkeit* (or *après-coup*) proved itself particularly helpful in analyzing Manet's multi-layered use of historical sources.

Following Freud's own suggestion that psychoanalysts should consult "Jokes and Their Relation to the Unconscious" (1905) for the analysis of an aesthetic work of any nature, I found that his methods for deciphering jokes are of particular relevance for the interpretation of a painting. Like the joke-work and the dream-work, it turns out that the art-work conflates diverse and often contradictory sources, impressions, ideas, and memories into a unified artifact. By the same token, a painting also uses the psychological mechanisms of displacement, condensation, indirect representation, and unification to combine into a single image a complex range of heterogeneous ideas and emotional strands. What distinguishes them from the dream, however, is that both the artwork and the joke are public and social products which strive to be understood even in and through their manifold disguises. It became increasingly evident how psychoanalytic theory provided the soundest methodology for exploring the subtle associative chains which Manet integrated into his paintings, as well as for interpreting the masked allusions, the puns and "visual" wordplays, the covert social commentaries which Manet embedded in his works. While the psychoanalytic method—which analyzes the unconscious meaning of the transformations, distortions and omissions and subject forms of remembered events—seems especially suitable to Manet's works, since these contain such explicit references to traditional and canonic pictorial scenes, I believe that the same method lends itself equally well to the analysis of other forms of artistic production. Although Manet made the reinterpretation of traditional art a vital aspect of his paintings, every artist in some way attempts to situate his work in the long genealogy of painting. That is, every artist, weaves together various memorial strings from the entire fabric of art history in order to open a space for his/her own piece in the constantly metamorphizing circuit of pictorial production.

It was Freud's paper "The Moses of Michelangelo" (1914) that originally led me to the third level of a psychoanalytic interpretation of Manet's works. In his essay, Freud unwittingly provided a detailed account of the spectator's identificatory desire vis-à-vis the figure(s) represented in a work of art. Because post-Freudians have discussed the Moses essay almost exclusively as an autobiographical document—relevant only to Freud's own ambitious longings—they have failed to realize how an analysis of the identificatory process can serve as a powerful model for the study of the spectator/art object/artist relationship.

Unlike traditional psychoanalytic aesthetic criticism—which is primarily concerned with how the content of a painting may reveal the artist's unconscious motives—, in his paper on the statue of Moses, Freud acknowledges that the *effect* of an artwork upon its beholder should be a constitutive part of any psychoanalytic aesthetic criticism. Although Freud did not analyze this identificatory process as such and only recorded the process in the Moses paper, it was his work "Jokes and Their Relation to the Unconscious," as well as his two papers on identification, "A Child is Being Beaten" (1919) and "Group Psychology and the Analysis of the Ego" (1921), that provided the theoretical basis for my own analysis of the spectator-painting-artist relationship in Manet's oeuvre.

A crucial stage of my argument became possible with the theoretical realization—and subsequent concrete demonstration—of how the effect an artist wishes to produce upon his observers could be paralleled with the effect a joke-teller intends to produce upon his listener when recounting a sexually or markedly tendentious joke. Both the joker and the artist produce their effect at the expense of whoever the joke is aimed at, or, in our case of who is represented on the canvas. Furthermore, the joker and the artist respectively address the listener's/spectator's unconscious identificatory desire to become an active participant in the scene related or depicted. Consequently, the joker and the artist mark out an empty space for the listener/spectator, a space in which to "complete" the scene referenced in the joke or artwork. By carefully examining the relationship Manet sets up between his painted figures and the spectator, his particular mastery in manipulating his spectator's identificatory desires became evident. The enigmatic quality of the gaze of his figures and their aloof, yet intimate relationship with their audience were in part determined by the artist's precisely marking-out the position for the viewer's imaginary presence within the painted spectacle. But as soon as the observers filled up or completed the gap made available for their imaginary presence, Manet barred any further advance, stanching whatever phantasmagoric desires arose, and reminded his audience that they were merely "visitors" in the fictional realm of the painting and could only view them from outside. Manet's careful manipulation of his audience is highly unusual, since by tradition painters have constructed their works either to absorb the spectators completely into the depicted scene, or to exclude them entirely, positioning them as passive beholders in front of the canvas. Although my demonstration of the value of a psychoanalytic study of the painter/art object/spectator relationship is based upon the example of Édouard Manet, a painter who, to my mind, intuitively rather than consciously recognized the importance of the spectator's desire with an imaginary Other and made this process a constitutive element of his paintings, I think that the psychoanalytic method could also be applied to other artists whose work may reveal analogous structures underlying the relationship between the artist, the painting, and the viewer.

My intent was not, as J.F. Lyotard once wrote in a similar context, to express "a concealed discourse," but rather to "reroute the perspective-creating potentialities these works contain."[5] One important question still remains to be considered at the conclusion of the psychoanalytic pictorial analysis which I have developed on the basis of Manet's oeuvre: Is the psychoanalytic method, a discipline developed to understand a subject's verbal discourse, really applicable to a visual depiction?[6] Although it is clear from this book that I believe that a psychoanalytic perspective can uncover significant meanings in a visual object which standard art-historical criticism would tend not to explore, one must nonetheless remember that any textual description of a painting, my own included, will inevitably be "missing something," similar to a verbal account of a dream:

5 Lyotard 1977: 98.

6 For an excellent discussion of the complexities involved in translating a visual image into a verbal account, see Donald Spence, *Narrative Truth and Historical Truth* (1982), especially Chapter III: 55–79.

> The reconstruction of the dream can take place only by reference to the order of the conscious discourse interpretation, and consequently the representations in the dream do not follow the same considerations of representability that organize the dream work in the order of the unconscious.[7]

By shifting from the visual to the verbal register and back, the syntax changes, with the effect that the very nature and structure of language will fail to reveal the disparate elements of a painted work, the full picture as it were. Of course, painting has its own syntax, since the limitations of the canvas, frame and paint itself, along with stylistic considerations, such as form, perspective, and dimensionality, impose their own laws upon the multiplicity of visual images. Despite these internal constraints to which painting must adhere, images are immediately more comprehensible than verbal statements because, as Marion Milner states, "they bring so much of the past into a single moment of present experience."[8] Moreover, unlike with a written text or a musical piece, in which we can comprehend or enjoy certain lines or movements and are obliged to follow the temporal succession of elements, with a painting the impression is at once simultaneous and total. This distinction is fundamental. As readers or listeners our fruition is commanded by the sequential logic of the material before us.

With the visual arts, our eyes follow their own logic. "[P]ictures, to be sure," observes Roland Barthes, "are more imperative than writing, they impose meaning at one stroke, without analysing or diluting it."[9] Although we can study and revisit a painting many times, as observers we can never fully dissect the many constituent pieces, nor retrace the successive stages in a painting's creation. Hence, when we transpose a visual image into a verbal account, we are shifting our perspective and distorting the structural framework in which the painting was created. That said, it seems to me that psychoanalysis—the discipline dedicated to exploring a realm of the human mind that had been assumed to be closed off to any rigorous examination—offers perhaps a

7 Judovitz 1979: 33.
8 Milner 1979: 123.
9 Barthes 1972: 108.

refined method for assessing this shift in perspective between a visual object and a verbal/written account. Analogous to the analyst—who not only interprets the content of the analysands' verbal description of their dream images, but who also pursues the associative paths leading back to memories connected to the reported dream, and who, moreover, interprets the meaning of the dream within the context of the transference/countertransference relationship—psychoanalytic art critics can investigate these same areas when they interpret a pictorial representation. Similar to the procedure of a dream or joke analysis, they can explore the memories the artist has woven into the picture plane and study the meanings issuing from the artist's specific transformations of those memories. Finally, psychoanalytic art critics—similar to taking note of the dynamics of the transference/countertransference relationship in an analysis—are particularly well equipped to identify the relationship with the spectators that the painters establish through their work. While a painting in itself is a "silent" object, its effect upon the public has often been loud. By focusing upon this "silent noise," a novel realm of study ushers in a new form.

END

Index

This index is in alphabetical, word by word order. It does not cover the Abstract. Location reference is to page number, given in plain type, and Plate number, given in bold. Abbreviations: n = footnote

Bibliography

Édouard Manet:

Austin, Nancy A. (1981): *Metaphor and Fact at Mid Century: Manet and Contemporary History Painting. Édouard Manet and the Execution of Maximilian*. An Exhibition by the Department of Art at Brown University, Providence, RI: Brown University Art Center.
Bailey, Colin B. (2020): "Suffering, Unfaltering Manet", in: *The New York Review of Books*, December 3, 2020.
Bataille, George (1955): *Manet*. New York: Rizzoli.
Bargelow, Raymond (1980): *Role, Emotion and Power in Manet: A Sartrean Examination,* unpublished paper, Berkeley: The Wright Institute, Berkeley: 1980.
Barthes, Roland (1972): *Mythologies,* translated by Annette Lavers, New York: The Noonday Press, Farrar, Strauss & Giroux.
Barthes, Roland (1971): "Style and Its Image", in: Chatman, Seymour (ed.): *Literary Style: A Symposium*, London, New York: Oxford University Press, 3-15.
Bazin, Germain (1974): *Edouard Manet,* Milan: Fratelli Fabbri.
Baudelaire, Charles (1965): *The Painter of Modern Life and Other Essays*, translated and edited by Jonathan Mayne, London, New York: Phaidon.
Baudelaire, Charles (1981): *Art in Paris 1845–1862: Salons and Other Exhibitions*, Oxford: Phaidon Press.
Baudelaire, Charles (1998): *The Flowers of Evil*, translated by James Mc Gowan, Oxford, New York: Oxford University Press.
Baudelaire, Charles (1869/1962): "Le désir de peindre", *Le Spleen de Paris,* Paris: Editions Garnier Frères
Baudelaire, Charles (2023): *Paris Spleen,* translated by Martin Sorrell, London: Alma Classics.
Baudelaire, Charles (1845–1867/1961): *Les Fleurs du Mal,* Paris: Edition Garnier Frères / *The Flowers of Evil,* translated by James Mc Gowan, Oxford: Oxford University Press.
Baudry, Jean-Louis (1974): "Ideological Effects of the Basic Cinematographic Apparatus", *Film Quarterly, Vol. XXVIII, No. 2*, 39–47.
Berl, Emmanuel (1976): *Interregatoire par Patrick Modiano suivi de il fait beau, allons au cimetière,* Paris: Gallimard.
Benjamin, Walter (1978): *Illuminations*, New York: Schocken Books.

Berger, John (1980): *Ways of Seeing*, London: Penguin Modern Classics. Zitat auf Seite 183 habe ich hier gefunden: Berger, John (2013): *Understanding a Photograph*, London: Penguin Books.

Bergson, Henri (1911): *Of the survival of Images, Memory and Mind,* translated by Nancy Margaret Paul & W. Scott Palmer, London: George Allen & Unwin.

Boime, Alfred (1970): *The Academy and French Painting in the Nineteenth Century,* Oxford: Phaidon Press.

Boime, Albert (1980): *Thomas Couture and the eclectic vision*, New Haven: Yale University Press.

Borges, Jorge Luis (1964): *Labyrinths,* translated by Donald Yates & James Irby, London: Penguin Books.

Brush, Kathryn (1981): "Manet's Execution and the Tradition of Histoire", in: Brown University (ed.): *Edouard Manet and the Execution of Maximilian, An Exhibition by the Department of Art*, Providence, RI: Brown University Art Center, 39-49.

Bryson, Norman (1983): *Vision and Painting, The Logic of the Gaze,* London: The Macmillan Press, LTD.

Büchner, Georg (1996): *Woyzeck*, translated by Gregory Motton, London: Nick Hern Boooks.

Büchner, Georg (1997): „Woyzeck", in: Georg Büchner: *Dichtungen und Schriften*, Köln: Könemann Verlag, 155–182.

Cachin, Françoise (1983): "Introduction à l'Éxhibition d'Édouard Manet", Avril-Aout, Galeries Nationales du Grand Palais, Paris.

Cezanne, Paul (1995): *Letters,* edited by John Rewald, translated by Marguerite Kay, New York: Da Capo Press.

Clark, Timothy J. (1980): "Preliminaries to a Possible Treatment of 'Olympia' in 1865", in: *Screen*, Spring, 21(1) 19–41.

Clark, Timothy J. (1973): *The Absolute Bourgeois: Artists and Politics in France 1848–1851,* Greenwich CT: New York Graphic Society Ltd.

Clark, Timothy J. (1982): *Image of the People: Gustave Courbet and the 1848 Revolution*, Princeton NJ: Princeton University Press.

Crichton, Michael (1977): *Jasper Johns,* New York: Abrams Publisher.

Courthion, Pierre and Pierre Cailler (1960): *Portrait of Manet by Himself and His Contemporaries,* New York: Roy Publishers.

Couture, Thomas (1867): *Méthode et entretiens d'atelier*, Paris: Rue Vintimille, N° 22.

Daix, Pierre (1983): *La Vie de peintre d'Édouard Manet*, Paris: Fayard.

Darragon, Eric (1983): "Manet et ses modéles", *Beaux Arts Magazine*, Avril 1983, 1, 399–445.

Darragon, Eric (1983): "Nus Equivoques", *Beaux Arts Magazine*, Avril 1983, 1, 46–49.

Derrida, Jacques (1976): *Of Grammatology,* translated by Gayatri Spivak, Baltimore: The John Hopkins University Press.

Dewey, John (1938): *The Logic, The Theory of Inquiry*, New York: Henry Holt & Company.

Duret, Theodore (1910): *Manet and the French Impressionists,* translated by J. E. Crawford Flitch, London: Grant Richards; Philadelphia: J. B. Lippincott Co.

Eliade, Mircea (1963): *Myth and Reality,* New York: Harper & Row.

Eliot, T. S. (1919/1982): 'Tradition and the Individual Talent", *Perspecta, No. 19*, Brian Healy (Editor), Nate McBride (Editor), Yale Architectural Journal Paperback – Illustrated.

Esslin, Martin (1971): *Brecht: the Man and his Work,* Garden City, New York: Anchor Books Doubleday & Company.

Farwell, Beatrice (1975): "Manet's Nymphe Surprise", *The Burlington Magazine, Vol. CXVII*, April 1975, 224–229.

Finley, M. I. (1965): "Myth, Memory, and History", in: *History and Theory,* Wiley for Wesleyan University, Vol. 4, No 3, 281–302.

Foucault, Michel (1970/1973): *The Order of Things, An Archaeology of the Human Sciences,* New York: Vintage Books Edition.

Foucault, Michel (1977): *Language, Counter-Memory, Practice. Selected Essays and Interviews,* edited & translated by Donald P. Bouchard, Ithaca: Corncll University Press.

Fried, Michael (1969): "Manet's Sources: Aspects of his Art, 1859–1865", *Artforum VII*, March 1969, 28–81.

Fried, Michael (1978): "The Beholder in Courbet: His Early Self Portraits and Their Place in Art", in: Weber, Samuel / Sussman, Henry (eds.): *Glyph 4, Johns Hopkins Textual Studies*,

Baltimore: The Johns Hopkins University Press, 85-130.
Fried, Michael (1980): *Absorption and Theatricality, Painting and the Beholder in the Age of Diderot,* Berkeley: University of California Press.
Fried, Michael (1984): "Painting Memories: On the Containment of the Past in Baudelaire and Manet", *Critical Inquiry, Vol. 10, No. 3*, March 1984, 510–542.
Gay, Peter (1976): *Art and Act: On Causes in History – Manet, Gropius, Mondrian,* New York: Harper & Row Publishers.
Goethe, Johann Wolfgang (1808/1970): *Faust I*, Frankfurt: Insel Verlag.
Goethe, Johann Wolfgang von (1900): *Faust*, translated by Bayard Taylor, New York: Arden Book Company
Growe, Bernd (1983): „Modernität und Komposition, Zur Krise des Werkbegriffs in der Französischen Malerei des 19. Jahrhunderts", *Kolloquium Kunst und Philosophie 3, Das Kunstwerk,* München: UTB Schöning, 173–174.
Hamilton, George Heard (1969): *Manet and his Critics*, New York: W. W. Norton, Inc.
Hammer, Langdon (2021): "Open Yale Courses", *The Use of Citations in Poetry, Modern Poetry, English 310 – Lecture 10 – T. S. Eliot.*
Hanson, Anne Coffin (1977): *Manet and the Modern Tradition*, New Haven, London: Yale University Press.
Harris, Jean Collins (1964): "A Little-known Essay on Manet by Stéphane Mallarmé", in: *Art Bulletin*, Vol. XLVI (4), 559–563.
Hauser, Arnold (1957/1999: *Social History of Art, Naturalism, Impressionism, Film Age, Vol. IV*, New York: Routledge.
Heath, Stephen (1973): "Difference", *Screen, Vol. 19, No. 3*.
Heidegger, Martin (1962): *Being and Time,* translated by J. Macquarmie & E. Robinson, New York: Harper and Row.
Hofman, Werner (1961): *The Earthly Paradise: Art in the Nineteenth Century*, New York: George Braziller.
Honour, Hugh (1979): *Romanticism*, New York: Harper & Row.
House, John (1983): "Seeing Manet Whole", *Art in America*, November 1983, 178–187.
Huet, Marie-Hélène (1983): "Living Images: Monstrosity and Representation", *Representation, No 4*, Autumn 1983, Berkeley: University of California Press, 73–87.
Iser, Wolfgang (1980): "The Reading Process: A Phenomenological Approach", *Reader-Response Criticism, From Formalism to Structuralism,* edited by Jane P. Tompkins, Baltimore: John Hopkins University Press.
Janson, H. W. (1973): *History of Art. A Survey of the Major Visual Arts From the Dawn of History to the Present Day,* Englewood Cliffs, N.J. Prentice Hall, Inc. and New York: Harry N. Abrams Inc.
Johnson, David E. (2012): *Kant's Dog: On Borges, Philosophy and the Time of Translation*, New York: Suny Press.
Judovitz, Dalia (1979): "Freud: Translation and/or Interpretation", in: *SubStance,* Vol.8 (1), Issue 22, 29–38.
Kaak, Joachim (2016): "Lehrjahre des Auges, Édouard Manet gesehen mit Werner Hofman", in: *Manet sehen. Der Blick der Moderne,* Hamburger Kunsthalle, Petersberg: Michael Imhof Verlag, 61–67.
Letheve, Jacques (1972): *Daily Life of French Artists in the Nineteenth Century,* New York: Praeger Publishers.
Locke, Nancy (2001): *Manet and the Family Romance,* Princeton: Princeton University Press.
Lüthy, Michael (2016): „Die Wendung des Blicks", in: Gaßner, Hubertus / Hildebrandt-Schat, Viola (ed.): *Manet · Sehen. Der Blick der Moderne.* Ausstellungskatalog Hamburger Kunsthalle, Petersberg: Michael Imhof Verlag, 13–19.
Lyotard, Jean-François (1977): "The Unconscious as Mis-en-scène", in: *Performance in Postmodern Culture,* translated by Joseph Maier, edited by Michel Benamou & Charles Caramello, Milwaukee, Madison: Coda Press, 87–98.
Mathieu, Marianne / d'Arnoult, Dominique / Gooden, Claire (2021): *Julie Manet – La mémoire impressionniste,* Catalogue, Paris: Musée Marmottan, Vanves: Editions Hazan.
Marx, Karl (1907): *The Eighteenth Brumaire of Louis Bonaparte*, translated by Daniel de Leon, Chicago: Charles H. Kerr & Company.
Mauner, George (1975): *Manet, Peintre-Philosophe, A Study of the Painter's Themes,* University Park

and London: Pennsylvania State University Press.
Merleau-Ponty, Maurice (1966): "La Doute de Cezanne", in: *Sens et Non-Sens,* Paris: Les Editions Nagel, 15–44.
Merleau-Ponty, Maurice (1964): *The Primacy of Perception,* Chicago: Northwestern University Press.
Morelli, Giovanni (1892): *Italian Painters. Critical Studies of their Works, Vol. I, II*, translated by Constance Foulkes, London: Spottiswoode and Co., New Street Square.
Muller, Josef Emile (1980): *Velázquez*, translated by Peter Komnitzer, Cologne: Edition Berend von Nottbeck.
Muller, Josef Emile (1976): *Velázquez,* London: Thames and Hudson
Mulvey, Laura (1975): "Visual Pleasure and Narrative Cinema", *Screen, Vol. 16*, Issue 3, 1 October 1975, Pages 6–18.
Murrell, D. (2018): *Posing Modernity: The Black Model from Manet and Matisse to Today,* New Haven, London: Yale University Press.
Nancy, Jean Luc (1977): "Larvatus pro Deo", *Glyph 2 – Johns Hopkins Textual Studies,* Baltimore and London: The Johns Hopkins University Press, 14–36.
Nancy, Jean Luc (1997): *The Sense of the World*, translated by Jeffrey S. Librett, Minneapolis: University of Minnesota Press.
Nochlin, Linda (1971): *Realism,* Hardmonthsworth, Middlesex, England: Penguin Books.
Nochlin, Linda (1983): "A Thoroughly Modern Masked Ball", *Art in America,* November 1983, 188–201.
Oxford Companion to Classical Literature (1959/1989): Oxford University Press.
Panovsky, Erwin (1962): *Studies in Iconology: Humanistic Themes in the Art of the Renaissanc*e, New York: Harper & Row Publishers.
Picon, Gaetan (1978): *The Birth of Modern Painting*, New York: Rizzoli.
Poussin, Nicolas (1964): *Lettres et propos sur l'art*, Paris: Les Éditions Hermann.
Praz, Mario (1970): *The Romantic Agony,* Oxford: Oxford University Press.
Proust, Marcel (1909–1922/1970): *Remembrance of Things Past,* translated by C. K. Scott Moncrieff, New York: Random House.
Proust, Marcel (1924): *Within a Budding Grove*, translated by C. K. Scott Moncrieff, New York: The Modern Library.
Riley, Robert (1938): *Manet*, translated by Eveline Byam Shaw, Paris, The Hyperion Press.
Richardson, John (1958): *Manet Paintings and Drawings*, London: Phaidon Press, Ltd.
Reff, Theodore (1977): *Manet: Olympia*, New York: Viking Press.
Reff, Theodore (1962): "The Symbolism of Manet's Frontispiece Etchings", *The Burlington Magazine, Vol. 54*, No. 710, May 1962, 182–186.
Reff, Theodore (1969): "On Manet's Sources", *Art Forum, VIII*, September, 40–48.
Reff, Theodor (1970): "Manet and Blanc's 'Histoire des Peintres'", in: *The Burlington Magazine, Vol. 62, No. 808*, July 1970, 456–458.
Reff, Theodore (1973): "Manet and Paris, Another Judgment", *Art News*, *LXXII*, 8 October, 50–56.
Reff, Theodore (1975): "Manet's Portrait of Zola", *The Burlington Magazine*, *Vol. 67, No. 862*, January 1975, 35–44.
Reid, Elisabeth A. (1981): "Realism and Manet. Edouard Manet and the Execution of Maximilian", *Exhibition by the Department of Art, Brown University*, Providence RI: Brown University Art Center.
Rey, Robert (1938): *Manet*, London: Phaidon Press, Ltd.
Rodowick, David Norman (1980): "Vision, Desire and Film", in: *Camera Obscura, No. 6* (Fall 1980), 54–89.
Rodowick, David Norman (1982): "The Difficulty of Difference", in: *Wide Angle, Vol. 5, No. 1*, 4–15.
Rosen, Charles / Zerner, Henri (1976): "The Revival of Official Art", in*: The New York Review of Books, March 18, 1976, XXIII, No. 4*, 30–39.
Rosen, Charles / Zerner, Henri (1982a): "What is, and is not Realism?", in*: The New York Review of Books,* February 18, 1982, XXIX, No. 2, 21–33.
Rosen, Charles / Zerner, Henri (1982b): "The Unhappy Medium", in*: The New York Review of Books,* May 27, 1982, XXIX, No. 2, 49–54.
Rosen, Charles / Zerner, Henri (1984): *Romanticism and Realism: The Mythology of*

Nineteenth Century Art, New York: Viking Press.
Rouart, Denis (1957): *The Correspondence of Berthe Morisot,* translated by Betty W. Hubbard, New York: George Wittenborn Inc.
Ruegg, Maria (1979): "Metaphor & Metonymy: The Logic of Structuralist Rhethoric", *Glyph 6*, 141–157.
Ruggiero, Marianne (1981): "Manet and the Image of War and Revolution 1851–1871", in: *Édouard Manet and the Execution of Maximilian: Exhibition by the Department of Art, Brown University, Providence, RI*: Brown. University Art Center.
Sandblad, Nils Gösta (1954): *Manet: Three Studies in Artistic Conceptions,* Malmö: Lund.
Santayana, George (1905): *The Life of Reason or The Phases of Human Progress,* Cambridge, Mass: MIT Press.
Sartre, Jean-Paul (1968): *Being and Nothingness,* New York: Washington Square Press.
Sartre, Jean-Paul (1976): *The Psychology of Imagination, Secaucus, N.J. Citadel Press.*
Sartre, Jean-Paul (1966): *Essays in Aesthetics*, *New York: The Citadel Press.*
Saxl, Fritz (1970): *A Heritage of Images,* London: A Penguin Book.
Schapiro, Meyer (1956): "Leonardo and Freud: An Art-Historical study", in: *Journal of The History of Ideas, Vol. XVIII, No. 2*, April 1956.
Schapiro, Meyer (1978): *Modern Art: 19th and 20th Centuries*, New York: George Braziller Inc.
Schneider, Pierre (1968): *The World of Manet, 1832-1883*, New York: Time Life Books.
Schweiker, William (1988): "Beyond Imitation: Mimetic Praxis in Gadamer, Ricoeur and Derrida", in: *The Journal of Religion, Vol. 68, No 1*, 21–38.
Sennett, Richard (1977): *The Fall of Public Man,* New York: Alfred A. Knopf.
Spector, Jack J. (1969): "The Method of Morelli and Its Relation to Freudian Psychoanalysis", in: *Diogenes*, Volume 17, Issue 66 (June 1969), 63-83.
Spector, Jack J. (1974): *The Aesthetics of Freud*, New York: Mc Graw Hill.
Stapleton (1978): *A Dictionary of Greek and Roman Mythology,* New York: Bell Publishing Company.
Starobinski, Jean (1982): *1789: The Emblems of Reason,* translated by Barbara Bray, Charlottesville: University Press of Virginia.
Stern, Alfred (1967): *Sartre: His Philosophy and Existential Psycho-analysis,* New York: Dell Publishing Company.
Stuckey, Charles (1983): "Manet Revised: Whodunit?", *Art in America*, November 1983, 159–177.
Valéry, Paul (1960) [1934]): *Pièces sur l'Art*, Paris: Gallimard.
Wolff, Janet (1981): *The Social Production of Art,* London: The Macmillan Press, Ltd.
Wollheim, Richard (1974): *On Art and the Mind.* Cambridge, Massachusetts: Harvard University Press.
Wollheim, Richard (1980): *Art and Its Objects,* Cambridge, Mass: Harvard University Press.
Zeldin, Theodore (1973): *France 1848–1945, Ambition, Love and Politics,* Oxford: Oxford University Press.
Zeldin,Theodore (1979): *France 1848–1945: Politics and Anger*, Oxford: Oxford University Press.
Zeldin, Theodore (1980*): France 1848–1945: Taste and Consumption,* Oxford: Oxford University Press.
Zeldin, Theodore (1981)*: France 1848–1945: Anxiety and Hypocrisy*, Oxford: Oxford University Press.
Zola, Emile (1866/2012): *Mes Haines,* Paris: Edition de Francois-Marie Mourad.

Psychoanalytic Literature:

Aniel, Martine (1984):): *A Return to the Scene of Penis Envy and Masochism: A Contribution to the Psychoanalytic Theory of Female Sexuality,* Doctoral Dissertation, Berkeley: The Wright Institute.
Anzieu, Didier (1970): „Éléments d'une théorie de l'interprétation", *Revue Française de Psychanalyse*, 755–820.
Avery, Nicholas C. (1982–1983): "Family Secrets", in: *The Psychoanalytic Review*, New York: The Guilford Press, Vol. 69, no. 4, 471–486.
Bell, Clive (1925): "Dr. Freud on Art", *The Dial, Vol. LXXVIII, No. 4*, April 1925, 280–284.
Bott- Spillius, Elisabeth (1989): *On Kleinian Language,* London: Free Association.
Bush, Marshall (1967): "The Problem of

Form in the Psychoanalytic Theory of Art", *Psychoanalytic Review, Vol. 54, No. 1*, Spring 1967, 5–35.
Ehrenzweig, Anton (1971): *The Hidden Order of Art*, Berkeley: University of California Press.
Fenichel, Otto (1935): „Schautrieb und Identifizierung", *Internationale Zeitschrift für Psychoanalyse, 21,* (4), 561–583.
Fenichel, Otto (1972): *The Psychoanalytic Theory of Neuroses*, New York: W. W. Norton & Company.
Freud, Sigmund (1954): *The Origins of Psychoanalysis*, New York: Basic Books.
Freud, Sigmund (1895): *Studies in Hysteria. The Standard Edition of the Complete Psychological Works of Sigmund Freud, Vol. II* (translated & edited by J. Strachey), 24. vols, London: Hogarth Press, 1978. Hereafter, references to the *Standard Edition* will be designated by *S.E.*
Freud, Sigmund (1899): Screen Memories, *S.E. III*, 301–322.
Freud, Sigmund (1900): The Interpretation of Dreams, *S.E. IV & V*, 1–630.
Freud, Sigmund (1905a): Three Essays on the Theory of Sexuality, *S.E. VII*, 125–248.
Freud, Sigmund (1905b): Jokes and Their Relation to the Unconscious, *S.E. VIII*, 9–248.
Freud, Sigmund (1907 [1906]): Delusions and Dreams in Jensen's *Gradiva*, *S.E. IX*, 3–96.
Freud, Sigmund (1908/1907): Creative Writers and Day-Dreaming, *S.E. IX.*, 141–154.
Freud, Sigmund (1909a): Analysis of a Phobia in a Five-Year-Old Boy, *S.E. X*, 3–152.
Freud, Sigmund (1909 b): Notes upon a Case of Obsessional Neurosis, *S.E. X*. 153–238.
Freud, Sigmund (1910 [1909]): Five Lectures on Psychoanalysis, Fifth Lecture, *S.E. XI*, 3–58.
Freud, Sigmund (1910 a): Leonardo da Vinci and a Memory of His Childhood, *S.E.* XI, 59–138.
Freud, Sigmund (1910 b): The Psychoanalytic View of Psychogenic Disturbance of Vision, *S.E. XI*, 209–218.
Freud, Sigmund (1914 a): Remembering, Repeating and Working Through, *S.E. XII*, 145–156.
Freud, Sigmund (1911): Formulations on the Two Principles of Mental Functioning, *S.E. XII*.
Freud, Sigmund (1913): The Claims of Psycho-Analysis to Scientific Interest, *S.E. XIII*, 165–192.
Freud, Sigmund (1914 b): The Moses of Michelangelo, *S.E. XIII*, 211–240.
Freud, Sigmund (1914 d): On the History of the Psychoanalytic Movement, *S.E. XIV*, 3–66.
Freud, Sigmund (1914 c): On Narcissism, An Introduction, *S.E. XIV*, 67–104
Freud, Sigmund (1915): Instincts and Their Vicissitudes, *S.E. XIV*, 109–140.
Freud, Sigmund (1917 [1915]): Mourning and Melancholia, *S.E. XIV*, 237–260.
Freud, Sigmund (1916 [1915]): On Transience, *S.E. XIV*, 303–308.
Freud, Sigmund (1916–1917): Introductory Lectures on Psychoanalysis: Lecture XXIII, The Path to the formation of Symptoms, *S.E. XVI*, 243–463.
Freud, Sigmund (1917): A Childhood Recollection from *Dichtung und Wahrheit S.E. XVII*, 145–156.
Freud, Sigmund (1919a): A Child is Being Beaten: A Contribution to the Study of Sexual Perversions, *S.E. Vol XVII*, 175–204.
Freud, Sigmund (1919b): The Uncanny, *S.E. XVII*, 217–252.
Freud, Sigmund (1940 [1922]): Medusa's Head, *S.E. XVIII*, 273–275.
Freud, Sigmund (1920 Beyond The Pleasure Principle, *S.E. XVIII*, 3–144.
Freud, Sigmund (1921): Group Psychology and the Analysis of the Ego, *S.E. XVIII*, 67–144.
Freud, Sigmund (1923): The Ego and the Id, *S.E. XIX*, 3–68.
Freud, Sigmund (1923): The Infantile Genital Organization: An Interpolation into the Theory of Sexuality, *S.E XIX*, 141–148.
Freud, Sigmund (1927): *Fetishism*, *S.E. XXI*, 149–158.
Freud, Sigmund (1933 [1932]): New Introductory Lectures on Psychoanalysis, *Lecture XXIX, S.E. XXII*, 192–209.
Freud, Sigmund (1937): Constructions in Analysis, *S.E. XXIII*, 255–269.
Freud, Sigmund (1934–1938, 1939): Moses and Monotheism, *S.E. XXI*, (3–140).
Fuller, Peter (1980): *Art and Psychoanalysis,* London: Writers and Readers Publishing Cooperation.

Fry, Roger (1924): *The Artist and Psychoanalysis*, London: The Hogarth Press.

Gaudillière, Jean-Max / Davoine, Françoise (2021): *Madness and the Social Link. The Jean-Max Gaudillière Seminars 1985–2000*, London/New York: Routledge.

Gedo Mary M. (1981): *Deciphering Picasso's Painted Autobiography: Comments on Method and Results. Dialogues: A Journal of Psychoanalytic Perspectives,* (Fall 1981), 3 (1), 37–47.

Greenacre, Phyllis (1970): "The Transitional Object and the Fetish with Special Reference to the Role if Illusion", in: *The International Journal of Psycho-Analysis*, 51 (4), 447-456.

Greenacre, Phyllis (1971): *Emotional Growth: Psychoanalytic Studies of the Gifted and a Great Variety of Other Individuals, Vol. 2,* New York: International Universities Press.

House, Jonathan & Slotnick, Julie (2015): "Après-Coup in French Psychoanalysis: The Long Afterlife of *Nachträglichkeit*, The First Hundred Years", 1893 to 1993, *Psychoanalytic Review 102 (5)*, 683–704.

House, Jonathan (2017): „The Ongoing Rediscovery of Après-Coup as a Central Freudian Concept", in: *Journal of the American Psychoanalytic Association 65(5)*, October 2017, 773-798.

Jones, Ernest (1953–1957): *The Life and Work of Sigmund Freud,* New York: Basic Books, three volumes, 1st volume (1953), 2nd volume 1957, 3rd volume 1957.

Jung, Carl Gustav (1971): "Psychology and Literature", *The Collected Works of C.G. Jung,* translated by R.F. C. Hall, edited by William McGuire, Vol. 15, Princeton: Princeton University Press.

Khan, Masud (1974): *The Privacy of the Self: Papers on Psychoanalytic Theory and Technique,* Madison, Connecticut: International Universities Press.

Kris, Ernst (1974): *Psychoanalytic Explorations in Art,* New York: Schocken Books.

Kris, Ernst (1956): "The Recovery of Childhood Memories in Psychoanalysis", *The Psychoanalytic Study of the Child, Vol. XI.*

Kristeva, Julia (1980): *Powers of Horror, An Essay on Abjection,* translated by Leon Roudiez, New York: Columbia University Press.

Kristeva, Julia (1986): "Word, Dialogue and Novel", in: *The Kristeva Reader*, Tovil Moi (ed.), New York: Columbia University Press.

Lacan, Jacques (1955): "The Purloined Letter", translated by Jeffrey Mehlman, in *The Purloined Letter*, edited by John Muller & William Richardson, Baltimore: John Hopkins University Press.

Lacan, Jacques (1978): *The Four Fundamental Concepts of Psycho-Analysis*, translated by Alan Sheridan, New York: W. W. Norton & Company.

Lacan, Jacques (1977): *Écrits: A Selection,* translated by Alan Sheridan, London: Tavistock Publications Limited.

Lacan, Jacques (1968): *The Language of the Self: The Function of Language in Psychoanalysis*, New York: Dell Press.

Lacan, Jacques (1975): *Encore, Seminar XX*, translated by Bruce Fink, New York: W. W. Norton & Company.

Laplanche, Jean & Pontalis, Jean-Bertrand (1973): *The Language of Psycho-Analysis,* translated by Donald Nicholson Smith, New York: W.W. Norton & Company.

Lemaire, Anika (1977): *Jacques Lacan*, translated by D. Macey, London/New York: Routledge& Kegan Paul.

Lemoine-Luccioni, Eugénie (1976): *Partage des femmes,* Paris: Le Seuil.

Lemoine-Luccioni, Eugénie (1987): *The Dividing of Women or Woman's Lot*, translated by Marie-Laure Davenport and Marie-Christine Réguis, London: Free Association Books.

Loch, Wolfgang (1977): "Some Comments on the Subject of Psychoanalysis and Truth", in: Smith, Joseph H. (ed.): *Psychiatry and the Humanities, Volume 2: Thought, Consciousness, and Reality,* New Haven and London: Yale University Press, 217-255.

Loewald, Hans (1976), "Perspectives on Memory", in: *Psychological Issues. Psychology versus Metapsychology: Psychoanalytic Essays in Memory of George S. Klein,* New York: International Universities Press, Vol. IX, No. 4, Monograph 36, 298-325.

Loewald, Hans (1976): *Papers on Psychoanalysis,* New Haven: Yale University Press.

Mahler, Margaret S. (1974) "Symbiosis and Individuation: The Psychological Birth of the

Human Infant", *The Selected Papers of Margaret S. Mahler, Vol. II,* New York: Jason Aronson, 149–168.

Mehlman, Jeffrey (1975): "How to read Freud on Jokes: The Critic as Schadchen", in: *New Literary History, Vol. 6, No. 2, On Narrative and Narratives* (Winter, 1975), Baltimore: University of Virginia, 439–461.

Major, Réne (1974): "The Revolution of Hysteria", *International Journal of Psychoanalysis 55, No. 3,* 385–392.

Milner, Marion (1979): *On Not Being Able to Paint,* New York: International Universities Press.

M'Uzan, Michel.de (1974): "Analytical Process and the Notion of the Past", *International Review of Psychoanalysis, 1,* 461–466.

Neale, Steven (1981): "Psychoanalysis and Comedy", *Screen, Vol. 22, No. 2,* 29–43.

Novey, Samuel (1968): *The Second Look: The Reconstruction of Personal History in Psychiatry and Psychoanalysis,* Baltimore: Johns Hopkins Press.

Nunberg, Hermann & Federn, Ernst (1976): *Minutes of the Vienna Psychoanalytic Society,* New York: International Universities Press.

Rank, Otto (1914): „Der Doppelgänger", *Imago III,* 2. April 1914, 97–164.

Rank, Otto (1979): *The Double,* translated by Harry Tucker, Jr., New York: New American Library

Rank, Otto (1975): *Art and Artist,* translated by Charles Francis Atkinson, New York: Agathon Press.

Ricoeur, Paul (1976): "Psychoanalysis and the Work of Art", in: Smith, Joseph H. (ed.): *Psychiatry and the Humanities,* Volume I, New Haven and London: Yale University Press, 3-33.

Ricoeur, Paul (1978): "Image and Language in Psychoanalysis", edited by J. Smith, *Psychiatry and Humanities, Vol. III.*

Segal, Hanna (1981a): *A Psychoanalytic Approach to Aesthetics, The Work of Hanna Segal,* New York, London: Jason Aronson Inc. 185–206.

Segal, Hanna (1981b): *Delusion and Artistic Creativity, The Work of Hanna Segal,* New York, London: Jason Aronson Inc., 207–216.

Sekoff, Jed (1982): *Remembering Against the Current: The Appropriation of the Past in transformative vision,* unpublished dissertation, Berkeley: The Wright Institute.

Spector, Jack (1969): *The Method of Morelli Psychoanalysis and Its Relation to Freudian Psychoanalysis, Diogenes, No. 66, Summer 1969, 63–68.*

Spector, Jack (1974): *The Aesthetics of Freud,* New York: Mc Graw Hill.

Spence, Donald P. (1982): "Narrative Truth and Theoretical Truth", *Psychoanalytic Quarterly, Vol. 1,* 49.

Steele, R.S. (1979): "Psychoanalysis and Hermeneutics", *International Review of Psychoanalysis, 6,* 389–411.

Strachey, Alix (1978): "Editor's Note" to *Leonardo da Vinci and a Memory of His Childhood,* in: *Standard Edition of the Complete Psychological Works of Sigmund Freud,* Volume XI (1910), London: The Hogarth Press and the Institute of Psycho-Analysis, 59-62.

Taiana, Cecilia (2022): "What does Poetry offer Psychoanalysis? T.S. Eliot's Concept of Tradition", in: *Canadian Journal of Psychoanalysis. Vol. 30., No. 2,* Fall 2022, 191–214.

Waelder, Robert (1965): *Psychoanalytic Avenues into Art,* London: The Hogarth Press.

Willbern, David (1979): "Freud and the Inter-Penetration of Dreams", *Diacritics, Volume 9, No. 1,* Spring 1979, 98–110.

Winnicott, D.W. (1980): *Playing and Reality,* Hardmonsworth: Penguin Books Ltd.

Winnicott, D.W. (1966): "The Location of Cultural Experiences", *International Journal of Psychoanalysis, 48,* 368–372.

Wolff Bernstein, Jeanne (1999): "Countertransference, our New Royal Road to the Unconscious?", *Psychoanalytic Dialogues, Vol. 9, No. 3,* 275–300.

Wolff Bernstein, Jeanne (2007): "Love, Desire and Jouissance, Two out of three ain't bad", *Psychoanalytic Dialogues, Vol 16, No. 6,* 711–724.

Wolff Bernstein, Jeanne (2012): "Jacques Lacan", *Textbook of Psychoanalysis,* 2nd edition, edited by Glen Gabbard, Bonnie Litowitz & Paul Williams, Washington DC: American Psychiatric Association Publishing, 225–238.

List of Plates